Essential Quantitative Methods

for business, management and finance

fifth edition

Les Oakshott

First edition 1998
Second edition 2001
Third edition 2006
Fourth edition 2009
Fifth edition 2012
Published by
PALGRAVE MACMILLAN

Palgrave Macmillan in the UK is an imprint of Macmillan Publisherss Limited,
registered in England, company number 785998, of Houndmills, Basingstoke,
Hampshire RG21 6XS

Palgrave Macmillan in the US is a division of St Martin's Press LLC,
175 Fifth Avenue, New York, NY 10010

Palgrave Macmillan is the global academic imprint of the above companies
and has companies and representatives throughout the world.

Palgrave and Macmillan are registered trademarks in the United States,
United Kingdom, Europe and other countries.

ISBN-13 978–0–230–30266–2 paperback

This book is printed on paper suitable for recycling and made from fully
managed and sustained forest sources. Logging, pulping and manufacturing
processes are expected to conform to the environmental regulations of the
country of origin.

A catalogue record for this book is available from the British Library.

A catalog record for this book is available from the Library of Congress.

10   9   8   7   6   5   4   3   2   1
21 20 19 18 17 16 15 14 13 12

Printed in China

For Vicky, Andrew, Kim, Joshua and Christina

Contents

List of tables and figures

Tables

Figures

Preface to the fifth edition

Many degree programmes these days include at least one compulsory course in statistics or quantitative methods and there are also many undergraduate and masters programmes that have an elective in these areas. Students are therefore getting more exposure to analytical techniques and, with the reduction in class contact time, need resources to help them with what many find a difficult subject.

As with the previous four editions, this edition guides the student through the maze of techniques that make up the quantitative methods syllabus. The in-text activities is one reason for the success of the previous editions and is continued and expanded in this edition. Also retained and expanded are the *Key points* at the end of each chapter as they have proven to be well liked by both students and lecturers. New for this edition are *Did you know* snippets which give some interesting facts that relate to but are separate from the topic being discussed. An example is the mention of Florence Nightingale as a brilliant statistician as well as a famous nurse (Chapter 4). Hopefully this will act as a motivating factor for students who will come to see these snippets both as a welcome distraction from the main topic and an incentive to discover more about the rich field of mathematics and statistics.

A little reordering of chapters has been made in this edition to help the subject material flow better. The chapter on investment appraisal has been moved to Section IV (Decision-making techniques) because it is concerned with making financial decisions. The chapters on inventory control and simulation have been moved to the companion website as they were quite small and only used on a few courses. The space that this has released has allowed more relevant material to be included. In the chapter on correlation and regression (Chapter 10) a new section on further topics of linear regression has been added. This has allowed the more advanced aspects of linear regression to be better integrated with the SPSS software that is used in this text. Another addition has been a section on problem formulation in the chapter on decision-making (Chapter 11). This text like most others assumes that a problem is well defined to enable a particular technique to be used. However in many real business problems this is not the case and we often need to do an investigation into the background of the problem first. One of the best ways of doing this is by the use of diagrams. This new section on problem formulation looks at several diagrams that can be used for this stage of decision-making. The section in Chapter 3 on secondary sources of data has been re-written to make it applicable to the internet age. It is now called 'Obtaining research data from on-line sources' and includes details on how to use search engines more effectively. Lastly the further reading section at the end of each chapter has been expanded so as to give general guidance on other texts to consult. These further reading sources are now summarized in a bibliography at the end of the text.

As before the comprehensive companion website (www.palgrave.com/business/Oakshott5e) will contain:

- Progress questions, Review questions, True/false questions and Multiple choice questions. Students will now be able to work through these questions online and get immediate feedback (including references to appropriate pages in the text).
- Additional material including further practice questions and assignments.
- Solutions to all practice questions in the text.
- A list of statistical and mathematical formula used in the book.
- Basic instructions for the novice on using Excel and SPSS.
- Excel and SPSS datasets used in the text.
- The chapters on inventory management and simulation.
- A password protected area for the exclusive use of lecturers who adopt this text. This area will contain answers to assignments and PowerPoint slides for teaching purposes.

Both Excel and SPSS have been updated in this latest edition. However, compared to the fourth edition, the changes in Excel are minimal so anyone familiar with Excel 2007 will not have any problems using Excel 2010. It is a similar situation with SPSS version 19.

Another success story with this text has been the inclusion of a real case study at the start of each chapter. Reviewers mentioned that students really like to see the relevance of the subject and were impressed with the range of cases provided. For the fifth edition, case studies have either been updated with more recent data or changed to something more relevant to today's economic and political climate. For example, there is a case on the UK 2010 General Election, as well as a case relating to the recent banking crisis and one on the 2012 Olympics.

Notes to the fifth edition

This edition, like the fourth edition, is divided into four parts:

Part I   Mathematical applications
Part II   Collecting and interpreting data
Part III   Probability and statistics
Part IV   Decision-making techniques

The purpose of this arrangement is to try to anticipate the way that lecturers organize their courses. Not all courses will cover all topics. Some introductory statistical courses only require basic statistical knowledge and may therefore require only Part II, while more advanced statistical courses may also require Part III. The material provided in Parts II and III is designed to be taught sequentially, whereas the chapters in Parts I and IV can be taught in any order. It is recommended, however, that students who do not feel confident with GCSE-level mathematics work through Chapter 1 (Revision mathematics) first, no matter what parts they study subsequently.

Although it is assumed that most students have used Excel before, it may not be the case that all students have met Excel 2010 or 2007 which have a different look and feel to them than earlier versions. To help these students more detailed instructions are provided as and when required. However, to avoid repetition it is suggested that students who have not met these versions of Excel before either read the relevant parts of Chapter 4 or go to the website before moving on to more advanced uses of Excel. Although both Excel and SPSS are used in Part II of the text, greater emphasis has been placed on SPSS in Part III because SPSS is superior to Excel when it comes to more advanced statistics. Excel is still used in many of the chapters in Part IV however.

 As before *Progress questions*, *Review questions*, *True/false questions* and *Multiple choice questions* can be found on the companion website (www.palgrave.com/oakshott). These questions can be answered online, where immediate feedback is provided. Solutions to selected *Practice questions* can again be found in Appendix 2 at the back of the text while the remaining solutions are on the website.

Acknowledgements

The author and publishers are grateful for permission to reproduce the following copyright material:

Energy Information Administration for reference to their 'Annual Energy Outlook 2010'

Operational Research Society for permission to include details of 'A model of railway efficiency', June 2010, Inside OR

BBC for reference to their web article on 14 February 2011, '2012 London Olympics still on budget'

Pearson plc for Table VII of *Statistical Tables for Biological, Agricultural and Medical Research*, 61e by R.A. Fisher and F. Yates

BBC for football World Cup goal statistics 2010

BP for data from their *Statistical Review of World Energy 2009*

John Haigh and plus maths magazine for ideas behind 'Is goal scoring a random event?'

World Resources Institute (WRI) for data on greenhouse gas emissions

Catalyze and CoRWM for reference to their joint work on the management of radioactive waste

Catalyze for permission to use and print results from their Hiview3 model

FAME database published by Bureau van Dfik Electronic Publishing

Department of the Environment, Food and Rural Affairs, for data from their Northern Ireland seat-belt survey

HMSO for material from the Office of National Statistics website and for Census data

Microsoft Corporation and SPSS Inc. for permission to incorporate screen shots of their software in the text

Interfaces for permission to include details of Donald L. Kiefer, 'Decision analysis to evaluate proof of principle trial design for a new drug candidate', *Interfaces*, 34(3), 2004, pp. 206–7

British Polling Council for a summary of the final poll taken in the UK 2010 General Election

Commercial Motor for reference to their article of November 2010 on pay settlements fro RDC managers

Straight Statistics for many ideas throughout this text

International Journal of Contemporary Hospitality for permission to include details from 'Guests' perception on factors influencing customer loyalty'

Every effort has been made to trace all copyright holders, but if any have been inadvertently overlooked the publishers will be pleased to make the necessary arrangements at the first opportunity.

Company names

Except where the author is quoting real company statistics, all company names in worked examples are intended to be fictitious. The use of any name that has been registered by a real company is accidental, and the author and publishers will be pleased to make any necessary changes at the first opportunity.

Guided tour of the book

Prerequisites outline subject matter that should have been covered before chapters are tackled

Introduction sets the chapter in context in terms of the book as a whole

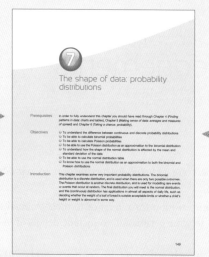

Objectives identify the concepts to be covered in the chapter and the knowledge and skills that students will obtain by reading it

Quantitative methods in action encourage students to apply learning to real-world situations

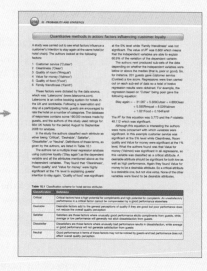

Activities illustrate points and test learning as each chapter is worked through

Did you know snippets give interesting facts that relate to the topic being discussed

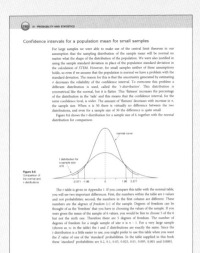

Examples offer contemporary scenarios in which the chapter subject matter may be empirically applied

Reflection rounds up the major themes of the chapter and reinforces their practical application

Key points summarize the fundamentals of each chapter and help to reinforce Objectives

Further reading gives guidance on texts to be consulted

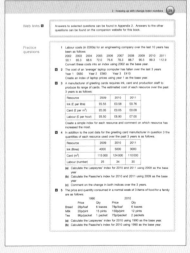

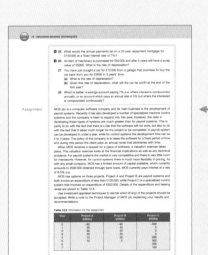

Assignments involve students in additional research activities in order to further develop their knowledge and skills; answers are provided for lecturers on the Companion Website

Practice questions are revision exercises designed to test learning once each chapter has been completed; answers are available at the back of the book or on the Companion Website

I

MATHEMATICAL APPLICATIONS

1

Revision mathematics

Introduction

The aim of this chapter is to provide the basic numeracy skills that will be needed in subsequent chapters. If you have any doubts about your knowledge of particular areas you are recommended to tackle the diagnostic tests that you will find throughout this chapter. If you do not achieve 100% success in any of these tests, try to find out where you went wrong by reading through the remainder of that section. The books listed in the further reading section may also be of help if you need additional practice.

Number and number operations

Activity 1.1

Write down the answers to the following questions (without a calculator).

1 $4 + (-2)$ 2 $4 - (-4)$ 3 $5 + (-2) - (-4)$

4 $2 \times (-3)$ 5 $-15 \div (-3)$ 6 $\dfrac{-10}{2}$

7 $\dfrac{5}{0}$ 8 $\dfrac{0}{5}$ 9 $3 \times 2 + 8 \div 4$

10 $3 \times (2 + 8) \div 4$

Answers

1 2   2 8   3 7

4 -6 5 5   6 -5

7 no solution (∞) 8 0   9 8

10 7.5

Number operations often confuse people, particularly when they involve positive and negative numbers. The easy rule is that like signs give a plus while unlike signs give a negative. This is summarized in Table 1.1.

Another problem is deciding the order in which to carry out a series of calculations. Questions 9 and 10 had the same numbers in the same order but in question 10 a bracket separated some of the figures. There is an order in which mathematical operations are performed. You may have come across the term '*bedmas*', which stands for 'brackets, exponent, division, multiplication, addition and subtraction'. This is not strictly correct as addition and subtraction have equal priority, as do multiplication and division. Where the operations have equal priority the order is taken from left to right. The main point to remember is that if you want a calculation to be done in a particular order you should use brackets to make the order clear. Most scientific calculators should use the bedmas system but it is worth checking with some simple calculations. These calculators will also have the bracket function to allow the order of calculation to be controlled.

Table 1.1 Number operations

Addition and subtraction	Multiplication	Division
$+(+) = +$	$+ \times + = +$	$+ \div + = +$
$-(-) = +$	$- \times - = +$	$- \div - = +$
$+(-) = -$	$+ \times - = -$	$+ \div - = -$
$-(+) = -$	$- \times + = -$	$- \div + = -$

Decimals, fractions and percentages

Activity 1.2

1   Convert the following decimals to fractions in their simplest form.
    (a) 0.2   (b) 0.5   (c) 0.33$\dot{3}$ (d) 0.125   (e) 0.375

2   Convert the following fractions to decimals.

   (a) $\dfrac{1}{10}$ (b) $\dfrac{1}{5}$ (c) $\dfrac{11}{3}$ (d) $\dfrac{2}{7}$ (e) $\dfrac{3}{8}$

   (f) $\dfrac{7}{3}$ (g) $\dfrac{1}{100}$ (h) $1\dfrac{3}{4}$

3   Convert the following fractions to percentages.

   (a) $\dfrac{1}{4}$ (b) $\dfrac{1}{2}$ (c) $\dfrac{1}{5}$ (d) $\dfrac{2}{3}$ (e) $\dfrac{3}{4}$

4   Convert the following percentages into fractions in their simplest form.
    (a) 40%   (b) 45%   (c) 60%   (d) 12%   (e) 19%

5   Carry out the following calculations.

   (a) $0.25 + 0.37$ (b) $\dfrac{1}{2} \times 3$ (c) $\dfrac{1}{2}$ of 46%

   (d) $\dfrac{4}{5} + \dfrac{2}{3}$ (e) $\dfrac{3}{4} \times \dfrac{3}{2}$ (f) $\dfrac{3}{4} \div \dfrac{3}{2}$

   (g) $0.25 \times \dfrac{1}{5}$ (h) 0.00025×3000

6   Round the following decimals to 3 decimal places.
    (a) 1.5432   (b) 1.5438   (c) 1.5435   (d) 0.000843   (e) 100.2003

7   Write the following numbers to 3 significant figures.
    (a) 1.5432   (b) 1.5438   (c) 1.5435   (d) 0.000843   (e) 100.2003
    (f) 13 256   (g) 1.000561

8   Write down the following numbers in scientific notation.
    (a) 25 438 176   (b) 1 600 000   (c) 0.00001776

Answers

1   (a) $\dfrac{1}{5}$ (b) $\dfrac{1}{2}$ (c) $\dfrac{1}{3}$ (d) $\dfrac{1}{8}$ (e) $\dfrac{3}{8}$

2   (a) 0.1   (b) 0.2   (c) 3.66$\dot{6}$ (d) 0.2857   (e) 0.375
    (f) 2.33$\dot{3}$ (g) 0.01   (h) 1.75

3   (a) 25%   (b) 50%   (c) 20%   (d) 66.66$\dot{6}$%   (e) 75%

4   (a) $\dfrac{2}{5}$ (b) $\dfrac{9}{20}$ (c) $\dfrac{3}{5}$ (d) $\dfrac{3}{25}$ (e) $\dfrac{19}{100}$

5   (a) 0.62   (b) 1.5   (c) 23%   (d) $1\dfrac{7}{15}$ (e) $1\dfrac{1}{8}$

   (f) $\dfrac{1}{2}$ (g) $\dfrac{1}{20}$ or 0.05   (h) 0.75

Activity 1.2 continued

6 (a) 1.543   (b) 1.544   (c) 1.544   (d) 0.001   (e) 100.200

7 (a) 1.54   (b) 1.54   (c) 1.54   (d) 0.000843   (e) 100
   (f) 13 300   (g) 1.00

8 (a) 2.5438176×10^7 (b) 1.6×10^6 (c) 1.776×10^{-5}

Fractions, decimals and percentages are used throughout this book and you need to be able to convert a number from one form to another. To convert from a fraction to either a decimal or a percentage all you need to do is to divide the numerator (the number above the line) by the denominator (the number below the line). For a percentage you also need to multiply by 100. To convert a decimal to a fraction you simply have to remember that the first digit after the decimal point is a tenth and the second digit is a hundredth and so on. For example, 0.2 is $\frac{2}{10}$ and this can be simplified by dividing the top and bottom by 2 to give $\frac{1}{5}$. The conversion of a percentage to a fraction is easier as the denominator of the fraction is always 100. So 40% is $\frac{40}{100}$ and this simplifies to $\frac{2}{5}$.

A frequent question asked by students is, how many decimal places should an answer be given to? There is no easy answer to this, although a good rule of thumb to use when analyzing data is to give one more place than in the original data. So if your data had one decimal place you should give your answer to two decimal places. Giving more decimal places implies that your answer is accurate to this number of decimals, which is misleading. However, numbers should only be rounded at the end of a calculation. If you round intermediate values you will introduce rounding errors into your calculations, which can cause major errors in your final figure.

When rounding, remember the rule that numbers below 5 are rounded *down* and numbers of 5 and above are rounded *up*. So 1.5432 is 1.543 to 3 decimal places but 1.5435 is 1.544 to 3 decimal places.

Another form of cutting down the number of digits in an answer is to give a stated number of *significant* figures. In many cases the two systems will give identical results, but the real difference with using significant figures is that zeros are only included when they are significant. Thus 0.01654 becomes 0.0165 to three significant figures while 1.01654 would become 1.02. Significant figures can also be used when handling large numbers. For example, 13 256 is 13 000 to 2 significant figures. The zeros have to be added to maintain the place value of the remaining numbers.

If very large or very small numbers are involved it is all too easy to make a mistake and accidentally lose a digit. To avoid this you can use *scientific* notation. Scientific notation is in the form of $a \times 10^b$ where a is a decimal number below 10 and b is the number of places the decimal point needs to be moved to arrive back at the original number. For example, 25 438 176 can be changed to 2.5438176×10^7 as the decimal place has been moved 7 places to the left. Scientific calculators use this method when the number exceeds a set number of digits, except that the base 10 is not displayed – a source of confusion among students!

Powers and roots

Activity 1.3

Write down the value of the following.

1 2^3 2 3^4 3 $\left(\dfrac{1}{2}\right)^3$ 4 2^{-3} 5 $\sqrt{81}$ 6 $\sqrt[3]{27}$

Answers

1 8   2 81   3 $\dfrac{1}{8}$ 4 $\dfrac{1}{8}$ 5 9   6 3

When a number is raised to a power (or exponent) the number is multiplied by itself that number of times. So 2^3 means $2 \times 2 \times 2 = 8$. Powers take precedence in an expression after any brackets. In the calculation of $2 + 6 \times 3^2 - 4$, the order of calculation is as follows.

$$3^2 = 9, \qquad 9 \times 6 = 54, \qquad 54 + 2 - 4 = 52$$

Elementary algebra

Activity 1.4

1 Simplify the following expressions.

(a) $x + x^2 + y + 2x + 3x^2$ (b) $\dfrac{2x}{x}$ (c) $\dfrac{2x}{y}$ (d) $\dfrac{x^3}{x^2}$

(e) $\dfrac{x^2 - 4}{(x + 2)}$

2 Evaluate the expressions given in question 1 when $x = 2$ and $y = 4$.

3 Solve the following equations.

(a) $4x - 5 = 9$ (b) $\dfrac{7x - 4}{2} = 2x + 4$ (c) $x^2 + 4 = 20$

(d) $\dfrac{1}{x} = 10$ (e) $x^2 - 4x + 3 = 0$ (f) $2x^2 - 6x - 3 = 0$

Answers

1 (a) $4x^2 + 3x + y$ (b) 2   (c) $\dfrac{2x}{y}$ (d) x (e) $x - 2$

2 (a) 26   (b) 2   (c) 1   (d) 2   (e) 0

3 (a) 3.5   (b) 4   (c) ± 4 (d) 0.1   (e) 1 or 3

(f) -0.436 or 3.436

Most students who have not studied mathematics beyond GCSE level find algebra difficult. The idea of replacing numbers by letters is quite abstract and many students do not understand the need for it. Unfortunately some understanding of algebra is essential if you are to successfully complete a quantitative methods course and many chapters in this book assume this understanding.

There are many algebraic techniques but the most important as far as this book is concerned is to be able to solve equations. To achieve this it is necessary to remember that whatever you do to one side of the equation you must do to the other. In solving

$$\frac{7x - 4}{2} = 2x + 4$$

the following steps are carried out:

1 Multiply both sides by 2. The equation then becomes $7x - 4 = 4x + 8$.
2 Subtract $4x$ from both sides to give $3x - 4 = 8$.
3 Add 4 to both sides to give $3x = 12$.
4 Divide both sides by 3.

This gives the answer $x = 4$.

When the unknown variable is raised to a power, the method of solving the equation becomes more complicated and in some cases it is necessary to resort to numerical methods. Quadratic equations are those involving x^2 and the method of solution depends on the equation. For $x^2 + 4 = 20$ the solution follows the method already described. That is, subtract 4 from both sides

$$x^2 = 16$$

and then take the square root of both sides

$$x = \sqrt{16}$$
$$= \pm 4$$

Notice that both $+4$ and -4 are solutions since $(-4)^2 = 16$.

Some quadratic equations can be *factorized*. To factorize an expression we need to find two factors that when multiplied together give the original expression. $x^2 + 2x = 0$ can be factorized by noting that x is a common factor to both terms. If we take out the x we get $x(x + 2) = 0$ and both x and $(x + 2)$ are factors of the original expression. The modified equation is easier to solve than the original as we can see that the equation is true when either $x = 0$ or $(x + 2) = 0$. That is, $x = 0$ or $x = -2$.

For $x^2 - 4x + 3 = 0$ we need to find two brackets that when multiplied together give these terms. Factorizing this type of expression can involve some trial and error but in this case it is fairly easy and will be

$$(x - 3)(x - 1) = 0$$

If you multiply the two brackets you get

$$x^2 - 3x - x + 3 = 0$$

which is the same as the original since $-3x - x = -4x$.

The solution to this equation is either

$$x - 3 = 0 \quad \text{or} \quad x - 1 = 0$$

So x is either 1 or 3.

Factorizing only works easily for a small number of quadratic expressions, and a more general method is to use a formula. If the expression is in the form $ax^2 + bx + c = 0$, the formula is:

$$x = \frac{-b \pm \sqrt{b^2 - 4ac}}{2a}$$

For example, to solve $2x^2 - 6x - 3 = 0$, we first note that $a = 2$, $b = -6$ and $c = -3$

$$\text{so} \quad x = \frac{-(-6) \pm \sqrt{(-6)^2 - 4 \times 2 \times (-3)}}{2 \times 2}$$

$$= \frac{6 \pm \sqrt{36 + 24}}{4}$$

$$= \frac{6 \pm 7.74597}{4}$$

$$= -0.436 \quad \text{or} \quad 3.436$$

Indices and logs

Activity 1.5

1 Simplify the following expressions.

(a) $2^3 \times 2^5$ (b) $3^2 \times 3^3$ (c) $2^3 \times 8^4$ (d) $\dfrac{10^5}{10^2}$

(e) $(2^3)^2$ (f) $a^x \times a^{2x}$ (g) $b^5 \times c^5$ (h) $\dfrac{a^x}{a^y}$

(i) $(a^x)^y$ (j) $\dfrac{a^{2x}}{a^{5x}}$ (k) $16^{3/2}$

2 Solve for x:

(a) $10^x = 15$ (b) $e^x = 1.6$ (c) $25 = 10 \times (1.1)^x$

(d) $1.8 = \dfrac{3^{5x}}{3^x}$ (e) $5^{2x+3} = 12 \times 6^{4x}$

Answers

1 (a) $2^8 = 256$ (b) $3^5 = 243$ (c) $2^{15} = 32\,768$ (d) $10^3 = 1000$

(e) $2^6 = 64$ (f) a^{3x} (g) $(bc)^5$ (h) a^{x-y}

(i) a^{xy} (j) a^{-3x} (k) 64

2 (a) 1.176   (b) 0.470   (c) 9.614   (d) 0.1338   (e) 0.5935

In Section 1.4 we saw that if a number is multiplied by itself a number of times then we can simplify the expression by the use of indices – so that $2 \times 2 \times 2 = 2^3$. In general the product of $a \times a \times a \dots$ is written as a^n. We say that the *base* (a) is raised to the power of n.

There are 3 important formulae for indices and these are:

$$a^m \times a^n = a^{m+n}$$
$$a^m \div a^n = a^{m-n}$$
$$(a^m)^n = a^{mn}$$

Therefore, providing the bases are the same, you can add or subtract the powers.

So $2^3 \times 2^5 = 2^{3+5}$

$$= 2^8$$
$$= 256$$

and $\dfrac{10^5}{10^2} = 10^{5-2}$

$$= 10^3$$
$$= 1000$$

If m and n have the same value (say x) then $a^x \div a^x = a^0$.

As this expression must also equal 1, it follows that $a^0 = 1$. Also $a^1 = a$.

The power can be negative or fractional. $1/a^n$ can also be written as a^{-n}, and $a^{1/2}$ is the same as $\sqrt{a}$.

We could simplify $16^{3/2}$ to $((16)^{1/2})^3$. Since the square root of 16 is 4, then $4^3 = 64$.

We can rewrite $Y = a^x$ as $x = \log_a Y$. The word *log* is short for *logarithm* and this expression is read as x equals log of Y to the base a. There are only two bases you need worry about; these are base 10 and base e. These bases can be found on all scientific calculators; log to base 10 is usually written as *log*, and log to base e is written as *ln*.

There are three important formulae for logs that apply to all bases and these are:

$$\log(uv) = \log u + \log v$$
$$\log(u/v) = \log u - \log v$$
$$\log x^n = n \log x$$

The importance of logs as far as this book is concerned is the ability to use the laws of logs to solve certain types of equations. For example, to solve $5^{2x+3} = 12 \times 6^{4x}$ you would carry out the following steps.

$$\log(5^{2x+3}) = \log(12 \times 6^{4x})$$
$$(2x + 3)\log 5 = \log 12 + \log 6^{4x}$$
$$2x \log 5 + 3 \log 5 = \log 12 + 4x \log 6$$
$$2x \log 5 - 4x \log 6 = \log 12 - 3 \log 5$$
$$2x(\log 5 - 2 \log 6) = \log 12 - 3 \log 5$$

$$2x = \frac{\log 12 - 3 \log 5}{\log 5 - 2 \log 6}$$

$$2x = \frac{1.0792 - 3 \times 0.6990}{0.6990 - 2 \times 0.7782}$$

$$2x = \frac{-1.0178}{-0.8574}$$

$$2x = 1.1871$$

$$x = 0.5935$$

Mathematical symbols

Activity 1.6

What do the following symbols stand for?

1   $<$ 2 $\leq$ 3 $>$ 4 $\geq$ 5 $\neq$ 6 $\cong$ 7 $\sum$

Answers

1   less than

3   greater than

5   not equal to

7   the sum of

2   less than or equal to

4   greater than or equal to

6   approximately equal to

We will be using all these symbols in later chapters of the book, particularly the summation sign. If you see the expression $\sum x$ it means you should add up all the values of x, while $\sum xy$ means multiply the pairs of x and y before summing them. For example, in Table 1.2 there are two columns of numbers which I have called x and y.

$$\text{From Table 1.2} \quad \sum x = 2 + 1 + 4 + 6 + 4 \quad = 17$$

$$\sum xy = 14 + 5 + 8 + 18 + 16 = 61$$

$$\sum x^2 = 4 + 1 + 16 + 36 + 16 = 73$$

If your calculator has the SD or Statistical Data function many of these calculations can be done automatically for you.

Table 1.2 Use of the summation sign

x	y	xy
2	7	14
1	5	5
4	2	8
6	3	18
4	4	16

Graphs and straight lines

Activity 1.7

Which of the following equations represent straight lines?

1 $y = 2x + 5$ 2 $y + 4x = 20$ 3 $y = 8$ 4 $y = x$ 5 $y = x^2$

Answers
All except equation 5.

The equation of a straight line is $y = mx + c$, where m is the gradient and c is the value of y when $x = 0$ (often referred to as the *intercept* on the y-axis). Equation 1 is obviously a straight line with $m = 2$ and $c = 5$. Equation 2 is also a straight line and this may be easier to see if you subtract $4x$ from both sides of the equation.

That is: $y = 20 - 4x$

or $y = -4x + 20$

This equation is now in the standard form and you should see that $m = -4$ and $c = 20$. Equation 3 is another straight line but this is a special one. This could be written as $y = 0x + 8$ and you will see that $m = 0$; that is, the gradient is zero. This can be therefore be represented as a *horizontal* line. Equation 4 can be written as $y = x + 0$, so this represents a straight line with a gradient of 1 and c of 0. This line passes through the origin of the graph (that is, $x = 0$, $y = 0$). Equation 5 is *not* a straight line since y increases as the *square* of x. The graphs of these equations are shown in Figure 1.1.

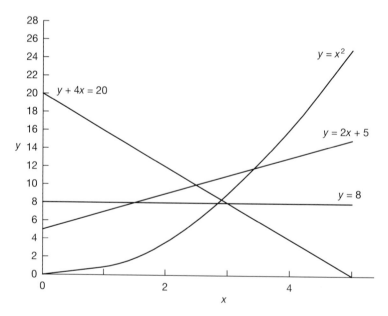

Figure 1.1
Graph for Activity 1.7

Solving linear equations graphically

Activity 1.8

Plot the equations $2y + x = 8$ and $y + 2x = 7$ on the same graph and write down the coordinates of the point of intersection.

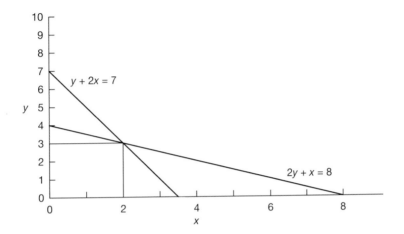

Figure 1.2
Solving equations
graphically

You should have obtained the graph shown in Figure 1.2. The point of intersection of the two lines is at the point $x = 2$, $y = 3$. This can be written as (2,3). In this example the coordinates of the point of intersection were both whole numbers, which made it easy to read from your graph. Unfortunately this is not always the case and accurately reading fractional values from a graph is difficult. A better method is the algebraic method of *simultaneous equations*.

Solving linear equations simultaneously

Activity 1.9

Solve the equations given in Activity 1.8 simultaneously.

All being well, your answer agreed with the graphical method. The method of solving simultaneous equations I prefer is the method of *elimination*. To use this method the two equations are written down as follows:

$$y + 2x = 7 \tag{1}$$

$$2y + x = 8 \tag{2}$$

The coefficients of either x or y must be equal in the two equations and this is achieved by multiplying *both* sides of equation (1) by 2.

The equations can now be *subtracted*:

$$2y + 4x = 14$$
$$2y + x = 8$$

$$3x = 6 \quad (y \text{ has now been 'eliminated'})$$

That is $\qquad x = 2$

This value of x can now be substituted back into either equation (1) or (2) to give the value of y. Using equation (2):

$$2y + 2 = 8$$
$$2y = 6$$

Therefore $\qquad y = 3$

Inequations

Activity 1.10

1   What do the following inequations mean?

   (a) $y + 2x \leq 7$ (b) $2y + x \geq 8$

2   How would you represent these two inequations graphically? And what does the term 'intersection' mean in this case?

Answers

1   Inequation (a) means that the sum of the left hand side of the equation must be less than or equal to 7; that is, the sum cannot be greater than 7. Inequation (b) means that the sum of the left hand side of the equation must be at least 8; it cannot be less.

2   Whereas an equation can be represented by a straight line, an inequation is represented by a *region*. The equation $y + 2x = 7$ forms the *boundary* of the region represented by the inequation $y + 2x \leq 7$. Similarly the equation $2y + x = 8$ forms the boundary of the region $2y + x \geq 8$. The region can only be on one side of the boundary and this can be found by inspection; that is, a point is investigated to see if it satisfies the inequation. The easiest point to try is the origin ($x = 0$, $y = 0$), except when the boundary passes through this point. When the region has been found it needs to be identified. This can be done by shading. The normal convention is to shade the *unwanted* region and this is the convention adopted in this book. You can see this in Figure 1.3.

   The intersection of regions is the area on the graph that satisfies *all* inequations. In this example, the area is represented by ABC. Any point within this area (including the boundaries) satisfies both inequations.

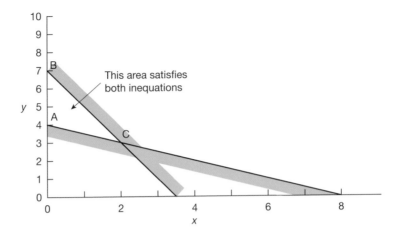

Figure 1.3
Graph for
Activity 1.10

Further reading

There are a number of texts that are designed to help the student with basic mathematics such as Rowe (2002) and Morris (2007). There are also many online sources such as the BBC's Skillswise (www.bbc.co.uk/skillswise/numbers/wholenumbers/) which is part of their online learning support series (www.bbc.co.uk/learning/subjects/maths/shtml).

Keeping up with change: index numbers

Objectives

- To be able to calculate a simple one-item index
- To be able to calculate the Laspeyres' index
- To be able to calculate the Paasche's index
- To understand how the different consumer price indices are calculated, and to be able to use the RPI to deflate financial data

Introduction

An index is a means of comparing changes in some variable, often price over time. This is particularly useful when there are many items involved and when the prices and quantities are in different units. The best-known index in the UK is the *retail price index* (RPI) although the *consumer price index* (CPI) is becoming more prominent now that it is the official measure of inflation when it comes to up-rating public sector pensions and benefits. Both indices compare the price of a 'basket' of goods from one month to another. This chapter looks at the construction and use of different types of indices.

As a start we will use the idea of an index to see how the price and consumption of oil have changed from 1986 to 2009. This type of index is called a *simple index* as only one variable is involved.

Quantitative methods in action: is the demand for oil increasing?

There are reckoned to be approximately 1333.1 thousand million barrels of oil reserves worldwide (source: BP). On current consumption, this should last for 46 years. Of course, if consumption increases this figure will fall, and if new sources of oil are found this figure will rise. What is not in doubt, though, is that oil is not a renewable resource – the world will eventually have to survive without oil.

Records of oil consumption and price for every country in the world are available since 1965 from the BP website (www.bp.com/sectionbodycopy.do ?categoryId=7500&contentId=7068481). Part of this data for the USA, China and the UK has been downloaded and is shown in Table 2.1. A chart of the consumption data is shown in Figure 2.1. Oil price is given at 2009 prices and you will see the reason for this later in the chapter.

What do these figures and chart tell us? It is immediately obvious that the USA has a far greater consumption than either China or the UK. It is also clear that China's consumption has increased considerably since 1986. However as the magnitude of the consumption for each country is so different it is difficult to make direct comparisons. We will see in this chapter how the use of index numbers can allow comparisons to be made even when the magnitude of the figures is so different.

Table 2.1 Oil price and oil consumption (in thousand barrels daily) since 1986

	1986	1987	1988	1989	1990	1991	1992	1993	1994	1995	1996	1997
Price[1]	28.25	34.82	27.06	31.53	38.94	31.51	29.54	25.20	22.90	23.95	28.26	25.52
USA	16281	16665	17283	17325	16988	16713	17033	17236	17719	17725	18309	18621
China	1941	2062	2211	2340	2323	2524	2740	3051	3116	3395	3702	4179
UK	1647	1608	1703	1744	1762	1758	1775	1791	1777	1757	1798	1752

	1998	1999	2000	2001	2002	2003	2004	2005	2006	2007	2008	2009
Price[1]	16.74	23.14	35.50	29.61	29.84	33.62	43.46	59.89	69.32	74.90	96.91	61.67
USA	18917	19519	19701	19649	19761	20033	20731	20802	20687	20680	19498	18686
China	4228	4477	4772	4872	5288	5803	6772	6984	7410	7771	8086	8625
UK	1741	1721	1697	1697	1693	1717	1764	1802	1785	1714	1681	1611

[1]Price in $ per barrel at 2009 prices
Source: BP Statistical Review of World Energy.

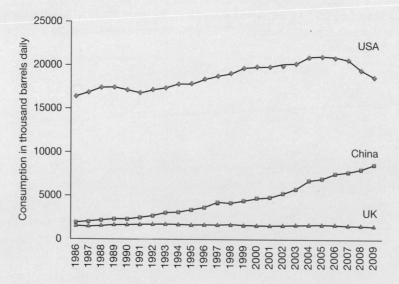

Figure 2.1
Line chart of oil consumption for the USA, China and the UK

Simple indices

From Table 2.1 we see that between 1986 and 2009 the price of a barrel of oil rose by $33.42. But how much had it gone up relative to the price in 1986? If 1986 is used as a *base*, it becomes possible to compare changes in price with this base. The base is given a value of 100: a price increase would result in a value greater than 100, while a price decrease would result in a value less than 100. Thus if $28.25 is equivalent to 100, then $61.67 is equivalent to:

$$\frac{100}{28.25} \times 61.67 = 218.3$$

The value 218.3 is called the *price index* and 1986 is the *base year*. In percentage terms, this means that the price in 2009 is 218.3% of what it was in 1986.

If p_n represents the price in the current year (year n) and p_0 represents the price in the base year, then the price index is:

$$\frac{100}{p_0} \times p_n$$

More normally this is expressed as:

$$\frac{p_n}{p_0} \times 100$$

The change in the oil consumption can also be represented by an *index number*. In this case we are calculating the change in quantity, so the formula is:

$$\frac{q_n}{q_0} \times 100$$

where q_0 represents the quantity at the base year and q_n the quantity at year n.

For the USA, the quantity index for 2009 using 1986 as the base year is therefore:

$$\frac{18\,686}{16\,281} \times 100 = 114.8$$

The USA has thus shown a 14.8% increase in oil consumption between 1986 and 2009.

Activity 2.1

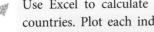

Use Excel to calculate both the price index and the quantity index for all three countries. Plot each index on the same chart, and explain what the chart tells you about the change in price and consumption over the 24-year span.

The chart in Figure 2.2 shows that from 1986 to 2003 the price of oil was fairly stable but after 2003 the price of oil (in today's prices) started to rise rapidly. The price fell in 2009 due to the world recession (and hence a reduction in the demand for oil). At the time of writing in mid-2011 we have seen another rise due to the Libya crisis. What is very clear from the chart is that China has shown a dramatic increase in consumption over the entire 24-year period.

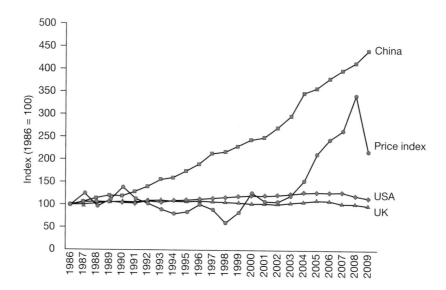

Figure 2.2
Index of oil price
and consumption
for the USA, China
and the UK

Example 2.1

The resources used in the manufacture of glass-fibre boats include resin, glass-fibre mat and labour. The price of each of these resources varies and the average price during each of the years 2009 to 2011 is shown in Table 2.2.

Table 2.2 Price data for Example 2.1

Item	2009	2010	2011
Resin	£0.25/l	£0.20/l	£0.18/l
Mat	£0.16/m^2	£0.16/m^2	£0.20/m^2
Labour	£5.50/hour	£5.85/hour	£8.30/hour

Activity 2.2

Calculate the index for each item using 2009 as the base year.

You should have obtained the table shown in Table 2.3.

Table 2.3 Price index for Activity 2.2

Item	2009	2010	2011
Resin	100	80	72
Mat	100	100	125
Labour	100	106	151

You can see that the index for resin has shown a decrease while labour has shown the largest increase. But what does this tell you about the cost of production? Is it possible to combine the data in some way so that an aggregate index can be obtained?

Activity 2.3

Could you obtain an aggregate index simply by adding the prices together for each year?

There are two problems with this approach: first, the items are in different units; you have litres, square metres and hours; and second, the importance of each item might be different. If labour is the dominant cost then the aggregate index should reflect this fact. To overcome these problems each item is weighted according to its importance. When this is done you have a *weighted aggregate index*.

Weighted aggregate indices

In order to weight an index it is necessary to have information on the importance of each item. For the boat example, this could be done by recording the quantities used in its production.

Example 2.2

The quantities required in the production of a boat vary from year to year as production methods change. This can be seen in Table 2.4.

Table 2.4 Quantity data for Example 2.2

Item	2009	2010	2011
Resin	50 l	48 l	48 l
Mat	200 m²	210 m²	215 m²
Labour	30 hours	27 hours	23 hours

Activity 2.4

How might you use the information in Examples 2.1 and 2.2 to create an aggregate index?

Since price × quantity equals the cost of that item, the aggregate index could be obtained as:

$$\frac{\text{Total cost of production at current prices}}{\text{Total cost of production at base year prices}}$$

There is, however, one problem with this definition. What quantities should we use? Both price and quantities have varied from year to year and for comparison purposes we need to use the same quantities for the numerator and denominator of the index. The choice is to use either the base year quantities or the current year quantities. When you use the former you have a base weighted or *Laspeyres'* index, and when you use the latter you have a current weighted or *Paasche's* index.

Laspeyres' index

The definition of the Laspeyres' index is:

$$\frac{\text{Total cost of base year quantities at current prices}}{\text{Total cost of base year quantities at base year prices}}$$

Using p to represent price and q to represent quantity, this definition can be expressed as:

Sum of current prices times base quantities

$$\text{Laspeyres' index} = \frac{\sum p_n q_0}{\sum p_0 q_0} \times 100$$

Sum of base prices times base quantities

In order to calculate this index for the boat example, you may find it useful to write the data from Examples 2.1 and 2.2 into another table (Table 2.5).

Table 2.5 Price and quantity combined

Item	2009		2010		2011	
	Price	Quantity	Price	Quantity	Price	Quantity
Resin	£0.25	50	£0.20	48	£0.18	48
Mat	£0.16	200	£0.16	210	£0.20	215
Labour	£5.50	30	£5.85	27	£8.30	23

Activity 2.5

Calculate the Laspeyres' index for 2010 and 2011 using 2009 as the base year.

Each year needs to be calculated separately. These calculations are tabulated in Tables 2.6 and 2.7.

Table 2.6 Calculation of Laspeyres' index for 2010

p_0	q_0	p_n	$p_0 q_0$	$p_n q_0$
0.25	50	0.20	12.5	10.0
0.16	200	0.16	32.0	32.0
5.50	30	5.85	165.0	175.5
		Sum	209.5	217.5

Table 2.7 Calculation of Laspeyres' index for 2011

p_0	q_0	p_n	$p_0 q_0$	$p_n q_0$
0.25	50	0.18	12.5	9.0
0.16	200	0.20	32.0	40.0
5.50	30	8.30	165.0	249.0
		Sum	209.5	298.0

So the Laspeyres' index for 2010 $= \dfrac{217.5}{209.5} \times 100 = 103.8$

and for 2011 it is $= \dfrac{298.0}{209.5} \times 100 = 142.2$

You can see from these calculations that there has been a dramatic increase in the index from 2010 to 2011. This was due to the large increase in labour costs that took place during 2010 to 2011.

Paasche's index

The definition of the Paasche's index is:

$$\frac{\text{Total cost of current year quantities at current prices}}{\text{Total cost of current year quantities at base year prices}}$$

This can again be expressed in algebraic form as:

Sum of current prices times current quantities

$$\text{Paasche's index} = \frac{\sum p_n q_n}{\sum p_0 q_n} \times 100$$

Sum of base prices times current quantities

Activity 2.6

Calculate the Paasche's index for the boat building example.

A table can again be used in the calculation. The calculations for 2010 are shown in Table 2.8.

Table 2.8 Calculation of Paasche's index for 2010

p_0	q_0	p_n	$p_0 q_0$	$p_n q_0$
0.25	48	0.20	12.00	9.60
0.16	210	0.16	33.60	33.60
5.50	27	5.85	148.50	157.95
		Sum	194.10	201.15

So the Paasche's index for 2010 $= \dfrac{201.15}{194.1} \times 100 = 103.6$

If you repeat these calculations for 2011 you should find that the sum of $p_0 q_n$ is 172.9 and the sum of $p_n q_n$ is 242.54. So the Paasche's index for 2011 is:

$$\frac{242.54}{172.9} \times 100 = 140.3$$

Both indices give similar results for this data and in general there will not be a great difference between the two unless the weights (quantities) are very different. Table 2.9 summarizes the advantages and disadvantages of each index.

Table 2.9 Comparison of the two indices

	Laspeyres' index	Paasche's index
Ease of calculation	Denominator only calculated once	Denominator recalculated each year
Quantities required each year	No, only base quantities required	Yes
Comparability	Direct comparison from year to year	No direct comparison
Accuracy	Weights quickly become out of date	Reflects consumption patterns in current year

In practice the Laspeyres' index is the most commonly used index and the base year is redefined at regular intervals. When the base year is redefined it is a good idea to recalculate the index for previous years. For example, the figures below represent an index for the years 2000 to 2008. The base year was 2000 but it has been decided to change the base year to 2008.

2000	2001	2002	2003	2004	2005	2006	2007	2008
100	105.6	108.9	121.2	142.3	145.1	147.9	148.8	153.1

The index in 2000 becomes

$$\frac{100}{153.1} \times 100 = 65.3$$

Activity 2.7

Calculate the index for each subsequent year.

You should have obtained the following figures:

2000	2001	2002	2003	2004	2005	2006	2007	2008
65.3	69.0	71.1	79.2	92.9	94.8	96.6	97.2	100

Consumer price indices

Two very important indices are the retail price index (RPI) and the consumer price index (CPI). They both show how prices have changed (usually upwards!) over the years and are a determining factor in deciding how interest rates, wages, pensions and tax allowances for instance are changed. Both indices measure the change in the price of a 'basket' of goods and are used as a measure of inflation although the government inflation target is based in the CPI. The RPI covers some 650 items divided into 14 groups, such as food, housing and motoring expenditure. Each component of the index is given a weight to represent the importance of that item and the weights are updated annually by the *family expenditure survey*. Prices of each item in the index are checked monthly. The weights used in the RPI are designed for the 'average' family and are not representative of high income groups or pensioners. The CPI is similar but excludes things like council tax and other housing costs but its weights cover all income groups. It also include some financial services and follows international definitions.

The current RPI is based on prices of goods in January 1987 and this date was given a value of 100. In January 2011 the RPI was 229.0 so a basket of goods costing £100 in 1987 would have cost £229.00 in January 2011. This means that prices have increased by 129.0% (229.0 – 100) during this period.

Did you know

In the 2010 June budget the Chancellor of the Exchequer George Osborne announced that in future public sector benefits and pensions will be linked to the CPI and not the RPI. Over the past 20 years the CPI has only been greater than the RPI on 3 occasions so in general annual increases will be lower than if the RPI had been used.

Activity 2.8

The RPI in January 2010 was 217.9 and the CPI was 112.9 in January 2010 and 116.9 in January 2011. Compare the rates of inflation as given by these two indices.

We know that the RPI in January 2011 was 229.0 so the change in this index has been $229.0 - 217.9 = 11.1$ and the percentage change relative to January 2010 is $11.1/217.9 \times 100 = 5.1\%$. An alternative way of calculating the percentage change is $229.0/217.9 = 1.051$ which is a 5.1% change.

Similarly for the CPI change we get $116.9/112.9 = 1.035$ which is a 3.5% change. So inflation is rising faster according to the RPI.

Inflation makes the value of a £1 now worth less in the future. Likewise a £1 in the past is worth less now. This means that a company's cash flow or a person's salary should be *deflated* to allow for inflation. When we do this we usually talk about the *real* change in cash flow or earnings.

The next example illustrates a company's turnover during a 6-year period.

Example 2.3

A company's turnover (in £m) since 2005 has been as follows:

2005	2006	2007	2008	2009	2010
2.3	3.3	4.1	4.2	4.4	4.7

It looks as if turnover has been steadily increasing, but at the same time the RPI has also been increasing. The average value of the RPI since 2005 has been as follows:

2005	2006	2007	2008	2009	2010
192.0	198.1	206.6	214.8	213.7	223.6

(*Source: Monthly Digest of Statistics*)

Although the turnover has increased from £2.3m to £3.3m between 2005 and 2006 the RPI has increased from 192.0 to 198.1. This means that the RPI has changed by $198.1/192 = 1.032$ or 3.2%. £3.3m is therefore only really worth £3.3/1.032 $= £3.20$m at 2005 prices. An easier way to deflate an amount is as follows

$$\text{Value now} = \frac{\text{value then} \times \text{RPI then}}{\text{RPI now}}$$

So using our example, the £3.3m turnover in 2006 becomes

$$3.3 \times \frac{192.0}{198.1} = £3.20\text{m}$$

Activity 2.9

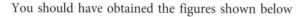

Calculate the deflated turnover for the remainder of the years.

You should have obtained the figures shown below

2005	2006	2007	2008	2009	2010
2.3	3.20	3.81	3.75	3.95	4.04

The picture is now one of steadily rising turnover until 2007 after which the turnover appears to level off. This can be seen clearly in Figure 2.3.

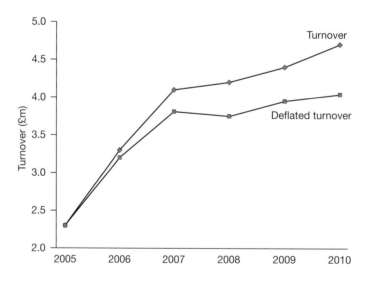

Figure 2.3
Chart for Activity 2.9

Reflection

Indices are as common today as averages, but as with averages many people do not really understand what an index is. For example, when inflation is quoted as (say) 3%, how many people really understand that this means that the retail price index has increased by 3%? The RPI in January 2011 was 229.0 while for the same month in 2010 it was 217.9, a change of 11.1 in the index. In percentage terms, however, this represents a change of 5.1%, and this is used as a measure of inflation.

Another complicating factor is that there are different measures of inflation. The RPI was the most common index. It was used to adjust pensions and showed the effect of inflation on household expenditure. However the UK government's preferred measure is the CPI and this is now used in up-rating pensions and benefits. There are several other indices used in the UK such as tax and price index (TPI) which includes income tax paid and allows the government to see what increase in pay is needed to compensate for tax rises.

Indices can be used to monitor all kinds of prices and commodities. The oil price data shown above in *Quantitative methods in action* might not be an obvious set of data to make into an index, but as you saw the index helps enormously in comparing the volumes of oil consumption in the different countries. From Figure 2.2 we can see clearly the rapid rise in China's oil consumption between 1986 and 2009. What this chart doesn't tell us is what the future consumption of oil will be. Although BP has estimated that there are 46 years of oil reserves remaining, this figure is based on current consumption. Others suggest that oil reserves will rapidly decline from 2011 ('UK firms fear collapse of oil supplies will mean devastation for economy' – *The Guardian* 30/10/08). We will consider forecasting in Chapter 13.

Key points

○ An *index* allows changes in a variable to be compared over a period of time.
○ The *base index* is given a value of 100, so an index value below 100 means a decrease and a value above 100 means an increase. As the base is 100, these changes can also be expressed in percentage terms.
○ For a single item or variable, a *simple index* can be used.
○ Where several items are involved, it is necessary to use a *weighted aggregate index*.
○ There are two main *weighted indices*. These are *Laspeyres' index*, which is a base weighted index, and *Paasche's index*, which is a current weighted index.
○ The Laspeyres' index is easier to use but soon gets out of date, while the Paasche's index reflects consumption patterns in the current year.
○ The *retail price index* (*RPI*) and *consumer price index* (*CPI*) use consumption patterns as weights. These are derived from a family expenditure survey.
○ The RPI and CPI are used as measures of *inflation*, and allow financial data to be *deflated*. The CPI is the index favoured by the UK government and is used to up-rate public sector pensions and benefits.

Further reading

Most general quantitative method texts have a chapter on index numbers. The text by Curwin and Slater (2008) gives a good coverage, particularly on the differences between RPI and CPI. There are many on-line sources particularly from the Office of National Statistics (ONS). The ONS website for all sources of economic data including the RPI and CP is www.ons.gov.uk.

Web links [W]

Answers to selected questions can be found in Appendix 2. Answers to the other questions can be found on the companion website for this book.

Practice questions

1   Labour costs (in £000s) for an engineering company over the last 10 years has been as follows

2002	2003	2004	2005	2006	2007	2008	2009	2010	2011
50.1	65.3	68.6	72.0	76.6	78.3	88.7	90.5	99.3	112.9

Convert these costs into an index using 2002 as the base year.

[W] 2   The cost of an 'average' laptop computer has fallen over the last 3 years
Year 1   £650   Year 2   £580   Year 3   £410
Create an index of laptop prices using year 1 as the base year.

[W] 3   A manufacturer of greeting cards requires ink, card and production staff to produce its range of cards. The estimated cost of each resource over the past 3 years is as follows:

Resource	2009	2010	2011
Ink (£ per litre)	£0.55	£0.58	£0.76
Card (£ per m²)	£0.05	£0.05	£0.08
Labour (£ per hour)	£6.50	£6.90	£7.00

Create a simple index for each resource and comment on which resource has increased the most.

[W] 4   In addition to the cost data for the greeting card manufacturer in question 3 the quantities of each resource used over the past 3 years is as follows.

Resource	2009	2010	2011
Ink (litres)	4000	5000	3000
Card (m²)	115 000	124 000	110 000
Labour (number)	25	34	30

(a) Calculate the Laspeyres' index for 2010 and 2011 using 2009 as the base year
(b) Calculate the Paasche's index for 2010 and 2011 using 2009 as the base year
(c) Comment on the change in both indices over the 3 years.

[W] 5   The price and quantity consumed in a normal week of 3 items of food for a family are as follows:

	1990		2010	
	Price	Qty	Price	Qty
Bread	28p/loaf	6 loaves	78p/loaf	6 loaves
Milk	20p/pint	15 pints	150p/pint	12 pints
Tea	96p/packet	1 packet	75p/packet	2 packets

(a) Calculate the Laspeyres' index for 2010 using 1990 as the base year.
(b) Calculate the Paasche's index for 2010 using 1990 as the base year.

W 6 A person has a portfolio of 4 shares. The price and quantity of shares held between 1998 and 2011 are as follows:

	1998		2011	
Share	Price	No. held	Price	No. held
Company A	160	200	520	500
Company B	350	650	265	250
Company C	105	600	140	400
Company D	53	100	159	200

(a) Calculate the Laspeyres' index for 2011 using 1998 as the base year.

(b) Calculate the Paasche's index for 2011 using 1998 as the base year.

W 7 The price of a house in a residential district fell from £140 000 in 2004 to £105 000 in 2008. What was the real drop in price if the retail price index changed from 186.7 in 2004 to 214.8 in 2008?

W 8 A company's turnover (in £m) since 2005 has been as follows:

2005	2006	2007	2008	2009	2010
15.3	10.3	12.1	15.2	24.4	34.7

What has been the real turnover if the value of the RPI for each of these years has been as follows?

2005	2006	2007	2008	2009	2010
192.0	198.1	206.8	214.8	213.7	223.6

9 The following table gives the number employed by each department and the average salary for that department. Calculate Laspeyres' index and Paasche's index for 2011 using 2003 as the base year.

	2003		2011	
	Number employed	Av. salary (£000s)	Number employed	Av. salary (£000s)
Sales	120	7.5	158	9.0
Admin.	41	10.0	52	12.5
Clerical	25	8.0	30	10.0
Managerial	21	18.0	25	22.4

(*Source*: Payroll Department)

10 Using the information on the price and quantities used of given materials in 2006 and 2011, calculate for these years:

(a) the Laspeyres' index

(b) the Paasche's index

	2006		2011	
Material	Price (£)	Quantity	Price (£)	Quantity
A	3.63	3	4.49	2
B	2.11	4	3.26	6
C	10.03	1	12.05	1
D	4.01	7	5.21	5

11 (a) For the following data on the price of a security over 6 months, construct a fixed base index (use August = 100).

Month	Aug	Sept	Oct	Nov	Dec	Jan
Price	155	143	120	139	165	162

(b) By what percentage has the security price changed between:
   (i) August and January?
   (ii) September and December?

12 The following table gives the average weekly wage and the average retail price index (RPI) for the years 2008–2010:

Year	2008	2009	2010
Av. weekly wage (£s)	255.1	271.3	290.7
Av. RPI	214.8	213.7	223.6

Deflate the wage figures to 2008 values. Comment on the 'real value' of wages over this period of time.

13 The price of a house in a residential district fell from £62 000 in 2008 to £57 500 in 2010. What was the real drop in price? (Use the RPI figures from question 12.)

14 **(a)** The RPI figures in Question 12 used January 1987 as the base period (that is, January 1987 = 100). Construct a table of RPIs using the 'average' figures quoted for the years 2008–2010 with 2008 as the base period.
   (b) By what percentage has the average RPI changed between:
      (i) 2008 and 2009?
      (ii) 2008 and 2010?
      (iii) 2009 and 2010?

....

Assignment

You are to use the internet to investigate the composition of the CPI and how it is updated. You should use graphs and diagrams to illustrate its composition and provide examples of how the index is calculated. Discuss how useful this index would be to:

(a) the government as a means of controlling inflation

(b) a union for wage negotiation purposes

(c) a pensioner in deciding how well off he or she is likely to be next year.

Finally, comment on the accuracy of the index and how it compares to the RPI.

II

COLLECTING AND INTERPRETING DATA

Collecting data: surveys and samples

Objectives

- To understand the difference between a sampling frame, a sample and a population
- To understand the difference between probabilistic and non-probabilistic sampling
- To know how to select the correct sampling method in different situations
- To understand how to design a questionnaire

Introduction

Many decisions made by business and by the government are the result of information obtained from sample data, as it is often too costly or impractical to collect data for the whole population.

Data may already exist or it may need to be collected. When we have to collect our own data we call it *primary data*. When it already exists, as in government statistics, we call it *secondary data*. The collection of data can take many forms, but in this chapter we will concentrate on data that is collected by carrying out surveys. During the UK General Election in 2010 many surveys were undertaken by market research companies. The purpose of these surveys was not just to try and understand how people might vote, but also to look at attitudes to issues and leaders, for example. Most of these surveys would have been conducted by telephone or face-to-face, although in some other less urgent surveys people are sent questionnaires by post or email or complete a questionnaire online.

In the surveys undertaken during the UK General Election a lot of care would have gone into selecting a representative sample of the target population. The samples had to be representative of the gender, age profile and ethnicity of the population being surveyed as well as other attributes that might be considered to affect people's voting intentions or views. The number of people being surveyed would also be calculated to ensure that a specified level of accuracy was obtained. A fuller discussion of accuracy issues when taking samples of data is given in Chapter 8.

As well as discussing ways of collecting samples of data this chapter also discusses questionnaire design because it is very important to ensure that the type and wording of questions is given proper attention if the analysis is to be of use. Finally we will look at sources of secondary data available on the internet, as well as how to use search engines more effectively.

Quantitative methods in action: the 2010 UK General Election

During the run-up to the 2010 General Election in the UK a large number of polls were conducted by several market research companies. Table 3.1 shows the results of the final polls taken by companies who are members of the British Polling Council.

The actual result is also shown and you can see that in general these polls were very accurate. All but one of the pollsters got the Conservatives' share of the vote to within 2%. However all pollsters under-predicted the Labour vote and over-predicted the Liberal Democrat vote. The average error is the average of the difference between the poll result and the actual result across all four estimates, so on this basis the Harris poll was the most accurate.

The British Polling Council was formed to foster the professionalism of market research companies and members have to demonstrate that they use appropriate sampling methods and weighting procedures that will accurately represent the target population. When a member organization makes a poll result available to the general public it must give the following details of the poll:

○ Client commissioning the survey
○ Dates of interviewing
○ Method of obtaining the interviews (e.g. in-person, telephone, internet)
○ The population effectively represented (e.g. all adults, voters)
○ The percentages upon which conclusions are based
○ Size of the sample and geographic coverage.

We will discuss some of these issues in this and subsequent chapters.

Source: British Polling Council

Table 3.1 Final poll for the 2010 General Election

	Conservative	Labour	Liberal Democrat	Other	Average error
	%	%	%	%	%
Angus Reid	36	24	29	11	3.25
Com Res	37	28	28	7	2.25
Harris	35	29	27	10	1.5
ICM	36	28	26	10	1.25
Ipsos MORI	36	29	27	8	1.75
Opinium	35	27	26	12	2.25
Populus	37	28	27	8	1.75
TNS BMRB	33	27	29	11	3.25
YouGov	35	28	28	9	2.25
Actual result	37	30	24	10	

Source: British Polling Council.

The basics of sampling

I am sure that you have been a *respondent* in a survey at least once in your life. Have you filled in a *questionnaire* or been stopped in the street and asked some questions? You no doubt know that the purpose of a survey is for some organization or person to obtain *information* about some issue or product. This information could range from what television programme you watched last night to your views on the government of the day.

A survey only collects information about a small subset of the *population*. The word 'population' can and often does refer to all the people in Britain or a town, but for statisticians it is also a general term used to refer to all groups or items being surveyed. For instance, it could refer to the viewing habits of all children in a town or, as you will see in a later chapter, it could refer to the weights of jars of coffee produced by a company during a week. The alternative to a survey is to question every member of the population, and when this is done it is called a *census*. Unfortunately it is expensive and very difficult to carry out a census, and also unnecessary. A survey of a small subset of the population, called a *sample*, can give surprisingly accurate results if carried out properly. Unfortunately, if not carried out correctly, the results can at best be unreliable and at worst misleading. Before you carry out a survey you need answers to several questions, such as:

- What is the purpose of this survey?
- What is my *target* population?
- Do I have a list of the population?
- How can I avoid bias in my sample?
- How accurate do I want my survey to be?
- What resources do I have at my disposal?
- How am I going to collect the required data?

Did you know

The 2011 census was estimated to have cost the taxpayer £460m (Cabinet Office estimate) – the most expensive ever.

There has been a census in the UK every 10 years since 1801.

The census in 2011 is expected to be the last one. Other sources of information such as the electoral roll, GP records, tax returns and school enrolments will probably be used instead.

It is crucial to be clear about the purpose of the survey. Not only will this dictate your target population but it will also allow you to formulate your questionnaire correctly. For example, if you are interested in consumers' opinion of a new alcoholic drink it would be pointless targeting people under 18 (and unethical). The target population should contain every person who is likely to buy your product or whose views you are particularly interested in.

Once you have selected your target population, you need to determine whether there is any list that would allow you to identify every member of the population. This list is called a *sampling frame*, and examples include the electoral register, a company's personnel records or even a list of all serial numbers of cars built by one car manufacturer last year. Sometimes a sampling frame is simply not available or is too difficult to obtain, in which case achieving a *representative* sample will be more difficult, but not necessarily impossible.

Activity 3.1

What would be your target population for a survey on motorway tariffs, and would there be a sampling frame available?

If you were only interested in the views of British car drivers then anyone holding a UK driving licence would form your target population. A suitable sampling frame would be records held by the DVLC at Swansea. It would not be 100% accurate as drivers might have changed address and not informed the DVLC, or they might have died.

Once your target population has been chosen and an appropriate sampling frame identified, it is necessary to choose your sample. If the sample is chosen badly your results will be inaccurate due to *bias* in your sample. Bias is caused by choosing a sample that is unrepresentative of the target population. For example, perhaps you wanted to discover people's views on whether a sports field should be sold to a property developer. If your sample contained a large number of people from the local football club, then the sample is likely to be biased in favour of one particular group! To avoid bias you need to ensure that your sample is *representative* of the target population. You will see how this can be achieved later.

Did you know   In the US Presidential Election in 1936 between Alfred Landon and Franklin Roosevelt the *Literary Digest* sent out 10 million post cards asking people how they would vote. The magazine received almost 2.3 million back, and the result suggested that Landon was leading Roosevelt by 57% to 43%. A young pollster named George Gallup also did a survey but on a much smaller sample. He correctly predicted that Roosevelt would win easily. In the event Roosevelt went on to win with 60% against just 37% for Landon. The reason why the *Literary Digest* did so badly was that they used a directory of car owners and the telephone directory, which gave them a biased sample because only the better-off had cars or telephones. Gallup had used a much more representative sample.

The purpose of a survey is to obtain information about a population. All other things being equal, the accuracy of the sample results will depend on the sample size; the larger the sample, the more accurate the results. A large sample will clearly cost more than a small one, although the method that is employed to collect the data will also determine the accuracy and cost of the survey. Methods of data collection range

Table 3.2 Methods of data collection

	Postal questionnaire	Telephone interviewing	Face-to-face interviewing	Online
Cost	Low	Moderate	High	Low
Response rate	Low	Moderate	High	Moderate
Speed	Slow	Fast	Fast*	Fast
Quantity of information collected	Limited	Moderate	High	Limited
Quality of information collected	Depends on how well the questionnaire has been designed	Good	High	Depends on how well the questionnaire has been designed

*The speed of collecting the data will be high but travelling time by the interviewers may need to be considered.

from the use of postal questionnaires to 'face-to-face' interviews. Some methods of data collection are expensive but guarantee a good response rate, while others are cheap to administer but are likely to produce quite a poor response. Table 3.2 compares the main methods of collecting data.

Activity 3.2

You have been asked to obtain the views of the student population at your institution regarding car parking facilities within the campus. What method of data collection would you use?

The best method would probably be face-to-face interviews, but it is unlikely that you would have the resources for this approach. Telephone interviewing is probably not realistic because of the cost and the fact that students' telephone numbers might be difficult to obtain. This leaves you with either a postal or online questionnaire, both of which should be quite reasonable for this relatively simple type of survey.

There are two types of sampling procedures for obtaining your sample. The first is *probabilistic* sampling, which requires the existence of a sampling frame. The second method is *non-probabilistic* sampling, which does not rely on a sampling frame. Probabilistic sampling is the most important form of sampling as it allows you to use probability theory to calculate the probability that a particular sample could have occurred by chance.

Did you know

During the 2010 General Election in the UK a crisp manufacturer was seen giving away packets of crisps outside King's Cross station. The crisp packets were coloured red (for Labour), blue (for the Conservatives) and yellow (for the Liberal Democrats). Each of these different coloured packets were in 3 identical bins which had the picture of the party leader on the front. This was a publicity stunt by the crisp manufacturer but could the number of the different coloured packets taken at any one time reveal the popularity of each of the leaders? (Source: BBC News Magazine, 6 January 2011).

Think of as many reasons as you can why the data might lie.

Questionnaire design

Questionnaire design is more of an art than a science and there is no universal design that would be suitable for all situations. The actual design will depend on factors such as:

- the type of respondent (for example, business, consumers, children)
- the method of data collection (postal, telephone, face-to-face or online)
- the resources available.

However, even though no two questionnaires will be identical, it is possible to make a list of some 'dos and don'ts' that should apply to most questionnaires. The most important ones are:

- Do make each question brief and the wording clear and concise with minimal use of jargon. It shouldn't be necessary to explain to the respondent the meaning of a particular question.
- Do keep the length of the questionnaire to a minimum. A maximum of around 20 questions is probably a good guide for most surveys.
- Do make the questions simple to answer.
- Do make the questions as specific as possible. A question such as '*Are you a heavy smoker?*' could be interpreted differently by different respondents. It would be much better to give ranges such as '*Do you smoke less than 10 cigarettes a day?*', '*Between 10 and 20?*' and '*Over 20?*'
- Do have a logical sequence to the questions.
- Do start with simple questions such as gender, leaving more complicated questions for later in the questionnaire.
- Don't leave the most important question to last. There is a risk that if a respondent becomes bored with answering a questionnaire he or she may not complete the final section.
- Don't use leading questions. For example, '*What are your views on the level of indirect taxation in the UK?*' is better than '*Do you agree that indirect taxation in the UK is too high?*'
- Do try and avoid asking personal questions. Even information on salary is considered by many people to be personal and most respondents prefer to have salary ranges to select. It is often better to ask this type of question later in the questionnaire. If it is necessary to collect really personal information, a face-to-face interview is essential using experienced interviewers.
- Do use a filtering method if not all questions are applicable to all respondents. For example, '*Did you watch Eastenders last night?*' may then be followed by questions relating to this episode. To avoid asking non-viewers these questions you will need to have an instruction that allows these non-viewers to jump to the next appropriate question.
- Don't ask two questions in one. A question such as '*Is your job interesting and well paid?*' is unlikely to be answered with a simple yes or no.

○ Don't ask questions that rely on memory. Asking respondents if they watched *Eastenders* last night is acceptable, but asking if they watched it last week or last month will not necessarily produce very reliable results.

○ Don't ask hypothetical questions. Asking someone what he or she would do under a hypothetical situation (such as winning the National Lottery) is unlikely to lead to reliable results. In some surveys this type of question cannot be avoided, but extra care should be taken in its wording.

○ It is generally better to use close-ended questions (see later) rather than allow open answers. However, do allow for the fact that your selection of responses might not be complete by having an 'other' category.

For example, '*What type of property do you live in?*'
Terraced house   Semi-detached   Detached   Flat
This question needs an '*Other*' category since you might find someone who lives on a boat or in a windmill!

○ Make the questionnaire attractive and easy to complete. Microsoft Word allows you to create forms for use as questionnaires and you can then distribute these forms as an email attachment if this is appropriate for your sample.

○ Do conduct a pilot survey on a small but *representative* sample of the target population. This will test out your design and allow you to fine tune it.

Having looked at some of the more important dos and don'ts of questionnaire design we now need to consider the format of the questions and the most effective method of obtaining reliable responses. Questions are of two forms: *close-ended* questions and *open-ended* questions. Close-ended questions give the respondents a choice of answers and are generally considered much easier to answer and to analyze. However, the limited response range can give misleading results. Open-ended questions, such as '*Why did you buy this product?*', allow respondents more flexibility in the type of response (you may get answers that you hadn't thought of), but of course this type of question is difficult to analyze. Close-ended questions are the most commonly used type and can take many forms, such as:

○ *Dichotomous questions* These are questions that have only two answers, such as yes or no.

○ *Numeric* Some questions ask for a single number, such as the distance travelled to work each day. Where the question is personal (for example, earnings or age) it is best to give a range, such as:

Less than £20 000   £20 000 to £30 000   Over £30 000

○ *Multiple choice* Respondents select from three or more choices (the question on salary above is an example of a multiple choice question).

○ *Likert scale* The question is a statement, such as '*Taxes should be increased to pay for a better health service*', and respondents indicate their amount of agreement using a scale similar to the one below.

Strongly agree	*Agree*	*Neither agree nor disagree*	*Disagree*	*Strongly disagree*

○ *Semantic differential* With this type of question only two ends of the scale are provided and the respondent selects the point between the two ends that represents his views. For example, '*The leisure facilities in my town are*':

Excellent _____ *Poor*

○ *Rank order* Respondents are asked to rank each option. This type of question is useful if you want to obtain information on relative preferences, but is more difficult to analyze. The number of choices should be kept to a minimum.

Once the questionnaire has been designed you need to decide how to collect the data. Some methods require a sampling frame while others do not.

Simple random sampling

With this method every member of the target population has an *equal* chance of being selected. This implies that a sampling frame is required and a method of *randomly* selecting the required sample from this list. The simplest example of this technique is a raffle where the winning ticket is drawn from the 'hat'. For a more formal application a stream of *random numbers* would be used. Random numbers are numbers that show no pattern; each digit is equally likely. A table of random numbers is given in Appendix 1. The method of simple random sampling using random numbers is quite easy to apply, although tedious, as you will see from Example 3.1.

Example 3.1

Table 3.3 is a part of a list of students enrolled on a business studies course at a university.

Say from this 'population' of 25 students you wanted to randomly select a sample of 5 students. How would you do it? You could use the student number (in this case conveniently numbered from 1 to 25) and then try and obtain a match using a stream of two-digit random numbers. For example, suppose you had the following random numbers: 78, 41, 11, 62, 72, 18, 66, 69, 58, 71, 31, 90, 51, 36, 78, 09, 41, 00, 70, 50, 58, 19, 68, 26, 75, 69, and 04. The first two numbers don't exist in our population but 11 does – it is student D. Jeffrey. The next two numbers do not exist but 18 does, and so on. The final sample is numbers 11, 18, 09, 19 and 04, which are students D. Jeffrey, S. Moore, G. Godfrey, F. Muper, and C. Meng.

The majority of random numbers were redundant in this case because the population was so small. In practice the population would be much larger, but the method remains essentially the same. Most sampling frames are held on computer these days so it is much easier to use the computer to select the sample.

Activity 3.3

Randomly select another sample of 5 students from the list in Table 3.3 using the random numbers: 09, 55, 42, 30, 27, 05, 24, 93, 78, 10, 69, 09, and 11.

Table 3.3 List of students enrolled on a business studies course

Number	Name	Gender
1	N. Adams	Male
2	C. Shah	Male
3	B. Booth	Female
4	C. Meng	Male
5	A. Ho	Male
6	D. Drew	Male
7	K. Fisher	Female
8	P. Frome	Male
9	G. Godfrey	Male
10	J. Bakoulas	Male
11	D. Jeffrey	Female
12	H. Jones	Male
13	M. Li	Male
14	N. King	Female
15	K. Lenow	Male
16	A. Loft	Female
17	T. Georgiou	Female
18	S. Moore	Female
19	F. Muper	Female
20	R. Muster	Female
21	A. Night	Male
22	J. Nott	Male
23	L. Nupper	Male
24	K. Khan	Male
25	O. Patter	Female

You should have noticed that number 09 occurs twice. What did you do in this case? For practical reasons you should have ignored the second 09 and chosen the next number, 11, instead. Your final sample should have been: G. Godfrey, A. Ho, K. Khan, J. Bakoulas and D. Jeffrey.

How representative of the target population are these samples? Since the population is so small it is a simple matter to compare each sample with the population. For instance, there are 15 male and 10 female students, which is a proportion of 60% males to 40% females. In the first sample there were 2 males out of 5, a proportion of 40%, and in the second there were 4 males, a proportion of 80%. From this you can see that the first sample was an underestimate of the true number of males, while the second was an overestimate. Another sample could be different again, and you may even get a sample of all the same sex. This variation is called *sampling error* and occurs in all sampling procedures. In Chapter 8 you will be shown how to quantify this error.

It is possible to reduce the sampling error by a slight modification to the simple random sample method. This is applicable when the target population can be categorized into groups or *strata*.

Stratified sampling

Many populations can be divided into different categories. For example, a population of adults consists of the two sexes, the employed and unemployed, and many other categories. If you think that the responses you will get from your survey are likely to be determined partly by each category, then clearly you want your sample to contain each category in the correct proportions.

Activity 3.4

Using the random numbers 09, 55, 42, 30, 27, 05, 25, 93, 78, 10, 69, 09, 11, 99, 21 and 01, obtain a sample of size 5 that contains the correct proportion of each sex.

You probably realized that your sample should contain 3 males (60% of 5). In order to ensure that you will get exactly 3 males, you should first of all have separated out the two sexes and then obtained two simple random samples, one of size 3 and one of size 2, as shown in Table 3.4.

Table 3.4 Table ordered by gender

Number	Name	Sex	Number	Name	Sex
1	N. Adams	Male	1	B. Booth	Female
2	J. Bakoulas	Male	2	K. Fisher	Female
3	D. Drew	Male	3	T. Georgiou	Female
4	P. Frome	Male	4	D. Jeffrey	Female
5	G. Godfrey	Male	5	N. King	Female
6	A. Ho	Male	6	A. Loft	Female
7	H. Jones	Male	7	S. Moore	Female
8	K. Khan	Male	8	F. Muper	Female
9	K. Lenow	Male	9	R. Muster	Female
10	M. Li	Male	10	O. Patter	Female
11	C. Meng	Male			
12	A. Night	Male			
13	J. Nott	Male			
14	L. Nupper	Male			
15	C. Shah	Male			

The two populations have been re-numbered, although this is not essential. The first sample consists of students 9, 5 and 10, that is K. Lenow, G. Godfrey and M. Li, while the second sample consists of students 9 and 1, that is R. Muster and B. Booth.

Stratified sampling is a very reliable method but it does assume that you have a knowledge of the categories of the population. Stratified sampling is often used in conjunction with the next method.

Multi-stage sampling

If the target population covers a wide geographical area then a simple random sample may have selected respondents in quite different parts of the country. If the method employed to collect the data is of the face-to-face interview type, then clearly a great deal of travelling could be involved. To overcome this problem the area to be surveyed is divided into smaller areas and a number of these smaller areas randomly selected. If desired, the smaller areas chosen could themselves be divided into smaller districts and a random number of these selected. This procedure is continued until the area is small enough for a simple random sample (or a stratified sample) to be selected. The final sample should consist of respondents concentrated into a small number of areas. It is important that the random sample chosen from each area is the same proportion of the population or bias towards certain areas could result. As it is, bias is likely to occur as a result of similarity of responses from people within the same area, but this is the price you pay for reduced travelling time.

Activity 3.5

You have been asked to obtain a representative sample of television viewers from across Britain using the multi-stage sampling method. How would you select the sample?

The country could be split into counties, or perhaps television regions might be more appropriate in this case. A number of these would be chosen at random, and these areas subdivided into district councils. A random sample of districts within each chosen region could now be selected, and the selected districts divided into postal areas. A random sample of residents within each chosen postal area could then be chosen using the register of electors.

Figure 3.1 illustrates this process in diagrammatic form. At each level you are taking a random sample. Note that it is not until you get to the individual elector that you carry out the actual survey.

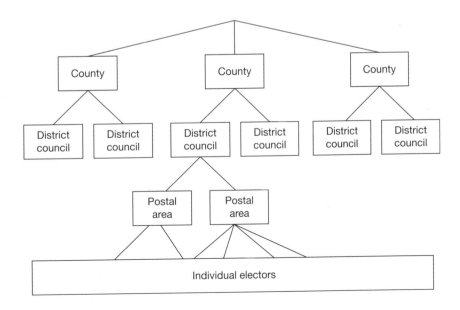

Figure 3.1
Multi-stage sampling

Cluster sampling

Cluster sampling is similar to multi-stage sampling and is used when a sampling frame is not available. Again a large geographical area is divided into a number of smaller areas called *clusters*. If necessary these clusters can be further subdivided to obtain clusters which are small enough for *all* members of the cluster to be surveyed. As with multi-stage sampling, a bias will result due to similarities in responses from members of the same cluster. The difference between cluster sampling and multi-stage sampling is that since individual members of a cluster cannot be identified in advance, it is necessary for all members to be surveyed. Random sampling is therefore *not* involved.

Activity 3.6

How would you apply cluster sampling to the population referred to in Activity 3.5?

You would carry out the same procedure to obtain a selected number of postal districts, but these districts could be further subdivided so that individual streets were identified. All households of selected streets would then be surveyed.

Systematic sampling

This method is normally used with a sampling frame but it can also be used where a sampling frame is not available. However, in this case the size of the population must be known. The idea is that every nth member of a population is selected, where the value of n is determined by the size of the population and by the required sample size. For instance, if a 5% sample is to be selected from a population of size 1000, then every 50th person will be selected. The start of the sequence is usually chosen at random. For example, if a 20% sample was to be selected from the student population given in Table 3.3, every 5th person would be selected. If you started with, say, the third student, your sample would consist of B. Booth, P. Frome, M. Li, S. Moore and L. Nupper.

Activity 3.7

You have been asked by a local newspaper to find out what people thought of a particular film that is showing at the local cinema. How would you obtain a sample of 10 people?

Clearly it would be pointless asking people who hadn't seen the film, so your target population would be those people who had recently seen it. The easiest method would be to wait outside the cinema and select people as they left. If there were 300 people watching the film then you would need to stop every 30th person.

Table 3.5 Details taken from a register office's records

Name	Date of marriage	Nationality
Mr A. Tan	21/3/93	British
Miss N. Taylor	21/3/93	British
Mr F. Barker	22/3/93	British
Miss F. Addai	22/3/93	Australian
Mr T. Barry	22/3/93	British
Ms K. Larch	22/3/93	Canadian

Systematic sampling is a very quick and efficient method of obtaining a sample. The sample should be random, provided there is no pattern in the way people are ordered in the population. For example, if a population consists of married couples then it is possible for the sample to consist of all husbands or all wives. To illustrate this point Table 3.5 refers to records taken from a register office. If you took a systematic sample that selected every second person and you started at F. Barker, all your sample would be males.

Quota sampling

I am sure that you have seen an interviewer in a town centre with a clipboard waiting to pounce on some unsuspecting individual! The interviewer is in fact looking for particular groups of individuals who meet the categories that he or she has been asked to interview. Within each group there will be a number or *quota* of people required and the survey is complete when the quotas have been reached. Quota sampling is a non-probabilistic version of stratified sampling. The quotas within each group should, like stratified sampling, reflect the proportions within the target population.

Activity 3.8

You want to obtain the views of the local population on the creation of an out-of-town shopping complex. You are told that 30% of the population is aged between 12 and 20, 60% is between 20 and 60, and 10% is over 60. You want a sample of 100 individuals. How would you go about choosing your sample?

Your first decision must be the location and time of the survey. An obvious choice would probably be the town centre on a Saturday when many people are out shopping. To reflect the fact that 30% of the population is aged between 12 and 20 you want a quota of 30 individuals in this age range. Similarly, for the other two age bands you would want 60 and 10 individuals respectively.

Quota sampling is a cheap and quick method of obtaining a sample. It is a particularly popular method for market research surveys and opinion polls. Its main disadvantage is that the sample could be heavily biased in favour of one particular group. For instance, in the case of the shopping centre the group of people who do not shop in the town centre will be omitted.

Other sampling methods

There are three other non-probabilistic sampling methods that are sometimes used. These are *judgemental, purposive* and *snowball* sampling. With judgemental sampling the researcher makes a judgement about what constitutes a representative sample. If a government agency was interested in the effects on people's health of car exhaust fumes they would choose areas near cities or motorways to obtain the sample. They would not choose rural areas, except perhaps for a control group.

Purposive sampling is where certain members of the population are purposefully chosen. For example, customers holding store loyalty cards might be asked about planned improvements to the store.

Snowballing is where a sample is chosen using one of the methods mentioned in this chapter and then additional members of the population are generated from this sample. An example could be in the investigation of the mis-selling of pensions that occurred in Britain during the late 1980s. A sample of pensioners could be obtained and any person who was persuaded to leave their occupational pension scheme would be asked to name other people they knew who were also affected. In this way the sample size could be increased.

Activity 3.9

A market research company is interested in consumers' reaction to a new brand of sun cream. What type of sampling method should they adopt?

Although most of the methods mentioned in this chapter would be suitable, judgemental sampling might be the best method to use in this situation. The researcher's judgement together with sales information could be used to select a few holiday resorts where it is likely that the product is being used. Once a resort has been chosen the researcher could use his or her judgement as to which age range should be sampled and at what time of the day the survey should be conducted.

Obtaining research data from on-line sources

In many cases it is unnecessary to carry out a survey as the relevant data has already been collected and published. When data has already been collected we say that it is *secondary data*. Much of the data collected by governments is available, free and usually reliable. In the UK the government has created a website, www.data.gov.uk, where links to 5600 datasets are made available. These include datasets for central and local government as well as for other public sector bodies. The project is ongoing and more datasets will be added in the future. In the USA the equivalent site is called www.data.gov. Most countries in the developed world publish some statistics. In China for instance the National Bureau of Statistics of China publishes economic statistics at www.stats.gov.cn/english. Census data is also available for many countries and in the UK this can be found through the www.data.gov.uk website.

The World Bank (http://data.worldbank.org/) has an open data policy and data on 200 countries can be found. Much of this data is related to developing countries and can be used in poverty assessment for example. The United Nations also has freely available datasets at http://data.un.org.

An interesting on-line source is 'Internet World Stats' (www.internetworldstats.com) which is an international website that features up-to-date world internet usage, population statistics and internet market research data for over 233 individual countries and world regions.

Another useful source is 'NationMaster' (www.nationmaster.com/index.php) an American-owned site which has a huge collection of data from such sources as the CIA World Factbook, UN and OECD. The site allows you to generate maps and graphs on all kinds of statistics.

Other sources of data include national newspapers, *Financial Times* and others for stock market and commodity prices, and the organizations themselves, for instance CAA for UK airline statistics. Whatever your interest there is almost certain to be data available somewhere, although not necessarily free and not necessarily in the format required.

You can of course use search engines to find relevant data or information. When searching for a particular on-line source of data you need to think carefully about the search terms to be used and the search engine you use. Google is currently the search engine of choice as it covers the largest number of website pages and is extremely fast. It also uses a 'crawler' engine that follows hyperlinks from page to page. When using Google or any other search engine it is useful to bear the following tips in mind.

- Keep it simple.
- Use terms that are more likely to be on a page rather than in a book or a person's memory, so if you are searching for 'statistical data on car manufacturers' you could type 'car manufacturer statistics'.
- Use as few terms as possible. Every word you use is included in the search and will limit the results you get. You can always add more words in subsequent searches. So for 'car manufacturer statistics' you might need to add the year of interest.
- You can use double quotes around groups of words and this will tell Google only to look for pages where these words are together. This will reduce the number of hits considerably but you may miss relevant pages (by searching on "car manufacturer statistics" the number of hits is reduced from about 75 million to 690 000!).
- Use a minus sign to omit pages that contain specific terms, so if you don't want to include Honda cars you would put '-honda' at the end of the search.
- If you want to search for car manufacturers or statistics you would put 'OR' between the search terms. This would look for pages with either car manufacturers or statistics. This can double the number of hits so should be used sparingly.
- You can limit the search to specific sites, so to search for Australian websites you would add 'site:au'.
- Google has an advanced search facility which makes it easy to include many of the above ideas.

(For further information on the technique of searching see www.google.com/support/websearch/?hl=en-GB)

The one disadvantage of on-line data (or even printed data) is that the quality is sometimes unknown. This is less of a problem with official sources, although it is still important to ensure that you know how the data was collected and any particular circumstances that have made the data inaccurate or distorted in some way. This information is usually given in notes at the end of the publication or in footnotes to the relevant table. Unfortunately the accuracy of unofficial sources of data is often of dubious quality and some checking may be needed to ensure it is acceptable to use. You should anyway give the full reference (URL) of the website, any authors mentioned and the date when you accessed it.

Reflection

Sampling is very important in today's complex society. Companies are always keen to find out what consumers think about their products, and governments need to obtain views on all kinds of issues. Surveys are very frequent around the time of elections and in the UK 2010 General Election market research companies carried out many surveys to find out people's views on election issues. The primary intention of these surveys was to try and predict the make-up of the future government. As it happened their predictions were very accurate, particularly with regard to the Conservative vote.

One issue with all surveys is whether the respondents have answered the questions truthfully. For example, when there is a question of income some respondents may have income they do not wish to disclose, particularly if they are on benefits. Face-to-face interviews will usually give more reliable results, provided that the questions are well thought-out and experienced interviewers are used.

Another issue with surveys is that they need a great deal of planning and research. It is easy to rush into a survey only to find later that a vital question has been missed. It is also easy to ask too many questions and either to find that the respondents do not complete the questionnaire or that the sample size is insufficient to provide meaningful analysis. This latter point is particularly important when you hope to analyze results by several categories and subcategories such as gender, age and income. Each additional category can double the number of respondents required.

To resolve many of these challenges it is essential that a pilot survey is conducted first. A pilot survey is a small-scale version of the full survey, although it must be large enough that some analysis can be attempted. The pilot survey should also allow the issue of non-response to be highlighted. Response rates vary from survey to survey, but 30% is usually considered to be quite good; for some methods, such as postal surveys, the response rate can be in single figures.

The type of survey method is of course another very important consideration. Probabilistic sampling methods are the most accurate but require a sampling frame and are generally more expensive than non-probabilistic methods. Election surveys normally use probabilistic sampling methods because accuracy is paramount. Non-probabilistic methods can be used when accuracy is not that important or when general patterns only are required. The crisp manufacturer which gave away packets of crisps during an election campaign was not doing it for scientific reasons, although some people might have interpreted the findings too literally. Just because one bin had less crisps in it than another doesn't necessarily mean that this leader was most popular – perhaps this bin was closest to the station and people came across it first. Of course we don't know how frequently the bins were refilled or whether the crisps were all the same flavour. This example though does highlight how important it is not to take statistics at their face value; you need to look behind the figures first. We will come back to this theme in later chapters.

Key points

- It is generally impractical to question or observe every member of the *target population*, so a sample of this population is selected instead.
- To obtain data from a population of people you normally carry out a survey. This survey can be done by post, by telephone, face-to-face and online. Each method has its advantages and disadvantages. A face-to-face survey normally gives you the best response rate but is more costly than other methods.
- Whatever method you use the sample should be representative of the target population.
- *Probabilistic* sampling methods will give you a representative sample but require a sampling frame.
- *Non-probabilistic* sampling is generally quicker to carry out but may not be completely representative of the target population.
- Table 3.6 summarizes the different sampling methods available.

Table 3.6 A summary of the sampling methods available

	Sampling frame available (probabilistic sampling)	Sampling frame not available (non-probabilistic sampling)
Population resides in one place	Simple random sampling Systematic sampling	Systematic sampling (if the size of the population is known) Judgemental sampling Purposive sampling
Population geographically scattered	Multi-stage sampling	Cluster sampling Judgemental sampling
Population is defined by categories	Stratified sampling	Quota sampling
Population is small and unknown		Snowballing

- When you carry out any sort of survey you need to use a questionnaire. The design of the questionnaire needs to be carefully formulated and tested using a pilot survey.
- Data that you collect yourself is called *primary* data. However data on all kinds of business issues are often available either in paper format or more likely on-line. Data obtained in this way is called *secondary* data. When searching for particular data using a search engine you need to think carefully about the search terms used.

Further reading

There are a huge number of quantitative methods and statistical texts that cover the collection of data. Some like Morris (2008) and Curwin and Slater (2008) cover similar material to this text. Collis and Hussey (2009) is a more general text on business research methods. Fowler (2009) is a very detailed text on survey research methods and would be ideal for anyone having to design their own survey.

Web links W

Answers to selected questions can be found in Appendix 2. Answers to the other questions can be found on the companion website for this book.

Practice questions

W **1** In a Business Studies course at a university there are 320 students in year 1, 250 students in year 2 and 230 students in year 3. There are approximately 60% female students and 40% male students in each year. A survey of 50 students is to be taken to find their views on a course change. How many students of each gender should be selected from each year?

W **2** A town with historical connections has received a grant of £20m in order to improve its tourist facilities. The town councillors have decided to ask a representative sample of residents how the money should be spent. Given that expenditure for the survey must be kept to a minimum suggest ways in which a representative sample of residents can be chosen.

W **3** In preparation for the London 2012 Olympics, a survey of the British public is to be undertaken into the form of the opening ceremony. What type of survey should be undertaken and how would the respondents be chosen?

4 Criticize the following questionnaire into people's smoking habits.

Questionnaire on smoking habits	
1 How old are you?	☐
2 What is your marital status?	Single/married/cohabiting
3 Does your partner smoke?	Yes/No
4 How many cigarettes do you smoke a day?	☐
5 Do you understand the health risks of smoking?	Yes/No
6 Would you consider giving up if	
The price increased	☐
A relative died of cancer	☐
There were financial incentives for doing so	☐
7 Did your parents smoke?	Yes/No
8 Which socio-economic class do you belong to?	
A	☐
B	☐
C1	☐
C2	☐
D	☐
E	☐

5 Which of the following are likely to have a sampling frame?
1 Students at a university
2 Employees of a company
3 Concert goers
4 Shoppers at a shopping mall
5 Members of a social networking group

6   Table 3.7 represents a target population.

Table 3.7 Population for Question 6

Name	Sex	Age	Newspaper read
Alan	M	23	*Guardian*
Steve	M	36	*The Times*
Jane	F	47	*Mirror*
Chris	M	36	*Mirror*
Julie	F	41	*Sun*
Stuart	M	37	*Mirror*
Jill	F	37	*Telegraph*
John	M	38	*Express*
Kim	M	48	*Sun*

(a) Using the random numbers 2, 9, 4, 3, 6, 7, select a simple random sample of sample size 3. What is the average age of your sample and what newspapers do they read?

(b) Stratify your sample by sex and repeat part (a).

(c) If a systematic sample of size 3 was required and the first person chosen was Steve, who would be the second person chosen?

W 7   You have been asked to conduct a survey into people's views of the council tax. What would be the target population and what would be a good sampling frame?

W 8   A football club wants to obtain the views of its supporters on a possible rise in admission charges. It has decided to obtain a simple random sample of members of the supporters' club. Comment on this proposal and suggest alternative target populations and sampling methods.

W 9   You have been asked to conduct a survey into the attitudes of school leavers to higher education. You intend to carry this out using the face-to-face interview method. How would you obtain your sample?

W 10   You have been asked to obtain the reaction to the proposal to pedestrianize your local town centre. What survey methods would you use?

11   A clothing company has just been approached by a students' union to supply a range of products suitable for the student market. However, the company wants some evidence that the market would be viable. You have been asked to help design a survey to discover if the students would be prepared to purchase their clothes from this company and what kind of price they would be prepared to pay.

(a) You are considering using either stratified or quota sampling to obtain your sample. Explain the differences between the two methods and discuss which method you think would be most suitable. State what categories or 'strata' you might want to consider for this problem, giving reasons why you think that these categories are important.

(b) Would multi-stage sampling be worth considering for this problem?

(c) Discuss the types of problems that might arise, both during the design phase and the survey itself. How might you overcome these problems?

W **12** A company wishes to carry out a survey of its employees to monitor their views on the future of the company. A departmental breakdown of the company's 200 employees is as follows:

Shop-floor/warehouse	80	Accounts	15
Service engineers	15	Personnel	10
Quality control	20	Administration	25
Marketing and sales	25	Catering	10

A survey of 40 employees is to be conducted. A sampling frame is available, listing the employees by surname in alphabetical order, independent of department.

(a) Explain how the following sampling methods could be carried out to obtain the sample of 40 employees:

- simple random sampling
- systematic sampling
- stratified sampling
- quota sampling.

(b) Discuss the benefits and drawbacks of using quota sampling to obtain the sample of 40 employees.

13 A university is considering introducing a third semester so that students can complete their degrees in 2 years by remaining at the university over the summer vacation. To help the university decide whether this would be acceptable to staff and students, it wants to conduct a survey to establish the views of a cross-section of the university community.

(a) In the context of this problem, describe the terms:

- target population
- sampling frame
- stratified sampling
- multi-stage sampling.

(b) Design 5 questions that you might ask the respondents to the survey. Explain how these questions would help you to satisfy the aims of the survey.

(c) What type of data collection method would you use (postal, telephone or face to face)?

14 Give as many reasons as you can why the scenario illustrated in *Did you know* on page 37 would not give an accurate picture of the popularity of each party leader.

....

Assignment

Conduct a survey on some aspect of the quality of current television programmes. It is important that you do some research into the relevant issues and then conduct a survey using a questionnaire of your own design.

Information that you collect from your respondents might include:

- Viewing habits (that is, number of hours spent watching television, favourite programmes, and so on).
- Views on the quality of the programmes watched.
- What improvements they would like to see.
- Demographic information such as age, gender, occupation, and so on.

Finding patterns in data: charts and tables

Prerequisites

Some understanding of sampling methods (Chapter 3: *Collecting data: surveys and samples*) would be useful but is not essential.

Objectives

- ○ To be able to distinguish between different types of data
- ○ To be able to tabulate data into an ungrouped or a grouped frequency table, as appropriate
- ○ To be able to use diagrams to present data, and to know how to draw appropriate conclusions from these diagrams
- ○ To be able to use Excel and/or SPSS to produce professional-looking charts

Introduction

The human brain finds it difficult to make sense of a large quantity of data. However, when data is organized and presented in a diagrammatic form we find it much easier to pick out patterns. This is the opposite to computers which can easily process vast quantities of data but find pattern recognition extremely difficult. This chapter first discusses the type of data that you may come across, and then looks at the best ways of displaying it.

Quantitative methods in action: climate change in pictures

The volume of articles and publications written about climate change in general and greenhouse gas (GHG) emissions in particular is enormous, and understanding the impact of all the statistics quoted is not easy, even for experts. However charts and diagrams can help make this understanding easier. The World Resources Institute (WRI) has published a wealth of data and graphics on GHG emissions. For instance the pie chart in Figure 4.1 allows us to see what proportion of GHGs is attributable to transportation. Another interesting chart is the multiple bar chart shown in Figure 4.2 which compares both countries and time frame. Finally Figure 4.3 is a kind of line plot that shows the aggregate contributions of major GHG emitting countries.

What can you summarize from these three charts?

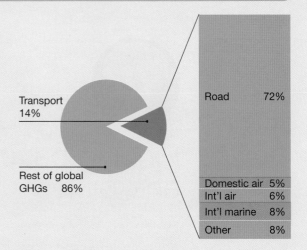

Figure 4.1 GHGs from transportation

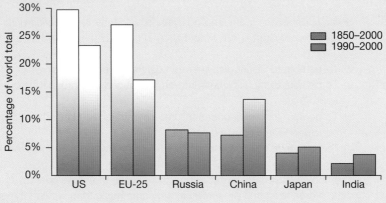

Figure 4.2
Cumulative CO2 emissions: comparison of different time periods

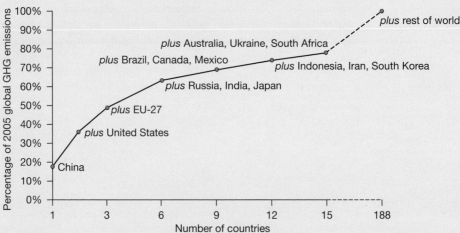

Figure 4.3
Aggregate contributions of major GHG emitting countries, 2005

Sources and notes: WRI, CAIT (http://cait.wri.org).Percentage contributions are for year 2005 GHG emissions only. Moving from left to right, countries are added in order of their absolute emissions, with the largest being added first. Figures exclude emissions from land-use change and forestry, and bunker fuels.
Adapted from Figure 2.3 in Baumert et al. (2005) 'Navigating the Numbers: Greenhouse Gas Data and International Climate Policy', http://pdf.wri.org/navigating_numbers.pdf.

Data classification

If your idea of data is simply lots of numbers then you may be surprised to learn that there are several different classifications or *levels of measurement*. Knowing which category your data falls into is very important as it determines what type of statistical analysis you perform. There are four levels of measurement. These are:

1 *Continuous data* Data that is measured on a scale, such as weight or temperature. The scale can be subdivided into as many intervals as required, depending on the accuracy of the measuring equipment. Using ordinary kitchen scales, for instance, you might record the weight of an item as 435 g; on more accurate scales the weight might be shown to be 434.8 g; and using laboratory-type scales you might be able to record the weight to three decimal places or more. Time is also continuous as it is measured using a clock, although it can be treated as discrete (see below). To complicate matters further, continuous data can be further subdivided into *interval-scale data* or *ratio-scale data*. An interval scale has no true starting (zero) point, so although it is possible to comment on the interval between measurements, it is not possible to compare the ratio of one to the other. For example, temperature (in Celsius and Fahrenheit) is measured on an interval-scale: you can say that 24C is twelve degrees hotter than 12C, but you cannot say that 24C is twice as hot as 12C. Ratio-scaled data, on the other hand, can be compared on a ratio basis as well as on an interval basis. For example, weight is measured on a ratio scale; 24 kg is twice as much as 12 kg, as well as being 12 kg different. For practical purposes this distinction makes little difference and most statistical packages (for example, SPSS) ignore this distinction.

2 *Discrete data* Data that takes on whole values. The obvious example of discrete data is data obtained by counting, such as the number of defective items in a batch. An important aspect of discrete data is that it cannot be subdivided (for example, you can't have half a defective item). Other examples of data that can be treated as discrete include the cost of an item or shoe size. Time is really a continuous measure, but for practical purposes it is often treated as discrete: people usually work a defined number of hours (or fractions of an hour), for example, and they give their age as a whole number of years. However, simply rounding a continuous quantity to a whole number doesn't make it discrete.

3 *Ordinal data* Data that can be arranged in some meaningful order. An example of this type of data is the assessment consumers might give to a product. They might be asked to rate the product using a score from 1 to 5, where 5 is 'excellent' and 1 is 'poor'. Although 5 is better than 1, it is not necessarily 5 times better or even 4 points better. One point that should not be forgotten is that just giving a numerical value to a category does not make it discrete data. You cannot do anything with this number apart from saying something like 'the higher the number, the better' (or 'the worse', for that matter).

4 *Nominal data* Data that does not have a numerical value and can only be placed in a suitable category. An example of this is hair colour or choice of newspaper. All we can do with nominal data is to separate it into its categories.

Ordinal and nominal data are usually referred to as *categorical data*.

To summarize:

- *Ratio data* Statistically the highest level of data. It has a defined zero so that data can be compared by interval and ratio.
- *Interval* There is no defined zero, so we can only compare intervals.
- *Discrete* It is meaningful to give data only in whole numbers. Discrete data is usually obtained by counting.
- *Ordinal* Ordinal data has order, but the interval between measurements is not meaningful.
- *Nominal* Nominal data has no order, and little statistical analysis can be done with this data.

The further you go down the hierarchy, the less the statistical analysis that can be carried out on the data. An important point to note, though, is that data can be manipulated downwards but not upwards. For example, data on ages could be placed into groups, such as: group 1, less than 20; group 2, from 20 to 30; etc. This could then be treated as ordinal data. It is of course not possible to give nominal data (such as mode of travel) a number, and then to treat the numbers as ordinal data.

Activity 4.1

How would you define the following sets of data?

(a) Measurement of the weights of jars of coffee.
(b) Choice of summer holiday.
(c) Weekly earnings by employees at a factory.
(d) Numbers of students following a business studies course.
(e) Market research survey into consumer reaction to a new product.

You should have defined (a) as ratio data since weight will be measured using either the metric or imperial system. (b) is nominal data since choice will be destination or home/abroad. (c) will be discrete since employees will earn an *exact* amount, such as £182.55. (d) is also discrete since the number can be found by counting. (e) could be either ordinal or nominal. It would be ordinal if you were asked to give a numerical score and nominal if you were simply asked to say whether you liked or disliked the product.

Tabulation of data

Example 4.1

A small survey was carried out into the mode of travel to work. The information in Table 4.1 relates to a random sample of 20 employed adults.

Table 4.1 Data for Example 4.1

Person	Mode of travel	Person	Mode of travel
1	car	11	car
2	car	12	bus
3	bus	13	walk
4	car	14	car
5	walk	15	train
6	cycle	16	bus
7	car	17	car
8	cycle	18	cycle
9	bus	19	car
10	train	20	car

Activity 4.2

How would you classify this data?

This data is categorical (nominal) since mode of travel does not have a numerical value. This information would be better displayed as a frequency table (Table 4.2).

Table 4.2 Frequency table

Mode of travel	Frequency	Relative frequency (%)
Car	9	45
Bus	4	20
Cycle	3	15
Walk	2	10
Train	2	10
Total	20	

Frequency is simply the number of times each category appeared. As well as the actual frequency, the *relative frequency* has been calculated. This is the frequency expressed as a percentage and is calculated by dividing a frequency by the total frequency and multiplying by 100.

The order in which you write these down is not important, although ordering by descending size of frequency makes comparison clearer.

Example 4.2

The data in Table 4.3 (overleaf) gives the number of foreign holidays sold by a travel agent over the past four weeks.

Activity 4.3

How would you classify the data in Table 4.3, and what can you deduce from the figures?

Table 4.3 Data for Example 4.2

Day	No. sold
Monday	10
Tuesday	12
Wednesday	9
Thursday	10
Friday	22
Saturday	14
Monday	11
Tuesday	18
Wednesday	10
Thursday	10
Friday	11
Saturday	9

Day	No. sold
Monday	13
Tuesday	10
Wednesday	12
Thursday	8
Friday	12
Saturday	12
Monday	11
Tuesday	13
Wednesday	10
Thursday	14
Friday	13
Saturday	12

Can the travel agent sell a fraction of a holiday? Assuming that a holiday is a holiday regardless of the duration or the cost, then this is clearly discrete data and would have been obtained by counting. By examining the figures you should see that 10 sales occurs most frequently, although there is a range from 8 to 22 sales. To enable this information to be seen more clearly you could aggregate the data into a table (Table 4.4).

Table 4.4 Frequency table for Example 4.2

Number sold	Frequency
8	1
9	2
10	6
11	3
12	5
13	3
14	2
More than 14	2

This table is called an *ungrouped frequency table*, since the numbers sold have not been grouped. This table is a useful way of summarizing a small set of discrete data. There are two extreme values or *outliers* of value 18 and 22 sales and these have been included by the use of a 'more than' quantity. From this table you can see that between 10 and 12 holidays are usually sold each day.

Example 4.3

Table 4.5 gives the number of bolts produced by a machine each hour over the past 65 hours, while Table 4.6 gives the length in mm of 80 of these bolts.

Table 4.5 Hourly rate of bolt production

184	250	136	178	231	158	197	159	141	218
223	156	124	177	298	175	231	218	117	149
169	119	174	171	191	202	214	138	127	254
177	181	189	201	198	165	140	100	147	188
296	237	223	267	147	112	238	139	165	125
165	188	230	150	127	251	182	139	159	179
230	183	166	163	194					

Table 4.6 Length of bolts (mm)

49.9	53.8	61.3	45.8	51.2	44.5	55.3	51.4	84.1
55.7	52.7	68.7	52.5	58.8	37.8	44.1	49.9	43.8
64.1	35.9	46.4	45.1	30.6	45.9	54.8	54.0	49.3
46.8	46.5	52.2	33.3	42.9	47.7	46.2	40.5	36.8
47.5	46.3	70.2	35.5	56.7	56.0	56.5	49.5	57.5
52.0	36.8	46.3	42.4	30.2	49.5	36.3	44.6	45.1
30.0	47.0	52.1	53.0	46.1	50.5	56.0	50.9	42.7
42.1	51.2	49.0	49.9	54.4	53.2	43.0	41.3	49.7
42.9	61.1	41.7	35.7	45.0	59.2	60.6	44.7	

Activity 4.4

Look at the data in Table 4.5 and Table 4.6. Can you deduce anything about how many bolts are produced each hour or the length of each bolt? Would it help if ungrouped frequency tables were created, as in Activity 4.3?

I expect that you found it quite difficult to draw many conclusions from the data. For Table 4.5 you might have identified the range of production as between 100 and 298 bolts per hour, but what is the 'normal' production rate? Similarly, the smallest bolt is 30.0 mm and the largest is 84.1 mm, but what size are the majority of the bolts? An ungrouped frequency table for either set of data would not be very helpful for two reasons: for both data sets the range of the data is large, which would necessitate a large table, and for Table 4.6 the data is continuous. Continuous data can, by definition, take on any value, so what values would you use in your table? To overcome these problems a *grouped frequency table* is produced. A grouped frequency table is similar to an ungrouped table except that intervals are defined into which the data can be grouped. The number and size of each interval depends on the quantity and range of your data. In general you would have between 8 and 15 intervals and the width of each interval, or the *class interval*, should be a convenient number such as 10, 20, 25 etc. In the case of Table 4.5 the range is $298 - 100 = 198$, and a class interval of 20 would give you 10 intervals, which is about right. The first interval would be 100 to 119; the second 120 to 139, and so on. Once you have decided on the size of each interval you need to allocate each value to one of the intervals. This can be done by using a *tally chart*. A tally chart is simply a foolproof means (or nearly) of ensuring that all items have been allocated. You start with the first value, in this case 184, and find the relevant interval, which is 180 to 199. A '|' is placed in this row. You then do the same with subsequent values, except that when you have four | s in a row you would draw a line through the group to make the total of 5. This has been done for you in Table 4.7.

Table 4.7 Tally chart

Class interval	Tally
100 to 119	||||
120 to 139	⊬⊤ |||
140 to 159	⊬⊤ ⊬⊤
160 to 179	⊬⊤ ⊬⊤ |||
180 to 199	⊬⊤ ⊬⊤ |
200 to 219	⊬⊤
220 to 239	⊬⊤ |||
240 to 259	|||
260 to 279	|
280 to 299	||

The next stage is to add up the tally in each interval to give you the frequency. The final grouped frequency table is as shown in Table 4.8. From this table it appears that the rate of production is quite variable, although the rate is unlikely to be less than 120 or more than 240 bolts per hour.

Table 4.8 Grouped frequency table

Interval	Frequency	Relative frequency (%)
100 to 119	4	6.2
120 to 139	8	12.3
140 to 159	10	15.4
160 to 179	13	20.0
180 to 199	11	16.9
200 to 219	5	7.7
220 to 239	8	12.3
240 to 259	3	4.6
260 to 279	1	1.5
280 to 299	2	3.1
Total	65	100

How would you group the data in Table 4.6? You might decide on a class interval of 5 mm, which would give you 11 intervals. Since the smallest length is 30 mm the first group would start at 30 mm; the second at 35 mm, and so on. But what should the end of each group be? If you used 34 mm you would not be able to allocate a value between 34 and 35 mm. You cannot use the same figure for both the end of one group and the start of the next because this would allow a value to be added to more than one group. It is essential that a value can go into *one, and only one,* interval, so the ranges must be designed to guarantee this. Since the data is continuous the length can be quoted to any degree of accuracy, so the end of each group would be defined as *under* 35 mm and under 40 mm, and so on. In this way a length of 34.9 mm would be in the first group while 35.0 mm would be in the second group.

Activity 4.5

Obtain the grouped frequency table for the data in Table 4.6. What can you deduce about the length of bolts produced?

You should have obtained Table 4.9. If you look at this table the *distribution* of the lengths is clearer. 77.5% of the values are between 40 mm and 60 mm, with few over 60 mm or less than 40 mm.

Table 4.9 Grouped frequency table for the length of bolts

Interval	Frequency	Relative frequency (%)
30 to under 35 mm	4	5.00
35 to under 40 mm	7	8.75
40 to under 45 mm	14	17.50
45 to under 50 mm	23	28.75
50 to under 55 mm	16	20.00
55 to under 60 mm	9	11.25
60 to under 65 mm	4	5.00
65 to under 70 mm	1	1.25
70 to under 75 mm	1	1.25
75 to under 80 mm	0	0
80 to under 85 mm	1	1.25

In both these examples the class intervals were the same for the whole distribution; that is, 20 in the first case and 5 in the second. However, it is not necessary for the intervals to be equal and you may have two or more different intervals in the same table. In Table 4.9 you might decide to condense the last four intervals into one since the frequencies in these intervals are small. If you do this your last interval will be 65 to under 85 mm, which has a frequency of 3. It is also possible to have an *open* interval at the beginning or end, such as greater than 70 mm or less than 30 mm. However, only use open intervals if you really have to and only if there is a relatively small number of items in this interval.

Diagrammatic representation of data

Although frequency tables can give you more information than the *raw* data, it can still be difficult to take in all the information that is inherent in the data. Diagrams can help provide this additional information and also display the data in a more visually attractive manner. You do lose some detail but this is a small price to pay for the additional information that diagrams provide. There are several types of diagram and the choice depends mainly on the type of data, but also on your intended audience.

These days most people will use a spreadsheet when producing diagrams. Spreadsheets can produce high-quality charts which can be easily updated if the data changes. However, some experience of drawing diagrams by hand is still useful.

Example 4.4

The sales by department of a high street store over the past three years are shown in Table 4.10.

Table 4.10 Sales by department and year

	2009	2010	2011
Clothing	£1.7m	£1.4m	£1.4m
Furniture	£3.4m	£4.9m	£5.6m
Electrical goods	£0.2m	£0.4m	£0.5m
Total	£5.3m	£6.7m	£7.5m

An inspection of the data in Table 4.10 reveals that the total sales have increased over the three years, although clothing has shown a decline. Diagrams should help bring out these and other differences more clearly.

Pie charts

When you want to compare the relative sizes of the frequencies a pie chart is a good choice of diagram. It is normally used for categorical data and each category is represented by a segment of a circle. The size of each segment reflects the frequency of that category and can be represented as an angle. It is rare for people to draw a pie chart by hand as a protractor is required to measure the angles, but if you need to, the angle is calculated by working out the percentage of the category and then multiplying by 360. For example, for the sales for 2011 in Example 4.4 the angle would be calculated as follows:

$$\text{Clothing as a percentage is } \frac{1.4}{7.5} \times 100 = 18.7\%$$

$$\text{The angle is therefore } \frac{18.7}{100} \times 360 = 67°$$

The complete pie chart for the sales for 2011 is shown in Figure 4.4. This diagram demonstrates that the furniture department has contributed the bulk of the total sales for this year.

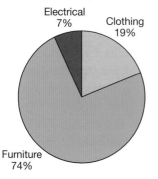

Figure 4.4
Pie chart for sales in 2011

Florence Nightingale was a respected statistician as well as a famous nurse in the Crimean War. Along with her colleague William Farr she did much pioneering work in showing how poor hygiene was killing soldiers unnecessarily. She used diagrams and charts extensively in her work and she developed a polar area graph which was a bit like a pie chart. Using her diagrams she was able to persuade the government to improve sanitation in both military and civilian hospitals. Florence was made a Fellow of the Royal Statistical Society in 1858.

Bar charts

Although pie charts tend to be a popular means of comparing the size of categories they have the disadvantage that they are not suitable for displaying several sets of data simultaneously. You would, for instance, need three separate pie charts to represent the data in Table 4.10. A *simple bar chart* is another useful method of displaying categorical data, or an ungrouped frequency table. For each category a vertical bar is drawn, the height of the bar being proportional to the frequency. The diagram in Figure 4.5 shows the total sales in the form of a simple bar chart.

When a category is subdivided into several subcategories the simple bar chart is not really adequate as you would need a different bar chart for each subcategory. A *multiple bar chart* is used when you are interested in changes in the components but the totals are of no interest. Figure 4.6 is a multiple bar chart for the data in Table 4.10.

If you are interested in comparing totals and seeing how the totals are made up a *component* bar chart is used. Figure 4.7 is a component bar chart for the data in Table 4.10. In this figure you can see the variation in total sales from year to year as well as seeing how each department contributes to total sales. If you are more interested in the proportion of sales in each department a *percentage* bar chart may be of more interest. This is shown in Figure 4.8. This chart is rather like the pie chart but has the advantage that several sets of data can be displayed simultaneously.

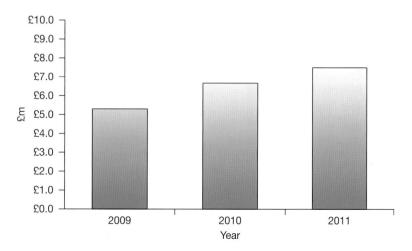

Figure 4.5
A simple bar chart of total sales

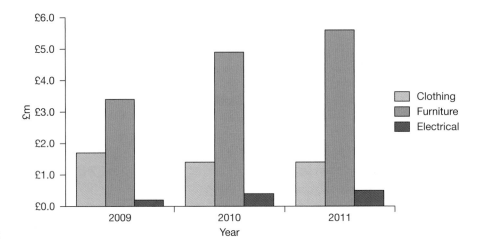

Figure 4.6
A multiple bar chart

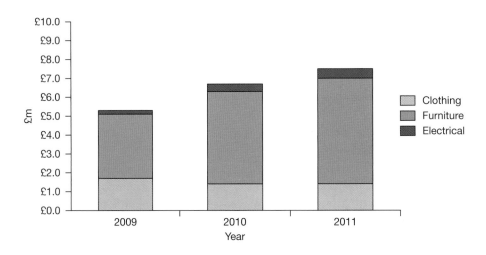

Figure 4.7
A component bar
chart

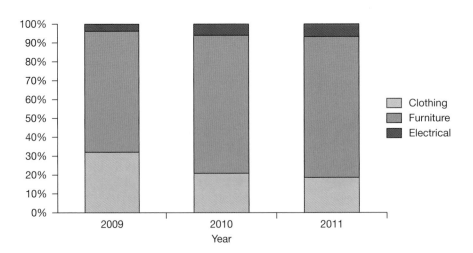

Figure 4.8
A percentage bar
chart

Line graphs

When data is in the form of a *time series* a line graph can be a useful means of showing any trends in the data. Figure 4.9 is a line graph for the total sales given in Table 4.10 and clearly shows the rise in sales over the three years. When this type of diagram is shown in company publications you will often find that the scale on the *y*-axis is broken. This will exaggerate the growth in sales or other measure and can be misleading unless you are aware of what is going on. This can be justified if none of the values are near zero, but in this case the break in the scale should be clearly shown. Figure 4.10 shows how this should be done.

We will be looking at line graphs in more detail in Chapter 13.

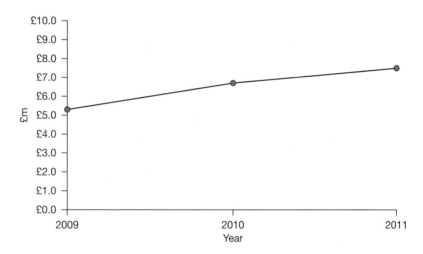

Figure 4.9
Line graph

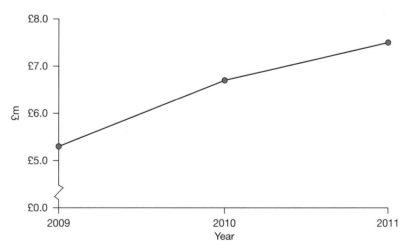

Figure 4.10
Line graph with
adjusted scale

Activity 4.6

Use Figures 4.4 to 4.10 to summarize how the sales have varied by department and year.

You should be able to deduce that:

- Total sales have increased over the three years, although the largest increase was between 2009 and 2010.
- Most of this increase has been the result of sales of furniture.
- Clothing has shown a decrease in sales from 2009 to 2010 but has then remained steady.
- The sales of clothing as a proportion of total sales has declined, while the proportion of electrical sales has increased.

Histograms

For grouped frequency tables a different type of diagram is normally used. This diagram is called a *histogram* and although it may look like a bar chart there are some important differences. These are:

- The horizontal axis is a continuous scale, just like a normal graph. This implies that there should not be gaps between bars unless the frequency for that class interval really is zero.
- It is the *area* of the bars that is being compared, not the heights. This means that if one class interval is twice the others then the height must be halved, since area = width × height.

The histogram shown in Figure 4.11 is for the lengths of bolts given in Example 4.3 and uses an equal class interval of 5 mm.

If the last four intervals were combined, the last class interval would be 20 mm. In this case the frequency of 3 should be *divided* by 4 (since 20 is 4 × 5) to give 0.75 and the histogram would have to be redrawn as shown in Figure 4.12. Where there are several different class intervals it is normal practice to divide each frequency by the

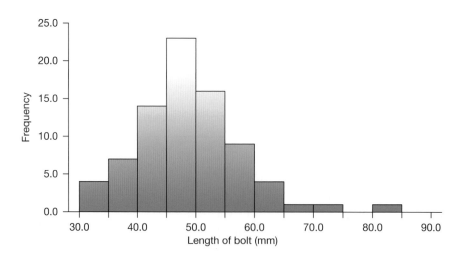

Figure 4.11
Histogram of length of bolt

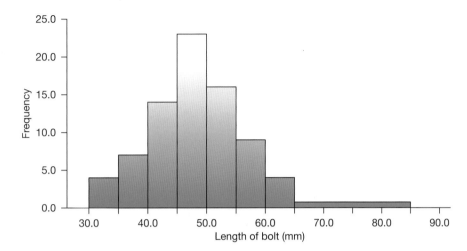

Figure 4.12
Histogram with unequal class intervals

corresponding class width. The resulting values are called the *frequency density* although it is usually better not to give the vertical axis a label.

When you draw histograms for discrete data there is a problem in that there is a gap between the end of one interval and the start of the next. You can get round this problem by extending each interval half way to the next or last interval. Thus for the example of the rate of production of bolts, the intervals would become 100.5 to 119.5 and 119.5 to 139.5, and so on.

Activity 4.7

Draw a suitable chart for the production rate data (Table 4.5).

You might either have drawn a histogram like the one in Figure 4.13 or a bar chart (Figure 4.14).

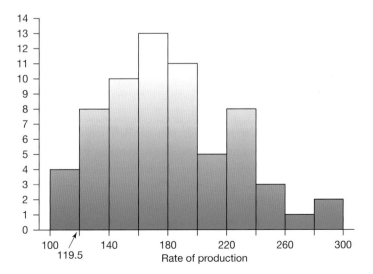

Figure 4.13
Histogram for discrete data

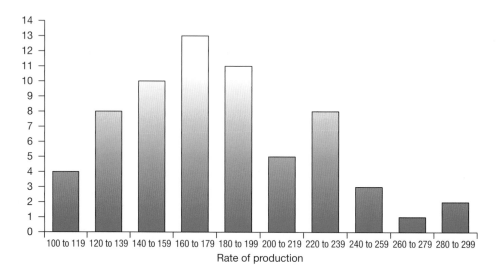

Figure 4.14
Bar chart of rate of
production

Frequency polygons

To get a better idea about how the data is distributed across the range of possible
values of the data, you can join up the mid points of the top of each bar of the
histogram. This is shown in Figure 4.15 for the bolt length data.

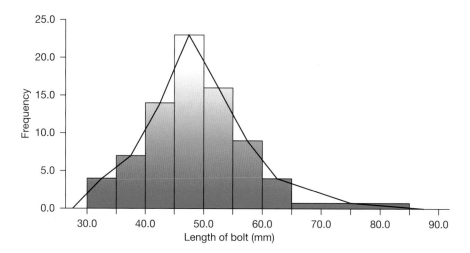

Figure 4.15
Histogram with mid
points joined up

If the bars are now removed, you are left with a picture of the shape of the
underlying distribution of the data. The area under the frequency polygon is the same
as the area under the original histogram (Figure 4.16).

This diagram can be quite useful if you want to compare different distributions, as
it is possible to plot more than one frequency polygon on the same graph. This is not
possible with the other diagrams you have met, as they would look too confusing.

Another important use of the frequency polygon is to categorize the shape of the
distribution in terms of its degree of symmetry. A distribution that is perfectly
balanced is called *symmetrical*, whereas a distribution which has its peak offset to one

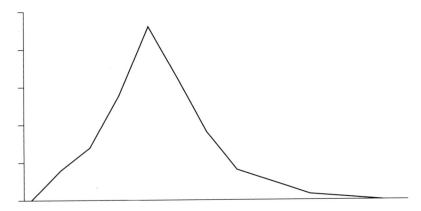

Figure 4.16
Frequency polygon

side is called *skewed*. If the peak is to the left, the distribution is called *right* or *positive* skewed, whereas if the peak is to the right, the distribution is called *left* or *negative* skewed. This may sound illogical but you will discover the reason for this convention in the next chapter. I find it easier to look at the *tail* of the distribution. If the tail is to the right it is right skewed and if the tail is to the left it is left skewed. The diagrams in Figure 4.17 may help you appreciate the differences.

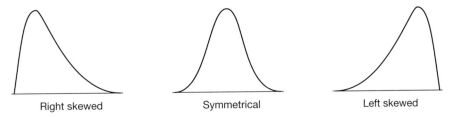

Figure 4.17
Distribution shapes

Right skewed   Symmetrical   Left skewed

Activity 4.8

How would you define the shape of the distribution of bolt lengths?

The distribution is approximately symmetrical, although it has a slight right skewness to it.

Ogive

Another diagram can be created by plotting the *cumulative* frequencies. Cumulative frequency is simply a running total of the frequencies. The cumulative frequencies for the bolt length data are shown in Table 4.11.

The percentage cumulative frequencies have also been calculated as you will find that the use of percentages has certain advantages. The cumulative frequency graph or *ogive* can now be drawn. The *upper* boundaries of each class interval are plotted against the (%) cumulative frequencies, as shown in Figure 4.18.

This is a very useful diagram and you will meet this again in the next chapter. For the purposes of this chapter you can treat this graph as a *less than* graph, since the upper-class boundaries were plotted against the cumulative frequencies. So, for example, 13.75% of the lengths are below 40 mm.

Table 4.11 Calculation of cumulative frequencies

Interval	Frequency	Cumulative frequency	% cumulative frequency
30 to under 35 mm	4	4	5.00
35 to under 40 mm	7	11	13.75
40 to under 45 mm	14	25	31.25
45 to under 50 mm	23	48	60.00
50 to under 55 mm	16	64	80.00
55 to under 60 mm	9	73	91.25
60 to under 65 mm	4	77	96.25
65 to under 70 mm	1	78	97.50
70 to under 75 mm	1	79	98.75
75 to under 80 mm	0	79	98.75
80 to under 85 mm	1	80	100.00

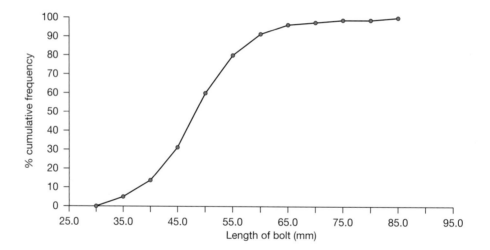

Figure 4.18
Ogive

Activity 4.9

Determine the proportion of lengths that are:
(a) below 50 mm   (b) below 41 mm   (c) above 63 mm

The answer to (a) can be read directly from the grouped frequency distribution and is 60%. However, for both (b) and (c) you should use the ogive to *interpolate* between two boundaries. To do this you should draw a vertical line up from the x-axis at the appropriate value to meet the ogive. You can then draw a horizontal line from this point until it meets the y-axis and then it is a matter of reading the cumulative frequency from this axis. This has been done for you in Figure 4.19.

You will see from the diagram that I have drawn lines for all three lengths. The cumulative frequency for (a) is 60% as it should be. The cumulative frequency for (b) is approximately 17%, so 17% of lengths are below 41 mm. The cumulative frequency for (c) is approximately 94% but, as you were asked to find the proportion above 63 mm, you then need to subtract 94 from 100, that is 6%.

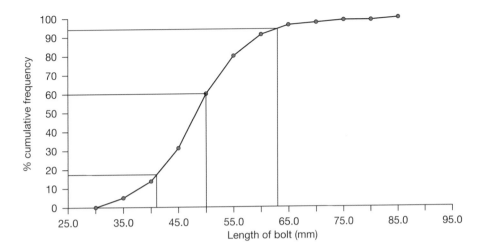

Figure 4.19
Using the ogive

Other diagrams

There are many other diagrams that can be used to represent data. The simplest is a pictogram which just uses a picture to represent a quantity. So for the sales at a high street store (Example 4.4) a picture of a money bag could be used to represent £200 000. So for clothing in 2009 you would need 8 and half bags to represent £1.7m. This is a popular diagram to use in magazines as it is visually appealing and requires little knowledge of statistics.

There are also *surface* charts, *area* charts, *doughnut* charts, *bubble* charts and *radar* charts as well as three dimensional bar charts. However apart for some specialized uses these charts don't generally provide any more information than the ones we have already met, and in some cases can even confuse.

One other diagram that can be useful, particularly when there is little data, is a *stem and leaf* plot. In this plot the most significant digit is the stem and the least significant digit is the leaf. So in the length of bolt data where the data varies between 30 mm and 80 mm the stem would be represented by the tens unit (3 to 8) and the leaf by the remaining digit (the decimal value would be ignored). We normally add the leaf values in the order they come in the data and then redraw the diagram with the leaves arranged in order on each stem.

Activity 4.10

Draw a stem and leaf plot for the length of bolt data.

If we used the values 3 to 8 as the stem we would only have 6 values making up the stem which is a little low. In these situations it is useful to split the stem unit into 2 so for the value 3 the first stem value would be used for values 30 to 34 and the second value used for the values 35 to 39.

After ordering the leaf values you should have got the 'diagram' represented by Table 4.12.

Table 4.12 A stem and leaf plot of the length of bolt data

```
Frequency      Stem & Leaf
     4.00         3 . 0003
     7.00         3 . 5556667
    14.00         4 . 01122222334444
    23.00         4 . 55555666666677799999999
    16.00         5 . 0011122222333444
     9.00         5 . 556666789
     4.00         6 . 0114
     3.00 Extremes   (>=68)
```

3|3 represents 33 mm

The 3 values above 65 mm can be represented as *outliers* as shown. This diagram clearly shows the shape of the distribution and can be quick and easy to produce. It can also be used when you are comparing two sets of data as you can use a *back to back* stem and leaf plot where one set of leaves is to the left of the stem and other to the right. As we will see later we can also use this diagram to obtain statistical information about the data.

Creating charts with Excel 2010

Very few people draw charts by hand these days, as it is much easier to use a spreadsheet, such as Excel. Charts produced by a spreadsheet also look more professional and they can be immediately updated if the data changes. When drawing charts in Excel you can choose whether to create the chart as an object in the same worksheet as the data or to create the chart in a new sheet. Being able to see the chart next to the data can be useful, but if you want to print out the chart or to copy and paste it in another document it is often easier to create it in a new sheet.

The version of Excel used in this text is Excel 2010. This version is similar to Excel 2007 and uses the idea of a 'Ribbon', which replaced the menus and toolbars used in earlier versions. The ribbon has 7 tabs which include Home, Insert, Page Layout, Formulas, Data, Review and View. Within each tab, commands are grouped logically so in the Insert tab there is a Charts group which contains all the charts found in earlier versions of Excel. When a chart is created a new set of tabs is visible. These are Design, Layout and Format tabs and allow you to change the layout or style of a chart. There is also a File button at the top left of the sheet which allows you to save, print and change options etc. There is a very comprehensive help facility within Excel (click on the blue question mark on the top right of the sheet). The Insert tab of the Excel 2010 is shown in Figure 4.20.

 If you are unfamiliar with spreadsheets, the activity in the website will take you through the basics of adding data to a worksheet. This will help you become familiar with Excel 2010. More experienced users should be able to try Activity 4.11.

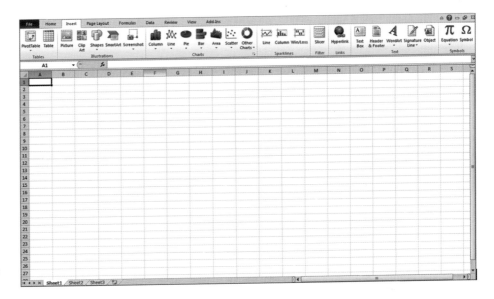

Figure 4.20
The Insert tab in
Excel 2010

Activity 4.11

Use Excel and data provided in Table 4.10 (page 62) to create:

1   A pie chart for sales in 2011
2   A simple bar chart of total sales for each of the three years
3   A multiple bar chart for sales by year and department
4   A component bar chart
5   A percentage bar chart
6   A line graph for the total sales over the three years

For each chart click on the Insert tab and choose the appropriate chart in the Charts group. The charts produced are the same ones that were shown earlier in the chapter and you will be referred back to these charts.

1 Pie chart

Highlight cells B6 to B8 and while holding down the <Ctrl> key on your keyboard highlight cells E6 to E8. Click on the Insert tab then Pie and choose the one you want. This screen is shown in Figure 4.21 overleaf. You can move the chart to a new sheet (recommended) or leave as an embedded chart. In both cases you will be able to choose a chart layout and format. The pie chart can be seen in Figure 4.4 (page 62).

2 Simple bar chart

Vertical bar charts in Excel are called Column charts and will be the first one in the list of charts. The first sub type can be used (Clustered Column), or you can use the second one (Stacked Column). Highlight cells C10 to E10 and then click on the Insert tab and Column and you should see the screen shown in Figure 4.22.

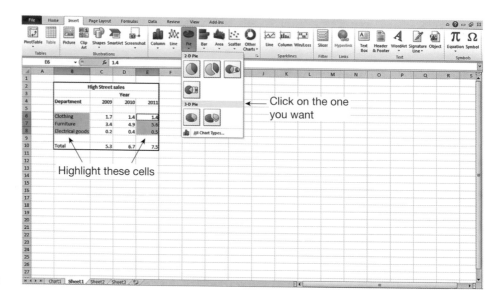

Figure 4.21
Creating a pie chart

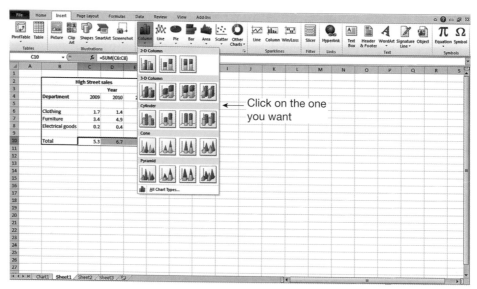

Figure 4.22
Creating a simple bar chart

In the Charts tab you can add the horizontal axis labels by clicking on the Data group, select Data and Edit under the Horizontal (Category) Axis labels (see Figure 4.23). You can also select an appropriate chart layout and add titles to both axes. The final chart can be seen in Figure 4.5 (page 63).

3 Multiple bar chart

Proceed as before, but this time highlight cells B6 to E8. Add the years to the horizontal axis and choose a chart layout as before. The final chart can be seen in Figure 4.6 (page 64).

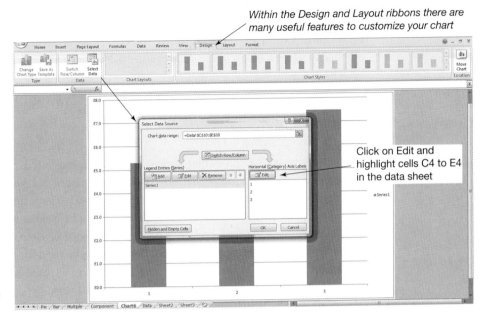

Within the Design and Layout ribbons there are many useful features to customize your chart

Click on Edit and highlight cells C4 to E4 in the data sheet

Figure 4.23
Adding horizontal axis labels

4 Component bar chart

A component bar chart is called a `Stacked Column` chart in Excel and is the second one in the row. Proceed exactly as before. The final chart can be seen in Figure 4.7 (page 64).

5 Percentage bar chart

This is exactly the same as before except that `100% Stacked Column` is chosen. This chart can be seen in Figure 4.8 (page 64).

6 Line graph

For this line graph you should choose `Line with markers` as shown in Figure 4.24.

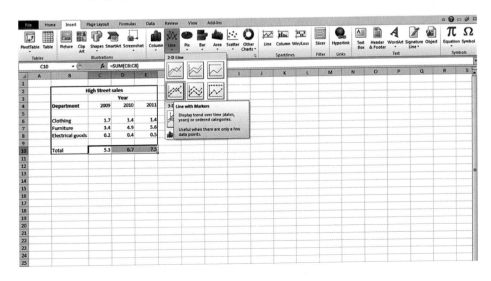

Figure 4.24
Creating a line chart

The chart can be seen in Figure 4.9 (page 65). Note that, as mentioned earlier, the y-axis for this chart need not be started at zero. However, when this is done it is good practice to show a break in the scale (Figure 4.10, page 65). Unfortunately this cannot be achieved automatically in Excel.

Creating charts with SPSS

The advantage with Excel is that almost every workplace has a copy of it and people are familiar with the package. The charts it produces are on the whole professional-looking and easy to create. Excel is a general-purpose package and does lots of things reasonably well. It can, for instance, do data analysis; be used as a simple database; be used as an optimizing tool; and even be used as a word processor! In addition it can, in conjunction with the powerful Visual Basic editor, be used for all kinds of advanced modelling purposes. Although Excel can (and often is) used as a word processor, however, most people would prefer to use a dedicated word processor package such as Microsoft Word^{TM}. So it is with statistical packages. Several packages are dedicated to statistical work, and one of the most popular is SPSS^{TM}.

Before getting started with SPSS, it is recommended that you become familiar with the basic principles of the package. There is a very good help facility within SPSS which contains an online tutorial. There is also a contextual help system within the package: this can be activated by pointing the mouse at the feature you are unsure about and right-clicking the mouse button. Information on specific SPSS functions will be provided as needed in this text; further information is provided on the companion website.

Basic ideas behind SPSS

SPSS is similar to other Windows-based packages, and features a title bar, a menu bar and a toolbar. The first screen you normally see is shown in Figure 4.25.

The basic outline looks similar to Excel in that there are rows and columns. This is where the similarity ends, however. The first difference you will notice is that there are two screens or views: a Data View and a Variable View (see Figure 4.25); you click on a tab to switch between views. Another major difference is the way you refer to data in SPSS. With Excel you can have a column or row of data, and it is possible to apply some limited formatting to the row, to the column, or to individual cells. In SPSS, in contrast, each row of data is called a *case* and each column is called a *variable*. This terminology has arisen because SPSS was originally designed to analyze survey data (SPSS stands for Statistical Package for the Social Scientist). In analyses of survey data, each case represented a respondent and each variable represented the response to a particular question. However, it is possible to analyze variables quite independently of each other.

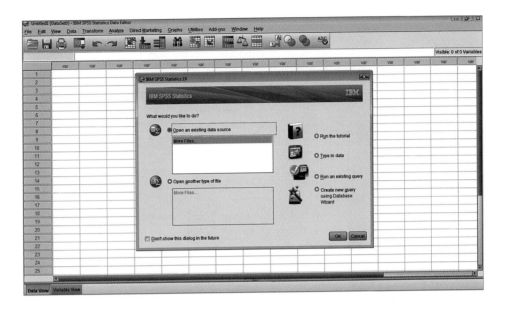

Figure 4.25
Opening SPSS screen

The data shown in Figure 4.26 contains information on a selection of companies in the UK (*Source*: FAME database). The information obtained included the following:

- *Company* Type of company ('Public quoted', 'Public not quoted', 'Private limited', 'Private unlimited' and 'Public aim').
- *Emp* Number of employees.
- *Turnover* (in £000s).
- *SIC* Standard industrial classification.

Before we look at the `Variable View` screen, a few words on how SPSS defines variables will be useful. The default type is `Numeric`, although there are several other categories that can be used, including `String` (text). For numeric data there is also a

	Type	Emp	Turnover	SIC
1	1	17441	3462800	6330
2	2	6934	3128300	5231
3	3	9	2077000	5010
4	3	78863	1930745	5552
5	1	5871	1841610	5010
6	3	5997	1763492	5010
7	3	6523	1671300	5010
8	3	2936	1595203	1596
9	1	37207	1560000	5540
10	3	34228	1492000	5540
11	3	2757	1137020	5010
12	1	3635	1093752	5010
13	3	1604	929680	5010
14	3	4650	870600	1589
15	3	4650	870600	1589
16	3	2728	839400	1596
17	3	2284	733711	1561
18	3	1585	704835	9
19	3	5233	678083	5530
20	3	1834	586254	5010
21	1	9209	578600	5030
22	3	9209	568100	5030
23	3	2246	563513	5010
24	3	18547	528252	5540
25	2	5081	517800	2212

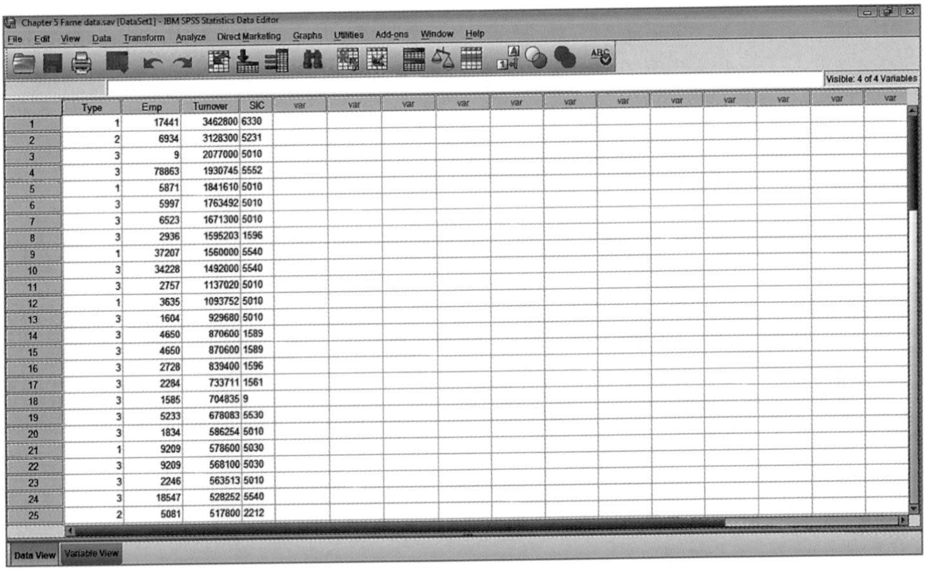

Figure 4.26
Company information

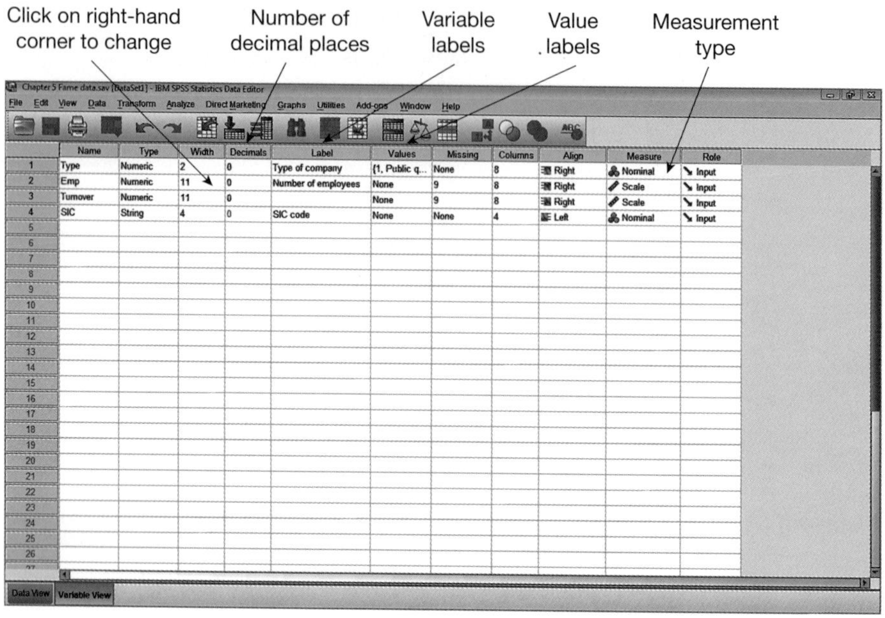

Figure 4.27
Variable details

sub-type or measurement type (Measure), which can be Scale, Ordinal or Nominal. (Note that SPSS does not distinguish between ratio, interval and discrete data.) If we want a *discrete* variable, we need to set the number of decimal places to zero. In our data, *Emp* and *Turnover* are scale variables, while *Company* and *SIC* are nominal.

Figure 4.27 is the Variable View and gives details of our four variables. Notice that the Label field allows us to give a longer description of the variable (Name is restricted to eight characters starting with a letter). The Values field allows us to add further information to ordinal or nominal data. In our case, codes were used for company type: 1 = *Public quoted*, 2 = *Public not quoted*, etc. These do not affect any calculations we do, but they make output clearer (see Figure 4.31). It is also possible to define missing values. In our case the number 9 was used to represent values that were missing in *Emp* and *Turnover*.

Charts in SPSS

There are two ways of getting charts in SPSS. The first and simplest way is through the Analyze menu. Click on Analyze, then Descriptive Statistics, then Frequencies (see Figure 4.28).

When you click on Frequencies you get the options shown in Figure 4.29. Highlight Type of company and click the right-facing arrow. Then click on Charts: you will be offered a choice of bar charts, pie charts and histograms. Bar charts and pie charts are applicable for ordinal and nominal data. We will choose Bar charts. You also have a choice of displaying the chart values as Frequencies or Percentages; we will choose Frequencies. Press Continue.

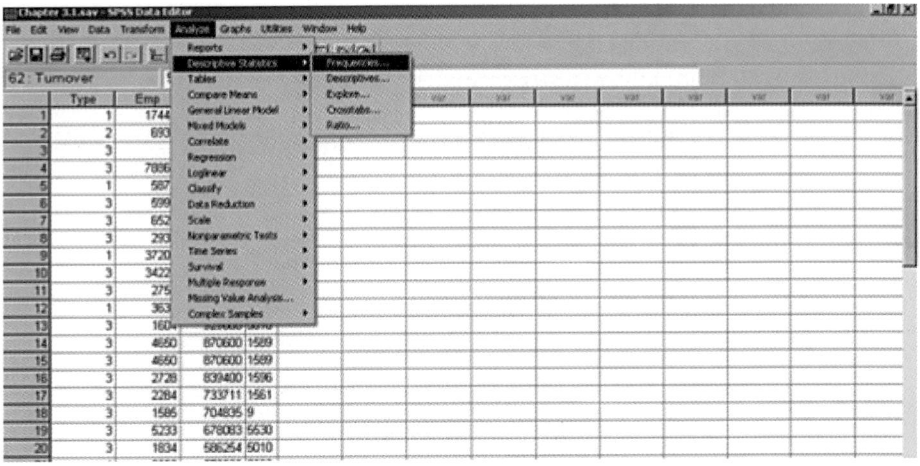

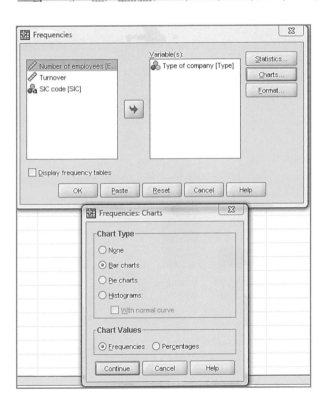

Figure 4.28
Drop-down menu for
Frequencies

Figure 4.29
Frequencies
dialog box

We don't need a list of frequencies, so we remove the tick from Display frequency tables. Press OK to initiate the SPSS processor.

All SPSS output is added to the Viewer window (Figure 4.30). This window has two sections or panes. The left-hand pane is called the outline pane, and the right-hand pane is the display pane. To see the bar chart properly, we need to scroll down the display pane. The bar chart is shown in Figure 4.31. You can see that the largest number of companies is *Private limited*.

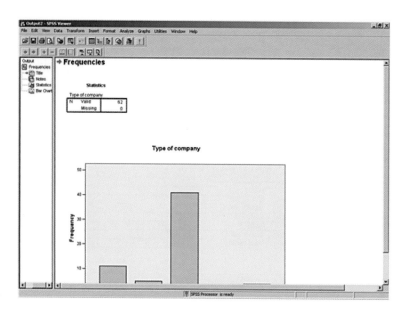

Figure 4.30
The Viewer window

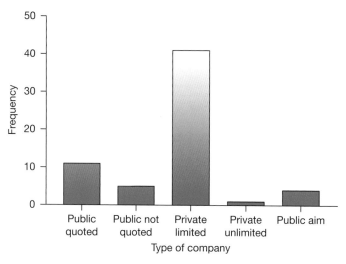

Figure 4.31
The bar chart for
Type of company

Activity 4.12

Create a pie chart of the variable *Type of company*.

Although you can create a pie chart in a similar way as we did for the bar chart, SPSS version 16 has a powerful chart builder that allows you to preview a chart as you are building it. Click on Graphs and then Chart Builder. Make sure that Gallery is selected and drag the picture of a pie chart into the preview screen (in other charts you will have a choice of chart subtype). Drag *Type of company* into Slice by? and in the Element properties change statistic to *percentage* and click Apply. You should get the screen as seen in Figure 4.32. You can add a title by clicking on Titles/Footnotes and adding a title into the Content box. Click OK.

Note: The preview only gives an example not the actual data

Change to percentage

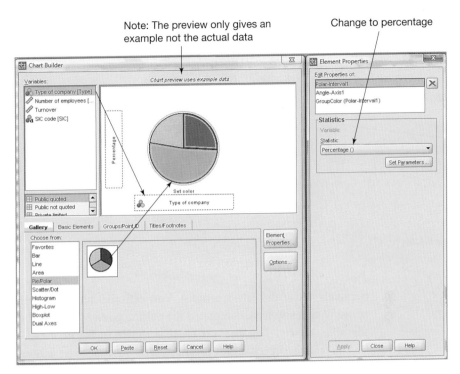

Figure 4.32
Define pie chart data

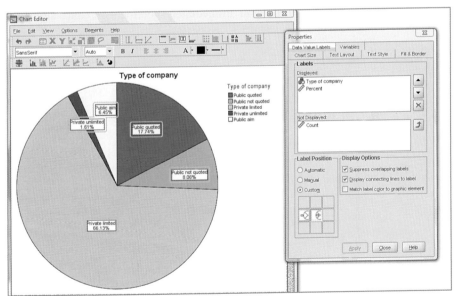

Figure 4.33
The chart editor

There are other formatting changes you can do but most other embellishments are carried out in the *chart editor* as shown in Figure 4.33. To enter the chart editor double-click the chart. Say we wanted labels and the percentages in each slice. Click Elements and then Show Data Labels. In the Labels boxes have *Type of company* and *percentages* in Displayed and *Count* Not displayed. If you want you can have the labels outside the pie and prevent labels from overlapping others and you can also

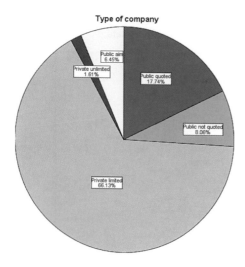

Figure 4.34
The final pie chart

manually move the labels around. You can also hide the legend from the options menu. When you have completed the editing go to `File` and then `Close` to return to the SPSS Viewer. The final pie chart is shown in Figure 4.34.

You can easily change the chart type in the chart editor by clicking on the `Variables` tab in the `Properties` window. Change the element type to `Bar` and click `Apply` and you immediately get the bar chart shown in Figure 4.35. Note

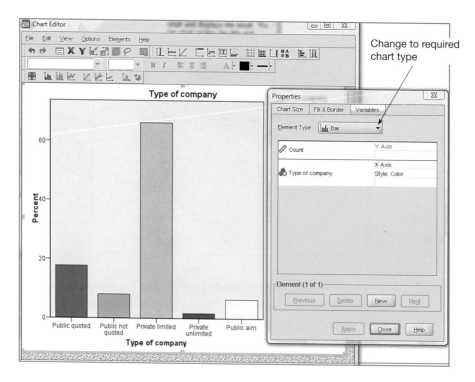

Figure 4.35
Changing chart type

however that not all chart types are suitable for all types of data and unsuitable ones will be greyed out. For instance you couldn't plot a histogram with *Type of company*!

The final chart we shall look at is a *Histogram*, which again can be built using the Chart Builder. As a histogram requires continuous data (called *scaled* data in SPSS) we will use *Turnover* for our histogram. The procedure is the same as for the pie chart except that we have a choice of 4 subtypes. We will use the first one – a simple histogram (see Figure 4.36). The histogram is shown in Figure 4.37. This chart clearly shows the (right) skewness of the distribution.

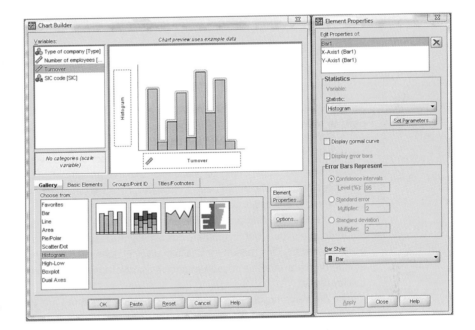

Figure 4.36
Using Chart Builder to plot a histogram

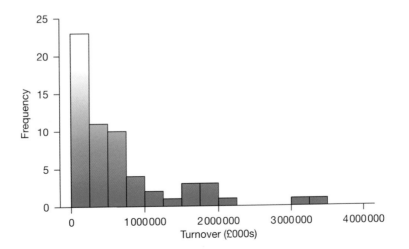

Figure 4.37
SPSS histogram for 'Turnover'

Did you know

Charts can be used to mislead as well as clarify. Figure 4.38 is taken from the US Environmental Law Institute. The idea of the diagram is to show that fossil fuels get a bigger tax break than renewables. The diagram looks a bit like a pie chart but is totally misleading, with nothing to scale. Either the data (there are only 16 values) could be represented simply as a table or as a component bar chart.

Source: Straight Statistics, May 2011
(www.straightstatistics.org/article/who-ate-all-pies)
Figure source: US Environmental Law Institute

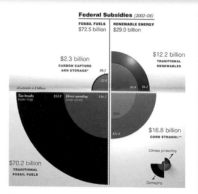

Figure 4.38 A misleading chart

Reflection

As you will have seen in this chapter, there are a number of different diagrams that can be used to represent a set of data. Choosing the most appropriate diagram is important if you want to be able to interpret the data correctly and to provide others with reliable information. A good chart should be technically correct but also visually stimulating. The use of Excel has made it easy to produce charts that are attractive to the eye, particularly if a limited amount of colour is used. However, SPSS is becoming more popular and can produce more professional looking charts.

Many published diagrams are misleading (sometimes intentionally!). One of the most common mistakes – but fortunately not usually misleading – is the use of bar charts for continuous data. One reason for this is that Excel does not have a histogram as one of its standard charts. Another reason might be that histograms are seen as too technical for the lay reader.

The diagrams produced by the World Resources Institute are visually attractive and convey a large amount of information. The Pie chart (Figure 4.1) shows clearly that transport is a relatively small amount of global GHGs and within this category it is road transport that is the biggest contributor to greenhouse gases with air transport contributing very little in comparison. Figure 4.2 illustrates that CO_2 emissions, as a percentage of world output, during the decade to 2000 have been as much as (and in some cases more than) those for the entire period since 1850. Figure 4.3 is even more revealing and shows that nearly 40% of global GHGs come from just 2 countries.

Key points

○ *Data* can be *continuous*, *discrete*, *ordinal* or *nominal*. The type of data determines the method to be used in its presentation.
○ Data is normally *aggregated* into *tables*. For continuous and discrete data, these tables can be either *ungrouped* or *grouped*.
○ For *group frequency tables*, the *class interval* needs to be decided and a *tally chart* used to help in the aggregation process.

○ Several different types of diagram can be used to display the data more effectively.

○ *Pie charts* can only be used for categorical data.

○ *Bar charts* are normally used for categorical data and for discrete data.

○ *Line graphs* can be used for time series data.

○ *Histograms* are used either for continuous or for discrete data that has been aggregated into a frequency table. A histogram gives you an idea of the shape of the underlying distribution, but a *frequency polygon* will show this more clearly.

○ If cumulative frequencies are plotted, a *cumulative frequency ogive* is obtained. This important graph allows you to obtain further information about the underlying distribution.

○ Another useful diagram is a stem and leaf plot. This diagram allows the shape of the distribution to be seen and outliers can be highlighted.

Further reading

As for the previous chapter all elementary statistical texts contain a chapter on presentation of data. Many texts such as Curwin and Slater (2008) use Excel but some cover SPSS or Minitab (another statistical package) as well. There are also a large number of texts that specialize in SPSS, such as the one by Field (2009) and another by Pallant (2010). For those of you interested in the subject of climate change see the excellent free publication from the Pew Centre on Global Change by Sussman and Freed (2008). This can be downloaded as a pdf file from www.pewclimate.org/docUploads/Business-Adaptation.pdf.

Web links 🆆

Answers to selected questions can be found in Appendix 2. Answers to the other questions can be found on the companion website for this book.

Practice questions

🆆 **1** How would you define the following sets of data?
   (a) The number of hours of sunshine each day at a seaside resort
   (b) The mean daily temperature at a seaside resort
   (c) Daily rainfall (in mm)
   (d) Scoring system for ice dancing

🆆 **2** In the context of a survey into internet usage give an example of
   (a) Ratio data
   (b) Interval data
   (c) Discrete data
   (d) Ordinal data
   (e) Nominal data

W. 3 A person keeps account of the number of text messages she has sent over the past 18 days and the results are shown in Table 4.13

Table 4.13 Data for Question 3

Day	Texts sent	Day	Texts sent	Day	Texts sent
1	2	7	10	13	8
2	5	8	20	14	6
3	5	9	0	15	30
4	12	10	10	16	12
5	1	11	4	17	1
6	5	12	2	18	9

Summarize this data in the form of a frequency table using suitable class intervals and plot the data.

4 A survey was carried out into consumers' preference for different types of coffee. A sample of 20 people gave the following replies:

Person	Preference	Person	Preference
1	instant	11	ground
2	filter	12	instant
3	instant	13	ground
4	filter	14	filter
5	instant	15	instant
6	filter	16	instant
7	ground	17	ground
8	instant	18	filter
9	filter	19	instant
10	filter	20	filter

(a) Aggregate this data into a suitable table.
(b) Draw a pie chart of the data.
(c) Draw a simple bar chart of the data.

5 Table 4.14 represents the sales by department of a high street store. Using Excel or otherwise, draw a component bar chart and a multiple bar chart of the sales.

Table 4.14 Sales information for Question 5

Department	2009	2010	2011
Menswear	£2.7m	£4.9m	£6.3m
Furniture	£3.4m	£2.3m	£1.5m
Household	£2.5m	£2.4m	£2.5m
Total Sales	£8.6m	£9.6m	£10.3m

What conclusions can you make about the sales for this store?

6 Table 4.15 shows how the sales of Marla plc were broken down between the company's four sales regions during the years 2007 to 2011. Using Excel or otherwise,

(a) Draw a simple bar chart to show the total sales for the four-year period.
(b) Draw a component bar chart to show the sales for the years and how they were broken down between the four sales regions.
(c) Draw a multiple bar chart to compare the sales for each region.

(d) Draw a pie chart to show the breakdown of total sales in 2011.

(e) What can you conclude about the sales of Marla plc?

Table 4.15 Sales information for Question 6

Sales region	Year (Sales £m)				
	2007	2008	2009	2010	2011
S. West	4.0	2.0	2.2	3.6	3.7
South	6.0	4.9	2.5	3.2	3.7
S. East	7.6	9.1	5.2	4.3	4.2
Wales	1.5	1.4	1.4	1.5	1.6
Totals	19.1	17.4	11.3	12.6	13.2

W. **7** The data below relates to the weight (in grams) of an item produced by a machine.

28.8	29.2	30.8	29.2	30.2	30.0	26.8	30.6	29.0	27.8	28.6
30.4	30.8	29.2	30.4	29.6	31.4	30.6	31.0	31.4	31.4	30.0
29.0	29.4	29.0	28.0	26.5	29.6	27.0	23.2	25.2	24.5	28.0
27.0	29.4	27.6	26.2	25.3	26.8	25.8	28.2	28.1	30.0	30.0
27.1	26.1	25.4	23.8	22.8	23.5	25.5	24.0	27.0	28.5	27.2
25.5	25.6	24.5	23.5	22.4	25.2	27.4	27.0	28.2	28.0	28.0
25.8	30.4	26.5	25.2	29.3	27.4	22.1	26.2	23.8	24.8	20.5
20.4	24.6	24.8								

(a) Aggregate this data into a suitable frequency table.

(b) Draw a histogram of the data.

(c) Draw a stem and leaf plot of the data.

(d) Draw a cumulative frequency ogive of the data and demonstrate how it could be used to provide further information about the distribution of weights.

(e) What conclusions can be made about the data from your diagrams?

W. **8** Using the data given in Table 4.13 for Question 3 plot the data using a histogram.

W. **9** The histogram in Figure 4.39 represents hours worked, taken from the British 2001 census. Describe what this histogram shows. How would you describe the shape of the histogram?

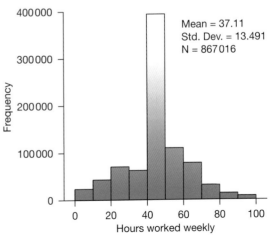

Mean = 37.11
Std. Dev. = 13.491
N = 867 016

Figure 4.39
Histogram of hours worked from the 2001 census

W 10 Table 4.16 shows the number of cars/vans per household taken from the 2001 British census. Using the Valid percentage column draw a pie chart and explain what this chart shows.

Table 4.16 Vehicles owned, taken from the 2001 national census

Cars/Vans Owned or Available for Use		Frequency	Percentage	Valid percentage	Cumulative percentage
Valid	No car	358 420	19.4	19.8	19.8
	1 car	761 398	41.3	42.1	61.8
	2 cars	537 155	29.1	29.7	91.5
	3 cars or more	153 602	8.3	8.5	100.0
	Total	1 810 575	98.2	100.0	
Missing	Not applicable (not in a household)	32 950	1.8		
Total		1 843 525	100.0		

W 11 Table 4.17 shows family type taken from the 2001 national census. Draw a bar chart using the Valid percentage column of this data and describe what it shows.

Table 4.17 Frequency table of family type taken from the 2001 national census

Family Type	Frequency	Percentage	Valid percentage	Cumulative percentage
Valid				
Lone parent – male	27 264	1.5	1.5	1.5
Lone parent – female	190 229	10.3	10.6	12.1
Married couple – no children	342 020	18.6	19.1	31.2
Married couple – children all belong to both members of couple	671 362	36.4	37.4	68.7
Married couple – children do not all belong to both members	63 983	3.5	3.6	72.2
Cohabiting couple – no children	80 237	4.4	4.5	76.7
Cohabiting couple – children all belong to both members	58 178	3.2	3.2	79.9
Cohabiting couple – children do not all belong to both members	46 005	2.5	2.6	82.5
Ungrouped individual (not in a family)	313 438	17.0	17.5	100.0
Total	1 792 716	97.2	100.0	
Missing				
Not applicable (not in a household/student living away)	50 809	2.8		
Total	1 843 525	100.0		

W **12** Table 4.18 is taken from the 2001 national census. It shows the highest qualification held by men and women. Using level of education qualification as x-axis labels:

Table 4.18 Level of highest qualifications (aged 16–74), England, Wales and Northern Ireland by sex

	Sex		
	Male	Female	Total
No qualifications	165	187	352
Level 1	99	99	198
Level 2	107	124	231
Level 3	48	50	98
Level 4/5	117	117	234
Other qualifications/level unknown (England and Wales only)	51	28	79
Total	587	605	1192

(a) Plot a multiple bar chart of the data
(b) Plot a component bar chart of the data
(c) Plot a percentage bar chart of the data
(d) Explain what these charts tells you about qualifications held by men and women in England, Wales and Northern Island

W **13** The sickness records of a company have been examined and Table 4.19 shows the number of days taken off work through sickness during the past year.

Table 4.19 Information for Question 13

Days off work	Number of employees
Less than 2 days	45
2 to 5 days	89
6 to 9 days	40
10 to 13 days	25
14 to 21 days	5
22 to 29 days	2

Draw a histogram to represent this distribution and comment on its shape.

14 A survey carried out into 605 small and medium-size companies (SMEs) in the South of England revealed the information in Table 4.20 (overleaf) on average sales growth during a period of recession.

(a) Using Excel, plot the following charts:

(i) A simple bar chart of the number of companies in each region
(ii) A multiple bar chart with year as the x-axis labels
(iii) A multiple bar chart with region as the x-axis labels
(iv) A line graph of the average change in sales growth from 2008 to 2010
(v) A pie chart of the sales growth for each region during 2008

(b) Write a paragraph summarizing your charts.

Table 4.20 Annual average % sales growth (from previous year) by region

Region	No. of companies	2008	2009	2010
South Western	63	17.3	−1.0	2.5
Southern	143	21.1	3.2	2.4
Eastern	77	11.9	7.6	0.6
South Eastern	48	50.5	25.5	−0.7
Outer London	78	17.3	1.7	2.3
Inner London	191	19.1	17.3	12.6

15 A high street store has gathered the following data about the value in £s of purchases made by a sample of 50 customers.

```
67.00   55.56   85.21   72.33   63.25   58.00   53.00   53.41   73.33   79.21
65.22   53.25   82.10   46.10   56.00   64.16   55.67   57.00   57.00   58.20
43.20   52.30   98.00   57.21   59.62   52.33   57.77   58.20   58.60   61.22
53.40   67.00   66.32   50.10   60.11   45.00   51.20   53.00   78.54   64.00
41.21   78.61   55.55   48.62   59.99   63.54   76.35   77.00   45.50   55.01
```

(a) Plot a histogram of the data using suitable class intervals and join up the mid points to form a frequency polygon. Describe the shape of the distribution.

(b) Plot a cumulative frequency ogive and find the following:

(i)   The percentage of sales in excess of £70

(ii) The percentage of sales between £52 and £72

(iii) The value of purchases that are exceeded by 10% of sales.

....

Assignment

Find examples (at least three) of diagrams in newspapers, company reports and statistical publications. You should write a paragraph on each diagram discussing the following points:

○ the conclusions that you can draw from the diagram

○ whether a different diagram would be more informative

○ how the diagram could be misleading (if applicable).

Making sense of data: averages and measures of spread

Prerequisites   In order to fully understand this chapter you should have read Chapter 4 (*Finding patterns in data: charts and tables*).

Objectives
- To be able to calculate measures of central tendency (measures of location) and variation in the data (spread around the central location)
- To understand the advantages and disadvantages of different measures
- To be able to draw suitable charts to help calculate some of these measures
- To be able to use Excel and SPSS to visualize some of these measures

Introduction   Although tables and diagrams allow important features of data to be displayed, these methods of summarizing information are generally *qualitative* rather than *quantitative*. In order to provide more quantitative information, it is necessary to calculate statistical measures that can be used to represent the entire set of data. Two important measures of the data are the *location* of the data, in terms of a typical or central value, and the *spread* or *dispersion* of the data around this central value.

Quantitative methods in action: pay settlements in a weak economy

Following the global financial crisis of 2008 most Western economies were weak, with large deficits. These deficits were tackled by austerity measures such as increases in taxation and reductions in capital expenditure. One consequence of these measures was the increase in unemployment and the reduced level of pay settlements. This was particularly true in the public sector in the UK where large numbers of workers expected to lose their jobs. A review of police pay (the *Winsor* review[1]) recommended that police officers should have their basic pay cut. This could result in 40% of police officers losing £4000 a year. Many other public sector organizations including the Post Office and local authorities either announced a pay freeze or job losses or both.

The private sector was not immune to the cuts because many businesses rely on government contracts or the spending power of consumers. This has resulted in strikes at several large companies such as Perkin Engines and Arriva Trains. The distribution sector (which includes companies such as Amazon,

IKEA and John Lewis) was one of the sectors hit hard by the recession, and pay rises there fell. A salary survey[2] showed that the average pay rise in 2010 was 2% – down from 2.6% in 2009 and 3.3% in 2008. However the average pay rise does not tell the full story because some groups saw a rise of 0.5% while others saw a rise of 4.4%. This survey showed that the average basic salary of a regional distribution centre (RDC) manager was £72 625 but 25% of managers were paid less than £60 900 and 25% were paid more than £82 438.

Low pay settlements in a low inflation climate is one thing but as inflation takes off people will notice a drop in their disposable income. Figure 5.1 shows how prices and wages changed between 2009 and 2010. You will see that during 2010 prices were increasing much faster than wages.

[1] http://review.police.uk/part-one-report/
[2] XpertHR Distribution Staff Salary Survey
Source: Commercial Motor, November 2010

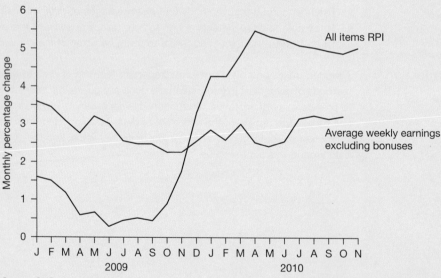

Figure 5.1
Prices and wages: monthly percentage changes compared with previous year
Source: ONS.

Measures of location

I am sure that you have heard of the word *average*. An average is some kind of representative item within a set of possible items. The word *location* is used because, for numerical data, an average *locates* a typical value of some distribution. This is not as easy as it may seem as there could be several different values that would serve as this average figure.

Example 5.1

The number of sales made by two salespersons over the past few days has been as follows:

Mike   3, 2, 1, 32, 2, 1, 1
Janet   0, 1, 4, 12, 10, 7, 8, 6

Activity 5.1

What would be a good measure of the daily number of sales by each salesperson?

Six out of the seven values for Mike are between 1 and 3 sales per day, while for Janet the values are fairly evenly spread between 0 and 12 sales per day. Do you choose one of the existing values to represent the number of sales per day or do you choose a value that is in between?

There are in fact three different averages and each can give you different values. The next section defines each one and discusses the advantages and disadvantages of each.

The mean, median and mode

The *mean* is defined as the sum of all the values divided by the total number of values. So for Mike the mean number of sales per day is:

$$\frac{3 + 2 + 1 + 32 + 2 + 1 + 1}{7} = 6$$

Notice that the mean is not one of the values in the set of data. (A mean value can also be a fractional value even if the data values are themselves whole numbers.)

The mean of a set of numbers is normally referred to as $\bar{x}$ (x bar) and in symbols the formula for the mean is:

Sum of the n values

$$\bar{x} = \frac{\sum x}{n}$$

Number of items

Activity 5.2

Find the mean number of sales per day for Janet.

You should have found that the mean for Janet is also 6. Is 6 sales a good measure of average for both data sets? Certainly for Janet a mean of 6 is quite a good representative value, but for Mike a value between 1 and 3 would be more typical. The problem with the mean is that it gives equal importance to *all* values, including any extreme values. In Mike's case the value of 32 is clearly influencing the mean. The *median* overcomes this problem by choosing the *middle* value of a set of numbers. In order to find this value the data is first ordered in ascending order as follows:

1, 1, 1, 2, 2, 3, 32

The middle value of this set of 7 numbers is 2, which is a more typical value.

Activity 5.3

Find the median sales for Janet.

You should have found a slight problem here in that there is no single middle number. There are two middle numbers though, which are 6 and 7 and in this case you would take the mean of these two numbers which is 6.5. This is close to the mean value of 6, so in this case either of the two averages are equally suitable.

Which is the better average? This is a difficult question to answer as both have their advantages and disadvantages, as you can see in Table 5.1.

Table 5.1 Comparison of mean and median

	Mean	Median
One of the actual data items?	Not usually	Usually
Equal contribution by all data items?	Yes	No
Influenced by extreme values (outliers)?	Yes	No
Easy to calculate?	Yes	No

The mean and median can both be used for numerical data but not for *categorical* data. The next activity illustrates this point.

Activity 5.4

In Chapter 4 data from a travel to work survey was provided. This data is summarized in Table 5.2.

Which is the most typical mode of travel?

Table 5.2 Results of a travel to work survey

Mode of travel	Frequency
Car	9
Bus	4
Cycle	3
Walk	2
Train	2

Clearly the car is the most common mode of travel. The category that occurs the most frequently is called the *mode*. The mode can also be quoted for numerical data.

Activity 5.5

What is the mode for the sales data of Example 5.1?

For Mike, 1 sale occurred most frequently so this is the mode for this group of numbers. However, there is no mode for Janet's sales data since each value occurs once only.

The mode has limited uses but it can be useful when the most common value or category is required. Can you imagine a shoe shop being interested in the mean or median size of shoe?

The mean, median and mode for a frequency distribution

It is relatively straightforward finding an average of a small set of data, but when large quantities of data are involved, or when the data is supplied in the form of a frequency table, the methods of calculation become more involved.

Example 5.2

The ungrouped frequency table in Table 5.3 gives the daily number of sales made by the sales force of a double glazing company.

Table 5.3 Ungrouped frequency table

No. of sales	Frequency
2	3
3	7
4	9
5	6
6	5
7	2
8	1

Activity 5.6

What is the mean number of sales made per day by the company's sales force?

The mean could be found by writing the value 2 three times, 3 seven times and so on. You would then add up all the values and divide by the total number of values, which is 33. However, a much easier method is to multiply 2 by 3, 3 by 7 and so on. This will give you the same sum as the longer method. If you let x be the number of sales and f the frequency, the procedure for calculating the mean can be seen in Table 5.4.

Table 5.4 Calculation of the mean

No. of sales x	Frequency f	f x
2	3	6
3	7	21
4	9	36
5	6	30
6	5	30
7	2	14
8	1	8
Total	33	145

The mean is therefore: $\dfrac{145}{33} = 4.4$ sales.

This calculation can be expressed in algebraic notation as follows:

$$\bar{x} = \frac{\sum fx}{\sum f}$$

← Multiply f by x and sum

← Sum of frequencies

Activity 5.7

What is the median number of sales made per day?

The median for this set of values can be found by remembering that the median is the middle value. Since the data is already in ascending order it is a simple matter of locating the middle value, which will occur at the 17th frequency. If you write down the cumulative frequencies as shown in Table 5.5, you will see that the median must occur when $x = 4$.

Table 5.5 Calculation of the median

x	f	Cumulative f
2	3	3
3	7	10
4	9	19
5	6	25
6	5	30
7	2	32
8	1	33

Activity 5.8

What is the modal value of sales?

The modal number of sales is easy to see since 4 sales occurs 9 times, which is the most frequent.

Example 5.3

The group frequency table shown in Table 5.6 refers to the length of 80 bolts produced by a machine.

Table 5.6 Grouped frequency table

Interval	Frequency
30 to under 35 mm	4
35 to under 40 mm	7
40 to under 45 mm	14
45 to under 50 mm	23
50 to under 55 mm	16
55 to under 60 mm	9
60 to under 65 mm	4
65 to under 70 mm	1
70 to under 75 mm	1
75 to under 80 mm	0
80 to under 85 mm	1

This is a similar table to that in Example 5.2, except that x does not have a single value. In order to calculate the mean, the *mid value* is used for x. So the mid value for the interval 30 to under 35 would be 32.5. (You can assumed that you can get as close as you like to 35mm.) Although this is an approximation, it is generally a very close one and is normally quite adequate.

Activity 5.9

Calculate the mean for the data in Table 5.6.

Table 5.7 shows how the mean is calculated by making x represent the mid point of the range.

Table 5.7 Calculation of the mean and median for a frequency distribution

Interval	Mid point (x)	Frequency f	fx	Cumulative frequency	% cumulative frequency
30 to under 35 mm	32.5	4	130.0	4	5.00
35 to under 40 mm	37.5	7	262.5	11	13.75
40 to under 45 mm	42.5	14	595.0	25	31.25
45 to under 50 mm	47.5	23	1092.5	48	60.00
50 to under 55 mm	52.5	16	840.0	64	80.00
55 to under 60 mm	57.5	9	517.5	73	91.25
60 to under 65 mm	62.5	4	250.0	77	96.25
65 to under 70 mm	67.5	1	67.5	78	97.50
70 to under 75 mm	72.5	1	72.5	79	98.75
75 to under 80 mm	77.5	0	0.0	79	98.75
80 to under 85 mm	82.5	1	82.5	80	100.00
	Total	80	3910.0		

The mean is:

$$\frac{3910}{80} = 48.875 \text{ mm}$$

The mean using the raw data is 48.652 mm, so the value obtained using the frequency table is quite a good one. (If you want to check this calculation, the raw data can be found in Example 4.3 (Table 4.6 on page 59).)

Activity 5.10

What is the median length of a bolt?

The problem with obtaining the median from a grouped frequency table is that the median is likely to lie within an interval. You could locate the required interval and then simply use the mid point as an estimate, but a better approximation is to interpolate within the interval. There are two methods of doing this extrapolation. The easiest method is graphical and if a cumulative frequency ogive is drawn the median frequency will be halfway up the y axis. It is often easier to use percentage cumulative frequency, as then the median frequency is 50%. Figure 5.2 is the cumulative frequency ogive for the length of bolts, and you will see that the median is around 48 mm, so 50% of bolts are below 48 mm in length and 50% above.

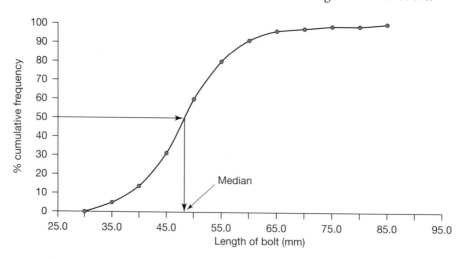

Figure 5.2
Ogive

An alternative method is by calculation. If we look at Table 5.7 we see that 25 bolts are below 45 mm and 48 below 50 mm so the median (the 40th bolt) must be in the interval 45 to 50 mm. That is, the median is 45 plus a proportion of the 5 mm interval. As the median is represented by the 40th bolt it must be $40 - 25 = 15$ into this interval and since there are 23 bolts in the interval then $15/23$ is the fraction of the interval. If we multiply this fraction by 5 we get the amount we must add on to 45. So the median will be:

$$45 + \frac{15}{23} \times 5 = 48.26 \text{ mm}$$

which agrees with the values obtained graphically.

We can write this calculation as a formula:

$$\text{Median} = l + w\left(\frac{\frac{n}{2} - F}{f}\right)$$

where l is the lower boundary of the median group, w is the width of the median group, n is the number of values, f is the frequency in the median group and F is the cumulative frequency up to the median group.

So in our example: $l = 45$; $w = 5$; $n = 80$; $f = 23$ and $F = 25$ and

$$45 + 5\left(\frac{40 - 25}{23}\right) = 48.26, \text{ as before.}$$

A further method is to use a stem and leaf plot. In Activity 4.10 (page 71) we obtained a stem and leaf plot for the length of bolt data (see Table 5.8). As there is an even number of values we must take the average of the two middle two values which will be the 40th and 41st value. Counting from either end we get 47 and 49 mm and the mean of these two numbers is 48 mm which again agrees with the other two methods.

Table 5.8 A stem and leaf plot of the length of bolt data

```
Frequency      Stem &  Leaf
     4.00         3 . 0003                      The middle two values
     7.00         3 . 5556667
    14.00         4 . 01122222334444
    23.00         4 . 5555566666667799999999
    16.00         5 . 0011122222333444
     9.00         5 . 556666789
     4.00         6 . 0114
     3.00 Extremes    (>=68)

               3|3 represents 33 mm
```

Activity 5.11

What is the modal value of the length of bolts?

It is normal to talk about a *modal class* in a grouped frequency distribution, although it is possible to estimate a single value. The grouped frequency table in Example 5.3 (Table 5.6) suggests that the interval 45 to under 50 mm has the highest frequency of 23. A single estimate of the modal value could be obtained using the geometric method illustrated in Figure 5.3. You should see that this modal value is approximately 48 mm. You might have noticed that all three averages are very similar. This is because the underlying distribution is approximately *symmetrical*. If the distribution were *right* skewed the mean would be displaced to the *right* of the mode, and if the distribution were *left* skewed the mean would be displaced to the *left* of the mode. The median is between the two but closer to the mean. (Skewness was first discussed in Chapter 4.) Earnings data is a good example of a distribution that is right skewed.

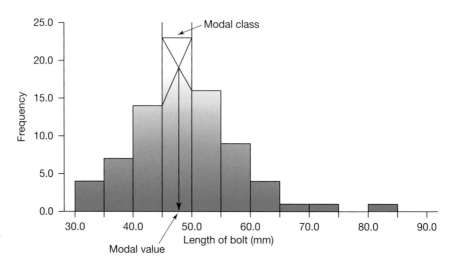

Figure 5.3
Graphical method for finding the mode

Activity 5.12

The grouped frequency table in Table 5.9 refers to the weight of jars of coffee. What is the average weight of a jar according to this data?

Table 5.9 Grouped frequency table with open classes

Class interval	Frequency
less than 96 g	5
96 to under 98 g	10
98 to under 99 g	15
99 to under 100 g	27
100 to under 102 g	11
more than 102 g	2

The problem with Table 5.9 is the open classes. A mean needs a mid point for each interval, which this data clearly does not have. There is no satisfactory way of calculating the mean for grouped frequency tables with open classes, although some people say you should use the width of the previous or next interval. So the mid point of the first interval would be 95 g and 103 g for the last interval. This approximation *may* be justified if the number of items in the open intervals is small relative to the closed intervals. I think that for open intervals the median is a far better average to use. The median only requires the upper value of each interval and it is not necessary for the ogive to be complete. This is illustrated in Figure 5.4 where you will see that the median is about 99.2 g.

In the calculation of the mean, each value was given an equal weighting. However, there are some circumstances where this is not correct. The next activity illustrates a typical example.

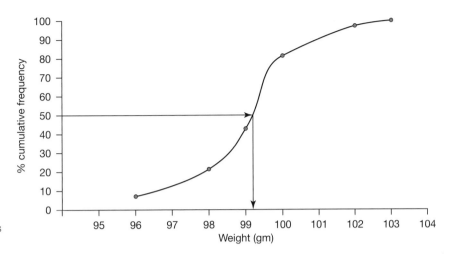

Figure 5.4
Median weight for jars
of coffee

Activity 5.13

The pay rises given to 1000 employees during the year were as follows:

Employee	Pay rise	No. of employees
Manual	1%	700
Clerical	3%	200
Management	8%	100

The company maintains that the average pay rise was 4%. Is this correct?

The company has ignored the fact that the majority of the employees have received 3% or less. To get a better idea of the true average the percentages should be *weighted* by the number of employees in each category, as follows:

$$\frac{1 \times 700 + 3 \times 200 + 8 \times 100}{1000} = 2.1\%$$

This figure is much more representative of the true average pay rise.

Did you know

How accurate should you give results from analyses? The *Guardian* newspaper reported a study by the Nationwide Building Society which apparently showed that parents are prepared to pay an extra £8670 for a house in the catchment area of a top local primary school. This figure was obtained by estimating that a top primary school will add 3.3% to the value of a house. They multiplied this figure by the average house price. As both the 3.3% and the average house price will have large margins of errors the final result will also be imprecise. Quoting the increase in house price to 3 significant figures is therefore wrong. A better figure would be £9000 but for some reason people are more influenced by a figure that looks precise.

Source: http://www.guardian.co.uk/education/2010/aug/02/parents-schools-house-prices-survey?INTCMP=SRCH

http://www.straightstatistics.org/article/spurious-accuracy-seduces-journalists-time-and-time-again

Measures of spread

An average is not always sufficient in describing how a set of data is distributed. The sales data given in Example 5.1 is a typical example. This data has been reproduced below.

Mike   3, 2, 1, 32, 2, 1, 1
Janet   0, 1, 4, 12, 10, 7, 8, 6

The mean number of sales per day in both cases was 6, yet the individual figures are quite different. In addition to a measure of location, a measure of *spread* or *dispersion* can also be provided. There are various measures of spread: the simplest is the *range*. The range is the difference between the smallest and largest and for Mike this is $32 - 1 = 31$ sales per day, while for Janet it is $12 - 0 = 12$. So there is a much larger spread in Mike's figures than in Janet's.

Unfortunately the range is too easily influenced by extreme values and is not a particularly good measure. Another measure is the *interquartile range* (IQR). To calculate the IQR the data is divided into quarters. If Q_1 is the lower quartile and Q_3 is the upper quartile, then

$$IQR = Q_3 - Q_1$$

(Q_2 is the median)

This method avoids the extremes and thus is more representative than the range. It is normally used with a group frequency table.

Activity 5.14

What is the IQR for the distribution of pay of RDC managers in 2010 (see *Quantitative methods in action* at the start of this chapter)?

As 25% get paid less than £60 900 and 25% get paid more than £82 438 this defines Q_1 and Q_3 so

$$IQR = 82\,438 - 60\,900$$
$$= 21\,538$$

So the range of the middle 50% of RDC managers is £21 538.

Activity 5.15

Calculate the IQR for the data given in Example 5.3 (page 97).

The easiest method is to draw a cumulative frequency ogive and mark the 25% and 75% limits. This has been done in Figure 5.5 and you will see that the IQR is about $54 - 44 = 10\,mm$.

Unfortunately this is still not ideal because you are just looking at the middle half of the data and ignoring the rest. A better method is the *standard deviation*.

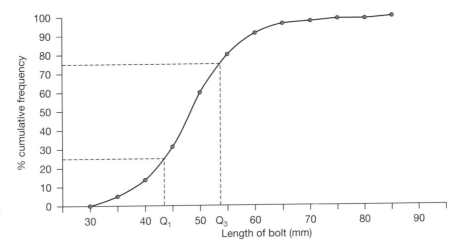

Figure 5.5
Graphical method for finding the interquartile range

The variance and standard deviation

Another measure of spread is a statistic called the *variance* – this is a better measure as it uses all the data. The procedure for calculating the variance is:

1 Find the difference between each value and the mean.
2 Square this difference (this removes the negative signs).
3 Add up all these squared differences.
4 Divide the total squared difference by one less than the number of data items (n). The reason for dividing by $n - 1$ and not n has to do with the fact that when you take a sample of data items the spread will be less than the spread of the population. To understand this, think of how many seven-foot people you know. There will be several seven-foot people in a country, and the spread of heights of the population will be influenced by these people. Yet if you take only a small sample, it is extremely unlikely that you will get any very tall or very short people, so the *sample* spread will be less than the *population* spread. Dividing by $n - 1$ helps to compensate for this. This adjustment is only really important for small sample sizes (n below 30). We will come back to this issue when we look at sample data in Chapter 8.

The statistic you have calculated – the variance – is one of the most important measures in statistics. However, as it is in squared units, it is usual to use the square root of the answer: this statistic is called the *standard deviation* and has the same units as the data. Standard deviation is a far more practical measure of spread and will be used extensively throughout this text.

The variance not only takes account of all data values but also magnifies the effect of values that are a long way from the mean. Data that is more spread out will have a larger variance than data that is clustered closer to the mean.

The procedure for calculating the variance for Mike's sales is shown in Table 5.10. Remember that the mean was 6.

Table 5.10 Calculation of the variance for Mike's sales

Sales	Difference	Difference squared
x	$x - 6$	$(x - 6)^2$
3	-3	9
2	-4	16
1	-5	25
32	26	676
2	-4	16
1	-5	25
1	-5	25
	Total	792

$$\text{Variance} = \frac{792}{7 - 1} = 132.0$$

The variance is usually represented by the symbol s^2:

$$s^2 = 132$$

The standard deviation, s, is $\sqrt{132}$

$$s = 11.5 \text{ sales per day}$$

Notice how the variance is affected by the outlier of 32 sales.

In algebraic terms the formula for the variance is:

Sum of the differences squared

$$s^2 = \frac{\sum(x - \bar{x})^2}{n - 1}$$

number of values – 1

The problems with this formula are that it is tedious and can be inaccurate if the mean has been rounded. A better formula is:

Sum of squared x Sum of x all squared

$$s^2 = \frac{\sum x^2 - \frac{(\sum x)^2}{n}}{n - 1}$$

Table 5.11 illustrates how this formula is used in practice.

$$s^2 = \frac{1044 - \frac{(42)^2}{7}}{6}$$

$$= \frac{792}{6}$$

$$= 132 \text{ as before}$$

Table 5.11 Calculation of the variance using the modified formula

x	x²
3	9
2	4
1	1
32	1024
2	4
1	1
1	1
42	1044

Activity 5.16

Calculate the variance and standard deviation for Janet's sales data.

Using the modified formula, you should have obtained Table 5.12.

Table 5.12 Calculation of the variance of Janet's data

	x	x²
	0	0
	1	1
	4	16
	12	144
	10	100
	7	49
	8	64
	6	36
Totals	48	410

$$s^2 = \frac{410 - \dfrac{(48)^2}{8}}{7}$$

$$= \frac{122}{7}$$

$$= 17.4$$

The standard deviation, $s = 4.2$ sales per day.

This calculation demonstrates that, compared with Mike, Janet has a much smaller variation in her daily number of sales.

Activity 5.17

It has been discovered that a mistake has been made in Janet's sales data given in Example 5.1. Her daily sales are all 3 less than they should be. What should the mean and standard deviation really be?

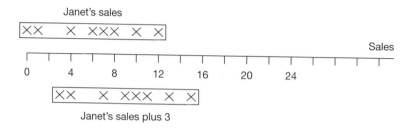

Figure 5.6
Standard deviation
remains unchanged

You should have found the mean to be 9, which is simply 3 more than originally quoted. However, the standard deviation hasn't changed at 4.2. Why is this? This can be explained if you look at Figure 5.6.

The original values have been shifted 3 units to the right. The spread of the new values has not changed so the standard deviation will be the same.

Activity 5.18

If Janet's sales should really be double the figures given in Example 5.1, what would the mean and standard deviation be in this case?

You should have found that both the mean and standard deviation have doubled. By doubling each value the spread has also doubled, as you can see in Figure 5.7.

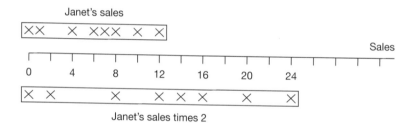

Figure 5.7
Standard deviation
doubles

The variance and standard deviation for a frequency distribution

A slightly different formula is used for a frequency distribution, to reflect the fact that frequencies are involved. The formula normally used for the variance is:

$$s^2 = \frac{\sum fx^2 - \dfrac{(\sum fx)^2}{\sum f}}{\sum f - 1}$$

As the sum of frequencies ($\sum f$) is likely to be large (greater than 30), it is not really necessary to subtract 1 from the denominator. The formula then becomes:

Sum of ($f \times x^2$)⟍   ⟋Sum of ($f \times x$)

$$s^2 = \frac{\sum fx^2}{\sum f} - \left(\frac{\sum fx}{\sum f}\right)^2$$

⟍ ⟋
Sum of f

This is a little easier to use.

Activity 5.19

Calculate the variance and standard deviation of the data in Table 5.6 (page 97).

The value of x takes the same mid point value as in the calculation of the mean (Activity 5.9). The calculation is shown in Table 5.13.

Table 5.13 Calculation of standard deviation for a frequency distribution

Interval	x	f	fx	x²	fx²
30 to under 35 mm	32.5	4	130.0	1 056.25	4 255.00
35 to under 40 mm	37.5	7	262.5	1 406.25	9 843.75
40 to under 45 mm	42.5	14	595.0	1 806.25	25 827.50
45 to under 50 mm	47.5	23	1092.5	2 256.25	51 893.25
50 to under 55 mm	52.5	16	840.0	2 756.25	44 100.00
55 to under 60 mm	57.5	9	517.5	3 306.25	29 756.25
60 to under 65 mm	62.5	4	250.0	3 906.25	15 625.00
65 to under 70 mm	67.5	1	67.5	4 556.25	4 556.25
70 to under 75 mm	72.5	1	72.5	5 256.25	5 256.25
75 to under 80 mm	77.5	0	0.0	6 006.25	0.00
80 to under 85 mm	82.5	1	82.5	6 806.25	6 806.25
	Total	80	3910.0	39 118.75	197 350.00

The variance is therefore:

$$\frac{197\,350}{80} - \left(\frac{3910}{80}\right)^2 = 2466.875 - 2388.7656$$

$$= 78.1094 \quad \text{or} \quad 78.1$$

and the standard deviation:

$$s = \sqrt{78.1094}$$
$$= 8.8 \ \text{mm}$$

Coefficient of variation

If two sets of data have similar means then it is easy to compare the variation by calculating their standard deviations. However, if the means are different then the comparisons of spread will not be so obvious.

Activity 5.20

A hospital is comparing the times patients are waiting for two types of operation. For bypass surgery the mean wait is 17 weeks with a standard deviation of 6 weeks, while for hip replacement the mean is 11 months with a standard deviation of 1 month. Which operation has the highest variability?

The problem here is not only that the means are quite different but also that the units are different (weeks in one case and months in the other). In order to compare the variability the coefficient of variation is calculated. This is defined as:

$$\frac{\text{standard deviation}}{\text{mean}}$$

This is usually expressed as a percentage by multiplying by 100.

For bypass surgery the coefficient of variation is:

$$\frac{6}{17} \times 100 = 35.3\%$$

while for hip replacement it is:

$$\frac{1}{11} \times 100 = 9.1\%$$

Therefore, relative to the mean, the bypass surgery has a larger spread or variation.

Box and whisker plots

A very useful diagram that summarizes information about the location and spread of a set of data is the *box and whisker plot*. The 'box' represents the middle 50% of the data and the extremities of the box are the quartiles Q_1 and Q_3. The median (Q_2) is marked and will obviously be inside the box. Each 'whisker' represents 25% of the data, and the extremities of the whiskers are the minimum and upper values of the data (or the class intervals).

Activity 5.21

Draw a box and whisker plot for the data given in Table 5.6 (page 97).

The median (Q_2) of this data is 48 mm (see Activity 5.10) and the values of Q_1 and Q_3 are 44 and 54 mm respectively (Activity 5.15). The box and whisker plot is shown in Figure 5.8.

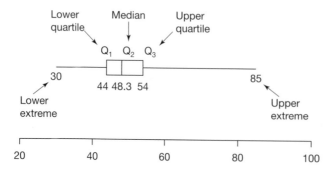

Figure 5.8
Box and whisker plot

Not only does this diagram give you an idea of the average and spread, it also tells you about the shape of the distribution of the data. If the box is small compared to the whiskers this indicates a distribution that is bunched in the middle with long tails. A box shifted to one side or the other indicates skewness, as does the position of the median within the box. In the case of the bolt lengths the right hand whisker is slightly longer than the left, suggesting a slight right skewness to the distribution. However, the median is close to the middle of the box so this skewness is small. The box and whisker plot is particularly useful when you have two or more distributions to compare.

Automatic methods of calculating measures of location and spread

You have probably realized by now that manual methods of calculating statistical measures are tedious and prone to error, particularly when a frequency distribution is involved. An alternative is to use either a scientific calculator or computer software, such as Excel or SPSS. However, a word of caution is necessary when you use either of these methods. You will find that your calculator has two standard deviation buttons, which may be labelled $x\sigma_n$ or $x\sigma_{n-1}$ or something similar. In the same way there are two spreadsheet functions that give you the standard deviation. In Excel these area STDEVP and STDEV, respectively. The difference between the two standard deviation values is that one is obtained by dividing by n and the other by $n - 1$. We briefly discussed the reason for dividing by $n - 1$ in *The variance and standard deviation* above, and we will look at this again in Chapter 9. However, to avoid confusion it is far easier to use one formula and in this text we recommend the $x\sigma_{n-1}$ key or STDEV function. The justification for this decision is that most of the data you have to analyze is sample data, the purpose of which is to estimate what the population parameters (such as the mean and standard deviation) are likely to be. The use of the formula involving $n - 1$ will give a more accurate and unbiased estimate of the standard deviation. A further justification is that for large values of n (greater than 30) there is very little difference between the results from the two formulae.

Activity 5.22

Use the statistical functions on your calculator to find the mean and standard deviation of the data in Example 5.1, page 93 (sales figures for Mike and Janet).

Statistical calculators vary both in the way that data is input and the keys that you press to find the required answers. The instructions below refer to the Casio fx83ES and the fx85ES models. These are both popular calculators (the 85ES is a solar/battery powered model) and can be bought for less than £10. If you have a different calculator you will need to refer to the instruction book. Whatever the make and model of your calculator, always repeat the calculation as a check that you have input the numbers correctly.

Before you start, clear the calculator by the following steps:

1 Press the keys `Shift` `9`

Choose to clear all by

2 Press `1` `=`

Then

3 Press `AC`

The data values for Mike are 3, 2, 1, 32, 2, 1, 1

To enter the STAT mode

Press `Mode` `2`

And `1` (for single variable)

Data can now be entered one value at a time, pressing the `=` key each time.

When all the data has been entered press `Shift` `1`

Then press `5` (for Variables)

This gives you a range of options where you can obtain n (= 7); $\bar{x}$ (= 6); $x\sigma_{n-1}$ (= 11.48912529 or 11.5 sales). Remember to delete the chosen statistic each time otherwise it gets included in the data.

Now clear the calculator and repeat for Janet's sales figures (0, 1, 4, 12, 10, 7, 8, 6). You should get a mean of 6 sales and a standard deviation of 4.174754056; that is, 4.2 sales.

Activity 5.23

Use the statistical functions on your calculator to find the mean and standard deviation of the data in Table 5.6 (page 97).

Table 5.6 is a frequency distribution and a calculator is essential for summarizing this kind of data. The method used by the Casio fx83ES and the fx85ES models is to specify a frequency column in the setup mode.

Press `Shift` and `Mode/Setup`

Then press the down arrow and select `3` (STAT)

Choose `1` (Frequency ON)

Now press `Shift` `1` `2` and you will get a screen as before except that you have a frequency column.

Add the mid points and frequency in the appropriate columns.

The mean and standard deviation is found in the same way as in Activity 5.22. ($\bar{x}$ is 48.875 and $x\sigma_{n-1}$ is 8.8937).

Note that the figure for the standard deviation without the $n-1$ correction is 8.8380, which agrees with Activity 5.19.

Activity 5.24

Table 5.14 shows data from the 2001 census on the travel to work question. What can you deduce from this data?

Table 5.14 Data from the 2001 census on travel to work

Description	Count	Percentage
Less than 2 km	185 781	25.13
2 km to less than 5 km	168 878	22.84
5 km to less than 10 km	151 639	20.51
10 km to less than 20 km	127 642	17.27
20 km to less than 40 km	65 983	8.92
40 km and over	39 385	5.33
Total	739 308	100.00

Source: 2001 Census Area Statistics. (Census output is Crown copyright and is reproduced with the permission of the Controller of HMSO and the Queen's printer for Scotland.)

The analysis was carried out in Excel and the worksheet is shown in Figure 5.9.

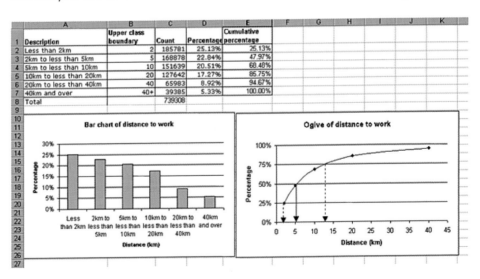

Figure 5.9
Excel worksheet for distance to work

What can you deduce from the bar chart in Figure 5.9? It is clearly right-skewed, with nearly 70% of people travelling less than 10 km to work. The modal range is the 'Less than 2 km' category, although there is not much difference in the height of the second bar.

We now need to try and calculate some statistics from the data. Unfortunately, the mean and variance cannot be calculated because of the '40 km and over' category. However, the median can be estimated from the ogive: it is just over 5 km. This means that for those people who travel to work, half the population travel less than 5 km and half travel more. The interquartile range can also be estimated from the ogive; this is about 12 km (14 − 2). This tells us that the middle 50% of the distribution covers a range of 12 km. This can perhaps be better seen in the box and whisker plot in Figure 5.10, where the skewness is clear.

Figure 5.10
Box and whisker
polot for distance
to work

2   5   14

0   50

Using Excel to calculate summary statistics

A scientific calculator is an essential piece of equipment for calculating the mean and standard deviation of a set of data. However, it is not much help if you want to calculate other statistical measures such as the median and interquartile range. For general statistical manipulation a spreadsheet is highly desirable and is now a fundamental part of a business person's 'toolkit'.

Before attempting Activity 5.25, you might want to go to the website to check that you understand how Excel deals with formulae and functions.

Activity 5.25

The following data sets show the sales made by the 20 staff in the sales department at the head office of Omega Computer Services plc, for the months of August and September 2008. Figures are in £s.

August 08   21 900   12 400   9800   6800   13 050   14 900   15 250   8 900   16 451   13 230   16 450   12 890   13 670   14 700   10 430   11 670   13 200   11 100   19 800   15 700

September 08   12 600   13 500   22 000   34 000   12 500   25 540   21 700   67 800   18 970   16 450   23 220   21 670   17 600   32 420   23 570   14 700   22 400   21 600   26 400   19 700

Use a spreadsheet to summarize both sets of data. In particular, find the mean sales for each salesman and the commission each would get in August based on a 1% commission rate.

The worksheet for Activity 5.25 is shown in Figure 5.11. Figure 5.12 shows the formulae used.

	A	B	C	D	E	F	G
1		Sales of Omega			Commission rate	1%	
2	Sales person	Aug-08	Sep-08	Mean sales	Commission in August		
3	1	£21,900	£12,600	£17,250	£219		
4	2	£12,400	£13,500	£12,950	£124		
5	3	£9,800	£22,000	£15,900	£98		
6	4	£6,800	£34,000	£20,400	£68		
7	5	£13,050	£12,500	£12,775	£131		
8	6	£14,900	£25,540	£20,220	£149		
9	7	£15,250	£21,700	£18,475	£153		
10	8	£8,900	£67,800	£38,350	£89		
11	9	£16,451	£18,970	£17,711	£165		
12	10	£13,230	£16,450	£14,840	£132		
13	11	£16,450	£23,220	£19,835	£165		
14	12	£12,890	£21,670	£17,280	£129		
15	13	£13,670	£17,600	£15,635	£137		
16	14	£14,700	£32,420	£23,560	£147		
17	15	£10,430	£23,570	£17,000	£104		
18	16	£11,670	£14,700	£13,185	£117		
19	17	£13,200	£22,400	£17,800	£132		
20	18	£11,100	£21,600	£16,350	£111		
21	19	£19,800	£26,400	£23,100	£198		
22	20	£15,700	£19,700	£17,700	£157		
23	Total sales	£272,291	£468,340				
24	Mean sales	£13,615	£23,417				
25	Median sales	£13,215	£21,685				
26	Modal sales	#N/A	#N/A				
27	Standard deviation	£3,546	£11,954				
28	Coefficient of variation	26.0%	51.0%				
29	Lower quartile	£11,528	£17,313				
30	Upper quartile	£15,363	£24,063				
31	IQR	£3,835	£6,750				

Figure 5.11
The completed worksheet

	A	B	C	D	E
1			Sales of Omega		Commission rate
2	Sales person	36739	36770	Mean sales	Commission in August
3	1	21900	12600	=(B3+C3)/2	=B3*$F$1
4	2	12400	13500	=(B4+C4)/2	=B4*$F$1
5	3	9800	22000	=(B5+C5)/2	=B5*$F$1
6	4	6800	34000	=(B6+C6)/2	=B6*$F$1
7	5	13050	12500	=(B7+C7)/2	=B7*$F$1
8	6	14900	25540	=(B8+C8)/2	=B8*$F$1
9	7	15250	21700	=(B9+C9)/2	=B9*$F$1
10	8	8900	67800	=(B10+C10)/2	=B10*$F$1
11	9	16451	18970	=(B11+C11)/2	=B11*$F$1
12	10	13230	16450	=(B12+C12)/2	=B12*$F$1
13	11	16450	23220	=(B13+C13)/2	=B13*$F$1
14	12	12890	21670	=(B14+C14)/2	=B14*$F$1
15	13	13670	17600	=(B15+C15)/2	=B15*$F$1
16	14	14700	32420	=(B16+C16)/2	=B16*$F$1
17	15	10430	23570	=(B17+C17)/2	=B17*$F$1
18	16	11670	14700	=(B18+C18)/2	=B18*$F$1
19	17	13200	22400	=(B19+C19)/2	=B19*$F$1
20	18	11100	21600	=(B20+C20)/2	=B20*$F$1
21	19	19800	26400	=(B21+C21)/2	=B21*$F$1
22	20	15700	19700	=(B22+C22)/2	=B22*$F$1
23	Total sales	=SUM(B3:B22)	=SUM(C3:C22)		
24	Mean sales	=AVERAGE(B3:B22)	=AVERAGE(C3:C22)		
25	Median sales	=MEDIAN(B3:B22)	=MEDIAN(C3:C22)		
26	Modal sales	=MODE(B3:B22)	=MODE(C3:C22)		
27	Standard deviation	=STDEV(B3:B22)	=STDEV(C3:C22)		
28	Coefficient of variation	=B27/B24	=C27/C24		
29	Lower quartile	=QUARTILE(B3:B22,1)	=QUARTILE(C3:C22,1)		
30	Upper quartile	=QUARTILE(B3:B22,3)	=QUARTILE(C3:C22,3)		
31	IQR	=B30-B29	=C30-C29		

Figure 5.12
The Excel worksheet with the formulae shown

Activity 5.26

What does the N/A mean for the mode in Activity 5.25?

The mode is the value that occurs most frequently. As all the values are different then the data does not have a mode. Excel will give N/A (not applicable) when this occurs.

Activity 5.27

What do the values of the mean and median tell you about the shape of the distribution of data?

If you look at the results you will see that the mean for both months is greater than the median. This means that the distribution is right skewed.

Activity 5.28

Which month has the greatest spread of data?

The standard deviation in September is greater than in August, but then so is the mean. If you look at the coefficient of variation you will see that this statistic is twice as large in September, so this is evidence that there is more variation in this month. The interquartile range is also nearly twice the value in September.

Using SPSS to calculate summary statistics

Summary statistics can be produced using the Analyze Descriptive Statistics/ Frequencies dialog box as for charts (see Chapter 4). Figure 5.13 shows the dialog boxes required to calculate the summary statistics for the data from Activity 5.25; the output can be seen in Figure 5.14.

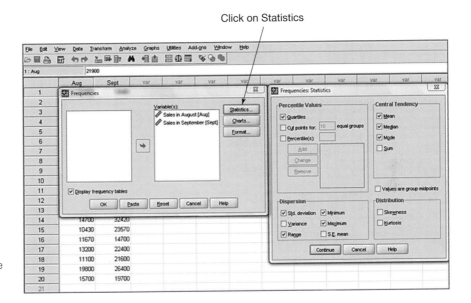

Figure 5.13
Dialog box to create summary statistics using SPSS

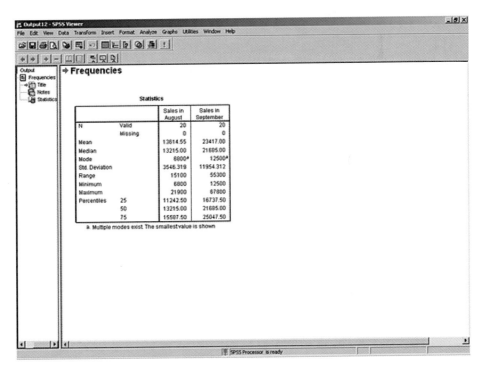

Figure 5.14
Summary statistics from SPSS

You can also use `Explore` under `Descriptive Statistics` in the `Analyze` menu (see Figure 5.15). This gives a wide range of statistics, most of which are not applicable to this chapter.

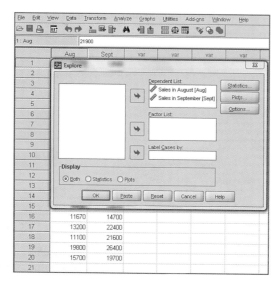

Figure 5.15
The `Explore` **menu**

SPSS will also produce boxplots for you, which Excel doesn't do. The simplest method is to use the `Explore` routine again (see Figure 5.16). Click `OK` and you will get the boxplots shown in Figure 5.17.

Click on Plots and then Dependents together

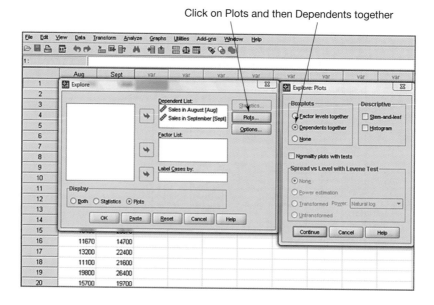

Figure 5.16
Creating a simple boxplot in SPSS

Activity 5.29

What can you conclude from the two boxplots about sales in August and September?

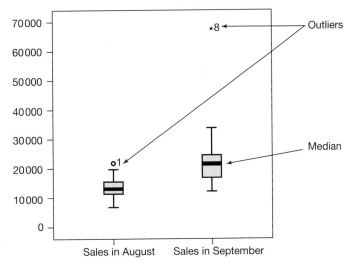

Figure 5.17
Boxplots for the sales data

Your answers here should be the same as your answers to Activity 5.27 and Activity 5.28. However, the boxplot compares the two sets of data quite nicely: you can clearly see that the sales are generally higher in September, and that the spread of sales in September is also higher. One extra feature that SPSS provides is the identification of outliers. As you can see in Figure 5.17, it has identified one value in August (£21 900) and one value in September (£67 800) as possible outliers. These are identified by case numbers (1 and 8).

Before we leave SPSS and boxplots, it is worth coming back to the way in which data is stored in SPSS. Remember that each row represents a case and each column a variable (see Chapter 4). In the data from Activity 5.25, each case represented a salesperson. However it could happen that the data is not matched in this way. If this is so, having two separate variables might not be the most appropriate way to represent the data. In such instances there could be a single variable (called 'Sales', say) and to differentiate between August and September a nominal variable (called 'Month', say) would be included. A code of 1 for August and 2 for September could be used and defined in the Values field. This procedure is shown in Figure 5.18.

	Name	Type	Width	Decimals	Label	Values	Missing	Columns	Align	Measure
1	Sales	Numeric	8	0		None	None	8	Right	Scale
2	Month	Numeric	8	0		[1, August]...	None	8	Right	Nominal
3										
4										
5										
6										
7										
8										
9										
10										
11										
12										
13										
14										
15										
16										
17										

Value Labels

Value Labels
Value: Spelling...
Label:

Add   1 = "August"
Change   2 = "September"
Remove

OK   Cancel   Help

Figure 5.18
Alternative data layout

Drag the simple boxplot into the chart preview area,
Sales into the Y-axis and Month into the X-axis

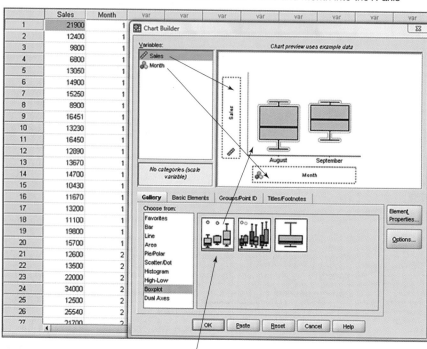

Figure 5.19
Using the chart
builder for boxplots

Simple boxplot

When data is in this form you use the `Chart Builder` option under `Graphs`. The
Y-axis is now 'Sales' and the `Category Axis` is 'Month', as you can see in Figure 5.19.
The boxplot you get is exactly the same as in the previous method. This method of
defining variables in SPSS will be used in subsequent chapters.

Reflection

We cannot escape averages! We hear the word on the radio and television, and see it in
newspapers. We hear about cricket averages, average alcohol consumption, average
wage, and average life expectancy. But do people really understand what the word
means? An understanding of the word 'average' is taken for granted; usually it refers to
the mean, even when the median would be more informative.

Even when the median is used, it is not always called an average. For example, in one
article the *Guardian* newspaper states, '50% of women have an independent income of
less than £100 per week' ('Has Labour Delivered?', *Guardian*, 31 January 2005). Of
course this means that 50% of women have an income greater than £100 per week, with
some women earning substantially more than this – that is, the distribution will be right-
skewed. The median is a very important measure of average, particularly when the data is
skewed. If you were told that that you had scored 56% in an assignment and that the
group mean was 60%, you might think that you had not done very well. However, if the
median was 55%, your score would be in the top half of the group.

Measures of spread are also conspicuous by their absence in newspapers and the media generally. Yet when comparing sets of data for which the averages are close, being given measures of spread does help to differentiate between the datasets. As we shall see in subsequent chapters, we need the variance when making inferences about one or more samples of data. We shall also discover that for distributions that are symmetrical, over 99% of the data is within plus and minus 3 standard deviations of the mean.

As well as calculating measures of average and spread, we must not forget the importance of charts in summarizing a set of data. A chart gives us a full picture of a set of data and should always be a first step, even when more complicated statistical techniques are used on the data. Charts can also provide information on measures of average and spread when these cannot easily be calculated from the data. For example, a cumulative ogive gives the median and interquartile range.

....

Key points

- The *mean*, *median* and *mode* are measures of average; they *locate* the data.
- In a *symmetrical distribution*, the mean, median and mode are equal. In a *right-skewed distribution* the mean and median are greater than the mode; and in a *left-skewed distribution* they are less than the mode.
- The median is the *50% quartile*, and can easily be found from a cumulative frequency ogive. The median exists even when not all values are available at either the lower or upper end of the distribution.
- To describe a set of data fully, a measure of *spread* is required. The *range* is the simplest measure, but a better measure is the *interquartile range* (*IQR*). The IQR uses the middle 50 per cent of the data and is therefore less influenced by extreme values.
- The best measure of spread is the *variance*. The square root of the variance is the *standard deviation*, which is in the same units as the data.
- When a constant figure is added to all the data items the standard deviation does not change, but it you multiply each data item by a constant figure the standard deviation will increase by the same proportion.
- When comparing the spread of two or more distributions, it is useful to compare the *coefficients of variation* for each as these take into account differences in the mean.
- A good visual summary of a frequency distribution is a *box and whisker plot*. This diagram can be used to compare several different distributions side by side.

Further reading

Most texts on quantitative methods and all elementary statistical texts will have a chapter on descriptive statistics. Straight Statistics and Sense about Science have produced a very useful free publication called *Making Sense of Statistics*. The pdf of this publication can be downloaded at www.straightstatistics.org/resources/making-sense-statistics. Another very interesting text and in the same vein is *The Tiger that Isn't: Seeing Through a World of Numbers* by Blastland and Dilnot (2007). Both these publications look at statistics from a commonsense perspective and show how statistics can often deceive unless we know what to look for.

Web links W

Answers to selected questions can be found in Appendix 2. Answers to the other questions can be found in the companion website for this book

Practice
questions

W 1 The weekly gross pay of 5 employees was as follows:

£160.24, £183.56, £155.00, £274.50, £174.34

(a) Calculate the mean and median of the data. Which average may be more appropriate, and why?
(b) Calculate the standard deviation of the data.
(c) Recalculate the mean and standard deviation if:
   (i) each value is increased by £20
   (ii) each value is increased by 5%

W 2 The temperature at a particular Mediterranean resort was taken the same day each month for a year. The temperature in C for each month was

16, 14, 19, 22, 25, 29, 33, 36, 30, 27, 24, 19.

(a) what is the mean, median and modal value of the temperature? From the point of view of a holiday maker are any of these averages any use?
(b) Calculate the standard deviation of the temperatures.
(c) It was later found that the temperature gauge used was under-reading by 2C. How would this affect the mean and standard deviation?
(d) Conversion of C to F is by the formula
$$°F = °C \times 9/5 + 32$$

Without converting each temperature find the mean and standard deviation of the temperature in F

W 3 Which average(s) is most appropriate in each case
(a) The test scores of a class of students
(b) The earnings of people in a particular industry
(c) The weights of pre-packed food
(d) Shoes stocked by a shoe shop
(e) Sizes of parts produced by a machine

W 4 Table 5.15 shows the number of rejects from a production process. Find the mean and standard deviation.

Table 5.15 Number of rejects from a production process

Number of rejects	Frequency
0	12
1	45
2	36
3	30
4	20
5	5
6	0

W 5 The following set of data refers to the daily Euro exchange rate to the British pound during the first 10 days of 2009

1.0471, 1.0473, 1.0457, 1.0458, 1.0573, 1.0886, 1.1104, 1.1092, 1.1168, 1.1260

(a) What is the mean and median of the exchange rate?
(b) What is the standard deviation of the exchange rate?
(c) Comment on the use of these statistics for this data

W 6 The histogram given in Figure 5.20 refers to the weekly hours worked of British people as taken from the 2001 national census.

(a) Estimate the mean, median and mode of hours worked

(b) Estimate the standard deviation of hours worked. What assumption are you making to arrive at your estimate?

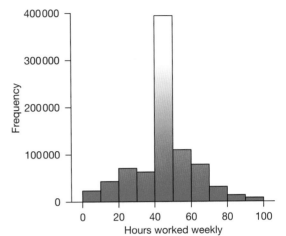

Figure 5.20
Histogram of hours worked from the 2001 census

W 7 The weighting given to coursework and exam for a quantitative methods course at a university is 40% coursework and 60% exam. If a student gets 74% for the coursework and 56% in the exam, what would be his or her average mark for the unit?

W 8 The average lifetime for 12 light bulbs is 180.6 hours. Another light bulb gave a lifetime of 200 hours. What would the mean lifetime be if this result was included?

9 The sickness records of a company have been examined and Table 5.16 shows the number of days taken off work through sickness during the past year.

Table 5.16 Data for Question 9

Days off work	Number of employees
Less than 2 days	45
2 to 5 days	89
6 to 9 days	40
10 to 13 days	25
14 to 21 days	5
22 to 29 days	2

(a) What is the mean number of days off work?
(b) What is the median number of days off work?
(c) What is the modal number of days off work?
(d) What is the interquartile range?

(e) What is the standard deviation?

(f) What is the coefficient of variation?

(g) Draw a box and whisker plot and comment on the shape of the distribution.

10　Items are manufactured to the same nominal length on two different machines, A and B. A number of items from each machine are measured and the results are shown in Table 5.17.

Table 5.17 Data for Question 10

Class interval (mm)	Frequency	
	Machine A	Machine B
20 to under 22	5	2
22 to under 24	12	5
24 to under 26	26	20
26 to under 28	11	25
28 to under 30	3	8
30 to under 32	0	2

(a) Find the mean, median and modal values for the two machines.

(b) Find the interquartile range and standard deviation for both machines.

(c) Calculate the coefficient of variation for both machines.

(d) Draw a box and whisker plot for both machines.

(e) Use your results from (a) to (d) to comment on the lengths of items produced by both machines.

11　Table 5.18 shows the wages paid last week to 45 part-time employees of a supermarket chain. Find the mean and the median wage.

Table 5.18 Data for Question 11

Wages (£s)	No. of employees
20 to under 30	2
30 to under 40	4
40 to under 50	6
50 to under 60	12
60 to under 70	11
70 to under 80	9
80 to under 90	1
	45

12　A company is involved in wage negotiations with the trade unions. The current gross weekly wages of the company's employees are summarized in the frequency table in Table 5.19. Two proposals are on offer:

Proposal 1: Give the employees an increase in pay equivalent to 10% of the current mean weekly wage.

Proposal 2: Give the employees an increase in pay equivalent to 12.5% of the current median weekly wage.

Compare the costs of the two proposals.

Table 5.19 Data for Question 12

Gross weekly wages (£s)	No. of employees
90 to under 110	14
110 to under 140	54
140 to under 160	16
160 to under 200	12
200 to under 240	2
	98

13 A firm purchases four main raw materials. Recently, the prices of these raw materials have increased by the percentages indicated in Table 5.20. This table also shows the estimated amount the company will spend per month on each raw material. The purchasing manager of the company has calculated that the average increase in raw material prices is 15%. Can you find an average that reflects more accurately the increase in costs that the company is likely to incur?

Table 5.20 Data for Question 13

Raw material	% increase in price	Mean expenditure per month (£)
Lead	10	3000
Copper	4	1000
Zinc	0	650
Adhesives	46	350

14 The production target of a manufacturer is 300 widgets per week. In the first ten weeks production has averaged 284.7 per week. What average must be reached in the final three weeks of the quarter for the original target to be achieved?

15 A salesperson travels 100 miles to Exeter at an average speed of 60 mph. She then returns home at a more leisurely 50 mph. What was the average speed over the 200 miles covered? (No, it's not 55 mph!)

16 Miracle Fashions has recorded the sales made during a particular day and these are shown in Table 5.21.

Table 5.21 Data for Question 16

Value of sales (£)	Number of sales in this range
5 to less than 10	50
10 to less than 20	75
20 to less than 30	45
30 to less than 40	38
40 to less than 60	27
60 to less than 100	18

(a) Using your calculator's statistical mode or a spreadsheet, estimate:
   (i)   the total sales (in £) during this day
   (ii) the mean value of sales
   (iii) the standard deviation of the value of sales
   (iv) the coefficient of variation of the value of sales

(b) Why are your answers in part (a) only estimates?

(c) A fashion shop across the road has also carried out similar calculations and its coefficient of variation of the value of sales is 40%.

(i) What can you deduce about the distribution of the value of sales between the two shops?

(ii) Is this other shop likely to be more or less expensive than Miracle Fashions?

(d) Using the data in the table, draw a percentage cumulative frequency ogive, and from your ogive deduce:

(i) the median value of sales

(ii) the interquartile range of the value of sales

(iii) the percentage of sales that were over £50

Assignment

A large bakery regularly takes samples of bread in order to ensure that its product meets quality specifications. Each loaf that is sampled is first weighed, and weight records of 765 'standard' sliced loaves have accumulated over the last few months. The Quality Control Manager would like these records analyzed and has aggregated the data into the frequency table in Table 5.22.

Table 5.22 Data for the assignment

Weight range	Number of loaves in this range
780 g to below 790 g	34
790 g to below 795 g	80
795 g to below 800 g	111
800 g to below 805 g	162
805 g to below 810 g	161
810 g to below 815 g	120
815 g to below 820 g	70
820 g to below 830 g	27

Analyze these figures and write a report to the Quality Control Manager. Your analysis should include graphs, diagrams and measures of location and spread of the data.

III

PROBABILITY AND STATISTICS

Taking a chance: probability

Objectives	
	○ To be able to calculate simple probabilities
	○ To be able to calculate probabilities of compound events using the rules of addition and multiplication
	○ To know how to use probability trees to solve problems
	○ To understand how to apply Bayes' theorem to modify probabilities when new information is received

Introduction	
	It is difficult to go very far in solving business problems without a basic understanding of probability. The 'laws of chance' underpin many decisions that are made in real life. For example, when we carry out a survey we need to know how the sample data relate to the target population. Our insurance premiums are determined by the chance of some mishap occurring, and quality control systems are built around probability laws. There are also many games of chance including card and dice games, horse racing and the National Lottery. This chapter contains all the basic rules and methods of probability that will be required in subsequent chapters.

Quantitative methods in action: POP design for a new drug candidate

Once a drug has passed human safety trials it still cannot be marketed until it has been shown to be effective. To do this a drug company will usually put a drug through a rigorous clinical testing programme called *proof of principle* (POP) clinical trials. Johnson & Johnson wanted to know whether they should put a new drug into their full development programme, which would cost around $200m over 5 years. A POP clinical trial for this particular drug would cost around $10m to $20m so, although an order of magnitude less than the full development programme, it is still a significant amount of money. There are a number of ways that such a trial could be conducted and not all methods will be cost effective. In this case the two main decisions were:

1 Whether or not to conduct a POP trial.
2 If a POP trial is to be conducted, what type and whether to include an '*active comparator arm*' in the trial. (A comparator is an existing drug that is known to be effective. An 'arm' is a group of patients.)

If the answer to the first decision is 'yes' then the researchers need to consider the type of clinical trial to use. In this particular case there were four alternatives. The first alternative (Design A) involved a placebo arm (a placebo is an inactive substance given to a control group), two trial arms with different dosing levels and an active comparator arm. The other three designs were variants on design A with different numbers of trial arms and different sample sizes. Figure 6.1 is an *influence* diagram showing the five random variables and their relationship with each other.

In this diagram the nodes represent uncertainties and an arrow between two nodes represents probabilistic dependencies between them. (Influence diagrams are discussed in Chapter 11.) Notice that

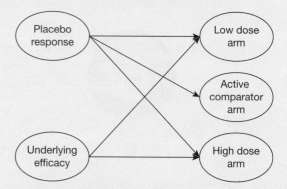

Figure 6.1 An influence diagram
Source: Donald L. Keefer, *Interfaces*, 2004.

outcomes of the two trial arms using the new drug are affected by the actual effectiveness of the drug and the placebo response. The comparator arm outcome is only affected by the placebo response. The advantage of using a comparator arm is that if this fails along with the test drug then the posterior probability of a false negative increases. (We will discuss this idea in this chapter.)

The probabilities for the various outcomes were found from a combination of expert judgements and *Bayesian* analysis. The research team used *decision trees* and *NPV* (net present value) to decide on the best course of action. (Decision trees are discussed in Chapter 11 and NPV in Chapter 12.) The NPV in this case was the difference between the mean commercial value and the development costs.

The analysis showed that a POP trial was beneficial and that design A was preferred as it gave a NPV of $9m more than the next best design.

Source: Interfaces, Vol. 34, No. 3, May–June 2004, pp. 206–7.

Basic ideas

The value of a probability can be given either as a fraction, as a decimal or as a percentage. An event with a probability of zero is termed impossible, while an event with a probability of 1 or 100% is termed certain. Figure 6.2 may help you to picture the idea of the probability measure.

Probability scale

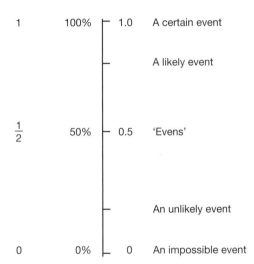

1	100%	1.0	A certain event
			A likely event
$\frac{1}{2}$	50%	0.5	'Evens'
			An unlikely event
0	0%	0	An impossible event

Figure 6.2
Probability scale

Probabilities can be obtained in a number of ways. The simplest is the *subjective* method where you estimate what you think the probability of a particular event will be. For example, a sales manager may estimate that the probability of high sales for a particular product is 60%. This figure may be based on market research or experience of a similar product, but it is unlikely to involve any calculations.

Another method is the *empirical* approach. This method uses measurement to estimate probabilities. For example, you may wish to determine the probability of a defective electrical component being produced by a particular process. If you test 100 components and find 5 defective, then you would say that the probability of a defective component being produced is $\frac{5}{100}$ or 0.05. That is,

$$\text{probability} = \frac{\text{number of times a particular event occurred}}{\text{total number of trials or 'experiments'}}$$

The particular event here is finding a defective component and the 'experiment' is picking, testing and classifying a component as either good or defective.

Activity 6.1

Toss a coin 10 times and use the above formula to calculate the probability of a head.

Did you get a probability of 0.5? This, as you will see shortly, is the 'correct' answer, but 10 tosses is a very small number of experiments. If you tossed the coin a further 10 times you would quite likely get a different answer. This is the basis of *sampling error*, which we shall come back to in Chapter 10. You will also see that the sampling error in this case could be reduced by tossing the coin a larger number of times; that is, the larger the number of tosses, the nearer you will get to a probability of 0.5.

However, to obtain the theoretical probability of a head you would use a different method, called the *a priori* approach. This is similar to the empirical approach, except that you can work out *in advance* how many times a particular event should occur. In the coin tossing activity you know that there is only one head, so that the probability of a head is $\frac{1}{2}$ or 0.5. If you picked a card from a pack, the probability of an Ace is $\frac{4}{52}$ or 0.0769, since there are 4 Aces in a pack. The definition can be written as:

$$\frac{\text{number of ways in which a particular event can occur}}{\text{total number of outcomes}}$$

This definition assumes that all outcomes are equally likely; that is, there is no bias associated with a particular outcome. This definition would not apply to, say, a race involving 10 horses, since the probability that any horse will win is unlikely to be 0.1. The *odds* would reflect such factors as form, jockey, trainer, etc.

Activity 6.2

You pick a card from a pack. What is the probability that it is a picture card?

To answer this question you would have listed the picture cards in a suit. These are Jack, Queen and King. Since there are 4 suits you should have decided that there will be $4 \times 3 = 12$ ways in which a particular outcome can occur. The probability of a picture card is therefore $\frac{12}{52} = 0.2308$.

The probability of compound events

It is frequently required to find the probability of two or more events happening at the same time. For example, an aircraft has many of its controls duplicated so that if one fails the other would still function. But what is the probability that both systems will fail? The way that probabilities are combined depends on whether the events are *independent* or whether they are *mutually exclusive*. Two (or more) events are said to be independent if the occurrence of one does not affect the occurrence of the other. The two aircraft systems will be independent if the failure of one system does not change the probability of failure of the other system. Two (or more) events are mutually exclusive if either event can occur, but not both. One card drawn from a pack cannot be a Jack and an Ace. However, a Jack and a Diamond are not mutually exclusive since the selected card could be both. When the set of all possible outcomes are known, they are said to be *mutually exhaustive*, and the sum of the probabilities of a set of outcomes that are mutually exclusive *and* mutually exhaustive must equal 1. For example, there are four suits in a pack of cards and the probability of selecting a card from a given suit is $\frac{13}{52}$ or 0.25. The sum of these probabilities is 1, since a card must come from one (and only one) of the suits. This idea will allow you to calculate a probability if the other or others are known. If, say, the probability of a defective component is 5%, then the probability that it is not defective is 95%.

Compound events can be more easily solved if a diagram is drawn. One useful diagram is the *Venn* diagram. A Venn diagram is made up of a square, the inside of which encloses all possible outcomes. The events of interest are represented by circles. The Venn diagram in Figure 6.3 represents two events, A and B. Event A is being dealt a Jack, which has a probability of $\frac{4}{52}$ or 0.0769, and Event B is being dealt an Ace, which also has a probability of $\frac{4}{52}$. The probability of being dealt either a Jack *or* an Ace is:

$$P(\text{Jack or Ace}) = P(\text{Jack}) + P(\text{Ace})$$
$$= 0.0769 + 0.0769$$
$$= 0.1538$$

However, if Event B is being dealt a Diamond then the two events overlap, as shown in Figure 6.4. If the two probabilities are now added, the intersection of the two events (shown shaded) will have been added twice. This intersection, which represents the case of being dealt a Jack of Diamonds (with a probability of $\frac{1}{52}$ or 0.0192), must be

A – a Jack   B – an Ace

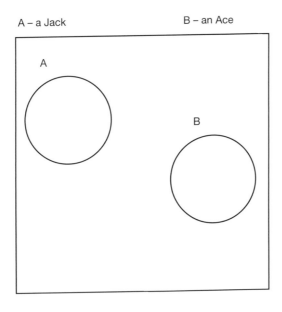

Figure 6.3
Venn diagram for mutually exclusive events

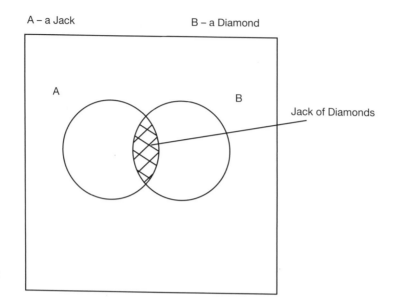

A – a Jack

B – a Diamond

A

B

Jack of Diamonds

Figure 6.4
Venn diagram for events that are not mutually exclusive

subtracted from the sum of the two probabilities. That is:

$$P(\text{Jack or Diamond}) = P(\text{Jack}) + P(\text{Diamond}) - P(\text{Jack of Diamonds})$$
$$= 0.0769 + 0.25 - 0.0192$$
$$= 0.3077$$

In general if $P(A)$ means the probability of Event A and $P(B)$ the probability of Event B then:

$$P(A \text{ or } B) = P(A) + P(B) - P(A \text{ and } B)$$

This is known as the *addition rule*.

NOTE: If the two events are mutually exclusive, as in the first example, then there is no intersection and $P(A \text{ and } B)$ is zero.

Activity 6.3

The police regularly carry out spot checks on heavy goods vehicles. During one particular month the results are as shown in Table 6.1.

Assuming that these results are typical of all heavy goods vehicles on the road, what is the probability that if a vehicle was stopped at random it would either be overweight or the driver would have exceeded the allowed driving time?

Table 6.1 Results from checks on heavy goods vehicles

	Overweight	Not overweight	Total
Driving time exceeded	15	25	40
Driving time not exceeded	20	40	60
Total	35	65	100

The key to this question is the word *or*. And since it is possible both for the vehicle to be overweight and for the driver to have exceeded the permitted driving time, the events are not mutually exclusive. Using the addition law you should have obtained the following result:

$$P(\text{time exceeded}) = \frac{40}{100} \quad \text{or} \quad 0.4$$

$$P(\text{overweight}) = \frac{35}{100} \quad \text{or} \quad 0.35$$

$$P(\text{time exceeded and overweight}) = \frac{15}{100} \quad \text{or} \quad 0.15$$

So the P(time exceeded or overweight) $= 0.4 + 0.35 - 0.15$

$$= 0.6$$

That is, there is a 60% chance that either the lorry would be overweight or the driver would have exceeded the driving time.

Conditional probability

If the probability of Event B occurring is dependent on whether Event A has occurred, you would say that Event B is conditional on Event A. This is written $P(B|A)$, which means the probability of B given that A has occurred.

When Event A and Event B are independent, $P(B|A) = P(B)$. Sampling without replacement is a good example of conditional probability. If two students are to be chosen randomly from a group of 5 girls and 4 boys, then the probability that the first person chosen is a girl is $\frac{5}{9}$ or 0.5556, and the probability that it is a boy is $1 - 0.556 = 0.4444$. The probability that the second person is a girl depends on the outcome of the first choice.

First choice	Probability of second choice being a girl
boy	$\frac{5}{8}$ or 0.625
girl	$\frac{4}{8}$ or 0.5

In the first case the number of girls remains at 5, but in the second case there are only 4 girls to choose from. Note that in both cases the total number of students left is 8, since one has already been chosen.

If you want to know the probability of the first student being a girl *and* the second student being a girl, you will need to use the *multiplication rule*. If the events are dependent, as in this example, the rule is:

$$P(A \text{ and } B) = P(A) \times P(B|A)$$

So P(girl and a girl) $= 0.5556 \times 0.5 = 0.2778$.

If two (or more) events are independent the rule simplifies to:

$$P(A \text{ and } B) = P(A) \times P(B)$$

For example, if an aircraft has a main and a back-up computer and the probability of failure of either computer is 1%, then the probability of both failing is $0.01 \times 0.01 = 0.0001$ or 0.01%.

Activity 6.4

A light bulb manufacturer produces bulbs in batches of 50, and it is known from past experience that 5 of each batch will be defective. If two bulbs are selected without replacement from a batch, what is the probability that both will be defective?

The probability that the first bulb is defective is $\dfrac{5}{50} = 0.1$, but the probability that the second is defective is $\dfrac{4}{49} = 0.0816$, since the total number of bulbs has been reduced by one and there must be one less defective bulb. The probability that both bulbs are defective is therefore:

$$0.1 \times 0.0816 = 0.00816$$

This probability is very small, so if you did in fact get two defective bulbs you should be suspicious concerning the claimed defective rate. (This idea forms the basis of some quality control schemes.)

Did you know

In 2003 Lucia de Berk, a children's nurse, was convicted of the murder of 4 patients and the attempted murder of 3 others. The only evidence was that she was on duty during the times these children died. A psychologist (Professor Henk Elffers) calculated that this number of deaths could only occur by chance 1 in 342 million times. This conviction was upheld in an appeal in 2004. However in April 2010 the conviction was squashed after a long campaign by Richard Gill (see www.math.leidenuniv.nl/~gill/lucia.html) and other leading statisticians who had shown that the statistical evidence was incorrect.

See also the case of Sally Clark discussed in the *Reflection* section.

Tree diagrams

A very useful diagram to use when solving compound events, particularly when conditional probability is involved, is the tree diagram. This diagram represents different outcomes of an experiment by means of branches. For example, in the student example the two 'experiments' of choosing an individual can be represented by the tree diagram in Figure 6.5. The first experiment is represented by a small circle or node, and the two possible outcomes are represented by branches radiating out from the node. The event and probability are written alongside the branch. The

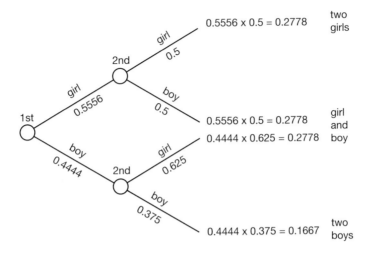

0.5556 x 0.5 = 0.2778   two girls

0.5556 x 0.5 = 0.2778   girl and boy

0.4444 x 0.625 = 0.2778

0.4444 x 0.375 = 0.1667   two boys

Figure 6.5
A tree diagram

second experiment is again represented by a node and you will notice that this node appears twice, once for each outcome of the first experiment. Branches again radiate out from each node, but notice that the probability is different depending on what happened in the first experiment.

You will see that the compound events have been written at the end of each route in Figure 6.5. If you add up these probabilities you will see that they sum to 1 (to 3 decimal places). This is because the routes are mutually exclusive and *mutually exhaustive*. They are mutually exclusive because one and only one of the routes can be followed, and they are mutually exhaustive because all possible routes have been shown. From this diagram various probabilities could be evaluated using the law of addition. For example, the probability of getting two students of the same sex is $0.2778 + 0.1667 = 0.4445$.

It is unlikely that you would use a tree diagram to solve a simple problem like this, but consider the problem in Example 6.1.

Example 6.1

The demand for gas is dependent on the weather and much research has been undertaken to forecast the demand accurately. This is important since it is quite difficult (and expensive) to increase the supply at short notice. If, on any particular day, the air temperature is below normal, the probability that the demand will be high is 0.6. However, at normal temperatures the probability of a high demand occurring is only 0.2, and if the temperature is above normal the probability of a high demand drops to 0.05. What is the probability of a high demand occurring if, over a period of time, the temperature is below normal on 20% of occasions and above normal on 30% of occasions?

The tree diagram is shown in Figure 6.6. Since the demand *depends* on temperature, the first node refers to temperature and there are three branches: below normal, normal and above normal. The probability of the temperature being normal is $1 - (0.2 + 0.3) = 0.5$. The compound probability for each route has been written

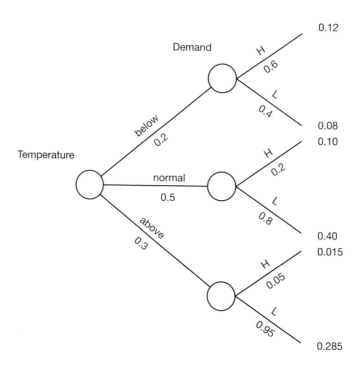

Figure 6.6
Tree diagram for
Example 6.1

at the end of the route, so that the probability of there being a high demand given that the temperature is below normal is $0.2 \times 0.6 = 0.12$. Since there are three routes where the demand could be high, the law of addition is used and the probability is:

$$0.12 + 0.10 + 0.015 = 0.235$$

Activity 6.5

A company purchases electronic components in batches of 100 and the supplier guarantees that there will be no more than 5 defective components in each batch. Before acceptance of a particular batch the company has a policy of selecting without replacement two components for testing. If both components are satisfactory the batch is accepted and if both are defective the batch is rejected. However, if only one is defective another component is selected and if this is satisfactory the batch is accepted, while if it is defective, the batch is rejected. If the probability that a component is defective is 5%, what is the probability that the batch will be accepted?

You could answer this question without a tree diagram, but it is strongly recommended that diagrams are used whenever possible. The diagram is shown in Figure 6.7 where it will be seen that each node has two outcomes: either OK or defective. At the start of the process the probability that the first selection will give a defective component is $\dfrac{5}{100}$ or 0.05, and the probability that it will be OK is 0.95. If the first component was defective, then the probability that the second is also defective is reduced to $\dfrac{4}{99}$ or 0.04040, since there is one less defective component *and*

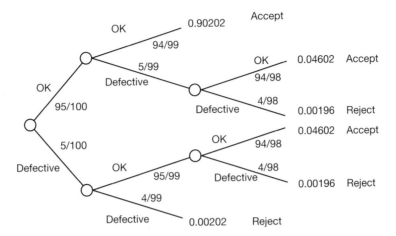

Figure 6.7
Tree diagram for
Activity 6.5

one less component in total. The remaining probabilities have been found using a similar reasoning.

The compound probabilities have been written at the end of each route together with the decision; that is, accept or reject. There are three routes where the decision is to accept, and the addition law can be used to give the probability that the batch will be accepted. That is:

$$0.90202 + 0.04602 + 0.04602 = 0.99406$$

The probability that the batch will be rejected is $1 - 0.99406 = 0.00594$. This can be confirmed by adding the probabilities separately.

As in Activity 6.4, it is unlikely that a batch would be rejected. However, if it was, you would have grounds to question the supplier about the true number of defective items in a batch. This type of problem comes under the category of quality control.

Bayes' theorem

This theorem is based on the idea that in many situations we begin an analysis with some *prior* or initial probability estimate for the event we are interested in. This probability can come from historical data, previous experience, a pilot survey, and so on.

Then, we receive additional information from a survey, test, report, and so on, so that we are able to update our prior probability and calculate, using Bayes' theorem, what is known as our *posterior probability*. Consider Example 6.2.

Did you know

Probability theory was developed in the early 18th century to answer questions on gambling and insurance issues. One of the statisticians' problems was how to calculate the probability of one person dying at a certain age given that, say, 5 people out of a sample had died. The Reverend Thomas Bayes came up with the solution and Bayes' theorem is named after him.

Example 6.2

You are a manager of a company that manufactures 'set top' boxes for digital TV. There is a large demand for these boxes and retailers are urgently asking for delivery. To speed up delivery you could cut out the time-consuming testing of each box, but you are worried that defective boxes would then be returned, which would tarnish the company's reputation. From past experience you know that about 5% of boxes would be expected to be faulty.

As the manager, you select a box. What is the chance that it is faulty? Clearly it is 5% or 0.05. This is our *prior* probability. Perhaps it is possible to do a 'quick and dirty' test on the box, but you know that this test is not very reliable. It is believed that the test will indicate that the box is defective 20% of the time when it is in fact perfectly OK. If the box is defective the test should get it right 90% of the time; that is, the test is better at getting it right when the box is defective. This means that the test is *biased*.

If you do this quick test on a box and it fails, how do you revise your prior probability in the light of this result?

Activity 6.6

Draw a probability tree showing the different outcomes when the test is applied to both a good and a defective box.

For each branch of the tree there are two outcomes of the test; either pass or fail. The probability tree with the probabilities added is shown in Figure 6.8.

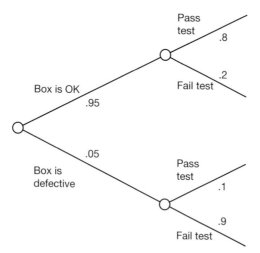

Figure 6.8
Probability tree diagram for Example 6.2

Activity 6.7

Imagine that you have 1000 boxes to test. How many boxes would you have along the different branches?

As there are 1000 boxes, then 950 of these will be good boxes and 50 will be defective. Of the 950 good ones, there will $950 \times 0.8 = 760$ that pass the test while the

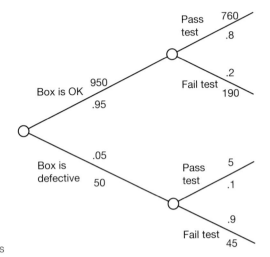

Figure 6.9
The tree with 1000 boxes split between the different branches

remaining 190 will fail. Of the 50 that are defective, there will be $50 \times 0.1 = 5$ that pass the test while the remaining 45 will correctly fail it. This information has been added to the probability tree and you can see this in Figure 6.9.

Activity 6.8

What is the probability that if you picked one of the 1000 boxes at random it would fail the test?

190 good boxes failed the test and 45 defective boxes failed the test. The total number that failed is therefore $190 + 45 = 235$, and the probability that a box would fail the test is

$$\frac{235}{1000} = 0.235$$

Activity 6.9

What is the probability that a box is defective given that it failed the test?

Out of the 235 boxes that failed the test, 45 came from boxes that were defective, so the probability that the chosen box is defective is $\dfrac{45}{235} = 0.1915$. So this new information has allowed us to revise our probability of a defective box from 5% to 19%.

Activity 6.10

Repeat the last three activities using 100 boxes.

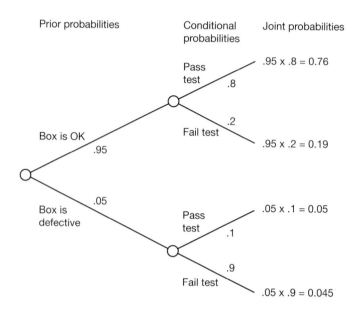

Figure 6.10
Calculation of joint probabilities

You should have found that you still get the same probabilities even though you are dealing with fractions of a box when the boxes are defective. In fact it is not necessary to even consider the number of boxes at all as all you are really doing is multiplying probabilities together. Figure 6.10 is the formal probability tree diagram for the problem using Bayes' theorem. The probability of the test being correct or not is the *conditional* probability as it is conditional on the first branch of the tree. The probabilities at the end of the tree are the *joint* probabilities as they are obtained by multiplying the prior and conditional probabilities together. The probability that a box would fail the test is the sum of the relevant joint probabilities; that is, $0.19 + 0.045 = 0.235$, and this is the same value as we obtained before. The probability that the a box is defective given that it failed the test is called the *posterior* probability, and for our problem it is

$$\frac{0.045}{0.235} = 0.1915$$

To summarize this procedure:

- Construct a tree with branches representing all the prior probabilities.
- Extend the tree adding the new information obtained. Write the conditional probabilities on these branches.
- Calculate the joint probabilities.
- To obtain the posterior probabilities, divide the appropriate joint probability by the sum of the corresponding joint probabilities.

As a formula this is:

$$P(B|A) = \frac{P(B \text{ and } A)}{P(A)}$$

where B is the event 'box is defective' and A is the event 'it failed the test'.

Bayes' theorem is a very powerful technique in solving probability problems and we will come back to an important application of this theorem when we look at decision trees in Chapter 11.

Permutations and combinations

Problems frequently exist where selections are made from groups of items. In these cases it is useful to be able to calculate the number of selections that are possible. The method used depends on whether the order of the selection is important or not. If it is, you should use *permutations*. The number of permutations, where r items are to be selected from a group of size n, is given by the formula:

$$^{n}P_r = \frac{n!}{(n-r)!}$$

where $n!$ is read as *factorial n* and means $(n-1) \times (n-2) \times (n-3) \times \ldots$ For example, $5! = 5 \times 4 \times 3 \times 2 \times 1 = 120$. (Note: $1! = 1$ and by definition $0! = 1$.) If you have a scientific calculator you should find that it has a $^{n}P_r$ button, which is much easier than using the formula.

Activity 6.11

Bank cheque cards usually have a 4-digit 'pin' number so that they can be used in a cash dispenser. What is the probability that a thief, finding your card, could hit on the correct combination at the first attempt?

The order is important here because, for example, 1234 is a different number from 4321. There are 10 possible digits (0 to 9) so the number of ways of selecting 4 from 10 is:

$$^{n}P_r = {}^{10}P_4$$
$$= \frac{10!}{(10-4)!} = \frac{10!}{6!}$$
$$= \frac{10 \times 9 \times 8 \times 7 \times 6 \times 5 \times 4 \times 3 \times 2 \times 1}{6 \times 5 \times 4 \times 3 \times 2 \times 1}$$
$$= 5040$$

So there is only a 1 in 5040 chance of the thief finding the correct permutation. As a probability this is:

$$\frac{1}{5040} = 0.000198$$

Where the order is *not* important, you would use *combinations*. The formula for this is as follows:

$$^{n}C_r = \frac{n!}{r!(n-r)!}$$

Again, most scientific calculators should contain this function.

Activity 6.12

What is the probability of winning the National Lottery (Lotto) jackpot?

To win the jackpot you must correctly guess the 6 numbers drawn from the numbers 1 to 49. These numbers can occur in any order, so you would use the combination formula for this calculation. In this case $n = 49$ and $r = 6$, so:

$$^nC_r = {}^{49}C_6$$

$$= \frac{49!}{6! \times (49 - 6)!}$$

$$= \frac{49 \times 48 \times 47 \times 46 \times 44 \times 43!}{6! \times 43!}$$

$$= 13\,983\,816$$

This is nearly 14 million to 1!

Expected value

If you toss a coin 100 times, you would *expect* 50 heads and 50 tails. That is, the expected number of heads is $0.5 \times 100 = 50$. In general it is a long-run average, which means it is the value you would get if you repeated the experiment long enough. It is calculated by multiplying a value of a particular variable by the probability of its occurrence and repeating this for all possible values. In symbols this can be represented as:

Expected value $= \sum px$

where $\sum$ means the 'sum of'.

Activity 6.13

Over a long period of time a salesperson recorded the number of sales she achieved per day. From an analysis of her records it was found that she made no sales 20% of the time, one sale 50% of the time and 2 sales 30% of the time. What is her expected number of sales?

The x in this case takes on values of 0, 1, and 2 and

expected value is $= 0.2 \times 0 + 0.5 \times 1 + 0.3 \times 2$

$= 0 + 0.5 + 0.6$

$= 1.1$ sales

This is just like working out the mean value of a group of numbers, where the probabilities are the frequencies or 'weights'. And, just like the mean, the expected value will not necessarily be a whole number.

Expected values are frequently used to calculate expected monetary values, or EMV. This is illustrated in the next activity.

Activity 6.14

An investor buys £1000 of shares with the object of making a capital gain after 1 year. She believes that there is a 5% chance that the shares will double in value, a 25% chance that they will be worth £1500, a 30% chance that they will only be worth £500 and a 40% chance that they will not change in value. What is the expected monetary value of this investment, ignoring dealing costs?

The EMV is found in a similar manner to the expected number of sales in Activity 6.1, that is:

$$0.05 \times 2000 + 0.25 \times 1500 + 0.3 \times 500 + 0.40 \times 1000$$
$$= 100 + 375 + 150 + 400$$
$$= £1025$$

So the EMV is £1025, an expected profit of £25.

Reflection

Probability affects all our lives. Most of us have bought a lottery ticket from time to time and know that the chance of winning the jackpot is very small. However, very few people know that the odds for the UK National Lottery are about 14 million to 1 against, and even fewer people would know how to calculate this figure. Even well-educated people find probability a difficult concept.

This is particularly so in court cases. An example in England from 1999 is the case of Sally Clark, who was convicted of killing two of her babies. The argument made by the paediatrician Sir Roy Meadow was that the chance of a baby from an affluent family dying from cot death was 1 in 8500, and that the chance of *two* babies in the same family dying from cot death is found by squaring this figure. This gives a probability of 1 in 73 million (or 0.000 000 013 7). The implication of this analysis is that two cot deaths in the same family should happen less than once a century in England – yet in fact double cot deaths occur almost every year. The problem with the initial analysis is its assumption that cot deaths in the same family are *independent*. Ray Hill, a Professor in the Mathematics Department at Salford University, has shown that such deaths are *not* independent, and has estimated that the chance is between 10 and 22 times greater that siblings of children who die of cot death will also die in the same way, as compared with children in the population as a whole ('Beyond reasonable doubt' by Helen Joyce: www.plus.maths.org/issue21/features/clark/). When his figure is taken into account, the probability of two children dying of cot deaths in the same family is around 1 in 130,000. As about 650,000 children are born every year in England and Wales, we would then expect around 5 double cot deaths a year.

In convicting Sally Clark, the jury committed what is known as the 'Prosecutor's Fallacy'. This fallacy invites people to believe that the chance of a rare event happening is the same as the chance that the defendant is innocent. In actual fact it is simply the chance that a family chosen at random will experience a double cot death. With such a large population, the expected number of double cot deaths will be finite, even if the probability of this event happening is infinitesimally small.

Of course, as the two events are *not* independent we should be using ideas based on conditional probability. This means that we should be using Bayes' theorem. And using Bayes' theorem it can be shown that the probability that Sally Clark's two babies died of natural causes was greater than 0.67 (see www.plus.maths.org/issue21/features/clark/). Unfortunately judges will not allow the use of Bayes' theorem to be used in evidence, as it is felt to be too difficult to understand!

On 29 January 2003, Sally Clark's conviction was quashed by the Court of Appeal.

Key points

- *Probability* is measured on a scale of 0 to 1.
- When two or more events can happen at the same time, the *addition rule* can be used to calculate the probability of either of the events occurring.
- When events occur in sequence, the *multiplication rule* is used.
- Conditional probability is when the probability of an event occurring is dependent on whether another event has occurred.
- Tree diagrams should be used for problems involving conditional probability.
- When we want to update some prior probability with new information, *Bayes' theorem* is used.
- Bayes' theorem allows the posterior probabilities to be calculated.
- In many probability problems it is necessary to calculate the number of ways an event can occur. In these cases the formulae for *permutations* and *combinations* can be used.
- Expected value is a long-run average; that is it is the average value you would get if you could repeat an experiment a large number of times.

Further reading

Probability is a wide subject and can be treated in many different ways. Students taking a maths or statistics degree would probably want a more mathematical text such as Swift and Piff (2010). A classic text is the one by Sheldon (2010). However this is only for students with a good background in mathematics. For those of you interested in sport and gambling there are a number of texts that show how probability can help improve your understanding of the issues involved. Examples are Haigh (2000) and Barboianu (2006). Haigh is a particularly easy to read text. There are also many resources that can help in your understanding of probability. The Plus magazine (http://plus.maths.org/content) is aimed at schools but will be of interest to university undergraduates too.

Web links W

Answers to selected questions can be found in Appendix 2. Answers to the other questions can be found on the companion website for this book

Practice
questions

1   What is the probability that if you toss 2 fair coins you get 2 tails?

2   What is the probability that if you toss 3 fair coins you get 3 tails?

3   What is the probability of 2 sixes when you throw 2 dice?

4   What is the probability of a score of 8 from throwing two dice?

5   Three cards are taken from a pack of cards (and not replaced). What is the probability that you get 3 aces?

W 6   Three cards are taken from a pack of cards (and not replaced). What is the probability that they are all red cards?

W 7   A bag contains 5 red discs, 3 yellow discs, and 2 green discs.
   (a) A disc is picked from the bag. What is the probability that the disc will be:
       (i)   red?
       (ii) yellow?
       (iii) not yellow?
   (b) Two discs are picked from the bag *with* replacement. What is the probability that the discs will be:
       (i)   both red?
       (ii) 1 red and 1 yellow?
   (c) Repeat part (b) if the discs are picked *without* replacement.

W 8   What is the probability that if you pick a card from a pack it will be:
   (a) an Ace?
   (b) a red card?
   (c) an Ace or a red card?

W 9   A box contains 50 light bulbs, of which 4 are defective. You purchase two bulbs from this box. What is the probability that both will be defective?

W 10 The probability that a double glazing salesperson will make a sale on a particular day is 0.05. What is the probability that over a three-day period the salesperson will make:
   (a) 3 sales?
   (b) exactly 1 sale?
   (c) at least 1 sale?

W 11 A mail order firm knows that it will receive a 20% response rate to any literature it circulates. In a new geographic location 8 circulars are mailed as a market test. Assuming that the response rate is still applicable to this new location, calculate the probability of the following events:
   (a) All 8 people respond
   (b) No one responds
   (c) Exactly 2 people respond

W 12 How might you try to assess the following probabilities?
   (a) the probability that the FT index will rise in value tomorrow
   (b) the probability that a jar of coffee, filled by an automatic process, will weigh less than the stated weight
   (c) the probability that you might win the top prize in the National Lottery
   (d) the probability that the ageing process will eventually be reversed

13 Three machines – A, B and C – operate independently in a factory. Machine A is out of action for 10% of the time, while B is out of action 5% of the time and C is out of action for 20% of the time. A rush order has to be commenced at midday tomorrow. What is the probability that at this time:

(a) All three of the machines will be out of action?

(b) None of the machines will be out of action?

14 A company is engaged in a civil engineering project.

The probability that the project will be delayed by bad weather is 0.3, while the probability that it will be delayed by geological problems is 0.2. What is the probability that the project will be delayed by both bad weather and geological problems?

15 A box contains 20 spark plugs, of which 6 are substandard. If two plugs are selected from the box without replacement, what is the probability that both will be substandard?

16 The probability of the FT 30 index rising on a particular day is 0.6. If it does rise then the probability that the value of shares in a publishing company will rise is 0.8. If the index does not rise then the publishing company shares only have a 0.3 probability of rising. What is the probability that tomorrow the publishing company's shares will rise in value?

W. 17 A confectionery company launches three new products. From its own market research the company believes that the probabilities that each of their current retailers will adopt the new products for sale are as follows:

Aunty Dolleys mixture	0.9
Battys allsorts	0.6
Minty mints	0.7

The adoption of any one product is independent of the adoption of any other.

(a) What is the probability that the retailer will adopt all three products?

(b) What is the probability that the retailer will adopt at least one product?

(c) What is the probability that the retailer will adopt none of the products?

18 **(a)** A light bulb is to be selected at random from a box of 100 bulbs, details of which are given below.

Type of bulb	Defective	Satisfactory
60 watts	20	40
100 watts	10	30

Find:

(i) P(bulb is defective)

(ii) P(bulb is defective|selected bulb is 60 watts)

(b) Suppose that the company receiving the bulbs has a policy of selecting, without replacement, two bulbs from each box when it is delivered. It then applies the following decision rules:

If both bulbs are satisfactory then the box will be accepted.

If both bulbs are defective, the box is returned to the supplier.

If one bulb is defective, a third bulb is selected and the box is only accepted if this bulb is satisfactory.

What is the probability that a box, referred to above, will be accepted?

19 Marla plc is trying to decide whether it markets its new car immobilizer nationwide. The sales of the product will depend to some extent on the demand for car immobilizers, and the marketing department has suggested that the probability of high demand is 0.2 and medium to low demand is 0.8. However, it is possible to modify these probabilities by a market research exercise, but the probability that the research will be correct is only 0.6. What is the probability that the demand is really high given that the market research indicates that it will be high?

W 20 A simple screening test can be conducted to indicate if someone has a particular medical condition or not. However the test sometimes gives incorrect results. A false positive result (when the person does not have the condition) occurs 5% of the time and a false negative result (when the person has the condition) occurs 10% of the time. It is estimated that 2% of the population have the condition.

Draw a probability tree of the situation and mark on it all given probabilities. What is the probability that a person tested at random will not have the condition given that they test positive and what is the probability that they will have the condition given they test negative?

....

Assignment

Car insurance companies are interested in the probabilities of different coloured cars getting involved in accidents. For example, red cars have historically been involved in a disproportionate number of accidents. Conduct a survey to find the proportion of the different coloured cars on a stretch of road near you. Convert these proportions into probabilities. These will be your prior probabilities.

You are now given access to recent accident records for that stretch of road and discover that the probability that a red car will be involved in an accident is 0.03; a blue car 0.015; and all others 0.023. Given that there is an accident, what is the probability that the car involved is red?

The shape of data: probability distributions

Prerequisites

In order to fully understand this chapter you should have read through Chapter 4 (*Finding patterns in data: charts and tables*), Chapter 5 (*Making sense of data: averages and measures of spread*) and Chapter 6 (*Taking a chance: probability*).

Objectives

- To understand the difference between continuous and discrete probability distributions
- To be able to calculate binomial probabilities
- To be able to calculate Poisson probabilities
- To be able to use the Poisson distribution as an approximation to the binomial distribution
- To understand how the shape of the normal distribution is affected by the mean and standard deviation of the data
- To be able to use the normal distribution table
- To know how to use the normal distribution as an approximation to both the binomial and Poisson distributions

Introduction

This chapter examines some very important probability distributions. The *binomial distribution* is a discrete distribution, and is used when there are only two possible outcomes. The *Poisson distribution* is another discrete distribution, and is used for modelling rare events or events that occur at random. The final distribution you will meet is the *normal distribution*, and this (continuous) distribution has applications in almost all aspects of daily life, such as deciding whether the weight of a loaf of bread is outside acceptable limits or whether a child's height or weight is abnormal in some way.

Quantitative methods in action: is goal scoring a random event?

In the 2010 football World Cup in South Africa there were 145 goals scored from 64 matches. The number of goals scored per game varied from 0 to 7 (the highest number was from the Portugal versus Korea match). If we look at the frequency of occurrence of goals scored we get Table 7.1.

If these are plotted on a bar chart you get Figure 7.1.

What do this table and chart tell us? The mean is 2.27 goals per match and the modal number of goals is 2. The distribution of goals scored is also right skewed. What we shall look at later in this chapter is whether the number of goals scored is a random event; that is, can you predict the number of goals scored from a history of recent matches? If the answer to this question is 'No' then the event is random.

(The author wishes to acknowledge the article 'Blast it like Beckham' by John Haigh published in http://plus.maths.org/issue21/features/haigh/ in September 2002 for the idea for this case.)

Table 7.1 Goals scored per World Cup match

No. of goals	0	1	2	3	4	5	6	7
Frequency	7	17	13	14	7	5	0	1

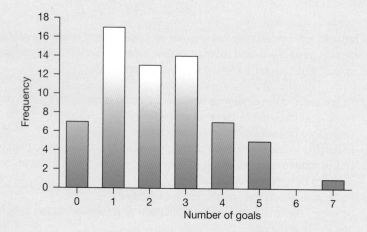

Figure 7.1
Bar chart of goals scored per World Cup match

Discrete and continuous probability distributions

The differences between discrete and continuous data were discussed in Chapter 4, but essentially discrete data is obtained by *counting*, whereas continuous data is obtained by *measurement*. So counting the number of loaves of bread baked over a period of time would give you data that only contained whole numbers (assuming that the bread is only sold as complete loaves), while recording the weight of each loaf of bread baked would give you data that could take on any value.

Example 7.1

Data on the number and weight of a 'standard' loaf of bread were collected over a period of time and aggregated into Table 7.2.

Table 7.2 Frequency table for the data on the number and weight of loaves of bread

Number of loaves baked		Weight of each loaf	
Number	Frequency	Weight range	Frequency
20	8	770g to below 775g	3
21	12	775g to below 780g	17
22	24	780g to below 785g	44
23	26	785g to below 790g	100
24	35	790g to below 795g	141
25	35	795g to below 800g	192
26	30	800g to below 805g	191
27	28	805g to below 810g	150
28	21	810g to below 815g	90
		815g to below 820g	42
		820g to below 825g	14
		825g to below 830g	9

In order to compare the two data sets in more detail, diagrams could be used. A *bar chart* would be appropriate for the number of loaves baked, while a *histogram* is necessary for the weight data (see Chapter 4). These diagrams are shown in Figures 7.2 and 7.3.

The histogram gives you an idea of the underlying distribution of the data; that is, it shows you how the data is *distributed* across the range of possible values. This kind of distribution is called an *empirical* distribution because it is obtained by measurement or observation. There are also distributions that can be derived mathematically. The three most common distributions are the binomial distribution, the Poisson distribution and the normal distribution.

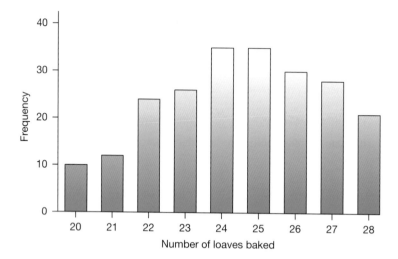

Figure 7.2
Bar chart for the number of loaves baked

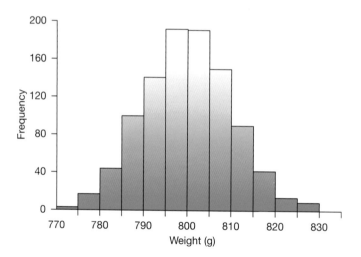

Figure 7.3
Histogram for the weight of a loaf

The binomial distribution

This is a discrete probability distribution and arises when

- a variable can only be in one of two states (an either|or situation)
- the probability of the two outcomes are known and constant from trial to trial
- the number of trials is known and constant
- successive events are independent.

The obvious example to use here is a coin since it can be in one of two states, either a head (H) or a tail (T). However, the binomial distribution can be used in many applications, such as quality control where an item can be either defective or not defective.

If a coin is tossed once, there are only two outcomes with equal probability, but if you toss a coin twice (or toss two coins once), the outcome could be one of the following:

2 heads, or

2 tails, or

a head and a tail

There are two ways of getting a head and a tail, since either toss could result in a head or a tail. The best way of illustrating the outcomes is by means of a tree diagram. Figure 7.4 shows that there are 4 'routes' to the tree. At the end of each route the number of heads has been indicated, together with the probability of that route. The number of ways of getting 2, 1, and 0 heads is 1, 2, and 1 respectively, and the probability of any route is $0.5 \times 0.5 = 0.25$ (or $(0.5)^2$). Therefore the probability of getting 1 head is $2 \times 0.25 = 0.5$.

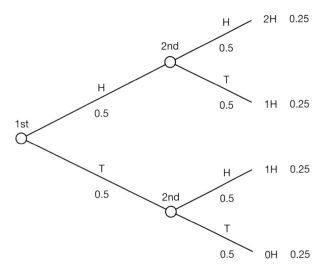

Figure 7.4
A coin tossed twice

Activity 7.1

Draw the tree for the case where a coin is tossed three times. What is the probability of

(a) one head, and

(b) two heads?

The tree has become a little more complicated and is shown in Figure 7.5. The number of ways of getting 3, 2, 1, or 0 heads is 1, 3, 3, and 1 respectively and the probability of following any route is now $(0.5)^3 = 0.125$. The probability of getting 1 head is therefore $3 \times 0.125 = 0.375$ and the probability of getting 2 heads is also 0.375.

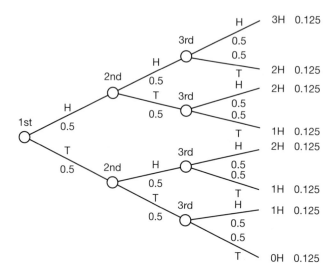

Figure 7.5
A coin tossed three
times

If you repeat this for 4 heads you should find that the number of ways of getting 4, 3, 2, 1, 0 heads is 1, 4, 6, 4, and 1 respectively, and the probability of following any route is $(0.5)^4 = 0.0625$. If you now write the number of ways of getting various combinations of heads in a table similar to the one below, you should see how easy it is to carry on the sequence.

1 toss			1	1		
2 tosses		1	2	1		
3 tosses	1	3	3	1		
4 tosses	1	4	6	4	1	

Activity 7.2

Continue the sequence for 5 tosses of the coin.

For 5 tosses the sequence will be 1, 5, 10, 5, 10, 5, 1 since $1 + 4 = 5$ and $4 + 6 = 10$. This is known as *Pascal's triangle* and it gives you the number of ways an event will occur. Although it is quite feasible to do this for a small number of tosses of the coin, what would happen if you tossed the coin 10, 20 or even 50 times? Fortunately, this series is the same as finding the number of ways of choosing r items from n (see Chapter 6 (page 141)) and is given by:

$$^nC_r = \frac{n!}{r!(n-r)!}$$

Activity 7.3

How many ways are there of getting 4 heads from 10 tosses of a coin?

Using the formula we get:

$$^{10}C_4 = \frac{10!}{4! \times (10 - 4)!}$$

$$= 210$$

This is fine for a coin where the probability of each event is 0.5, but what about more general problems? Where an item can be in one of two states and the probability of both states is known and constant, the ideas just discussed can be used. For example, about 5% of people are in blood type AB, so the probability that any one person has this blood type is 0.05. What is the probability that in a group of 10 people, 4 will have this blood type? This is a binomial problem because a person either does or does not have this blood type. The probability that a person doesn't is 0.95 $(1 - 0.05)$. If 4 people have this blood type then it follows that 6 do not, so the probability of a route of the probability tree giving this combination is:

$$(0.05)^4 \times (0.95)^6 = 0.00000459$$

Since there are 210 ways of getting this combination ($^{10}C_4$, see above), the probability of 4 people out of 10 with blood type AB is:

$$210 \times 0.00000459 = 0.00096$$

In general if p is the probability of a 'success', where success is defined as a person or item being in a particular state, then the binomial distribution can be defined as follows:

$$P(r) = {}^nC_r p^r (1 - p)^{n-r}$$

where n is the number of trials and r the number of successes. To use this formula you simply need to know the values of p, n and r. For example, suppose that you wanted to find the probability that 2 or more people in the group of 10 had blood of type AB. You could find the probability of 2, 3, 4, and so on, and then add the probabilities together. However, there is an easier way – this is to use the fact that the probabilities must sum to 1, so $P(r \geq 2) = 1 - (P(0) + P(1))$. This reduces the number of calculations from 9 to 2. (With larger values of n, the saving is even more pronounced.)

Activity 7.4

Calculate the probability of $P(r \geq 2)$ for the example above.

The calculation of $P(0)$ is easy since there is only one route in this case and $^{10}C_0 = 1$. So:

$$P(0) = (0.5)^0 \times (0.95)^{10}$$

$$= 0.59874$$

(Note: anything raised to the power of 0 is 1.)

For the calculation of P(1), $^{10}C_1 = 10$, so:

$$P(1) = 10 \times (0.05)^1 \times (0.95)^9$$
$$= 0.31512$$

and

$$P(r \geq 2) = 1 - (0.59874 + 0.31512)$$
$$= 0.08614, \text{ or about } 8.6\%$$

An easier method is to use the cumulative binomial function in Excel. The function name is

```
BINOMDIST(number_s,trials,probability_s, Cumulative)
```

where:

Number_s is the number of successes in trials [that is, r]
Trials is the number of independent trials [that is, n]
Probability_s is the probability of success on each trial [that is, p]
Cumulative is a logical value that determines the form of the function. If cumulative is true, then BINOMDIST returns the cumulative distribution function, which is the probability that there are at most number_s successes; if false, it returns the probability mass function, which is the probability that there are number_s successes.
(*Taken from the Help facility in Excel.*)

By setting Cumulative as true we get the cumulative probability of r successes or less in n trials. So, in the above example, to find the probability that 2 or more had blood group AB you would first need to use the BINOMDIST function to find the probability of 1 or less. The function would therefore be:

```
BINOMDIST(1,10,0.05,true)
```

Excel returns a probability of 0.9139, so if we subtract this from 1 we get 0.0861, which is the same as we got above. To avoid using Excel repeatedly, a table for selected values of n, r and p is provided in Appendix 1. This table gives you the probability of r successes or less, so to find the probability for $n = 10$ and $r = 1$ you would need to subtract the probability from 1 as before. Part of the binomial table is shown in Table 7.3 where the probability of 0.9139 has been highlighted.

Table 7.3 Part of the binomial table in Appendix 1

		p		
n	r	0.01	0.05	0.1
10	0	0.9044	0.5987	0.3487
10	1	0.9957	**0.9139**	0.7361
10	2	0.9999	0.9885	0.9298

Activity 7.5

The UK government's guideline is that hospital death rates that are 60% above the norm are unacceptable. Say a hospital performs 100 operations and the chance of dying in any one of these operations is 5%, which also happens to be the government's norm for this particular operation. Find the probability that the government's guidelines are exceeded.

Either a patient dies or lives so this is a binomial problem. The mean number of deaths in 100 operations will be 5, so 60% above the norm is 8 (that is, $5 + 5 \times .6$). You need to find the probability of 0 up to 7 deaths and subtract the sum from 1. Using Excel you should get the probability of 7 or less as 0.87. Therefore there is a chance of 0.13 that the hospital death rate will be unacceptable even if appears to meet the norm. This means that 13% of hospitals will fail the government's guideline by chance.

Activity 7.6

Use Excel to find the probability of P(0), P(1), P(2), P(3), P(4) and P(5) when $n = 5$ and $p = 0.2$. Plot these values in the form of a bar chart. How would you describe the shape of the distribution?

We would now set Cumulative as false, and the results using Excel are:

```
BINOMDIST(0,5,0.2.false) = 0.32768
BINOMDIST(1,5,0.2.false) = 0.40960
BINOMDIST(2,5,0.2.false) = 0.20480
BINOMDIST(3,5,0.2.false) = 0.05120
BINOMDIST(4,5,0.2.false) = 0.00640
BINOMDIST(5,5,0.2.false) = 0.00032
```

The chart in Figure 7.6 shows that the distribution is *right skewed*.

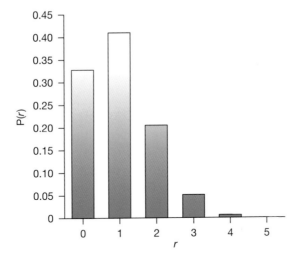

Figure 7.6
Bar chart for
Activity 7.6

Activity 7.7

Repeat Activity 7.6 for $n = 20$ and $p = 0.2$ (stop when P(r) is zero to 4 decimal places).

You should have obtained a chart similar to the one in Figure 7.7. Notice that the distribution is now much less skewed. (We shall return to the shape of the binomial distribution later.)

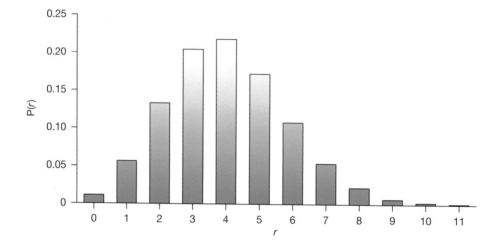

Figure 7.7
Bar chart for
Activity 7.7

The mean and standard deviation of the binomial distribution

The mean of a binomial distribution is np.

The standard deviation is given by the formula:

$$\sigma = \sqrt{np(1 - p)}$$

Activity 7.8

What is the mean and standard deviation of the binomial distribution with $n = 5$ and $p = 0.2$? (That is, for Activity 7.6.)

The mean is $5 \times 0.2 = 1.0$.

The standard deviation is $\sqrt{5 \times 0.2 \times 0.8} = 0.894$.

As the standard deviation is a measure of spread it would be interesting to see how many standard deviations would be needed to cover the distribution. One standard deviation would give a range of $1.0 \pm 0.894 = 0.106$ to 1.894. Looking at Figure 7.6 we can see that this includes $r = 1$ only. The probability for $r = 1$ is

0.4096

So about 41% of the distribution is covered by one standard deviation.

Activity 7.9

What proportion of the distribution is covered by two standard deviations?

In this case we have $1.0 \pm 2 \times 0.894 = -0.788$ to 2.788
This covers the first 3 values of r and the probabilities add to 0.94208. So about 94% is covered by two standard deviations, which is a high proportion of the distribution.

Activity 7.10

Repeat Activity 7.9 for the case where $n = 20$ and $p = 0.2$ (that is, Activity 7.7).

The mean is $20 \times 0.2 = 4$

The standard deviation is $\sqrt{20 \times 0.2 \times 0.8} = 1.789$

For two standard deviations we get a range of $4 \pm 2 \times 1.789 = 0.422$ to 7.589

This covers the distribution from $r = 1$ to $r = 7$ and adding the probabilities for these values of r we get 0.9563, which is almost 96%.

You will find that most observations rarely fall outside the range of the mean plus or minus two standard deviations. You will meet this idea again when we look at the normal distribution.

The Poisson distribution

The Poisson distribution is another example of a discrete probability distribution. Like the binomial distribution the Poisson distribution again models the either|or situation but in this case the chance of a particular event occurring is very small. That is, the event is 'rare'. Also, we are normally only given the mean occurrence of the event instead of the probability. The Poisson distribution is often used in situations where the event is unlikely (accidents, machine failures) or where the event occurs at random (arrivals of calls at a switchboard, for example).

The formula for the Poisson is less complicated than the binomial, and the probability of r events in a given unit (of time or length, and so on) is as follows:

$$P(r) = \frac{e^{-m}m^r}{r!}$$

where m is the mean number of events in the same unit and e is the constant 2.7182818 ... and can be found on many scientific calculators (usually in the form e^x).

A typical example of the Poisson distribution is as follows. The number of calls to a switchboard is random, with a mean of 1.5 per minute. What is the probability that there are no calls in any one minute?

All we need to do is to substitute $r = 0$ and $m = 1.5$ into the equation. That is:

$$P(0) = \frac{e^{-1.5}(1.5)^0}{0!} = 0.2231$$

(because $e^{-1.5} = 0.2231$, $1.5^0 = 1$ and $0! = 1$).

Did you know

Simeon Denis Poisson was born in 1781 in France. He was a gifted mathematician and the first mention of the Poisson distribution was in his paper titled 'Researches on the probability of criminal and civil verdicts' in 1837. His distribution has been used in many fields, particularly the military, and in the Second World War it was used to see whether the pattern of bombs landing on London was random or not. (If it was not random that would have suggested that the Germans had a sophisticated targeting mechanism in the bombs.)

Activity 7.11

Using a mean of 1.5 calls a minute, what is the probability that:

(a) There are more than 2 calls in any one minute?
(b) There are less than 6 calls in a 5-minute period?

It is not possible to calculate the answer to (a) directly since the maximum number of calls that could be received is not specified (in fact there is no maximum). However, as in the binomial distribution the probability can be found by noting that the sum of the probabilities must equal 1.

So, $P(r > 2) = 1 - (P(0) + P(1) + P(2))$

That is, $P(r > 2) = 1 - (0.2231 + 0.3347 + 0.2510) = 0.1912$

Question (b) is a little more difficult since the time period has been changed from a minute to 5 minutes. However, all that needs to be done is to work out the average rate over 5 minutes, which is 7.5 (5×1.5), and then continue as before. That is:

$P(r < 6) = P(0) + P(1) + P(2) + P(3) + P(4) + P(5)$

To make this calculation easier we could use Excel. The function for the Poisson distribution is:

`POISSON(x,mean,cumulative)`

where:

x is the number of events [that is, r]
Mean is the expected numeric value [that is, m]
Cumulative is a logical value that determines the form of the probability distribution returned. If `Cumulative` is `true`, `POISSON` returns the cumulative Poisson probability that the number of random events occurring will be between zero and x inclusive; if `false`, it returns the Poisson probability mass function that the number of events occurring will be exactly x.
(*Taken from the Help facility in Excel.*)

Using Excel we get:

`POISSON(5,7.5,true) = 0.2414`

So $P(r < 6) = 0.2414$

Table 7.4 Part of the Poisson table in Appendix 1

mean	r	
	5	6
0.1	1.0000	1.0000
7.2	0.2759	0.4204
7.3	0.2640	0.4060
7.4	0.2526	0.3920
7.5	**0.2414**	0.3782
7.6	0.2307	0.3646

An alternative to using Excel is to refer to the cumulative Poisson probability table in Appendix 1. This table gives you the probability of *r* or less events. Part of the Poisson table is shown in Table 7.4, where the probability of 0.2414 has been highlighted.

Activity 7.12

In the *Quantitative methods in action* case at the start of this chapter we looked at the number of goals scored in each match of the 2010 World Cup. Use the Poisson distribution to calculate the expected frequency that 0, 1, 2... goals are scored and compare with the actual.

The mean number of goals per match was 2.27 and we can use the Poisson distribution to calculate the probability of 0, 1, 2... goals. The Excel function is

`Poisson(x,2.27,false)` where *x* takes on the values 0, 1, 2...

The Excel screen print can be seen in Figure 7.8.

	B10		fx	=1-SUM(B2:B9)	
	A	B	C	D	E
1	**Goals**	**Probability**	**Expected**	**Actual**	
2	0	0.1033	6.6	7	
3	1	0.2345	15.0	17	
4	2	0.2662	17.0	13	
5	3	0.2014	12.9	14	
6	4	0.1143	7.3	7	
7	5	0.0519	3.3	5	
8	6	0.0196	1.3	0	
9	7	0.0064	0.4	1	
10	8 or more	0.0024	0.2	0	
11		**Sum**	64.0	64	
12					

Notice that the probability of 8 or more is 1 – probability of 7 or less

Figure 7.8
Use of Excel for
Activity 7.12

The second column gives the probability using the Poisson function. These probabilities are then multiplied by 64 (the number of matches played) to give the expected frequency that this number of goals was scored. So we can see that the expected number of times a match would be goalless is 6.6 and this compares well with the actual of 7. The largest discrepancy is for 2 goals where there is a difference of 4. You will also notice that to ensure that the expected values added to 64 we had a category of 8 or more goals.

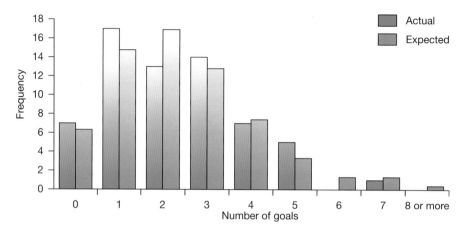

Figure 7.9
Comparison of actual
and expected goals
scored in the 2010
World Cup

A chart would give a better comparison and Figure 7.9 uses a multiple bar chart to compare the actual and expected frequencies.

This chart indicates that there is quite a good match which suggests that the number of goals scored is random. Therefore, it wouldn't be possible to predict the number of goals scored from a history of previous matches. In Chapter 9 we will see how we can do a more formal test on how close the two distributions are.

The use of the Poisson distribution as an approximation to the binomial distribution

As you will probably have noticed it is a little easier to calculate probabilities using the Poisson distribution than it is using the binomial distribution. In some circumstances it is possible to use the Poisson distribution instead of the binomial distribution. The error you will get as a result will be quite small providing the following conditions are met:

○ The number of trials, n, is large (greater than 30)
○ The probability of a success, p, is small (less than 0.1)
○ The mean number of successes, $n \times p$, is less than 5.

Activity 7.13

A batch contains 1% defective items and a sample of size 40 is chosen. What is the probability that there are exactly 2 defective items? Are the conditions for using the Poisson distribution instead of the binomial met for this problem?

This is a binomial problem and the answer using the binomial distribution is:

$$P(2) = 40C_2 \times (0.01)^2 \times (1 - 0.01)^{38}$$
$$= 780 \times 0.00006826$$
$$= 0.0532$$

However, we can also use the Poisson to solve this problem because n is large, p is small and the mean number of defects is 0.4 (40×0.01) which is less than 5.

Using the Poisson distribution for $r = 2$, we get:

$$P(2) = \frac{e^{-0.4} \times (0.4)^2}{2!}$$

$$= 0.0536$$

which is an error of less than 1%.

The mean and standard deviation of the Poisson distribution

The *variance* of the Poisson distribution is equal to the mean. So the standard deviation, which is the square root of the variance, is equal to the square root of the mean. In symbols this becomes:

$$\sigma = \sqrt{m}$$

For example, if the mean is 1.5 then the standard deviation will be $\sqrt{1.5} = 1.225$.

The normal distribution

Many observations that are obtained from measurements follow the normal distribution. For example, the heights of people and the weights of loaves of bread are approximately normally distributed. The normal distribution is completely symmetrical or bell shaped. The mean, mode and median of this distribution all lie at the centre of the bell, as you can see in Figure 7.10.

The normal curve has the following properties:

1 The curve is symmetrical about the mean.
2 The total area under the curve is equal to 1 or 100%. This means that probability can be equated to area.
3 The horizontal axis represents a continuous variable such as weight.
4 The area under the curve between two points on the horizontal axis represents the probability that the value of the variable lies between these two points.
5 As the distance between two points gets less, the area between the two points must get less. Taking this to its logical conclusion, the probability of a specific value is zero. It is therefore only meaningful to talk about ranges, such as 800 g to 810 g.

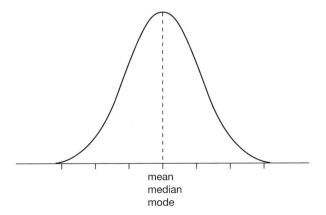

Figure 7.10
The normal
distribution

mean
median
mode

6 The position and shape of the curve depends on the mean and standard deviation of the distribution. As the standard deviation gets larger, the curve will get flatter and extend further on either side of the mean.

Did you know

> The normal distribution was first derived mathematically by DeMoivre in 1733. Laplace used the curve in 1783 to describe the distribution of errors and in 1809 Gauss used the curve to analyze astronomical data. (This is the reason it is often called the Gaussian curve.) The normal distribution is now the most commonly used distribution in statistics.

Activity 7.14

The average weight of a 'standard' loaf of bread is 800 g and the weights are normally distributed. If a loaf is selected at random, what is the probability that it will weigh less than 800 g?

Property 1 above says that the normal curve is symmetrical about the mean, so that 50% of the loaves will be below the mean weight of 800 g and 50% will be above. Hence the probability will be 0.5 or 50%.

Activity 7.15

What proportion of loaves weigh more than 815 g?

This problem has been illustrated diagrammatically in Figure 7.11, where the area representing all loaves with a weight exceeding 815 g has been shaded.

This shaded area is clearly a small proportion of the total area, but it would be difficult to estimate the actual figure from the diagram alone. Tables are used to obtain this area but, before you can do this, you need to understand the properties of the *standard normal distribution*.

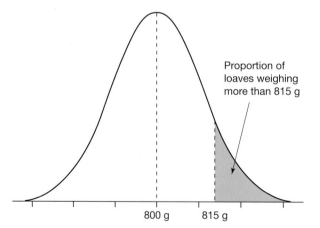

Figure 7.11
Distribution of the weight of a loaf of bread

The standard normal distribution

The standard normal distribution has a mean of zero and a standard deviation of 1. This is illustrated in Figure 7.12. The figures along the horizontal axis are the number of standard deviations and are called the Z values. You will see from the diagram that the majority of the distribution is covered within 3 standard deviations either side of the mean.

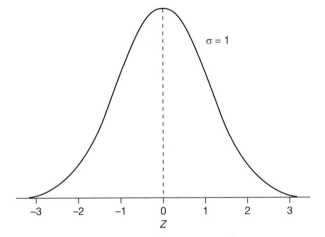

Figure 7.12
The standard normal distibution

To demonstrate the use of the normal table you should now refer to the table provided in Appendix 1. The table provided in this book gives you the area in the *right hand tail* of the distribution, but other tables may give the area in a different way. (Once you have used one table you should find it a simple matter to use a different type.)

The first column gives the Z value to one decimal place and the first row gives the second place of decimals. For example, for a Z value of 0.55, you would look down the first column until you found 0.5 and then across until you were directly under 0.05. The area is 0.2912, or 29.12%. This is the area in the tail for Z being greater than 0.55. Since the distribution is symmetrical, the area being less than $Z = -0.55$ is also 29.12%. You will see these areas shaded in Figure 7.13.

Activity 7.16

What is the area between a Z value of 1 and -1?

The area of the curve for Z greater than 1 is 0.1587 or 15.87%. To find the area from the mean ($Z = 0$) to any Z value you need to use the fact that half the distribution has an area of 0.5. So to find the area from $Z = 0$ to $Z = 1$ you would subtract this from 0.5. That is, $0.5 - 0.1587 = 0.3413$. Since the distribution is symmetrical, the area from 0.0 to -1.0 is also 0.3413. The area from -1 to $+1$ is therefore 0.6826. In other words, 68.26% of the normal curve is covered by ± 1 standard deviations. This area can be seen in Figure 7.14.

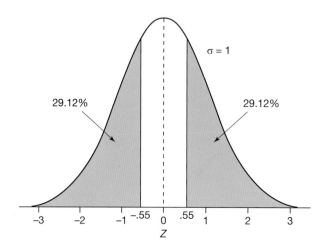

Figure 7.13
Areas under the
normal distribution

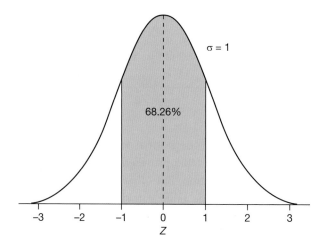

Figure 7.14
Diagram for
Activity 7.16

If you repeat this for $Z = 2$ and $Z = 3$, you should find that just over 95% (95.44%) of the normal distribution is covered by ± 2 standard deviations, and almost 100% (99.73%) is covered by ± 3 standard deviations.

Activity 7.17

What is the value of Z if the area of the upper tail is 5%?

This problem is illustrated in Figure 7.15. To solve this problem the normal table is used in reverse. That is, the table is inspected to find the area of 0.05. This figure does not exist, but you should find that a Z value of 1.64 gives an area of 0.0505, while a Z value of 1.65 gives an area of 0.0495. The most accurate value of Z would be the average of these two values, which is 1.645.

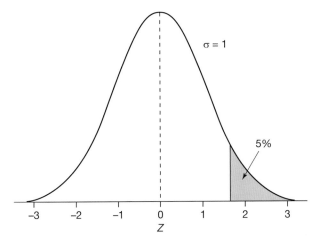

Figure 7.15
Diagram for
Activity 7.17

Standardizing normal distributions

Unfortunately, most normal distribution problems do not have a mean of zero or a standard deviation of 1, so the normal table cannot be used directly to solve general problems. However, all you have to do is to calculate the number of standard deviations from the mean, and this can be done quite easily, as follows:

- subtract the mean value from the particular value (x) that you are interested in
- divide this value by the standard deviation.

For example, if the mean is 5 and the standard deviation is 2, then a value of 9 is two standard deviations from the mean. This calculation is called the *Z transformation* and is given by:

$$Z = \frac{x - \text{mean}}{\text{standard deviation}}$$

If x is less than the mean, the value of Z will be negative. This negative value simply indicates that x is to the left of the mean. Since the distribution is symmetrical about the mean, you can ignore the sign when using the table.

Activity 7.18

A batch of loaves is baked. The weight of the loaves is normally distributed with a mean of 800 g and a standard deviation of 10 g. What proportion of loaves will weigh more than 815 g?

This is the same problem that you met in Activity 7.15 (see Figure 7.11), but you now should be able to solve this using the normal table. However, you first have to transform the problem using the Z formula. You should first note that:

$$Z = \frac{815 - 800}{10} = 1.5$$

That is, 815 g is 1.5 standard deviations away from the mean.

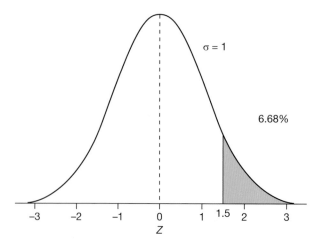

Figure 7.16
Diagram for
Activity 7.18

It is now a simple matter of looking up $Z = 1.5$ in the normal table. If you do this you should get an area of 0.0668 or 6.68%, which means that 6.68% of all loaves weigh more than 815 g. This is represented in Figure 7.16.

The problem can become slightly more difficult, as illustrated in the next activity.

Activity 7.19

A loaf is chosen at random. What is the probability that the weight will lie between 810 g and 812 g?

To find the probability it is necessary to find the shaded area in Figure 7.17. This area cannot be found directly, but it can be found by *subtracting* the area greater than 812 from the area greater than 810. To do this it is necessary to calculate two Z values as follows:

$$\frac{810 - 800}{10} = 1.0$$

$$\text{and} \quad \frac{812 - 800}{12} = 1.2$$

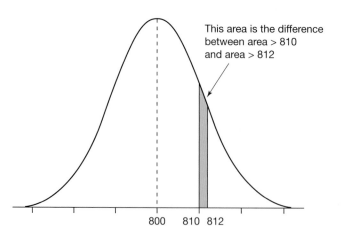

Figure 7.17
Diagram for
Activity 7.19

The areas from the normal table are 0.1587 and 0.1157 and the required area is:

0.1587 − 0.1151 = 0.0436

The probability that the weight will be between 810 g and 812 g is therefore 0.0436 or 4.36%. Alternatively you could say that 4.36% of all loaves weigh between 810 g and 812 g.

Activity 7.20

What proportion of loaves weigh between 790 g and 805.5 g?

To solve this problem you should note that the required area is the *sum* of the two areas A and B in Figure 7.18.

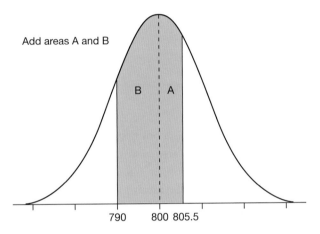

Add areas A and B

B   A

790   800 805.5

Figure 7.18
Diagram for
Activity 7.20

To calculate area A it is necessary to find the area greater than 805.5 and then subtract this from 0.5. (Don't forget that the tables used in this book give the area in the *right hand* tail of the distribution.) The calculation is as follows:

$$Z = \frac{805.5 - 800}{10} = 0.55$$

This gives an area of 0.2912 and area A is therefore 0.5 − 0.2912 = 0.2088.
Area B is found in a similar manner.

$$Z = \frac{790 - 800}{10} = -1.0$$

The negative sign indicates that the area is to the left of the mean and can be ignored for the purposes of obtaining the area from the normal table. Area B is therefore 0.5 − 0.1587 = 0.3413.

The combined area is 0.2088 + 0.3413 = 0.5501 or 55.01%, which is the proportion of loaves with weights between 790 g and 805.5 g.

In addition to calculating the probability or proportion of a variable having a value between specified limits, it is possible to carry out the reverse process. This is illustrated in the next activity.

Activity 7.21

The baker wishes to ensure that no more than 5% of loaves are less than a certain weight. What is this weight?

The diagram for this problem can be seen in Figure 7.19.

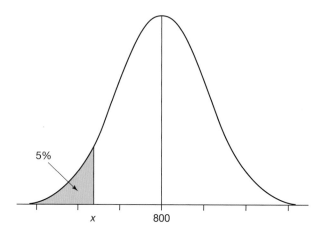

Figure 7.19
Diagram for
Activity 7.21

It is necessary to calculate the value x, but first the Z value corresponding to an area of 5% must be found. Although this area is in the lower tail, the method is identical to that used when the area in the upper tail has been given. (Don't forget that the distribution is symmetrical about the mean.) The value of Z for an area of 5% is 1.645, but because it is to the left of the mean, the value is negative; that is, -1.645. Substituting this value into the formula gives:

$$-1.645 = \frac{x - 800}{10}$$

Multiplying both sides by 10 gives:

$$-16.45 = x - 800$$

Then adding 800 to both sides:

$$x = 800 - 16.45$$

$$= 783.6 \text{ g}$$

So no more than 5% of the batch should weigh less than 783.6 g.

Although the preceding activities cover the most common applications, it is possible to use the Z formula to calculate either the mean or the standard deviation. This is demonstrated next.

Activity 7.22

A large number of loaves were weighed and it was found that 8% weighed less than 783.6 g. Assuming that the standard deviation hasn't changed, what has happened?

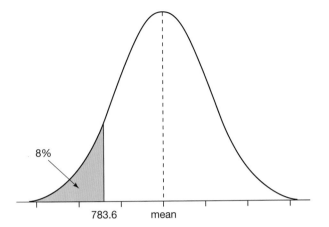

Figure 7.20
Diagram for
Activity 7.22

This problem is illustrated in Figure 7.20. If the standard deviation hasn't changed, then the only explanations are that the mean has changed or that it is not what it was thought to be. Again, it is necessary to work backwards. The Z value corresponding to a proportion of 8% is 1.405, which will again be negative. The value of x is 783.6 and it is required to find the value of the mean.

$$-1.405 = \frac{783.6 - \text{mean}}{10}$$

Multiplying both sides by 10 gives:

$$-14.05 = 783.6 - \text{mean}$$

Then adding 14.05 to both sides:

$$0 = 797.7 - \text{mean}$$

that is: mean $= 797.7 \, \text{g}$

The normal distribution as an approximation to the binomial distribution

If a particular binomial distribution is symmetrical it is possible to use the normal distribution to solve binomial problems. The conditions that make the binomial distribution symmetrical are that both $n \times p$ and $n \times (1 - p)$ are greater than 5. This means that p needs to be near to 0.5 and n should be large.

Activity 7.23

Use Excel to plot the binomial distribution for $n = 30$ and $p = 0.3$.

You should have obtained Figure 7.21 and you should notice that the distribution is approximately symmetrical.

The next activity will show you how to use the normal distribution as an approximation to the binomial.

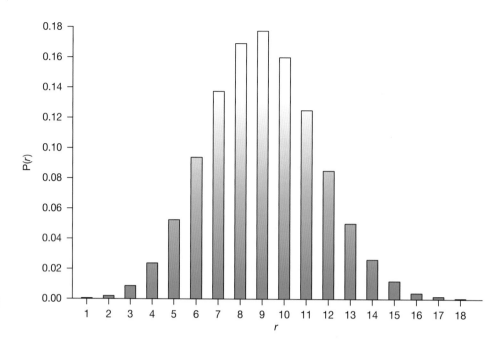

Figure 7.21
Binomial distribution
with $n=30$ and
$p=0.3$

Activity 7.24

The probability of a defective item is 0.3. If a sample of 30 were taken, what is the probability that at least 5 were defective?

Using the binomial table in Appendix 1 we would find the probability of 4 or fewer defectives, which is 0.0302.

The probability of at least 5 defectives is then:

$$P(r \geq 5) = 1 - 0.0302$$
$$= 0.9698$$

To solve this problem by the normal distribution it is first necessary to calculate the mean and standard deviation. The mean is $n \times p = 30 \times 0.3 = 9.0$ and the standard deviation is:

$$\sqrt{30 \times 0.3 \times 0.7} = 2.51$$

It is then necessary to make a *continuity correction*. This is because the binomial distribution is a discrete probability distribution whereas the normal distribution is a continuous one. To get around this problem it is assumed that the discrete value 5 is a continuous variable in the range 4.5 to 5.5. To find the probability greater than 4, the value 4.5 is used, as you can see in Figure 7.22.

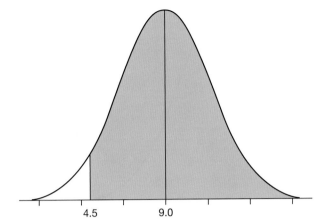

Figure 7.22
Normal
approximation to
the binomial for
Activity 7.24

This problem now becomes one of finding $P(r > 4.5)$, which is $1 - P(r < 4.5)$, and

$$Z = \frac{4.5 - 9}{2.51}$$

$$= -1.79$$

$$P(Z < -1.79) = P(Z > 1.79)$$

and from the normal table the probability is 0.0367, so the required probability is: $1 - 0.0367 = 0.9633$, which compares well with the correct value of 0.9698.

The normal distribution as an approximation to the Poisson distribution

The normal distribution can also be used to solve Poisson problems. This is valid provided the mean is greater than about 10.

Activity 7.25

The number of calls to a switchboard is random, with a mean of 1.5 per minute. What is the probability that there are fewer than 6 calls in a 5-minute period?

We looked at this problem in Activity 7.11 where we calculated the probability to be 0.2414. To solve this problem using the normal distribution you would note that the mean is 7.5 calls in a 5-minute period. (The mean of 7.5 is less than the recommended level, so it will be interesting to see how good the approximation will be in this case.)

To use the normal distribution, the continuity correction again needs to be applied. In this case the probability of less than 5.5 calls needs to be found. The standard deviation is the square root of the mean (7.5), which equals 2.739.

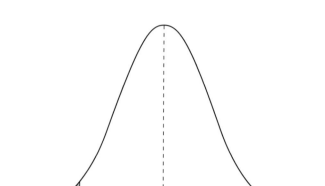

Figure 7.23
Normal
approximation to the
Poisson distribution
for Activity 7.25

The calculation is straightforward using the normal distribution:

$$Z = \frac{5.5 - 7.5}{2.739} = -0.7302$$

$$P((r < 5.5) = P((Z < -0.7302) = P((Z > 0.7302)$$

$$= 0.2327 \text{ (from the normal table)}$$

This represents an error of under 4% (the difference between 0.2414 and 0.2327 as a percentage of 0.2414).

Reflection

We have looked at only a few probability distributions: there are many, many more. Some are quite simple, such as the uniform distribution which can be used when values between the smallest and largest are constant. Other distributions are quite complex, however, and their shape may depend on two or more parameters.

Because it is so much easier to work with a mathematical distribution than with raw data, we often need to 'fit' a distribution to a set of data. We must remember, however, that mathematical distributions are usually only approximations. Further, some sets of data cannot be represented by a mathematical distribution – an example is data that is bimodal.

The World Cup example illustrated that probability distributions can be used for quite ordinary situations. You can also use the Poisson distibution to show that the number of goals scored during the game is also random (see Activity 7.12). However the most useful distribution is the normal as it can be used for such a wide range of situations. It is used in quality control, weights of animals and the distribution of errors to name just a few examples. It is also believed that the distribution of death rates amongst doctor's patients is also normal and it has been proposed that, if this analysis had been conducted during the 1980s and 1990s, the Shipman tragedy might have been avoided (*The Lancet*, vol. 362, August 2003). The analysis required some transformation of the data as there were many non-random factors involved (for example, age). The resulting transformed data had a mean of 0 and a standard deviation of 1 and, as we know, we expect almost the entire distribution to be covered by ±3 standard deviations. When researchers analyzed the Shipman data they found that in 1998 his mean death rate corresponded to a Z value of 6.6 which is well above what could have occurred by chance

An important use of the normal distribution is in sampling and we will come back to this in Chapters 8 and 9.

....

Key points

- Data can be plotted in the form of a *histogram* to give us a picture of how the data is distributed from the smallest to the largest value.
- Distributions can be either *discrete* or *continuous*.
- The shapes of many naturally occurring datasets appear to be very close to shapes defined by mathematical distributions.
- Examples of these distributions include the *binomial distribution* and the *Poisson distribution*, which are discrete distributions, and the normal distribution, which is a continuous distribution.
- The binomial distribution is used when an event can either happen or not happen.
- The Poisson distribution is used when the chance of an event happening is very small (it is a rare event). It is used where events occur at random such as arrivals to a queue.
- The normal distribution is the most widely used distribution in statistics. Before a normal distribution problem can be solved it needs to be transformed into the standard normal form which has a mean of zero and a standard deviation of 1.

Further reading

Like probability there are a large number of texts on probability distributions, ranging from introductory level to more advanced texts. Morris (2008) gives a good general description of the common distributions (binomial, Poisson and normal) without using many equations. Most other texts aimed at the business student such as Curwin and Slater (2008) give a similar treatment to this text.

Web links W

Answers to selected questions can be found in Appendix 2. Answers to the other questions can be found on the companion website for this book.

Practice questions

1 If a coin is tossed 5 times, how many ways are there of getting 3 heads?

2 What is the probability of getting 3 heads if a coin is tossed 5 times?

W 3 A job hunter is applying for nine jobs and believes that she has in each of the nine jobs a constant and independent 0.48 probability of getting an offer.
   (a) What might make you think that you are dealing with a binomial situation?
   (b) What is the probability that she will get at least three job offers?

4 The sex ratio of newborn infants is about 105 males to 100 females. If 4 infants are chosen at random, what is the probability that:
   (a) All four are males?
   (b) Exactly three are male?
   (c) Two are male and two are female?

5 The quality control manager of a company is concerned at the level of defective items being produced. Out of a batch of 20 items, 2 were found to be defective. Should the quality control manager be concerned given that in the past the defective rate has been 3%?

6 A shopkeeper finds that 20% of the cartons containing 6 eggs he receives are damaged. A carton is picked at random, checked and returned to the consignment. The procedure is repeated a further 3 times. What is the probability that out of the 4 cartons inspected
(a) none were undamaged?
(b) at least 3 were undamaged?

7 Calls arrive at a switchboard according to the Poisson distribution. If the average number of calls received in a 5-minute period is 6.7, find the probability that:
(a) There are fewer than 4 calls received in a 5-minute period.
(b) There are more than 7 calls received during a 5-minute period.
(c) There are no calls received in a 1-minute period.

8 Several lengths of plastic tubing are examined for the number of flaws in intervals of given length. If 1500 flaws are found in 1000 intervals each of 1 mm, find the probability, assuming a Poisson distribution of
(a) at least 2 flaws in an interval of 1 mm
(b) an interval between two consecutive flaws being greater than 5 mm.

W 9 A coffee shop has an average arrival rate of 3.2 customers every 4 minutes. These random arrivals are Poisson distributed. What is the probability of getting
(a) no customers in a 4 minute interval?
(b) at least 3 customers in a 4 minute interval?
(c) less than 5 customers in an 8 minute interval?

W 10 What is the area in the tail of the distribution for a Z value of 1.25?

W 11 What is area between the Z values of 1.45 and 2.45?

W 12 What is the area between Z values of -0.67 and 1.05?

W 13 A particular normal distribution has a mean of 5 and a standard deviation of 1.5. What is the area corresponding to a value:
(a) greater than 6?
(b) less than 4?
(c) between 4 and 6?
(d) between 6.5 and 7.5?

W 14 The daily demand for petrol at a garage is normally distributed with a mean of 20 000 litres and a standard deviation of 7200 litres. What is the probability that the demand in any one day is:
(a) greater than 25 000 litres?
(b) greater than 17 000 litres?
(c) between 20 000 and 25 000 litres?
(d) between 30 000 and 35 000 litres?

W 15 A recent large survey found that the average annual salary in the banking industry was £45,121 with a standard deviation of £24,246. If an employee is chosen at random what is the probability that he will earn more than £80,000? If there are 500,000 people working in the banking industry how many of them will earn more than £100,000?

W 16 Suppose that the time taken by a switchboard to answer a call is normally distributed with a mean of 48 seconds and a standard deviation of 10 seconds. What is the probability that a call will be answered within one minute?

W 17 The length of a special type of bolt is normally distributed with a mean diameter of 5.5 mm and a standard deviation of 0.4 mm. Bolts are only acceptable if their diameter is between 4.5 and 6 mm. What proportion of bolts will be accepted?

18 The specification for the length of an engine part is a minimum of 50 mm and a maximum of 55 mm. A batch of parts is produced that is normally distributed with a mean of 54 mm and a standard deviation of 2 mm. Parts cost £10 to make. Those that are too short have to be scrapped; those that are too long are shortened at a further cost of £8.
  (a) Find the percentage of parts that are
   (i) undersize
   (ii) oversize.
  (b) Find the expected cost of producing 1000 usable parts.

19 As an incentive for customers to spend more money on its credit card a bank has decided to award high spending customers with a free gift. However, it doesn't want to give gifts to more than 5% of customers. If the mean spend per customer is £135 with a standard deviation of £55, what balance should the company specify? However, at the end of the first month it was found that 8% of customers qualified for the free gift. What has happened? Assuming that the standard deviation hasn't changed, calculate the new mean spend per customer.

W 20 Crumbly Biscuits produces golden cream biscuits which are sold in notional 300 g packets. The weights of these packets are normally distributed with a mean of 320 g and a standard deviation of 10.4 g.
  (a) What is the probability that if you select a packet at random it will weigh:
   (i) less than 300 g?
   (ii) more than 325 g?
   (iii) between 318 and 325 g?
  (b) Out of a batch of 500 packets, how many would weigh less than 300 g?
  (c) It has been decided to reduce the mean weight to 310 g. What would the standard deviation need to be if no more than 3% of packets must weigh less than 300 g?

21 A company that is considering the launch of a new product estimates that the possible demand for the product, in its first year, will be approximately normally distributed with a mean of 2000 units and a standard deviation of 500 units. What is the probability that the first-year demand will be:
  (a) over 2500 units?
  (b) over 2800 units?
  (c) less than 1600 units?

W 22   A large departmental store has analyzed the monthly amount spent by its credit card customers and found that it is normally distributed with a mean of £100 and a standard deviation of £15. What percentage of people will spend:

(a) over £130?

(b) over £120?

(c) below £70?

(d) between £100 and £130?

(e) between £115 and £130?

What is the minimum amount spent of:

(f) the top 10%?

(g) the top 3% of customers?

23   If IQ scores for a certain test are approximately normally distributed with a mean of 100 and a standard deviation of 15, find the probability of a randomly selected individual scoring:

(a) 115 or more

(b) 130 or more

(c) between 115 and 130

24   The weekly demand for a liquid oil-based product that is marketed by a company is normally distributed with a mean of 2000 gallons and a standard deviation of 500 gallons. How many gallons of the product must the company have in stock at the start of the week to have only a 0.06 probability of running out of stock, assuming that no further supplies of the product are available during the week?

W 25   The weights of articles produced by a machine are normally distributed with a mean of 16 g and a standard deviation of 0.5 g. Only articles that have weights in the range 15.75 g to 16.75 g are acceptable and the remainder must be scrapped.

(a) What percentage of output will be scrapped?

(b) If an average of 10 000 units are produced per week and each scrapped unit costs £7, what will be the average weekly cost of scrapped units?

(c) A new machine can be hired at a cost of £10 000 per week. This would also produce articles with a mean of 16 g, but the standard deviation of the weights would be only 0.2 g. Is it worth hiring the new machine? (Assume that the old machine would have no scrap value.)

W 26   A company has to decide which of two possible new products, A or B, it should launch. A computer risk analysis package suggests that the profit that will result if A is developed is normally distributed with a mean of £15 million and a standard deviation of £9 million. The profit that would be generated by developing product B is also normally distributed, with a mean of £10 million and a standard deviation of £5 million. Which product should the company launch to minimize its chances of incurring a loss?

27   Solve Activity 7.5 using both the Poisson and the normal approximation to the binomial. Comment on the suitability of both approximations.

Assignment

Goodtaste Ltd, a coffee manufacturer, has recently been prosecuted for selling an underweight 100 g jar of coffee. You have been asked to give assistance to the quality control manager who is investigating the problem.

Jars are filled automatically and the filling machine can be preset to any desired weight. For the 100 g jars of coffee a weight of 101 g is set. There is no subsequent checking of the weight of individual jars, although samples are occasionally taken to check for quality. The standard deviation will depend to a certain extent on the mean weight, but for weights between 90 g and 110 g it is virtually constant at 1.5 g.

You have been asked to apply your knowledge of the normal distribution to the problem. In particular you have been told that prosecution only occurs when the product is underweight by more than 2%, so you need to find the probability that such a weight could happen by chance.

(a) Assuming that the mean weight is 101 g, what proportion of jars are:

    (i)   under 100 g in weight?

    (ii) under 98 g in weight?

    (iii) under 97 g in weight?

    (iv) over 100 g?

    (v) within 2 g of the marked weight?

(b) What should the mean weight be set to in order that the probability of a jar weighing less than 98 g is less than 0.1%?

(c) Write a short note to the quality control manager summarizing your results.

Interpreting with confidence: analysis of sample data

Prerequisites In order to fully understand this chapter you should have read through Chapter 3 (*Collecting data: surveys and samples*) and Chapter 7 (*The shape of data: probability distributions*).

Objectives
- To be able to calculate best estimates of the mean and standard deviation of a population
- To be able to calculate confidence intervals for a population mean
- To be able to calculate confidence intervals for a population percentage

Introduction You were introduced to the idea of sampling in Chapter 3, where the problems of recording information about the whole 'population' were discussed and the need for sampling became apparent. Information from a sample is subject to *error*, and the purpose of this chapter is to be able to *quantify* this error. This is achieved by stating the margin of error that accompanies the sample estimate of a given population parameter. Thus it would be possible to calculate the margin of error for opinion polls for example.

Quantitative methods in action: how many road accidents involve personal injury?

This sounds a silly question. Surely this data should be recorded somewhere? The police database called *STATS19* records all accidents reported to the police, but not all accidents are reported to the police and those that are might not be recorded or injuries misdiagnosed. Another source of data comes from hospital admissions (*Hospital Episode Statistics* or HES). Interestingly when serious injuries from these two data sources are compared they show a contrary picture, with the police data showing a reduction over the past 10 years and the hospital data showing an increase (see Figure 8.1)

Another source of data is the *National Travel Survey* (NTS). This survey asks a sample of people if they have suffered an injury as a result of a road accident. The results from this survey are very different from those obtained from STATS19 or HES. In particular STATS19 indicates that 26 000 people were seriously injured in 2007/8 while NTS suggests the true figure is around 220 000, which is a big difference. Of course the

survey data is subject to two main sources of error. The first is sampling error which occurs whenever a random sample is chosen. The second is non-sampling errors and occurs for a number of reasons such as non-response bias or incorrect interpretation of what constitutes a serious injury. Using hospital data and an analysis of the NTS a table of road casualties during 2007/8 was calculated by the Department for Transport (DfT) and is given in Table 8.1

The 95% confidence intervals indicate the possible sampling error and we will show in this chapter how this interval can be calculated. As you can see, the intervals are very wide, reflecting the uncertainty in the central estimates.

Source: DfT (http://www.dft.gov.uk/adobepdf/162469/221412/221549/227755/rrcgb2008articles.pdf); Straight Statistics (www.straightstatistics.org)

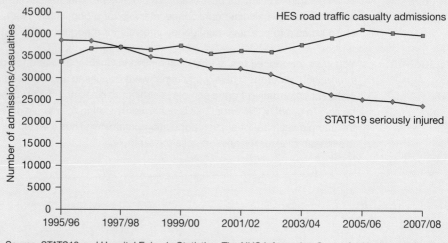

Figure 8.1
Comparison of STATS19 seriously injured casualties with hospital admissions: England, 1995/96 to 2007/08

Source: STATS19 and Hospital Episode Statistics, The NHS Information Centre for Health and Social Care.

Table 8.1 Estimates of non-fatal road casualties using the National Travel Survey data 2007/8 (in thousands rounded to nearest ten thousand)

	Central estimate	Approx. 95% confidence limits	
		Lower	Upper
All road casualties	800	680	920
Adults	720	620	820
Children	80	40	120
Seriously injured	80	40	120

Samples and sampling

Sampling is an extensive and in many cases controversial technique. Whenever there is a general election in the UK the question of sampling accuracy is raised and this was most evident in the 1992 election where the polls incorrectly forecast a Labour majority. However, sampling people's views and intentions is notoriously difficult and even the best sampling plan can fail in these circumstances. Fortunately, when sampling is done by measurement, the results tend to be much more reliable. Sampling in industry and business tends to be of the measurement kind, and it will be this aspect of sampling that will be emphasized here.

Activity 8.1

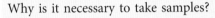

Why is it necessary to take samples?

The alternative to taking samples is to measure or test every member of the population. (The word 'population' in this context doesn't necessarily mean people; it is used to define all the items or things that are of interest, such as all television sets produced by a company in a day.) It is impractical to measure or test every member of the population for the following reasons:

- *It would take too long.* Measuring or testing can be time consuming and it is simply not always feasible to find the necessary time.
- *It is too expensive.* Testing costs money as inspectors need to be employed and goods that are to be tested take up space and cannot be sold until the testing is complete.
- *Some tests are destructive.* Sometimes goods have to be tested to destruction, and if all the goods were tested there would be nothing left to sell!
- *The total population is unknown.* There are occasions when the size of the population is so large as to be considered infinite (without limit). In other cases the size of the population is simply unknown.

Activity 8.2

You work for a company that manufactures plastic containers. The raw material is supplied in granular form and is delivered in 100 kg bags. The granules have to be tested for fire resistance and you are given the job of selecting the material for testing. How would you go about this task?

Since this is likely to be destructive testing, the only option available to you is to test a sample from each consignment. It is important that more than one bag is tested, since one particular bag may not be typical of the rest of the batch. Perhaps this bag happens to be old stock, or is different in some way. Whenever you take samples you must ensure that the samples are selected at *random*; that is, every member of the population must have an equal chance of being selected. (See Chapter 3.) In this case you would need to randomly select a number of bags and then test a small quantity from each of the bags selected. The number of bags chosen and the amount of material tested from each bag would depend on the specific requirements of the test.

Point estimates

The whole purpose of obtaining a sample from a population is to obtain estimates of various population *parameters*, such as the mean, the standard deviation or percentage.

These parameters can also be obtained for the sample, and it is the purpose of this section to show how the population parameters and the sample *statistics* are related. However, before continuing, it is necessary to define the symbols that are to be used throughout this (and the next) chapter.

The convention is to use Greek letters for the population parameters and normal letters for the sample statistics. The various symbols used are given below.

Parameter	Population	Sample
Mean	μ	$\bar{x}$
Standard deviation	σ	s
Percentage	π	P

The one exception to this rule is that the size of the population is usually referred to as N and the sample size as n.

Example 8.1
10 samples of plastic granules were tested for fire resistance and the combustion temperatures (in C) are as follows:

Sample no.	1	2	3	4	5	6	7	8	9	10
Temperature	510	535	498	450	491	505	487	500	501	469

Activity 8.3

What are the mean and standard deviation of the figures in Example 8.1, and what can you conclude about the whole batch?

You should have found the mean to be 494.6C, with a standard deviation of 23.03C. (See Chapter 5 if you are not sure about these calculations.) These figures are *best estimates* of the population mean and standard deviation. At this point it would be worth reminding ourselves of the reason why the variance and standard deviation are calculated using $n - 1$ instead of n.

The population of temperatures will follow some distribution. This distribution will probably have a few extreme values, but most of them will be clustered around the mean. The standard deviation of the population is a measure of spread; and all values, including the extreme ones, contribute to this value. However, if a sample is chosen at random, the sample is most unlikely to include any of the extreme values, so the spread of the sample will be less than that of the population. It has been found that dividing by $n - 1$ instead of n will compensate for this. As the sample gets larger, of course, the difference between the results of dividing by n or $n - 1$ diminishes; when n is greater than 30, the difference is very small.

The bigger the sample size n, the more accurate we would expect the sample mean to become as an estimate for the population mean. But how is information about the sample size taken into consideration in estimating the population parameters? Read on to find out.

Sampling distribution of the mean

Imagine that you took lots and lots of samples and calculated the mean of each. Each mean is an estimate of the population value, and therefore the 'mean of the means' should be an even better estimate. If you then plotted the distribution of the means, what shape would you expect the distribution to be? The answer is that the shape would tend towards the *normal* curve. The degree of agreement with the normal curve depends on two factors:

- the distribution of the population values
- the sample size.

If the population values are normally distributed, the 'sampling distribution of the means' would also be normal. If the population is not normally distributed, the agreement with the normal distribution depends on the sample size; the larger the sample size, the closer the agreement. This very important result is known as the *central limit theorem*.

In addition, the spread of this sampling distribution depends on the sample size; the larger the sample size, the smaller the spread (that is, the standard deviation). The standard deviation of the sampling distribution is called the *standard error*, as it measures the error that could arise in your estimate due to the spread of the sampling distribution. To avoid confusion with the standard error of the sampling distribution of a percentage, which will be discussed later, the standard error of the sampling distribution of the means will be referred to as STEM (the STandard Error of the Mean). Is it necessary to collect many samples in order to calculate the value of STEM? Fortunately not, as there is a relationship between σ and STEM. This relationship is as follows:

$$\text{STEM} = \frac{\sigma}{\sqrt{n}}$$

So the larger the sample size (n), the smaller the value of STEM, which makes sense.

These ideas are illustrated in Figure 8.2. Two sampling distributions are shown: one for a sample size of 4, and one for a sample size of 16. The population distribution (assumed normal in this case) has been superimposed on to the diagram.

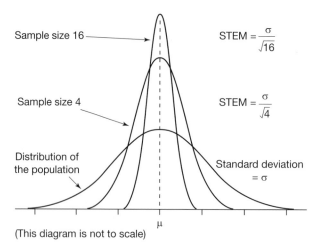

Figure 8.2
Sampling distribution
of the means

(This diagram is not to scale)

You will see that the mean of each sampling distribution is the same and equal to the population value. You would normally only take one sample, and from Figure 8.2 you can see that the mean of a sample can lie anywhere within the relevant sampling distribution, although it is more likely to be near the centre than in the tails. This variation depends on the value of STEM, so the smaller this figure, the more reliable your estimate of the population mean will be.

Activity 8.4

The standard deviation of the population of combustion temperatures for the plastic granules is known to be 23.75C. What is the value of STEM for a sample of size 10 and for a sample of size 40?

The value of STEM when $n = 10$ is:

$$\text{STEM} = \frac{23.75}{\sqrt{10}}$$
$$= \frac{23.75}{3.1623}$$
$$= 7.510$$

That is, 7.510C.

When $n = 40$, STEM becomes:

$$\text{STEM} = \frac{23.75}{\sqrt{40}}$$
$$= \frac{23.75}{6.3246}$$
$$= 3.755$$

That is, 3.755C. Notice that to halve the value of STEM, the sample size was increased fourfold. Calculation of the sample size necessary to give a prescribed level of accuracy will be discussed later.

Confidence intervals for a population mean for large samples

Rather than simply quote the value of STEM, a much better idea of the reliability of your estimate is to specify some limits within which the true mean is expected to lie. These limits are called *confidence limits* or *intervals*.

When calculating confidence intervals it is necessary to decide what level of confidence you wish to use. The most common level is 95%, which means that you are 95% confident that the true mean lies within the calculated limits. Or, put another way, there is a 5% chance that the true mean doesn't lie within these limits. Other limits are frequently used, such as 90%, 99% and 99.9%; but remember that as the confidence level gets closer to 100%, the interval gets larger and larger (at 100% it would be infinitely large).

The *normal distribution* (see Chapter 7, page 163) can be used to calculate these limits when the sample size is large as, according to the central limit theorem, the sampling distribution of the sample mean will be approximately normal. A large sample is generally considered to be 30 or over.

Figure 8.3 illustrates the Z values that enclose 95% of the standard normal distribution. The values ± 1.96 have been found from the normal table (Appendix 1) by noting that the area (or probability) in either tail is 0.025 ($= 0.05/2$).

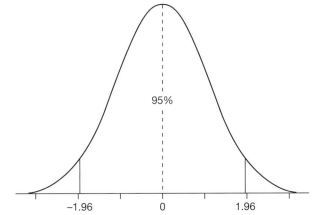

Figure 8.3
95% confidence interval for the standard normal distribution

From your knowledge of the normal distribution, you will know that any normal distribution can be transformed into the standard normal distribution using the formula:

$$Z = \frac{x - \mu}{\sigma}$$

However, this formula is for individual x values. For a sampling distribution of the means, the x needs to be replaced by $\bar{x}$ and σ needs to be replaced by STEM. The formula then becomes:

$$Z = \frac{\bar{x} - \mu}{\text{STEM}}$$

If you rearrange this formula to make μ the subject, you will get:

$$\mu = \bar{x} \pm Z \times \text{STEM}$$

This is the equation you would use to calculate confidence intervals using the normal distribution. For 95% confidence intervals, the Z value is 1.96 and the formula becomes:

$$\mu = \bar{x} \pm 1.96 \times \text{STEM}$$

How would you use this formula? The next example should help you.

Example 8.2

Imagine that you work for the quality control unit of a sugar producer. One of your tasks is to weigh samples of 1 kg bags of sugar, and from a sample of 36 bags you obtain a mean weight of 0.985 kg and a standard deviation of 0.056 kg.

Activity 8.5

What is the 95% confidence interval for the true mean weight of bags of sugar?

From the discussion on point estimates, you know that the best estimate of the true mean is 0.985 kg. That is:

$$\mu = 0.985 \text{ kg}$$

As we have a large sample the population standard deviation can be approximated by the sample standard deviation, and so the value of STEM is:

$$\frac{\sigma}{\sqrt{n}} = \frac{0.056}{\sqrt{36}}$$
$$= 0.00933$$

Therefore the 95% confidence interval for the true mean is:

$$0.985 \pm 1.96 \times 0.00933$$
$$= 0.985 \pm 0.018$$
$$= 0.985 - 0.018 \quad \text{and} \quad 0.985 + 0.018$$
$$= 0.967 \quad \text{and} \quad 1.003 \text{ kg}$$

The 0.967 kg is the *lower* limit and 1.003 kg is the *upper* limit. The ± 0.018 is often called the *half width* of the confidence interval. It is usual to write this confidence interval as:

$$0.967, \quad 1.003 \text{ kg} \quad (\text{or} \quad 0.967 \text{ to } 1.003 \text{ kg})$$

If you took another 36 bags you would get a slightly different sample mean and therefore the confidence interval would be different. It is likely that both these confidence intervals would contain the true mean, but if you took 20 different samples you would expect that *one* of these intervals would *not* contain the true mean. That is, there is a 1 in 20 or 5% chance that your confidence interval would not contain the true mean. This is illustrated in Figure 8.4, where confidence intervals for 5 sample means have been drawn, two of which do not contain the true mean.

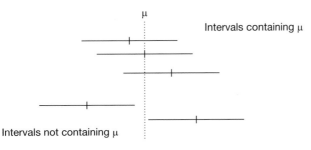

Figure 8.4
Diagram to illustrate
confidence intervals

If you wanted to reduce the chance of the interval not containing the true mean you could calculate 99% confidence intervals. From the normal table, the value of Z for 0.005 (1% divided by 2) is 2.58, so the 99% confidence interval is:

$$0.985 \pm 2.58 \times 0.00933$$
$$= 0.985 \pm 0.024$$
$$= 0.961, 1.009 \, \text{kg}$$

The interval is wider, which was expected. Now there is only a 1% chance that the true mean will be outside these limits. If these limits are too wide, the only way to reduce them (for the same confidence level) is to increase the sample size.

Did you know

There are many graphical ways of representing uncertainty in an estimate. The Bank of England uses a *fan* chart to represent uncertainty in its forecasts. In Figure 8.5 the forecast of CPI is quite uncertain and gets larger with time. The chart is drawn in such a way that there is an expected probability of 10% that the CPI will lie within the darker part of the fan and 90% that it will lie within the complete fan.

See www.bbc.co.uk/news/magazine-12632770 and www.bankofengland.co.uk/publications/inflationreport/ir11feb.pdf.

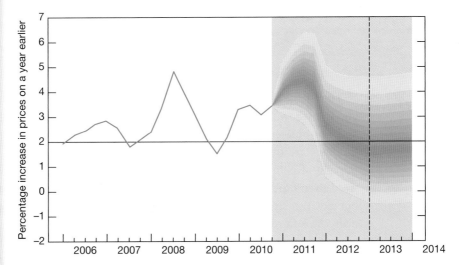

Figure 8.5 CPI inflation projection based on market interest rate expectations and £200 billion asset purchases

Confidence intervals for a population mean for small samples

For large samples we were able to make use of the central limit theorem in our assumption that the sampling distribution of the sample mean will be normal no matter what the shape of the distribution of the population. We were also justified in using the sample standard deviation in place of the population standard deviation in the calculation of STEM. However, for small samples neither of these assumptions holds, so even if we assume that the population is normal we have a problem with the standard deviation. The reason for this is that the uncertainty generated by estimating σ decreases the reliability of the confidence interval. To overcome this problem a different distribution is used, called the '*t-distribution*'. This distribution is symmetrical like the normal, but it is flatter. This 'flatness' increases the percentage of the distribution in the 'tails' and this means that the confidence interval, for the same confidence level, is wider. The amount of 'flatness' decreases with increase in n, the sample size. When n is 50 there is virtually no difference between the two distributions, and even for a sample size of 30 the difference is quite small.

Figure 8.6 shows the *t*-distribution for a sample size of 6, together with the normal distribution for comparison.

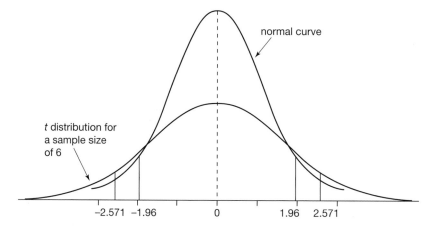

Figure 8.6
Comparison of the normal and *t*-distributions

(graph labels: normal curve; *t* distribution for a sample size of 6; −2.571 −1.96   0   1.96   2.571)

The *t*-table is given in Appendix 1. If you compare this table with the normal table, you will see two important differences. First, the numbers within the table are *t*-values and not probabilities; second, the numbers in the first column are different. These numbers are the *degrees of freedom* (ν) of the sample. Degrees of freedom can be thought of as the 'freedom' that you have in choosing the values of the sample. If you were given the mean of the sample of 6 values, you would be free to choose 5 of the 6 but not the sixth one. Therefore there are 5 degrees of freedom. The number of degrees of freedom for a single sample of size n is $n - 1$. For a very large sample (shown as ∞ in the table) the t and Z distributions are exactly the same. Since the *t*-distribution is a little easier to use, you might prefer to use this table when you want the Z value of one of the 'standard' probabilities. In the table supplied in this book these 'standard' probabilities are 0.2, 0.1, 0.05, 0.025, 0.01, 0.005, 0.001 and 0.0001.

To use this table you would first decide on the probability level. For a 95% confidence interval you would choose the 0.025 level, since this represents 2.5% in each tail. For a sample size of 6, the degrees of freedom is 5, so the t-value for 5 degrees of freedom at 95% confidence level is 2.571. This value has been shown in Figure 8.6. (Remember that the t-distribution is symmetrical about the mean of zero, so the equivalent value in the left hand side of the distribution is -2.571.)

The formula for calculating confidence intervals using this distribution is the same as when the normal distribution was used, except that Z is replaced by t, and is therefore:

$$\mu = \bar{x} \pm t \times \text{STEM}$$

Activity 8.6

In Activity 8.3 you calculated the mean and standard deviation of the combustion temperatures of a sample of size 10 to be 494.6C and 23.03C respectively. Calculate the 95% confidence intervals for the true mean combustion temperature of the entire batch.

The best estimate of σ is 23.03C, so the value of STEM is:

$$\frac{23.03}{\sqrt{10}} = 7.283$$

To find the 95% confidence interval for the true mean, you would use the t-table in Appendix 1 to find the appropriate value of t. The value of t for 9 degrees of freedom, with a probability of 0.025, is 2.262. Substituting this value into the equation for μ gives you:

$$494.6 \pm 2.262 \times 7.283$$
$$= 494.6 \pm 16.5$$
$$= 478.1, \quad 511.1 \, \text{degC}$$

So the true mean combustion temperature of the whole consignment lies between 478.1C and 511.1C at the 95% level of confidence.

Confidence interval of a percentage

Percentages occur quite frequently in the analysis of survey results; for example, the percentage of people who like a particular product, or the percentage of students over the age of 25. Provided n is large and the percentage is not too small or too large, the sampling distribution of a percentage can be approximated by the normal distribution.

The standard error of the sampling distribution of percentages (STEP) is:

$$\text{STEP} = \sqrt{\frac{P(100 - P)}{n}}$$

where P is the sample percentage.

The calculation of a confidence interval for a percentage is similar to that of the mean, that is:

$$\pi = P \pm Z \times \text{STEP}$$

Activity 8.7

A survey among 250 students revealed that 147 were female. What is the 95% confidence interval for the true percentage of female students?

The value of P is $\dfrac{147}{250} \times 100 = 58.8\%$

That is, the survey suggested that 58.8% of the student population is female. The value of STEP for this problem is:

$$\sqrt{\frac{58.8 \times (100 - 58.8)}{250}}$$

$$= 3.113$$

The value of Z for 95% confidence is 1.96, so the confidence interval becomes:

$$58.8 \pm 1.96 \times 3.113$$

$$= 58.8 \pm 6.1$$

$$= 52.7, 64.9$$

That is, the true percentage lies somewhere between 52.7% and 64.9%.

Did you know

People generally find it difficult to give estimates of how long a job will take or the time taken to drive to an unfamiliar destination. Two behavioural scientists, Tversky and Kahneman (1974), performed experiments on individuals in which they were first given a random number and then asked to estimate the values for various quantities, such as the percentage of African nations that were members of the United Nations. Surprisingly the subjects gave values close to their random number. This bias is called the *anchoring and adjustment heuristic* as people tend to anchor to a number from some similar situation and then fail to make sufficient adjustment for the new situation.

Source: http://lesswrong.com/lw/j7/anchoring_and_adjustment/

Calculation of sample size

Since the value of both STEM and STEP depend on the sample size, the width of the confidence interval for the same confidence level can be reduced by increasing the value of n. For the sugar example (Activity 8.5) the half width of the interval – that is, the difference between the lower or upper limit and the sample mean – is 0.018 kg for a confidence level of 95%. This was obtained by multiplying STEM by 1.96; that is:

Half width of confidence interval $= 1.96 \times$ STEM

$$= 1.96 \times \frac{\sigma}{\sqrt{n}}$$

If you wanted to reduce this half width to, say, 0.015 kg, then you would need to calculate the value of n required to achieve this reduction. That is:

$$1.96 \times \frac{0.056}{\sqrt{n}} = 0.015$$

since $\sigma = 0.056$ (see Example 8.2).

Rearranging this equation gives:

$$\sqrt{n} = \frac{1.96 \times 0.056}{0.015}$$
$$= 7.3173$$

so $n = 53.5$.

So a sample size of about 54 would be required to achieve an accuracy of ± 0.015 kg.

Activity 8.8

What sample size would be required to reduce the half width for the percentage of female students from 6.1% to 1%?

The calculation is similar to that for the mean. That is:

$$1.96 \times \text{STEP} = 1.0$$

The value of P is 58.8%, so:

$$1.96 \times \sqrt{\frac{58.8 \times (100 - 58.8)}{n}} = 1.0$$

Dividing both sides by 1.96 and squaring gives:

$$\frac{58.8 \times 41.2}{n} = 0.2603$$

Therefore:

$$n = \frac{58.8 \times 41.2}{0.2603}$$
$$= 9306.8$$

That is, a sample of about 9000 students would need to be selected to ensure this level of accuracy!

Finite populations

The assumption that has implicitly been made in this chapter is that the population is infinitely large, or at least much larger than the sample. The reason for this is that all sampling is done *without* replacement. That is, you would not measure or test the same person or item twice. This has no effect when the population is large, but for small populations, the probability that an item will be selected will change as soon as one item has been selected. (See Chapter 6.) To overcome this problem, the standard error (either STEM or STEP) is modified. This is achieved by multiplying the value by the *Finite Population Correction Factor*, which is:

$$\sqrt{\frac{(N - n)}{(N - 1)}}$$

where N is the size of the population.

Activity 8.9

In the sugar example (Example 8.2) STEM was 0.00933. What is the value of STEM if the size of the population is 100?

The value of STEM is multiplied by the correction factor, that is:

$$0.00933 \times \sqrt{\frac{(100 - 36)}{(100 - 1)}}$$

$$= 0.00933 \times 0.8040$$

$$= 0.00750$$

This is a *reduction*. (Since STEM is reduced, confidence intervals will also be reduced.)

As N gets larger relative to n, the correction factor approaches 1 and can therefore be ignored. For example, if you try $N = 10\,000$ and $n = 10$, you should get a value of 0.9995.

Reflection

> As a society we are always hungry for information. Whether it is a business that wants to find out how consumers are rating its product, or a newspaper that wants to find out how we are going to vote, the key issue is how to obtain *reliable* information. Although most serious surveys are conducted scientifically, any information obtained from a sample is subject to sampling error. Being able to quantify this error is one of the most important contributions of statistics.
>
> Even the most carefully conducted survey can give erroneous results, however. The classic case of this was during the General Election in 1992 in the UK, when the five main opinion polls predicted a Labour lead of 0.8%. The exit polls conducted by the BBC and ITV suggested a Conservative lead of 4%, but when the actual result was declared the Conservatives won by 7.5%. The error in the opinion polls was more than 8% – far higher

than the expected 2% or 3% margin of error. An enquiry afterwards put the error down to three main factors: a late swing, wrong quotas, and a high refusal rate (polled voters who declined to say how they would vote). Later investigation showed that Conservative voters were more likely to give a 'don't know' than Labour voters. Various methods have been used since to compensate for this problem, including the assumption that 60% of those who say that they don't know will in fact vote for the same party that they voted for in the previous election. (See www.alba.org.uk/polls)

....

Key points

- A sample can be used to provide estimates of population parameters such as the mean, proportion and standard deviation.
- Every estimate of these parameters will have a sampling error associated with them. We can reduce this error by taking a larger sample but we can never eliminate the error entirely.
- The central limit theorem allows us to calculate this error because we can assume that the sample mean (or proportion) comes from a normal distribution.
- We normally express this error in the form of a confidence interval. The confidence is expressed in percentages and the common values are 95% and 99%.
- We can calculate the sample size required to give a specific minimum error.
- For small samples we use the t-distribution because for the same confidence level we get a slightly wider interval.
- We usually assume an infinitely large population but when this is not true we can make a simple adjustment.

Further reading

All statistical texts and many quantitative methods texts will have a chapter on confidence intervals. Texts aimed at the business student will treat the material in a similar way to this text while those texts aimed at maths or stats students will be much more mathematical and probably beyond the ability of most business students. Morris (2008) is very descriptive and uses few equations apart for STEM and STEP.

Web links Ⓦ

Answers to selected questions can be found in Appendix 2. Answers to the other questions can be found on the companion website for this book.

Practice questions

Ⓦ 1 A university contains 16 000 students and it is required to find out how many students have part-time jobs. 50 students are selected at random and of these, 20 admitted to working during term time. What is the value of:
   (a) the size of the population?
   (b) the sample size?
   (c) the sample percentage?
   (d) the estimate of the true percentage?
   (e) the 95% confidence interval of the true percentage?

2 A sample of six packets of tea is selected from a production line. The contents of these packets are 9.4, 9.1, 10.2, 8.9, 10.9 and 9.2 g respectively. Obtain the 95% confidence interval estimate of the mean net weight of a packet, if the weights are normally distributed.

W **3** A random sample of 100 adult females from the population of a large town has a mean height of 169.5 cm with a standard deviation of 2.6 cm. Construct a 95% confidence interval for the mean height of all adult females in the town.

4 A sample of 60 people was asked if they thought that if children watched video 'nasties' they were more likely to commit a crime. Out of the sample, 45 thought that they would. Calculate the 95% confidence interval for the true percentage.

W **5** The weight of each of 10 specimens of carbon paper was found to be (in grams):
7.4, 8.3, 10.9, 6.9, 7.9, 8.2, 8.6, 9.1, 9.9, 10.0
Given that the weights are normally distributed, construct (a) 95% and (b) 99% confidence intervals for the true mean of the population weights.

6 A credit card company wants to determine the mean income of its card holders. A random sample of 225 card holders was drawn and the sample average income was £16 450 with a standard deviation of £3675.
(a) Construct a 99% confidence interval for the true mean income.
(b) Management decided that the confidence interval in (a) was too large to be useful. In particular, the management wanted to estimate the mean income to within £200, with a confidence level of 99%. How large a sample should be selected?

W **7** From a population of 200, a sample of 40 people were asked for their views on capital punishment. 12 people thought that hanging should be imposed for certain crimes. Estimate the 95% confidence interval for the true percentage.

8 A company involved in a market research survey takes a random sample of 800 orders which were delivered in a given month. Of these orders, 320 went to customers aged under 21. Estimate the percentage of all the company's orders which went to this age group during the month in question, with 95% confidence.

W **9** In a sample of 200 of a company's business customers, 160 say that they are likely to make a further purchase within the next 12 months. Estimate the percentage of all the company's customers who will make a further purchase within the next year with 95% confidence.

10 An insurance company is concerned about the size of claims being made by its policy holders. A random sample of 400 claims had a mean value of £230 and a standard deviation of £42.
Estimate the mean size of all claims received by the company:
(a) with 95% confidence
(b) with 99% confidence

11 A quality control inspector wishes to estimate the mean weight of bags of cement leaving a production line on a particular day to within 2 g at the 95% level of confidence. It is known that the standard deviation of the weights remains fairly constant at 60 g. How large a sample should the inspector take?

W **12** A company wants to estimate, with 95% confidence, the percentage of people in a town who have seen its press advertisements. The company would like its estimate to have a margin of error of $\pm 4\%$. How large a sample of people will they need to take if:

(a) a preliminary estimate suggests that the true percentage is about 10%?

(b) no preliminary estimate is available?

W **13** A survey of 16 houses in a particular district found the mean value to be £129 500 with a standard deviation of £55 524.

(a) Give a 95% confidence interval for the average value of all properties in the district.

(b) If it is required to halve the confidence interval for the same confidence level, what sample size would be required?

(c) If it is known that there are only 200 houses in the district how will this affect your answer to part (a)?

W **14** A survey of 200 people found that 89 were in favour of joining the Euro currency. Find the 95% confidence interval for the percentage of all people interested in joining the Euro.

....

Assignment

The latest internal accounts for an off-licence chain showed that the annual sales of wines and spirits had fallen by more than 30%. This fall has been blamed on the relaxation of the limits of duty free goods that can be brought into Britain from EU countries from 1993.

In order to test this theory it was decided to ask a random sample of shoppers if they intend to travel to France this year. Of the 75 shoppers questioned, 27 were certain to go to France at least once. It was also decided to ask a random sample of 60 returning holiday makers how much they had spent on duty free alcohol. Of these 60, 8 refused to answer, and for the remaining 52 people the average spend was found to be £37.26, with a standard deviation of £35.97.

(a) What is the percentage of shoppers who said they were definitely making at least one trip to France this year?

(b) Calculate the 95% confidence interval for the true percentage of shoppers who intend to travel to France this year. Interpret this interval.

(c) Calculate the 95% confidence interval for the true mean amount spent on duty free alcohol for all holiday makers returning from France.

(d) Calculate the number of shoppers to be questioned so that the half width of the confidence interval for the percentage of shoppers who intend to travel to France is no more than 3%.

(e) The half width of the confidence interval for the average spend on duty free alcohol must be reduced to £5. How many holiday makers need to be sampled?

(f) What reservations (if any) do you have about this kind of survey?

Checking ideas: testing a hypothesis

Prerequisites To complete this chapter successfully you should have read through Chapter 8 (*Interpreting with confidence: analysis of sample data*)

Objectives
- ○ To understand the ideas behind hypothesis testing
- ○ To know how to perform tests of hypothesis on the mean of a population
- ○ To know how to perform tests of hypothesis on a percentage
- ○ To know how to perform a 'goodness-of-fit' test
- ○ To be able to apply the chi-square test to categorical data
- ○ To know how to use Excel and SPSS to perform tests of hypothesis

Introduction In Chapter 8 you saw how to analyze a sample so that estimates of some population parameters, such as the mean or percentage, could be obtained. In this chapter the emphasis is slightly different in that you are told the value of the population parameter and then use the sample to confirm or disprove this figure. For example, you may want to determine the effect on fuel consumption of a particular make of car by modification to the carburation system, or you may want to determine if a trade union can be sure that, if a ballot was called, the majority of the membership would vote for strike action. In both these examples a *hypothesis* would be made concerning the population and this hypothesis tested using the sample data.

Quantitative methods in action: toxic waste and birth defects

A little over 60 years ago Corby was just another small village in the county of Northamptonshire but once the ironstone deposits were found the village soon became a large town and by the 1930s it was a major steel making centre. By the 1960s Corby had become one of the most industrialized areas of the Midlands covering 680 acres, with four blast furnaces, two coke oven complexes and other facilities. However by the 1980s steel-making became unprofitable as a result of cheap imports from the Far East and the plant was closed down by the owners, British Steel.

During its 50 year life the land on which the steel plant was based had been contaminated with waste material, much of it toxic. Following its closure Corby Borough Council bought the site and spent the next 15 years redeveloping it as part of its regeneration programme. This involved transporting thousands of tons of contaminated waste material in open lorries through the town. In subsequent years a number of children were born with deformities. The families of the affected children brought an action against Corby Borough Council for compensation. Their claim was that the number of birth deformities was three times that of children born in surrounding areas and eight to ten times higher than a town the size of Corby should expect.

Following the High Court case bought in 2005, the judge (The Hon Mr Justice Akenhead) ruled that there was a 'statistically significant' cluster of birth defects between 1989 and 1999. His ruling was based on the incidence of upper-limb deformities of babies born in Corby compared to the rest of the former Kettering Health Authority (KHA). There were 14 upper limb defects in the whole of KHA between 1989 and 1999 from 35 627 births and 6 of these were in Corby from 7736 births. One expert calculated that the one sided p-value (the probability of getting such a high number by chance alone) was 0.033. The reason the judge gave for using a one sided p-value was that they were only interested in excess risk. If a two sided test had been used the result wouldn't have been significant.

Other experts have thought that the judgement was flawed. They would want to calculate the probability of getting such an extreme result in Corby or another area. This could have been done by splitting KHA into 4 smaller areas of similar size to Corby. They have shown by computer simulation that there is a 22% chance of getting an apparent cluster of at least 6 birth defects by chance. (See http://www.straightstatistics.org/article/question-marks-over-corby-judgement)

Source: http://www.bailii.org/ew/cases/EWHC/TCC/2009/1944.html

The purpose of hypothesis testing

Activity 9.1

The light bulbs manufactured by Bright Lights are designed to last for 1000 hours on average. How can the company be sure that the average lifetime of a large batch of bulbs really is 1000 hours?

The mean lifetime could be found by testing a sample of bulbs and constructing a confidence interval within which the true mean is likely to lie. If the interval does contain 1000 hours, then you could assume that the true mean really is 1000 hours.

Alternatively, you could construct a confidence interval for the supposed true mean of 1000 hours and see if the sample mean was contained within this interval.

However, there is a third approach. This approach makes the *hypothesis* that any departure from the supposedly true mean by the sample mean is simply due to chance effects. It is then a matter of calculating the probability that this sample result could have occurred by chance. This is the general idea of hypothesis testing – it assumes that the hypothesis is true and then tries to disprove it. This hypothesis is known as the *null* hypothesis. If the null hypothesis is rejected, an *alternative* hypothesis is accepted. The null hypothesis is called H_0 and the alternative hypothesis H_1.

The null hypothesis is tested at a particular *significance level*. This level relates to the area (or probability) in the tail of the distribution being used for the test. This area is called the *critical region*, and if the *test statistic* lies in the critical region, you would infer that the result is unlikely to have occurred by chance. You would then reject the null hypothesis. For example, if the 5% level of significance was used and the null hypothesis was rejected, you would say that H_0 had been rejected at the 5% (or the 0.05) significance level, and the result was *significant*.

These ideas apply to all types of hypothesis tests. The precise form of each hypothesis and the calculations necessary to test H_0 depend on the test being carried out. There are very many tests that can be applied to samples. The most important group are *parametric* tests. These tests compare sample statistics with the population parameters and make assumptions about the form of the sampling distribution. *Non-parametric* (or distribution-free) tests are more general and do not insist on such stringent conditions. They can also be used where the data can only be ordered (ordinal data) rather than measured. However, non-parametric tests are less discriminating; that is, the results tend to be less reliable.

Whatever the test, the steps for checking the hypothesis are the same. This is:

Step 1 Set up the null and alternative hypotheses and determine (usually from tables) the boundaries of the critical region. These boundaries are called the *critical values*.

Step 2 Calculate the test statistic.

Step 3 Decide whether to accept or reject H_0.

Did you know

A placebo is an inert substance that should not cause a patient's condition to change. A placebo was first used in a medicinal context in the 18th century. Nowadays all trials of drugs use a placebo as a control mechanism. A trial of a new drug needs to show that it performs significantly better than either no treatment or by a patient taking a placebo. However there have been several studies that show the *placebo effect* can have a beneficial effect on many conditions, particularly if patients are told that they will improve. This is thought to be the result of dopamine release in the brain (see http://www.sciencemag.org/content/293/5532/1164.short).

Large sample test for a population mean

The normal distribution can be used to solve problems involving means if the population is normal *and* the standard deviation of the population (σ) is known. If normality cannot be assumed then a large sample size will ensure that the sampling distribution of the means is approximately normal.

However, as in the calculation of confidence intervals (see Chapter 8) σ may be unknown and has to be estimated from the sample. In these cases the normal distribution can be used as an approximation, provided the sample size is large.

The formula for Z is also the same as that used in the derivation of the formula for confidence intervals. That is:

$$Z = \frac{\bar{x} - \mu}{\text{STEM}}$$

where $\bar{x}$ is the mean of the sample, μ is the mean of the population, and STEM is the standard error of the sampling distribution of the means, and is given by:

$$\text{STEM} = \frac{\sigma}{\sqrt{n}}$$

where n is the sample size.

Activity 9.2

The distribution of the lifetime of all bulbs made by Bright Lights is normal, and the standard deviation of the population is known to be 120 hours. A sample of 30 bulbs were tested and the mean lifetime was found to be 1100 hours. Is this consistent, at the 5% level of significance, with the supposed true mean of 1000 hours?

Step 1

Set up H_0 and H_1 and decide on the critical values.

The null hypothesis in this case is that the true mean lifetime is 1000 hours. The alternative hypothesis can be one of three statements. These are:

The true mean is *not* equal to 1000 hours

or   The true mean is greater than 1000 hours

or   The true mean is less than 1000 hours

Using symbols, the null and alternative hypotheses become:

$$H_0 : \mu = 1000 \text{ hours} \quad H_1 : \mu \neq 1000 \text{ hours}$$
$$or \quad H_1 : \mu > 1000 \text{ hours}$$
$$or \quad H_1 : \mu < 1000 \text{ hours}$$

(The ':' is the mathematical shorthand for 'such that')

The first form of the alternative hypothesis is used for a *two tailed* (or a two sided) test and the other two forms are used for *one tailed* tests. The two tailed test is used when you have no reason to suppose that the true mean could be either greater than or less than the value given by the null hypothesis. The one tailed test is used when you are more interested in one side of the supposed mean than the other. The golden rule when carrying out hypothesis tests is that H_0 and H_1 are set up *before* the test is carried out (and preferably before the data is collected). You may find the diagrams in Figure 9.1 and Figure 9.2 helpful in clarifying the situation.

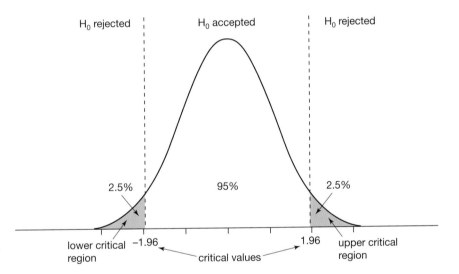

Figure 9.1
Two tailed test at the
5% significance level

In Figure 9.1 the critical values of ± 1.96 mark the boundaries of the two critical regions at the 5% significance level. These values are found from the normal table in Appendix 1. If the test statistic (Z) is either greater than the right hand critical value or less than the left hand value, then H_0 is rejected. If Z lies in between the two critical values then H_0 is accepted – *or you should really say that you do not have sufficient information to reject H_0.*

The left hand diagram of Figure 9.2 illustrates the case where the alternative hypothesis is of the 'less than' kind. There is only one critical region in this case and you would reject H_0 if Z was *less* than the critical value of -1.645. The reason that the critical value is different than for the two tailed case is that the area in the one tail is now the full amount (5% in this example) and not half as it was before. The right hand diagram is for the 'greater than' case, and the same reasoning applies here as in the left hand diagram. That is, H_0 would be rejected if Z was *greater* than 1.645.

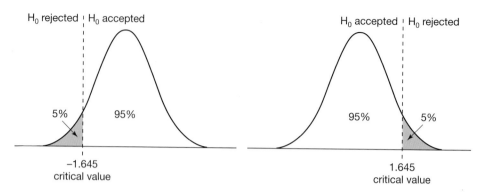

Figure 9.2
One tailed test at the
5% significance level

The light bulb example would be a two tailed test because there is nothing in the wording of the problem that suggests that you are more interested in one side of the mean. So the null and alternative hypotheses for this example are:

$$H_0 : \mu = 1000 \text{ hours} \qquad H_1 : \mu \neq 1000 \text{ hours}$$

and the critical values are ± 1.96.

Step 2

Calculate the test statistic.

In this problem, $n = 30$, $\mu = 1000$, $\sigma = 120$, and $\bar{x} = 1100$. Therefore

$$\text{STEM} = \frac{\sigma}{\sqrt{n}} = \frac{120}{\sqrt{30}}$$
$$= 21.9089$$

and:

$$Z = \frac{\bar{x} - \mu}{\text{STEM}}$$
$$= \frac{1100 - 1000}{21.9089}$$
$$= \frac{100}{21.9089}$$
$$= 4.56$$

This is your test statistic.

Step 3

Decide whether to accept or reject H_0.

It is now necessary to decide if this value of Z could have happened by chance, or if it is indicative of a change in the population mean.

Since Z (4.56) is greater than 1.96 and is therefore in the critical region, you can reject H_0 at the 5% level of significance. This is shown clearly in Figure 9.3, where the 0.1% significance level ($Z = 3.3$) has also been added. The result is significant, and you would conclude that there has almost certainly been a change in the mean lifetime of light bulbs.

The following activity illustrates the use of one tailed tests.

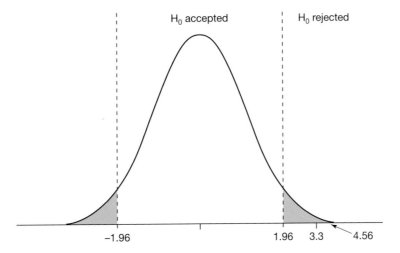

Figure 9.3
Diagram for
Activity 9.2

Activity 9.3

The mean fuel consumption for a particular make of car is known to be 33 mpg with a standard deviation of 5.7 mpg. A modification to this car has been made that should reduce fuel consumption. 35 cars are fitted with this device and their fuel consumption is recorded over 12 months. At the end of this period the mean fuel consumption of the 35 cars is found to be 34.8 mpg. Is there any evidence, at the 5% level of significance, that the fuel consumption has been improved?

This is a one tailed test since it is hoped that the modification will improve the fuel consumption – there is nothing to suggest that fuel consumption will be made worse. The Z-test can be used without assuming normality because the sample is 'large' (over 30).

The null and alternative hypotheses for this problem are:

$$H_0 : \mu = 33 \text{ mpg} \qquad H_1 : \mu > 33 \text{ mpg}$$

and the critical value of Z at the 5% significance level is 1.645.

$$\sigma = 5.7 \text{ mpg}, \ \bar{x} = 34.8 \text{ and } n = 35$$

Therefore:
$$\text{STEM} = \frac{5.7}{\sqrt{35}}$$
$$= 0.9635$$

and the test statistic is:
$$Z = \frac{34.8 - 33.0}{0.9635}$$
$$= 1.868$$

Since 1.868 is greater than the critical value of 1.645, you would reject the null hypothesis. That is, there is a *significant* difference between the mean fuel consumption before and after the modification has been fitted. You would conclude that the modification appears to have improved the fuel consumption of this particular make of car.

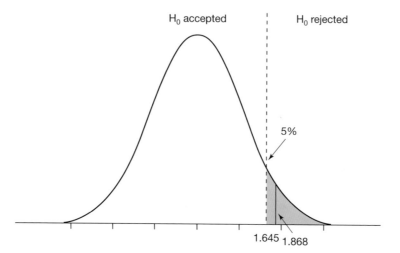

Figure 9.4
Diagram for
Activity 9.3

It is important to draw a diagram when carrying out hypothesis tests. The diagram for this problem is shown in Figure 9.4.

This diagram clearly shows that the test statistic is in the critical region, and H_0 should therefore be rejected. You may have noticed that H_0 would *not* have been rejected if the test had been two tailed. (Compare this diagram with Figure 9.1.) This is why it is so important to ensure that you are justified in using a one tailed test, as the chance of rejecting H_0 is greater in the one tailed case.

Small sample test for a population mean

As in the case of confidence intervals, it is necessary to assume that the population is normal and to use the t-distribution instead of the normal distribution. The formula for the t-statistic is:

$$t = \frac{\bar{x} - \mu}{\text{STEM}}$$

which is identical to the expression for Z. The formula for STEM is also the same, except that the standard deviation used is the estimate obtained from the sample. That is:

$$\text{STEM} = \frac{\sigma}{\sqrt{n}}$$

The same considerations apply concerning the critical region, except that the critical value is obtained from the t-distribution on $n - 1$ degrees of freedom (Appendix 1). For example, the critical value on 7 degrees of freedom at the 5% significance level is ± 2.365 for a two tailed test, and ± 1.895 for a one tailed test.

The following activity may help you understand the differences between the Z- and t-tests.

Activity 9.4

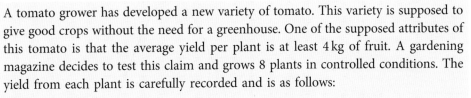

A tomato grower has developed a new variety of tomato. This variety is supposed to give good crops without the need for a greenhouse. One of the supposed attributes of this tomato is that the average yield per plant is at least 4 kg of fruit. A gardening magazine decides to test this claim and grows 8 plants in controlled conditions. The yield from each plant is carefully recorded and is as follows:

Plant	1	2	3	4	5	6	7	8
Yield	3.6	4.2	3.3	2.5	4.8	2.75	4.2	4.6

Does this data support the grower's claim at the 5% level of significance? (It can be assumed that the yield per plant is normally distributed.)

This is a one tailed test, since the claim is that the yield should be *at least* 4 kg. The null and alternative hypotheses are therefore:

$$H_0 : \mu = 4\,kg \qquad H_1 : \mu < 4\,kg$$

(The alternative hypothesis is less than 4 kg because the gardening magazine is attempting to disprove the claim.)

The critical value on 7 degrees of freedom at a significance level of 5% for a one tailed test is -1.895. (This figure was obtained from the *t*-table in Appendix 1).

Estimates of the mean and standard deviation of the yield from this sample are:

$$\bar{x} = 3.74 \qquad \sigma = 0.8466$$

$$\text{and} \qquad STEM = \frac{0.8466}{\sqrt{8}}$$

$$= 0.2993$$

The test statistic is therefore:

$$t = \frac{3.74 - 4}{0.2993}$$

$$= -0.869$$

Since -0.869 is *greater* than -1.895, you cannot reject H_0. (You may find it easier to ignore the negative signs and just compare 0.869 with 1.895, in which case 0.869 is *less* than 1.895.) Alternatively, you could draw a diagram as shown in Figure 9.5.

This diagram confirms that the test statistic is not in the critical region, and therefore it is not possible to reject H_0. That is, it hasn't been possible to disprove the grower's claim.

NOTE: In practice the *experimental design* for this example would be a little more involved than has been suggested here.

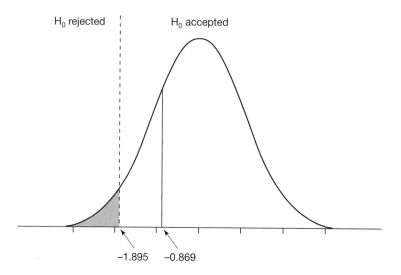

Figure 9.5
Diagram for
Activity 9.4

The *Z*-test for a population percentage

Testing a sample percentage against some expected or hypothesized value (π) is another important test. The test given here is based on the assumption that n is large and π is not too large or too small.

The standard error of the sampling distribution of a percentage (STEP) was given in Chapter 8 as:

$$\sqrt{\frac{P(100 - P)}{n}}$$

where P is the sample percentage.

However, for hypothesis testing it is the population parameter, π, that must be used. With this substitution, the equation for STEP becomes:

$$\text{STEP} = \sqrt{\frac{\pi(100 - \pi)}{n}}$$

The Z statistic is similar to that used for the test on a mean and is:

$$Z = \frac{P - \pi}{\text{STEP}}$$

The following activity illustrates how the test would be carried out.

Activity 9.5

A trade union is considering strike action and intends to ballot its large membership on the issue. In order to gauge the likely result of the ballot, a survey was conducted among a random sample of members. Of the 60 people surveyed, 36 were in favour of a strike. Would the ballot give the required simple majority for a strike?

For a strike to be called, at least 50% of the membership must agree. Anything less would not be good enough. The null and alternative hypotheses should therefore be:

$$H_0 : \pi = 50\% \qquad H_1 : \pi > 50\%$$

The cut-off point for the decision is 50% and the test will determine whether the sample percentage (P) of $\dfrac{36}{60} \times 100 = 60\%$ is significantly *greater* than 50%.

The critical value for a one tailed test at the 5% level is 1.645. So:

$$STEP = \sqrt{\dfrac{50 \times (100 - 50)}{60}}$$
$$= 6.455$$

and the test statistic is:

$$Z = \dfrac{60 - 50}{6.455}$$
$$= 1.549$$

Since 1.549 is less than 1.645, H_0 cannot be rejected. That is, it appears that there may not be a majority for strike action. However, the critical value and test statistic are quite close, and therefore the result is hardly conclusive. (Don't forget that the survey result is only a 'snapshot' of people's opinion at one instant in time. Some people may not have been entirely honest with their answers and others may change their opinion before the ballot.)

Figure 9.6 confirms that the test statistic is just inside the acceptance region.

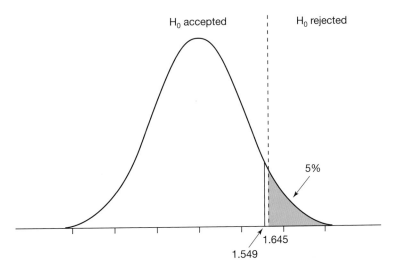

Figure 9.6
Diagram for
Activity 9.5

Hypothesis tests involving two population means

The tests we have looked at so far are for a single sample. In many situations we may have collected two samples and we want to test to see if the two population means are the same. As in the single sample case we have different tests for large and small samples. We also have another factor to consider: are the samples independent of each other or not? Samples that are independent mean that the measurements of one sample are not influenced by the second sample. In some situations, once we have (randomly) chosen the members of the first sample the members of the second sample will not be independent. For example, you might want to compare the reading ability of children before and after following a reading programme. The reading scores of a group of children represent the first sample and the second sample is represented by the reading scores of the *same* children at the end of the reading programme. The second sample is therefore related to the first sample by the identity of the child. There are good reasons why you should use this *paired* approach but it requires a test that doesn't demand independence. The mathematics involved in applying all these tests are more complicated than for the single sample case and the use of statistical software such as SPSS is recommended. However, although SPSS is better, it is also possible to use Excel to carry out some of the tests.

Large sample tests for two independent population means

We normally wish to set up the null hypothesis that the difference in the means of the two populations will be zero; that is:

$$H_0 : \mu_1 - \mu_2 = 0$$

The alternative hypothesis can be either one or two tailed. That is:

$$H_1 : \mu_1 - \mu_2 \neq 0 \text{ for a two sided test, and}$$
$$H_1 : \mu_1 > \mu_2 \text{ or } \mu_1 < \mu_2 \text{ for a one sided test.}$$

For a large sample we can assume that the difference between the means of the two sampling distributions is normally distributed with a mean equal to the difference of the population means and a standard error of:

$$\sigma_{(\bar{x}_1 - \bar{x}_2)} = \sqrt{\left(\frac{\sigma_1^2}{n_1} + \frac{\sigma_2^2}{n_2} \right)}$$

As in the single sample case, the population standard deviations are required, but provided that each sample size (n_1 and n_2) is at least 30 we can use the estimate given by the samples as an approximation.

The test statistic will be

$$Z = \frac{(\bar{x}_1 - \bar{x}_2) - (\mu_1 - \mu_2)}{\sigma_{(\bar{x}_1 - \bar{x}_2)}}$$

Activity 9.6

A high street store was interested in discovering whether credit card customers spent more or less than cash customers. A random sample of 50 credit card customers were found to have spent £55.30 on average with a standard deviation of £18.45, while a random sample of 40 cash customers were found to have spent £52.75 on average with a standard deviation of £17.22. Is there any evidence at the 5% significance level that there is any difference between the mean amounts spent by the two types of customers?

This is a two tailed test and the null and alternative hypotheses will be:

$$H_0 : \mu_1 - \mu_2 = 0 \qquad H_1 : \mu_1 - \mu_2 \neq 0$$

The standard error will be
$$\sqrt{\left(\frac{18.45^2}{50} + \frac{17.22^2}{40}\right)} = 3.7711$$

and the test statistic will be
$$\frac{(55.30 - 52.75) - 0}{3.7711} = 0.676$$

Since this is less than 1.96 we cannot reject H_0 and must conclude that there is no evidence to suggest that credit card customers spend more or less than cash customers.

Small sample tests for two independent population means

Just as in the single sample case we need to use the t-distribution instead of the normal. Both populations from which the samples have been taken should be approximately normally distributed with equal variances (variance is the square of the standard deviation). If the conditions of normality cannot be met it is possible to use *non-parametric* tests, details of which can be found in McClave and Sincich (2006). A modified test is available if the equality of variance cannot be assumed. The standard error for the small sample case is slightly different from that for large samples. It is:

$$\sigma_{(x_1 - x_2)} = \hat{\sigma}\sqrt{\left(\frac{1}{n_1} + \frac{1}{n_2}\right)}$$

where $\hat{\sigma}$ is the estimate of the *pooled* standard deviation of the populations and is given by:

$$\hat{\sigma} = \sqrt{\frac{(n_1 - 1)s_1^2 + (n_2 - 1)s_2^2}{n_1 + n_2 - 2}}$$

The test statistic is given by:

$$t = \frac{(\bar{x}_1 - \bar{x}_2) - (\mu_1 - \mu_2)}{\sigma_{(\bar{x}_1 - \bar{x}_2)}}$$

The critical value at a particular significance level and $(n_1 + n_2 - 2)$ degrees of freedom can be found from t-tables (see Appendix 1).

Activity 9.7

A health magazine has decided to test the claim of the makers of a new slimming pill that has just come on the market. The company claims that the pill will allow people to lose weight if taken daily. The health magazine obtained a sample of 14 people who agreed to take the pill for a month. This group was split into two, a sample of 8 who would be given the slimming pill and a control group of 6 who would (unknown to them) be given a placebo (a fake slimming pill). The weight change at the end of the month is given in Table 9.1 where a minus indicates a loss of weight and a positive figure indicates a gain in weight.

Table 9.1 Weight change (in lbs) data for Activity 9.7

Sample 1	Sample 2 (control group)
−2	−2
−6	5
3	−5
−10	8
0	4
2	0
−4	
−9	

It would of course be possible to apply the single sample test on the sample of 8 people to see if the mean weight change is different to zero. However, the use of a control group is quite common in medical research as it allows unknown factors such as people's 'belief' in a product to be taken into account.

If we assume that the health magazine is not biased in its opinion of the pill, this is a two tailed test and the null and alternative hypotheses will be:

$$H_0 : \mu_1 - \mu_2 = 0 \qquad H_1 : \mu_1 - \mu_2 \neq 0$$

The mean and standard deviation for sample 1 are −3.25 and 4.862, respectively. The equivalent figures for the control group are 0.833 and 4.579, respectively. The pooled standard deviation is therefore:

$$\hat{\sigma} = \sqrt{\frac{(8-1)4.862^2 + (6-1)4.579^2}{8+6-2}}$$
$$= 4.746$$

and the standard error is

$$4.746\sqrt{\frac{1}{8} + \frac{1}{6}} = 2.563$$

The test statistic is:

$$t = \frac{(-3.25 - 0.833) - 0}{2.563}$$

$$= -1.593$$

The critical value on 12 degrees of freedom at 5% significance level is -2.179. As the test statistic is greater than this value we cannot reject H_0, so we conclude that there is no evidence that the slimming pill has any effect on weight change.

This test could be performed either in Excel or in SPSS, but SPSS is far superior to Excel when it comes to tests of hypotheses. To carry out the test you need to put your data in one column, which has been called 'Weight'. The next column, called 'Group', tells SPSS which group each of the weight values is in. Value 1 is for sample 1 and 2 for sample 2 (see Chapter 4 for the way that SPSS organizes data). The t-test can be found in the Compare Means under the Analyze main menu. The test you want is the Independent Samples T-Test (see Figure 9.7). Add 'Weight' as your test variable and Group as your grouping variable (see Figure 9.8). Then click OK. The output you get is shown in Figure 9.9.

SPSS first checks whether the variances of the two samples are equal. As they are, we only need look at the top row of the table. The t-value of -1.593 agrees with our calculated value. The Sig (2-tailed) is 0.137: this is the probability of obtaining a test statistic at least as extreme as the one obtained. It is the area in the tail or tails of the distribution for this value of the test statistic. This probability is often called the *observed significance level* or *p-value*. If we were testing at the 5% (0.05) level, then a *p*-value less than this figure would be significant and we would reject the null hypothesis. However, in our case 13.7% is greater than 5%, so we cannot reject H_0. The Confidence Interval of the difference is also given, and as this straddles zero it again confirms that there is no difference in means.

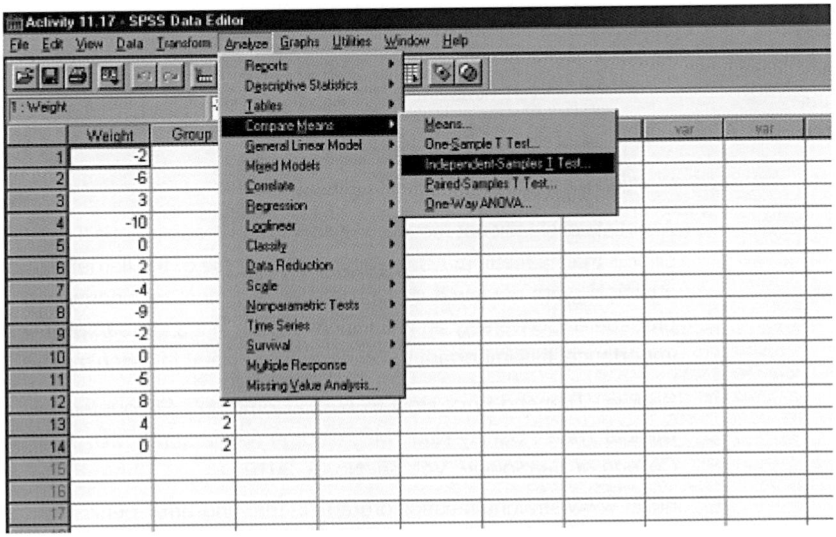

Figure 9.7
Independent samples
t-test using SPSS

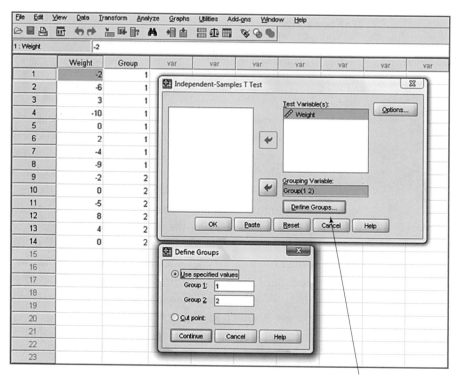

Figure 9.8
Setting up the test
in SPSS

Grouping variable defines
the sample. Click Define
Groups to specify 1 or 2

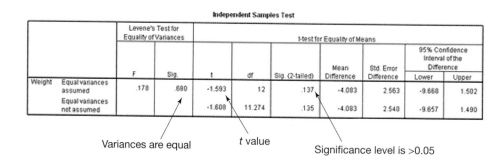

Independent Samples Test

		Levene's Test for Equality of Variances		t-test for Equality of Means						
									95% Confidence Interval of the Difference	
		F	Sig.	t	df	Sig. (2-tailed)	Mean Difference	Std. Error Difference	Lower	Upper
Weight	Equal variances assumed	.178	.680	-1.593	12	.137	-4.083	2.563	-9.668	1.502
	Equal variances not assumed			-1.608	11.274	.135	-4.083	2.540	-9.657	1.490

Figure 9.9
SPSS output

Variances are equal   *t* value

Significance level is >0.05

Did you know

A statistical significant result does not always mean practical significance. For example in clinical trials a result may be significant because of the (large) size of the sample but from a clinical point of view it doesn't prove its clinical superiority over an existing drug or procedure. Conversely an insignificant result in a small sample might in fact be of clinical importance. It is important to consider the context in which a statistical test is carried out.

Source: 'Trial and Error How to Avoid Commonly Encountered Limitations of Published Clinical Trials', Sanjay Kaul, MD, George A. Diamond, MD. *Journal of the American College of Cardiology*, Vol. 55, No. 5, 2010.

http://www.straightstatistics.org/article/trial-and-error-perils-p-value

Paired samples

We have already mentioned that the two-sample t-test is only valid when the two samples are independent. In many cases this assumption is not valid as the data is *paired*; that is, each observation of one sample is paired with an observation in the other sample. This can occur if identical conditions apply to pairs of observations. The null hypothesis is that the *difference* of the population means, μ_d, is zero and the alternative hypothesis can be either one or two tailed, depending on whether we believe the difference could be positive, negative or not equal to zero. The test statistic for this test is:

$$t = \frac{\bar{x}_d - \mu_d}{\sigma_{\bar{d}}}$$

where $\bar{x}_d$ is the sample mean of the n differences and μ_d is the population mean difference if the null hypothesis is correct (usually zero). $\sigma_{\bar{d}}$ is the standard error of the differences and is given by:

$$\sigma_{\bar{d}} = \frac{s_d}{\sqrt{n}}$$

where s_d is the standard deviation of the differences.

Activity 9.8

A publishing company has developed a new reading scheme that is supposed to improve the reading ability of children. In order to be able to justify its claim, 12 children were first given a standardized reading test before taking part in the programme. At the end of the programme they were tested again. The test scores before and after the programme can be found in Table 9.2. Does this data support the company's claim?

Table 9.2 Test scores for Activity 9.8

Child	Before	After	Difference
A	110	108	−2
B	121	122	1
C	95	98	3
D	80	90	10
E	130	132	2
F	100	105	5
G	105	105	0
H	85	90	5
I	95	96	1
J	100	98	−2
K	82	85	3
L	135	132	−3

The data are not independent because each member of the 'before' sample is related to a member of the 'after' sample by the attributes of the child. The advantage of this design is that it only looks at the differences between each child; it ignores the variation between children, which could be large. If the reading programme had had no effect you would expect the true average difference in test scores to be zero. The null hypothesis is therefore:

$$H_0 : \mu_d = 0$$

The alternative hypothesis is one tailed because we are testing to see if the programme improves reading ability (it is unlikely to make it worse), so:

$$H_1 : \mu_d > 0$$

The differences (after–before) can be found in Table 9.2, and the mean of the differences is 1.92 with a standard deviation of 3.655. The standard error of the differences is:

$$\sigma_{\bar{d}} = \frac{3.655}{\sqrt{12}}$$
$$= 1.055$$

and the test statistic is:

$$t = \frac{1.92 - 0}{1.055}$$
$$= 1.820$$

The critical value of t at the 5% significance level and on 11 $(12 - 1)$ degrees of freedom is 1.796. We can therefore reject H_0 at the 5% significance level and conclude that there is some evidence that the new reading programme does increase reading ability as represented by the testing method. Of course, a child's reading ability may well have increased without following the programme, so in practice a control group would be involved in the *experimental design*.

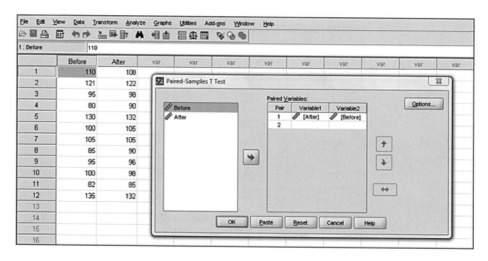

Figure 9.10

Setting up the paired *t*-test in SPSS

p value for two tailed test

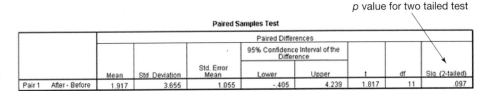

Paired Samples Test

		Paired Differences							
					95% Confidence Interval of the Difference				
		Mean	Std. Deviation	Std. Error Mean	Lower	Upper	t	df	Sig. (2-tailed)
Pair 1	After - Before	1.917	3.655	1.055	-.405	4.239	1.817	11	.097

Figure 9.11
Output for the paired
t-test

The paired t-test can be performed using SPSS and again it can be found under Compare Means (Paired Samples T-Test). Figures 9.10 and 9.11 give the relevant screen shots. The p-value for a two tailed test is 0.097, so for a one tailed test it will be half this, which is 0.048. As this is less than 0.05, H_0 is rejected. It is interesting to note here that had our alternative hypothesis been two sided ($\mu_d \neq 0$), then we would not have rejected H_0.

Hypothesis tests involving two population percentages

As well as conducting tests between two means it is possible to conduct tests between two percentages. Provided the sample sizes are large, the difference between the two percentages ($\pi_1 - \pi_2$) will be normally distributed. The null hypothesis will be:

$$H_0 : \pi_1 - \pi_2 = 0$$

and H_1 can be either one or two sided.
The standard error of the differences between the two percentages is:

$$\sigma_{(P_1 - P_2)} = \sqrt{\hat{P}(100 - \hat{P})\left(\frac{1}{n_1} + \frac{1}{n_2}\right)}$$

where $\hat{P}$ is the estimate of the population proportion and is given by:

$$\hat{P} = \frac{n_1 P_1 + n_2 P_2}{n_1 + n_2}$$

P_1 and P_2 refer to the two sample proportions.

The test statistic is:

$$Z = \frac{(P_1 - P_2) - (\pi_1 - \pi_2)}{\sigma_{(P_1 - P_2)}}$$

Activity 9.9

A top hairdresser has just opened two hairdressing salons in a large town and he is interested in whether there are any differences in the type of customers who use these two salons. During one month a random sample of customers at both salons were asked to complete a questionnaire. From the analysis of the questionnaire it was discovered that out of 200 customers at Top Cuts, 56 were under the age of 25. At Smart Cuts, 54 out of 150 were in this age bracket. Is there any difference in the percentage of under 25s at the two salons?

This is a two tailed test and the null and alternative hypotheses are:

$$H_0 : \pi_1 - \pi_2 = 0 \qquad H_1 : \pi_1 - \pi_2 \neq 0$$

$$P_1 = \frac{56}{200} \times 100 \qquad P_2 = \frac{54}{150} \times 100$$

$$= 28\% \qquad\qquad = 36\%$$

So:

$$\hat{P} = \frac{200 \times 28 + 150 \times 36}{200 + 150}$$

$$= 31.4\%$$

The standard error of the differences is:

$$\sigma_{(P_1 - P_2)} = \sqrt{31.4(100 - 31.4)\left(\frac{1}{200} + \frac{1}{150}\right)}$$

$$= 5.013$$

The test statistic is:

$$Z = \frac{(28 - 36) - 0}{5.013}$$

$$= -1.596$$

As this is greater than -1.96 we cannot reject H_0 and therefore conclude that there is no evidence to suggest that the percentage of customers in the under 25 age group is different in the two salons.

The chi-square hypothesis test

All the tests discussed so far in this chapter are called *parametric* tests in that they are testing a parameter (either the mean or proportion). However, there are also *non-parametric* tests and the text by McClave and Sincich (2006) contains many tests in this category. Perhaps the most useful non-parametric test is the chi-square test and there are two forms of this test. The first form, called the '*goodness of fit test*', tests to see if the data fits some distribution. The second form of the test is called the *test of association* and tests to see if there is any association between categories in a two-way table. For both forms of the test you have to count the number of data items that are observed to be in a particular category. The test statistic is calculated using the following formula:

$$\sum \frac{(O - E)^2}{E}$$

where O represents the observed count and E represents the expected count. The formula simply says: 'Find the difference between the observed and expected frequency of one category, square this value to remove any negative signs and then divide by the expected frequency for that category. Repeat this for all categories and sum the individual answers.'

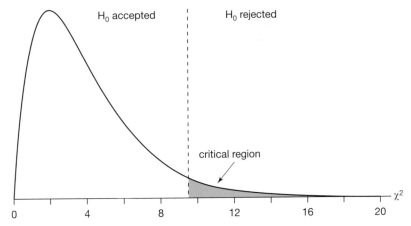

Figure 9.12
The chi-square
distribution on
4 degrees of freedom

This test statistic follows the χ^2 distribution (pronounced *chi-square*). The shape of this distribution depends on the degrees of freedom of the data. For example, for 4 degrees of freedom you would get the shape shown in Figure 9.12.

The area under the curve is again 1, but only one tail is used for the critical region – the upper tail. The area representing 5% has been indicated, and H_0 would be rejected if the test statistic was in this region.

The critical value of χ^2 is found from the χ^2 table that you will find in Appendix 1. For example, the critical value on 4 degrees of freedom at the 5% (0.05) significance level is 9.488. The test statistic follows the χ^2 distribution providing the expected values are not too small. We normally consider anything below 5 to be too small and if this occurs it is necessary to combine categories until this minimum number is achieved. We will meet this situation in Activity 9.11.

The 'goodness of fit' test

Suppose you threw a six-sided die 36 times. You would *expect* the faces numbered 1 to 6 to appear the same number of times; that is, 6. However, you might *observe* a rather different frequency.

Activity 9.10

Try this experiment for yourself and record the number of times each face appeared.

Suppose you got the following:

Face	1	2	3	4	5	6
Frequency	4	6	9	5	4	8

Is your observed frequency due to chance effects or does it indicate that the die is biased in any way? (In this example, face 3 occurs most.) The null hypothesis is that the die is fair and the alternate hypothesis is that it is biased; that is:

H_0 : die is fair H_1 : die is biased

Since the sum of the frequencies is fixed, you are 'free' to choose 5 of them; therefore the degrees of freedom is 5. From the χ^2 table, the critical value on 5 degrees of freedom and at the 5% significance level is 11.070. If the test statistic is greater than this value, H_0 will be rejected.

To calculate the χ^2 statistic you need to subtract the observed values from 6, square the result and then divide by 6. This calculation is shown in Table 9.3.

Table 9.3 Chi-square calculation for Activity 9.10

O	E	(O – E)	(O – E)²	$\dfrac{(O - E)^2}{E}$
4	6	–2	4	0.667
6	6	0	0	0.000
9	6	3	9	1.500
5	6	–1	1	0.167
4	6	–2	4	0.667
8	6	2	4	0.667
			Sum	3.668

The sum of these values is 3.668 and this is compared with the critical value of 11.070. H_0 cannot be rejected and you would have to assume that the die was fair. The diagram in Figure 9.13 demonstrates that the test statistic is not in the critical region.

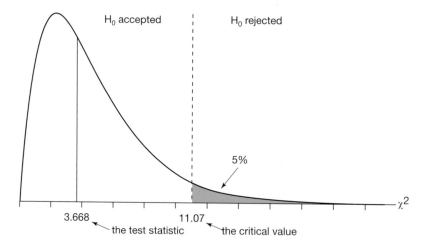

Figure 9.13
Diagram for
Activity 9.10

Activity 9.11

The *Quantitative methods in action* case in Chapter 7 used the goals scored in the 2010 football World Cup as an example of a Poisson distribution. In that chapter we used the Poisson distribution to calculate the expected number of times 0, 1, 2... goals were scored. The result of this calculation is repeated in Table 9.4. Use the chi-square test (at the 5% level of significance) to see if actual data does fit a Poisson distribution, that is goals scored are random.

Table 9.4 Using the Poisson distribution on goals scored

Goals	Probability	Expected	Actual
0	0.1033	6.6	7
1	0.2345	15.0	17
2	0.2662	17.0	13
3	0.2014	12.9	14
4	0.1143	7.3	7
5	0.0519	3.3	5
6	0.0196	1.3	0
7	0.0064	0.4	1
8 or more	0.0024	0.2	0
	Sum	64.0	64

Combine the last 4 goal categories as expected values are less than 5

Our hypothesis is that the data follows a Poisson distribution so H_0 and H_1 will be

H_0 : The goals scored follow a Poisson distribution

H_1 : The goals scored do not follow a Poisson distribution

Before we set up the chi-square test we should note that the expected values of 5, 6, 7 and 8 or more goals are below 5 so we should combine these categories to give us an expected value of 5.2 ($3.3 + 1.3 + 0.4 + 0.2$) and actual of 6 ($5 + 0 + 1 + 0$). We set up the chi-square test in the normal way and we get a test statistic of 1.461 (see Table 9.5).

Table 9.5 Chi-square calculation for Activity 9.11

Goals	O	E	(O – E)	$(O - E)^2$	$\dfrac{(O - E)^2}{E}$
0	7	6.60	0.40	0.16	0.024
1	17	15.00	2.00	4.00	0.267
2	13	17.00	−4.00	16.00	0.941
3	14	12.90	1.10	1.21	0.094
4	7	7.30	−0.30	0.09	0.012
5 or more	6	5.20	0.80	0.64	0.123
				Sum	1.461

As we have 6 categories and we have to estimate the mean for the Poisson distribution the degrees of freedom is $6 - 1 - 1 = 4$. The critical value at a significance level of 5% with 4 degrees of freedom is 9.488 and as the test statistic is below this we cannot reject the null hypothesis. We therefore conclude that the goals scored do follow a Poisson distribution and the number of goals scored is random.

The test of association

Example 9.1

The Personnel Manager of a company believes that monthly paid staff take more time off work through sickness than those staff who are paid weekly (and do not belong to the company sickness scheme). To test this theory, the sickness records for 561 randomly selected employees who have been in continuous employment for the past year were analyzed. Table 9.6 was produced, which placed employees into 3 categories according to how many days they were off work through sickness during the past year. For example, 95 monthly paid employees were off sick for less than 5 days.

Table 9.6 Number of days off sick by type of employee

Type of employee	Number of days off sick		
	Less than 5 days	5 to 10 days	More than 10 days
Monthly paid	95	47	18
Weekly paid	143	146	112

Activity 9.12

Is there any association between type of employee and numbers of days off sick?

Table 9.6 is a *contingency table*. The null and alternative hypotheses are:

H_0 : There is no association between type of employee and number of days off sick.
H_1 : There is an association between type of employee and number of days off sick.

In order to calculate the χ^2 test statistic it is necessary to determine the expected values for each category. To do this you first have to work out the row and column totals, as shown in Table 9.7.

Table 9.7 Table for Activity 9.12

Type of employee	Number of days off sick			Total
	Less than 5 days	5 to 10 days	More than 10 days	
Monthly paid	95	47	18	160
Weekly paid	143	146	112	401
Total	238	193	130	561

You now need to apply some basic ideas of probability (see Chapter 6) to the problem. If an employee were chosen at random, the probability that he or she was monthly paid would be $\dfrac{160}{561}$ and the probability that he or she would have been off sick for less than 5 days is $\dfrac{238}{561}$. Therefore, using the multiplication rule for two probabilities, the probability that the person is both monthly paid *and* in the 'less than 5 days' category is $\dfrac{160}{561} \times \dfrac{238}{561}$. Since there are 561 employees in total, the *expected* number of employees with both these attributes is

$$\dfrac{160}{561} \times \dfrac{238}{561} \times 561$$

$$= \dfrac{160 \times 238}{561}$$

$$= 67.9$$

This could be written as:

$$\text{Expected value} = \dfrac{\text{Row Total} \times \text{Column Total}}{\text{Grand Total}}$$

and is applicable for all cells of a contingency table. The rest of the expected values can now be worked out and a table set up similar to the one used for the 'goodness of fit' test (Table 9.8).

Table 9.8 Calculation of the chi-square test statistics

O	E	(O – E)	(O – E)^2	$\dfrac{(O - E)^2}{E}$
95	67.9	27.1	734.41	10.816
47	55.0	−8.0	64.00	1.164
18	37.1	−19.1	364.81	9.833
143	170.1	−27.1	734.41	4.318
146	138.0	8.0	64.00	0.464
112	92.9	19.1	364.81	3.927
			Sum	30.522

The sum of the χ^2 values is 30.522, and this is the test statistic for this problem. The critical value depends on the degrees of freedom of this table. As you know, degrees of freedom relates to the number of values that you are free to choose. If, for example, you chose the value for the top left hand cell in Table 9.7, the bottom left hand cell is determined since the two cells must add to 238. Likewise, you could choose the next cell along, but then all other cells are determined for you. So, for this problem, there are 2 degrees of freedom. Fortunately, there is a formula for calculating the degrees of freedom which is:

$$(\text{number of columns} - 1) \times (\text{number of rows} - 1)$$

In Table 9.7, there are 3 columns (excluding the total column) and 2 rows, so the degrees of freedom are:

$$(3 - 1) \times (2 - 1) = 2$$

The critical value for 2 degrees of freedom at the 5% significance level is 5.991, and at the 0.1% significance level it is 13.815. Therefore, since the test statistic is greater than 13.815, H_0 can be rejected at the 0.1% significance level, and you could conclude that there does seem to be an association between staff category and the number of days off sick.

It is possible to be more specific about this association by looking at the individual χ^2 values and also the (O − E) column. The two largest χ^2 values are 10.816 and 9.883. These both relate to the monthly paid staff, which suggests that this group of employees has a higher frequency in the 'less than 5 days category' than expected, but a lower frequency in the 'more than 10 days' category.

Activity 9.13

A survey is regularly carried out on mobile phone usage and Table 9.9 is one example from Northern Ireland.

Is there any association between gender and whether a driver is using a mobile phone?

Table 9.9 The percentage of drivers observed using a mobile phone by gender

All cars	Type of phone			
	Hand-held	Hands-free	Neither	Total
Base = 100	%	%	%	Count
Male	1.3	0.4	98.3	10 068
Female	0.5	0.4	99.1	6 976
Total	1.0	0.4	98.6	17 044

Source: Central Survey Unit, Department of the Environment for Northern Ireland.

The null and alternative hypotheses are:

H_0 : There is no association between gender and whether a driver uses a mobile phone.

H_1 : There is an association between gender and whether a driver uses a mobile phone.

Rather than do another manual calculation, we will look at how we can use Excel to carry out the test. The first thing we must do is to convert the data to *counts* rather than *percentages*. This is easily done as the total counts are provided. However, because the percentages in the original table had been rounded, the counts might give fractional values. To prevent this happening, Excel's ROUND function is used. For example, the formula for 'male' and 'handheld' is =ROUND((C4*$F$4/100),0).

 The spreadsheet containing the calculations is shown in Figures 9.14 and 9.15, and can also be found on the companion website.

The number of degrees of freedom is $(3 − 1) \times (2 − 1) = 2$.

The critical value for 2 degrees of freedom is 5.991 (as in the previous activity).

	A	B	C	D	E	F
1						
2				Table of percentages		
3			Hand-held	Hands-free	Neither	Total
4		Male	1.3	0.4	98.3	10068
5		Female	0.5	0.4	99.1	6976
6		Total	1	0.4	98.6	17044
7						
8						
9				Counts		
10			Hand-held	Hands-free	Neither	Total
11		Male	131	40	9897	10068
12		Female	35	28	6913	6976
13		Total	166	68	16810	17044
14						
15						
16				Chi-Square calculations		
17		Observed	Expected	O-E	(O-E)^2	(O-E)^2/E
18		131	98.06	32.94	1085.22	11.07
19		40	40.17	-0.17	0.03	0.00
20		9897	9929.77	-32.77	1074.18	0.11
21		35	67.94	-32.94	1085.22	15.97
22		28	27.83	0.17	0.03	0.00
23		6913	6880.23	32.77	1074.18	0.16
24					Total	27.31

Figure 9.14
Spreadsheet for Activity 9.13

Table of percentages

	Hand-held	Hands-free	Neither	Total
Male	1.3	0.4	98.3	10068
Female	0.5	0.4	99.1	6976
Total	1	0.4	98.6	=SUM(F4:F5)

Counts

	Hand-held	Hands-free	Neither	Total
Male	=ROUND((C4*$F$4/100),0)	=ROUND((D4*$F$11/100),0)	=ROUND((E4*$F$11/100),0)	10068
Female	=ROUND((C5*$F$12/100),0)	=ROUND((D5*$F$12/100),0)	=ROUND((E5*$F$12/100),0)	6976
Total	=SUM(C11:C12)	=SUM(D11:D12)	=SUM(E11:E12)	=SUM(F11:F12)

Table of percentages

Observed	Expected	O-E	(O-E)^2	(O-E)^2/E
=C11	=$F$11*C13/$F$13	=B18-C18	=D18^2	=E18/C18
=D11	=$F$11*D13/$F$13	=B19-C19	=D19^2	=E19/C19
=E11	=$F$11*E13/$F$13	=B20-C20	=D20^2	=E20/C20
=C12	=$F$12*C13/$F$13	=B21-C21	=D21^2	=E21/C21
=D12	=$F$12*D13/$F$13	=B22-C22	=D22^2	=E22/C22
=E12	=$F$12*E13/$F$13	=B23-C23	=D23^2	=E23/C23

Figure 9.15
Excel formulae for Activity 9.13

The test statistic of 27.31 is greater than the critical value, so the null hypothesis is rejected – the results show that there *is* an association between gender and whether drivers use a mobile phone. If you look at the table closely, in fact, you can see that females are much less likely than males to use a mobile phone while driving.

SPSS and the chi-square test

SPSS has a routine called Crosstabs which can create a contingency table from raw data and calculate various inferential test statistics, including the chi-square statistic. To demonstrate the use of Crosstabs we will use the samples of anonymized individual records (SARs) from the 2001 census (see www.ccsr.ac.uk/sars/). The census collects data on every individual in the UK: it asks questions on gender, health, employment, housing and ethic origin, to name just a few. Datasets from the census are extremely large (with millions of records) and are therefore difficult to handle.

The SARS dataset is a sample from the census: while still very large (1 843 525 records), it can easily be handled with SPSS. To demonstrate the use of Crosstabs in SPSS we will attempt to see whether there is an association between distance to work and gender.

The null and alternative hypotheses are:

H_0 : There is no association between distance to work and gender.
H_1 : There is an association between distance to work and gender.

The Crosstabs routine is found within the Analysis/Descriptive statistics menu, as you can see in Figure 9.16. If you click on Crosstabs you get the dialog boxes shown in Figure 9.17. In the Cell display we will request the observed and expected counts (frequencies), percentage by Column, and Unstandardized and Adjusted standardized residuals. The Unstandardized residuals are simply the difference between the observed and expected counts $(O - E)$. The Adjusted standardized residuals are similar to the $(O - E)^2/E$ statistic we calculated before. This statistic is used when H_0 is rejected, as any cell with a value outside the range of -2 to 2 could be the possible reason for the rejection.

The Statistic dialog box allows you to request particular inferential statistics. The Chi-square is the obvious one, but the other statistic to request is Phi and Cramer's V. Statisticians prefer these other two statistics as the chi-square statistic is influenced by the sample size; as the sample size increases, so does the value of the chi-square statistic. The absolute value of both Phi and Cramer's V statistic varies between 0 and 1, with 0 representing no association and 1 perfect association.

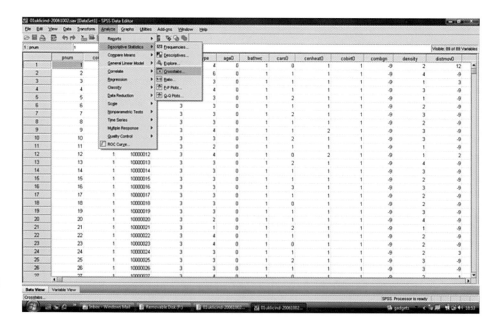

Figure 9.16
The SARS data and the Crosstabs routine

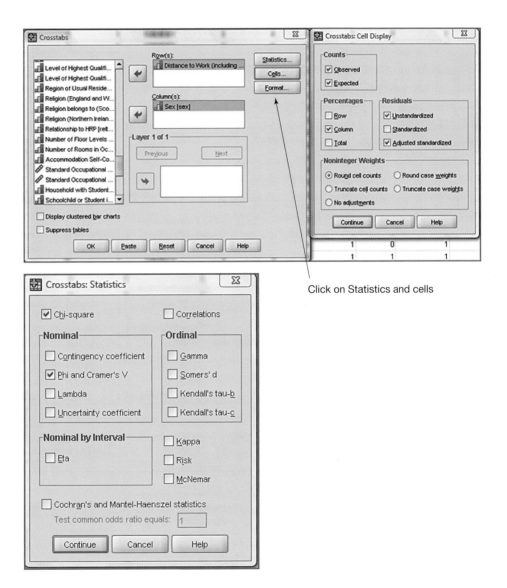

Click on Statistics and cells

Figure 9.17
The Crosstabs
dialog boxes

Both the Statistics and Cell Display dialog boxes are closed by clicking on Continue. The Crosstabs routine is executed by clicking on OK. Part of the contingency table output is shown in Figure 9.18; the statistical output is shown in Figure 9.19.

You will see from Figure 9.19 that all the significance levels (or p-values) are zero. In fact the zero really means 'less than 0.001', which is highly significant. H_0 is rejected and we conclude that there *is* an association between distance to work and gender. If you look at Figure 9.18, in fact, you will see that the largest adjusted standardized residuals are for less than 2 km and over 40 km. From this table you should be able to conclude that men travel further to work than women. However, both Phi and Cramer's V statistics are only 0.2, which does not suggest a very strong association.

More women in this category

			Sex		
			Male	Female	Total
Distance to Work (including study in Scotland)	less than 2km	Count	79618	106159	185777
		Expected Count	100083.2	85693.8	185777.0
		% within Sex	17.2%	26.8%	21.7%
		Residual	-20465.2	20465.2	
		Adjusted Residual	-107.6	107.6	
	2km to less than 5km	Count	80343	88534	168877
		Expected Count	90978.7	77898.3	168877.0
		% within Sex	17.4%	22.4%	19.7%
		Residual	-10635.7	10635.7	
		Adjusted Residual	-57.9	57.9	
	5km to less than 10km	Count	78749	72892	151641
		Expected Count	81693.2	69947.8	151641.0
		% within Sex	17.0%	18.4%	17.7%
		Residual	-2944.2	2944.2	
		Adjusted Residual	-16.7	16.7	
	10km to less than 20km	Count	73130	54519	127649
		Expected Count	68768.0	58881.0	127649.0
		% within Sex	15.8%	13.8%	14.9%
		Residual	4362.0	-4362.0	
		Adjusted Residual	26.5	-26.5	
	20km to less than 40km	Count	42131	23850	65981
		Expected Count	35545.8	30435.2	65981.0
		% within Sex	9.1%	6.0%	7.7%
		Residual	6585.2	-6585.2	
		Adjusted Residual	53.5	-53.5	
	40km and over	Count	28202	11179	39381
		Expected Count	21215.6	18165.4	39381.0
		% within Sex	6.1%	2.8%	4.6%
		Residual	6986.4	-6986.4	
		Adjusted Residual	72.3	-72.3	

Observed frequency

Difference between observed and expected

Adjusted residual gives information on form of association

More men in this category

Figure 9.18
Part of the
Crosstabs output

Chi-Square Tests

	Value	df	Asymp. Sig. (2-sided)
Pearson Chi-Square	34440.792[a]	10	.000
Likelihood Ratio	35964.794	10	.000
Linear-by-Linear Association	29350.732	1	.000
N of Valid Cases	857649		

a. 0 cells (.0%) have expected count less than 5. The minimum expected count is 24.45.

p values

Symmetric Measures

		Value	Approx. Sig.
Nominal by Nominal	Phi	.200	.000
	Cramer's V	.200	.000
N of Valid Cases		857649	

a. Not assuming the null hypothesis.

b. Using the asymptotic standard error assuming the null hypothesis.

Figure 9.19
Statistical output from
Crosstabs

The chi-square test for association is a very important and useful test in the area of statistics in particular, and decision-making in general. However, there are a couple of problems that you need to be aware of.

Two by two tables

The χ^2 distribution is a continuous distribution, whereas the sample data is discrete. Normally the sample size is sufficient to avoid making a continuity correction, but this will be needed for 2×2 tables. The correction required is to *subtract* 0.5 from the *absolute* value of the difference between the observed and expected values. For example, if the difference was -2.7, the corrected value would be -2.2 (not -3.2).

Tables of percentages

The χ^2 test is applied to tables of frequencies, *not* percentages. If you are given a table of percentages you will need to convert it to frequencies by multiplying each percentage by the total frequency. If you are not given the total frequency then it is not possible to use this test.

Reflection

Hypothesis testing is another very important statistical concept. Without being able to test ideas in a scientific manner, we would never be confident, for example, that a new drug or procedure was a significant improvement on a previous one.

Hypothesis testing originated from work carried out in the 1930s and 1940s by three famous statisticians, R.A. Fisher, J. Neyman and E. Pearson. The approach by Fisher was different from those of Neyman and Pearson, and resulted in quite heated debates in academic journals. Even today argument still rages on the reliance on arbitrary significance levels, and a few statisticians believe that conventional hypothesis testing should be abandoned in favour of probability values based on some *a priori* expectation of results. Most statistical software, including SPSS, gives *p*-values, which can be more helpful than test statistics and critical values.

Whenever you do hypothesis tests, be careful about 'accepting' the null hypothesis. John Tukey (1991) gives the following good reason why it is dangerous to accept a null hypothesis:

Statisticians classically asked the wrong questions – and were willing to answer with a lie, one that was often a downright lie. They asked 'Are the effects of A and B different?' and they were willing to answer 'no.'

All we know about the world teaches us that the effects of A and B are always different – in some decimal place – for any A and B. Thus asking 'Are the effects different?' is foolish.

What we should be answering first is 'Can we tell the direction in which the effects of A differ from the effects of B?' In other words, can we be confident about the direction from A to B? Is it 'up,' 'down' or 'uncertain'?

If the third answer to this first question is that we are 'uncertain about the direction' – it is not, and never should be, that we 'accept the null hypothesis'.

Key points

○ A *hypothesis* is formulated, and a *test* conducted on a sample of data in order to either accept or reject the hypothesis.

○ The test can either be two sided or one sided. We only use a one sided test when we are only interested in one side of the mean or proportion.

○ Apart from the chi-square test, the tests applied in this chapter are *parametric tests* – they test a parameter of a population.

○ The *population parameters* tested in this chapter include the mean and percentage.

○ For tests of percentages, the sample size must be large.

○ For tests on the mean, a large sample allows the *Z-distribution* to be used; otherwise it is necessary to use the *t-distribution*.

○ We can test a single mean or proportion or we can test two means or proportions. For a mean the test can either be two independent means or the samples can be paired.

○ The *chi-square test* is used to test whether a frequency distribution follows some expected distribution, and can also be used to test whether there is an association between categories.

○ Figure 9.20 summarizes the different tests applicable to means and proportions.

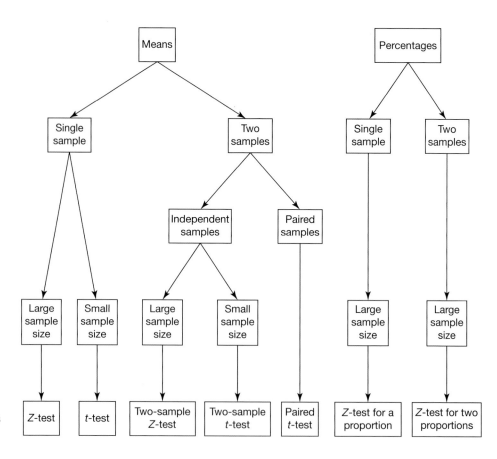

Figure 9.20
Summary of tests applicable to means and proportions

Further reading

As with confidence intervals there are a large number of texts aimed at the business student. However if you want to take the subject further McClave and Sinich (2006) is the 'gold standard' in this area. There is also an interesting article in *Statistical Science* by Tukey (1991).

Web links W

Answers to selected questions can be found in Appendix 2. Answers to the other questions can be found on the companion website for this book

Practice questions

W **1** What is the critical value for a two sided Z-test at 5% significance?

W **2** What is the one sided critical t-value at 1% significance for a sample size of 12?

W **3** What is the critical chi-square value for a contingency table of size 4×3 at 5% significance?

W **4** A company has analyzed the time its customers take to pay an invoice over the past few years and has found that the distribution is normal, with a mean of 5.8 weeks and a standard deviation of 2.3 weeks. In order to speed up payment the company threatened to charge interest if bills were not paid within 3 weeks. A sample of 10 customers was then analyzed and the mean time to pay had been reduced to 4.9 weeks. Is there any evidence that the mean time for *all* its customers had actually been reduced?

W **5** A motorcycle is claimed to have a fuel consumption which is normally distributed with mean 54 mpg and a standard deviation of 5 mpg. 12 motorcycles are tested and the mean value of their fuel consumption was found to be 50.5 mpg. Taking a 5% level of significance, test the hypothesis that the mean fuel consumption is 54 mpg.

W **6** The lifetime of electric light bulbs produced by a given process is normally distributed; the bulbs are claimed to have a mean lifetime of 1500 hours. A batch of 50 was taken, which showed a mean lifetime of 1410 hours. The standard deviation of the sample is 90 hours. Test the hypothesis that the mean lifetime of the electric light bulbs matches the claim.

W **7** A company has been accused of selling underweight products. This product is supposed to weigh 500 g; a sample of 6 was weighed and the results were:

495, 512, 480, 505, 490, 502

Is there any evidence that the mean weight is less than 500 g? (The weight of the product is known to be normally distributed.)

W **8** The Speedwell Building Society has claimed that there has been a significant increase in the percentage of its customers taking out fixed-rate mortgages. In the past, 30% of customers had this type of mortgage, but during the past week 60 out of 150 new mortgages have been at a fixed rate. Is the claim by the building society correct?

W 9 The number of accidents occurring at a large construction site during the past week has been as follows:

Mon	Tue	Wed	Thu	Fri
6	5	6	8	12

Is there any evidence that accidents are more likely on certain days of the week?

W 10 In Britain a survey was carried out of 171 radio listeners who were asked what radio station they listened to most during an average week. A summary of their replies is given in Table 9.10, together with their age range.

Table 9.10 Data for Question 10

	Age range		
	Less than 20	20 to 30	Over 30
BBC	22	16	50
Local radio	6	11	16
Commercial	35	3	12

(a) Is there any evidence that there is an association between age and radio station?

(b) By considering the contribution to the value of your test statistic from each cell and the relative sizes of the observed and expected frequencies in each cell, indicate the main source of the association, if any exists.

11 A component produced for the electricity industry is supposed to have a mean outside diameter of 10 cm. The mean diameter of a sample of 36 components taken from today's output is 9.94 cm with a standard deviation of 0.018 cm. Does this suggest that the production process is not meeting the specifications?

12 Before a special promotion, the percentage of customers who bought your product at a certain supermarket was 36%. After the promotion a random sample of 200 shoppers at the supermarket revealed that 80 of them had bought the product. Is there evidence of a significant change?

13 In the week before Christmas it was hoped that the mean takings of a shop's branches would be £40 000. However, 40 randomly sampled branches had mean takings of only £37 000 with a standard deviation of £6000. Does this suggest that the mean takings of all the branches were significantly different from the target figure?

14 A bank claims that 60% of people who apply for a personal loan will be granted it. However, a random sample of 500 loan applications contains only 250 which were successful. Does this suggest that the success rate is significantly different from 60%?

15 You are approached one day by a sales manager who has used a computer package to calculate the mean size of order placed by all the company's customers last year. His calculations show that the mean size of order placed was £36.90 with a standard deviation of £4.20. The manager wants advice on how to carry out a hypothesis test to see if the mean size of order placed last year was significantly different from the previous year's figure (this was £30.58). What would your advice be?

16 An inspection by the Environmental Health Department has recently taken place at a company that processes and packs cooked food. The inspectors expressed concern at the amount of dust that was detected in the air within the Cooked Meat department. Although the quantity of dust does not exceed the legal limit, the inspectors recommended that the extractor fans be replaced as soon as possible.

The company looked at various types of extractor fans on the market at the current time and reduced the choice to just two: the Ameba and the Bewax. In order to decide which one to purchase, the manufacturers have loaned the company one unit of each type so that a comparison can be made.

Ameba was installed first, and each week for the next six weeks the filters within the fan were weighed, cleaned and replaced. The Ameba unit was then removed and the Bewax unit placed in the same position and the experiment repeated. The amount of dust (in grams) collected by the two units was as follows:

Ameba   5.7   6.4   6.1   4.8   7.2   2.9
Bewax   2.9   4.7   6.3   3.0   7.0   3.5

Which extractor fan should the company purchase? (Use a 5% significance level.)

17 In an experiment, a sample of 400 consumers are simultaneously presented with four test packages.

Package A carries a competition offering the chance to win £10 000
Package B carries a token for a free gift
Package C simply carries a message '10% off normal price'
Package D carries a token offering 20 pence off the next purchase of the product

The consumers are then asked to choose the package which they find to be the most attractive. The results of the experiment are given below:

Package	No. of consumers selecting it
A	106
B	92
C	102
D	100

Are these results consistent with the hypothesis that consumers are equally likely to select each package?

18 In a market research survey 200 people are shown the proposed design of a new car and they are asked if they like the design. The responses, broken down by age groups, are shown in Table 9.11. Is there any evidence that age is associated with attitude to the proposed design?

Table 9.11 Data for Question 18

	Age		
	Under 21	21–35	Over 35
Liked design	20	40	80
Disliked design	30	20	10

W 19 A telephone company has found in the past that 60% of requests from business customers for new installations are for direct lines, 25% are for switchboard connections and 15% for fax machine and other connections. However, a random sample of 300 customers taken last month reveals that 120 are requesting direct lines, 80 are requesting switchboard connections and the remainder are requesting fax machine and other connections. Does this sample suggest that a significant change in the pattern of demand has occurred?

20 You have been asked to help in the design and analysis of a sales campaign involving a selected number of supermarkets. Janet Graves, the Marketing Manager, believes that it is the 'caring image' of the business that attracts customers rather than price cuts alone. To test this idea Janet obtained approval to invest in staff training and other expenditure to generate a friendly atmosphere within a supermarket. Advertising on television and local radio was also to be increased during the campaign. You randomly selected 8 supermarkets throughout the country representing different areas and spending patterns. Following staff training, the campaign was started and continued for a month. The sales turnover (in £000s) for each supermarket for the month before and after the campaign was noted and is as follows:

Supermarket	A	B	C	D	E	F	G	H
Sales Before	150	75	110	300	120	560	350	185
After	178	50	150	400	180	540	350	235

Is there any evidence at the 5% significance level that sales have improved as a result of the sales campaign?

21 In 2003 an educational researcher sampled 250 students to find out how many hours a week they spent in paid employment. Out of this 250, 30 said that they worked for more than 20 hours a week. The researcher repeated this survey in the year 2008 with a group of 220 students and found that 40 worked for more than 20 hours a week. Is there any indication that students were spending more time working in 2008 than they did in 2003?

W 22 A company has just relocated to a new site and managers are interested in whether the new site has changed staff's lunch preferences. At the old site 39% said that they brought their own lunch to work, 12% said that they skip lunch altogether, 18% responded that they bought it from the local shop and 31% said they bought it from the staff canteen. After a survey of 227 staff at the new site into their lunch habits the following data was obtained (Table 10.12).

Table 9.12 Data for Question 22

Category	Observed frequency (new site)
Bring lunch to work	42
Skip lunch	95
Buy from local shop	27
Use canteen	63

Use the chi-square goodness of fit test at the 5% significance level to determine whether staff have changed their lunch habits since moving to the new site.

W **23** MyBook is a social networking website and the organizers of the site wish to discover if a recent advertising campaign has changed the demographic mix of its users. A survey was conducted among its current users and the results are shown in Table 9.13. This table also gives the previous percentage of people in each category.

Table 9.13 Data for Question 23

Age group	Before campaign	Number after campaign
Less than 18	2.7%	6
18–19	29.9%	118
20–24	53.4%	102
Older than 24	14.0%	26
Total	100%	252

Use the chi-square test at the 5% level to see if there has been a change in the demographic mix of the users.

Assignment

In order to assess the effectiveness of a company training programme, each employee was appraised before and after the training. Based on the comparisons of the two appraisals, each of the 110 production staff were classified according to how well they had benefited from the training. This classification ranged from 'worse', which means they now perform worse than they did before, to 'high', which means they perform much better than they did before the training. The results of this appraisal can be seen in Table 9.14, where you will notice that employees have been further classified by age.

Table 9.14 Data for the assignment

Age of employee	Level of improvement				Total
	Worse	None	Some	High	
Below 40	1	5	24	30	60
40+	4	5	31	10	50
Total	5	10	55	40	110

(a) Is there any association between level of improvement at the job and age?

(b) What is the 95% confidence interval for the percentage of employees who showed a high level of improvement at their job?

Cause and effect: correlation and regression

Prerequisites Knowledge of hypothesis tests (Chapter 9: *Checking ideas: testing a hypothesis*) would be useful

Objectives
- To be able to draw and interpret scatter diagrams
- To be able to calculate Spearman's rank correlation coefficient
- To be able to calculate Pearson's product moment correlation coefficient
- To understand and know how to use the least squares regression line
- To understand the limitations of these techniques
- To know how to use SPSS to analyze multi-variate data

Introduction The statistical analysis that you have covered so far has been concerned with the characteristics of a single variable. However, in some circumstances it might be of interest to look at two variables simultaneously – for instance, you might suspect that cost of production is dependent on the quantity produced, or that sales of a product are related to price. This chapter introduces two techniques: *correlation*, to measure the association between two variables, and *regression*, to obtain the relationship between the variables. It is also possible to develop relationships between several variables, as indicated in the *Quantitative methods in action* case study. This chapter will show how SPSS can be used for this technique, which is called *multiple regression*.

Quantitative methods in action: factors influencing customer loyalty

A study was carried out to see what factors influence a customer's intention to stay again at the same hotel (or hotel chain). The authors looked at the following factors:

1   Customer service ('Cutser')
2   Cleanliness ('Clean')
3   Quality of room ('Rmqual')
4   Value for money ('Valmon')
5   Quality of food ('Food')
6   Family friendliness ('Famfr')

These factors were dictated by the data source, which was 'Laterooms' (www.laterooms.com). Laterooms is an online booking system for hotels in the UK and worldwide. Following a reservation and stay at a participating hotel, guests are encouraged to rate the hotel on a number of categories. The database of responses contains some 190 000 reviews made by guests, and the authors of the study used ratings for 664 UK hotels for the period August to September 2008 for analysis.

In the study the authors classified each attribute as either being 'Critical', 'Desirable',' Satisfier', 'Dissatisfier', or 'Neutral'. Definitions of these terms, as given by the authors, are listed in Table 10.1

The authors ran a multiple linear regression analysis using customer loyalty ('Stay again') as the dependent variable and all the attributes mentioned above as the independent variables. They found that 'Cleanliness', 'Room quality' and 'Value for money' were highly significant at the 1% level in explaining guests' intention to stay again. 'Quality of food' was significant at the 5% level while 'Family friendliness' was not significant. The value of R^2 was 0.609 which means that the independent variables are able to explain 60.9% of the variation of the dependent variable.

The authors next produced sub-sets of the data depending on whether the independent variables were below or above the median (that is, poor or good). So, for instance, 201 guests gave customer service (Custser) a low score. Regressions were then carried out on each sub-set of data so a total of twelve regression results were obtained. For example, the regression based on 'Cutser' being poor gave the following equation:

$$\text{Stay again} = -31.067 + 5.309\text{Cutser} + 4.880\text{Clean} + 5.590\text{Rmqual} + 8.029\text{Valmon} + 1.021\text{Food} + 0.164\text{Famfr}$$

The R^2 for this equation was 0.773 and the F-statistic 48.112 which was significant.

Although this equation is interesting the authors were more concerned with which variables were significant. In this example customer service was significant at the 5% level while Cleanliness, Room quality and Value for money were significant at the 1% level. What the authors found was that Value for money ('Valmon) was significant in all regressions, so this variable was classified as a critical attribute. A desirable attribute should be significant for both low as well as high performance. Again they found Value for money to be a desirable attribute. So a critical attribute is a desirable one, but not vice versa. None of the other variables were found to be desirable attributes.

Table 10.1 Classification scheme for hotel service attributes

Classification	Definition
Critical	Critical factors have a high potential for compliments and high potential for complaints. An unsatisfactory performance in a critical factor cannot be compensated by a good performance elsewhere
Desirable	Desirable factors add to the general perceptions of quality if they are good but poor performance does not reduce the overall quality perception
Satisfier	Satisfiers are those factors where unusually good performance elicits compliments from guests, while average or low performance will generally not elicit dissatisfaction from guests
Dissatisfier	Dissatisfiers are those factors where unusually bad performance results in dissatisfaction, while average or good performance will not generate satisfaction from guests
Neutral	Good performance in terms of these factors may not be noticed by guests and bad performance does not affect overall quality perception

For a variable to be classified as a satisfier attribute the regression with this variable should be significant at high performance but insignificant at low performance. In all twelve regressions there were no satisfier attributes. To be classified as a 'dissatisfier' the variable should be significant at low performance but insignificant at high performance. Customer service, room quality and food were found to be in this category. The remaining attributes (Cleanliness and Family friendliness) were insignificant at both low and high performance and so were classed as neutral attributes. Table 10.2 summarizes the findings.

The overall conclusion of this analysis was that 'Value for money' was critical in getting guests to want to stay again at a hotel. However 'Customer service' and 'Room quality' are considered dissatisfiers which mean that a poor performance in this attribute would not encourage guests to stay again. 'Cleanliness', 'Food quality' and 'Family friendliness' do not play much part in a guest's decision to stay again.

Source: International Journal of Contemporary Hospitality Management, Vol. 23, No. 1, 2011.

Table 10.2 A summary of the twelve regressions

	Critical	Desirable	Satisfier	Dissatisfier	Neutral
Customer service				X	
Cleanliness					X
Room quality				X	
Value for money	X				
Quality for food				X	
Family friendliness					X

Scatter diagrams

A scatter diagram is simply a way of representing a set of bivariate data by a scatter of plots. One variable is plotted on the x-axis and the other on the y-axis. Normally the x variable (the *independent* variable) is the one that you believe influences the y variable (the *dependent* variable). That is y *depends on* x.

Examples of scatter diagrams are given in Figures 10.1 to 10.4. Figure 10.1 indicates a *positive correlation* because as the number of deliveries increases, so apparently does the delivery time. Figure 10.2 indicates a *negative correlation* because as the air temperature increases, the heating cost falls. Figure 10.3 suggests that no correlation exists between salary and age of employees. Figure 10.4 suggests that the quantity produced and the efficiency of a machine are correlated but not linearly.

When categorizing scatter diagrams you may find it easier to draw a closed loop around the points. This loop should be drawn so that it encloses all the points but at the same time makes the area within the loop as small as possible. If the loop looks like a circle, this suggests that there is little, if any, correlation, but if the loop looks more like an ellipse then this suggests that there is some correlation present. An

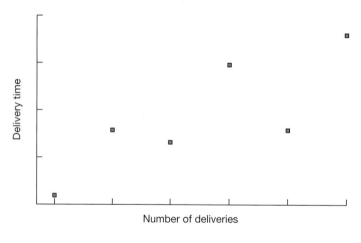

Figure 10.1
Positive correlation

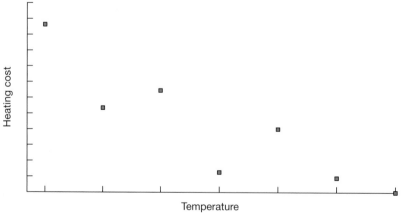

Figure 10.2
Negative correlation

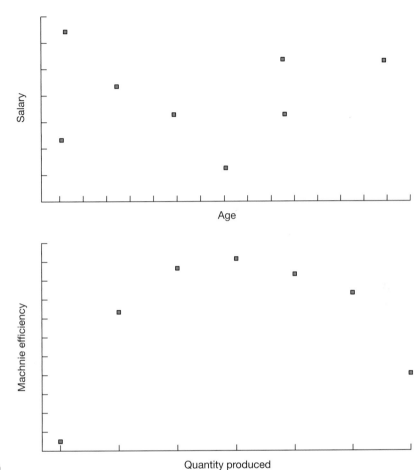

Figure 10.3
No correlation

Figure 10.4
Non-linear correlation

ellipse pointing upwards would represent a positive correlation and one pointing downwards would represent a negative correlation. If you try this with Figures 10.1 to 10.3 you will see that this agrees with the statements already made. A loop around the points in Figure 10.4 would clearly show the non-linear nature of the association.

The closer the ellipse becomes to a straight line, the stronger the correlation. If the ellipse became a straight line you would say that you have perfect correlation (unless the straight line was horizontal, in which case there can be no correlation since the dependent variable has a constant value).

Example 10.1

The Production Manager at Lookwools Engineering suspects that there is an association between production volume and production cost. To prove this he obtained the total cost of production for different production volumes and the data are as follows:

Units produced (000s)	1	2	3	4	5	6
Production costs (£000s)	5.0	10.5	15.5	25.0	16.0	22.5

Activity 10.1

Draw a scatter diagram for the data in Example 10.1 and comment on the association (if any).

Since production cost depends on volume, the horizontal (x) axis represents volume (units produced) and the vertical (y) axis represents cost. The scatter diagram for this data is shown in Figure 10.5.

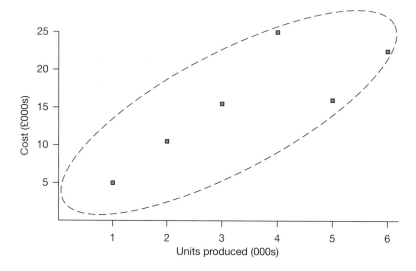

Figure 10.5
Scatter diagram for
Activity 10.1

A closed loop has been drawn around the points and from this you should be able to make the following observations:

- There is a positive correlation between volume and cost.
- The loop is a fairly narrow ellipse shape suggesting that, for the range of data provided, the association is reasonably strong (but not perfect).
- If the point representing 4000 units was omitted the ellipse would be narrower.
- There is no evidence of non-linearity in the data.

Although these observations are valid, the sample size is rather small to make definite conclusions. In practice a larger sample size would be advisable (at least twelve pairs) and the cost of 4000 units would be checked. Sometimes these 'rogue' results suggest that other factors are influencing the dependent variable and further investigation is necessary.

Correlation

The technique of *correlation* measures the strength of the association between the variables. There are two widely used measures of correlation. These are *Spearman's rank correlation coefficient* and *Pearson's product moment correlation coefficient*. Both give a value between -1 and 1 so that -1 indicates a perfect negative correlation, 1 a perfect positive correlation and zero indicates no correlation. This is illustrated in Figure 10.6.

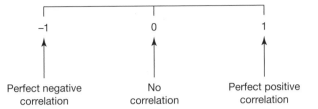

Figure 10.6
Range of values of
the correlation
coefficient

Spearman's rank correlation coefficient (R)

This method involves ranking each value of x and y and using the following formula to calculate the coefficient R.

$$R = 1 - \frac{6 \sum d^2}{n(n^2 - 1)}$$

where d is the difference in rank between pairs and n is the number of pairs. The value of R lies between 1 and -1.

The procedure to calculate this coefficient is as follows:

1 Rank both variables so that either the largest is ranked 1 or alternatively the smallest is ranked 1.
2 For each pair obtain the difference between the rankings.
3 Square these differences and sum.
4 Substitute the sum of these differences into the formula.

If during Step 1 you find you have equal rankings for the same variable, it is the *mean* of the rankings that is used. For example, if rank 3 occurs twice then both should be given a ranking of 3.5. The next ranking is 5.

Activity 10.2

Calculate Spearman's rank correlation coefficient for the data given in Example 10.1.

Step 1
Rank both variables.

If you use rank 1 as being the lowest and rank 6 as the largest value, then the 'Units Produced' are already ranked for you. 'Production Costs' start at 5.0 (£000s) and this will have a rank 1, while 25.0 is the largest and will be given a rank of 6. This can be seen below.

Units produced (000s)	1	2	3	4	5	6
Rank	1	2	3	4	5	6
Production costs (£000s)	5.0	10.5	15.5	25.0	16.0	22.5
Rank	1	2	3	6	4	5

Steps 2 and 3
Calculate differences, then square and sum them. You will find it easier if you set out the calculations in a table similar to Table 10.3.

Table 10.3 Calculation of R for Activity 10.2

No. of units	Cost	Difference (d)	d^2
1	1	0	0
2	2	0	0
3	3	0	0
4	6	−2	4
5	4	1	1
6	5	1	1
		Sum	6

Step 4

Substitute the sum of d^2 into the formula. The sum of d^2 is 6 and there are 6 pairs of values, so Spearman's rank correlation coefficient is:

$$R = 1 - \frac{6 \times 6}{6 \times (6^2 - 1)}$$
$$= 1 - \frac{36}{6 \times 35}$$
$$= 0.829$$

This value is close to 1 which supports the assessment made from the scatter diagram that there is a fairly strong positive relationship between cost of production and production volume.

Data do not always consist of actual measurements. For example, in market research, data may consist of opinions on a particular product. This kind of data is called *ordinal* data. Ordinal data has the property that although it does not have actual numerical values, it can be ranked.

The next example should help you understand how to apply Spearman's method to ordinal data.

Example 10.2

BSL Marketing has been asked to conduct a survey into the public's attitude to a new chocolate bar. A pilot survey was carried out by asking 5 people of different ages to try the product and give their reaction. The result of this survey is shown in Table 10.4.

Table 10.4 Survey results for Example 10.2

Person	Age range	Response
A	below 10	very good
B	15 to 20	fair
C	20 to 25	fair
D	10 to 15	excellent
E	over 25	disliked

Activity 10.3

Is there any evidence of an association between age and preference for the product?

Both the age range and response can be ranked. It doesn't really matter how you rank them as long as you take your method into account when you come to interpret your coefficient. In the calculations that follow I have used low rankings for low age range and low rankings for the low response ratings (that is, 'disliked' has a ranking of 1). Using this method the rankings are as shown in Table 10.5.

Table 10.5 Rankings for data in Activity 10.3

Person	Age range	Rank	Response	Rank
A	below 10	1	very good	4
B	15 to 20	3	fair	2
C	20 to 25	4	fair	2
D	10 to 15	2	excellent	5
E	over 25	5	disliked	1

Notice that both B and C are ranked equal second in their responses. To compensate for the missing third rank a *mean* rank of 2.5 is used instead of rank 2. You can see this in Table 10.6.

Table 10.6 Calculation of R for Activity 10.3

Person	Age range	Response	Difference (d)	d^2
A	1	4	−3	9
B	3	2.5	0.5	0.25
C	4	2.5	1.5	2.25
D	2	5	−3	9
E	5	1	4	16
			Sum	36.5

The sum of the square of the differences is 36.5, and substituting this value into the formula gives:

$$R = 1 - \frac{6 \times 36.5}{5 \times (5^2 - 1)}$$

$$= 1 - \frac{219}{120}$$

$$= -0.825$$

This value is fairly large, which suggests an association between age and response. Since the coefficient is negative, it would appear that younger people are more likely to react favourably to the product.

Pearson's product moment correlation coefficient (r)

This measure of correlation tends to be the most popular, but it can only be used when the data is on the interval scale of measurement, that is, when the data consists of actual measurements. The formula for r is:

the sum of x times y → / ← the sum of x times the sum of y

$$r = \frac{n \sum xy - \sum x \sum y}{\sqrt{\left[n \sum x^2 - (\sum x)^2 \right] \left[n \sum y^2 - (\sum y)^2 \right]}}$$

the sum of x^2 ↗ ↖ the sum of x all squared

This formula looks daunting at first sight but it is quite straightforward to use, as you will see by attempting Activity 10.4.

Activity 10.4

Calculate the Pearson's product moment correlation coefficient for the data given in Example 10.1 (page 241).

To obtain this coefficient you are advised to set out the calculations in tabular form, as shown in Table 10.7.

Table 10.7 Calculation of r for Activity 10.4

Units produced x	Production cost y	xy	x^2	y^2
1	5.0	5.0	1	25.00
2	10.5	21.0	4	110.25
3	15.5	46.5	9	240.25
4	25.0	100.0	16	625.00
5	16.0	80.0	25	256.00
6	22.5	135.0	36	506.25
$\sum x = 21$	$\sum y = 94.5$	$\sum xy = 387.5$	$\sum x^2 = 91$	$\sum y^2 = 1762.75$

The summations can then be substituted into the formula for r:

$$r = \frac{6 \times 387.5 - 21 \times 94.5}{\sqrt{\left[6 \times 91 - (21)^2 \right] \left[6 \times 1762.75 - (94.5)^2 \right]}}$$

$$= \frac{340.5}{\sqrt{(105 \times 1646.25)}}$$

$$= \frac{340.5}{415.7598} = 0.8190$$

This calculation agrees with Spearman's calculation (see Activity 10.2) in that there is a strong positive correlation between production volume and cost.

Pearson's product moment correlation coefficient is a more accurate measure of the correlation between two *numeric* variables. However, it cannot be applied to non-numeric data.

Did you know

'The General Lifestyle Survey (formerly the General Household Survey) has run continuously since 1971' but is now under threat from the spending cuts. It is an important survey that provides vital data on lifestyle behaviour particularly on drinking and smoking. 'In 2009 more than 8000 households took part and 15 000 interviews were conducted. [The survey currently] collects data on

- demographic information about households, families and people
- housing tenure and household accommodation
- access to and ownership of consumer durables, including vehicles
- employment
- education
- health and use of health services
- smoking
- drinking
- family information, including marriage, cohabitation and fertility'

From this data health professionals have been able to identify correlations between lifestyles and health-related issues. For instance, people in routine and manual jobs smoke twice as much as people in managerial and professional groups. However people in managerial and professional jobs have a higher weekly alcohol intake (see www.statistics.gov.uk/pdfdir/ghs0111.pdf)

Source: 'Smoking and alcohol time series under threat', Straight Statistics (http://www.straightstatistics.org/article/smoking-and-alcohol-time-series-under-threat)

Activity 10.5

How large does Pearson's correlation coefficient have to be before we are convinced that there is real association between two variables?

There is no easy answer to this question as it depends on the number of data points. If we went to the extreme and only had 2 data points we would find that the correlation would be perfect as there is no scatter around the imaginary line between the two points. Conversely, the more data points we have the larger the scatter and therefore the smaller the value of r. In order to allow for the number of data points when assessing the value of r we can apply a *significance test* (see Chapter 9) to the result. The null hypothesis is that there is no association or the two variables are unrelated. That is:

$$H_0 : \rho = 0$$

and

$$H_1 : \rho \neq 0 \quad \text{where } \rho \text{ is the population coefficient}$$

The test is simple to apply. The *test statistic* is our calculated value of r and the *critical value* can be found from the table in Appendix 1. These tables are based on ν *degrees of freedom* and for bivariate data $\nu = n - 2$.

Activity 10.6

Carry out a test of significance on the value of r calculated in Activity 10.4.

The value of r was 0.8190, which is our test statistic. The critical value on 4 $(6 - 2)$ degrees of freedom at a 5% significance level is 0.8114. We can therefore reject H_0 (just) and conclude that there is a significant correlation between the number of units produced and the production cost.

Linear regression

The technique of *linear regression* attempts to define the relationship between the dependent and independent variables by the means of a linear equation. This is the simplest form of equation between two variables and, fortunately, many situations can at least be approximated by this type of relationship.

The scatter diagram for the production cost data of Example 10.1 has been reproduced in Figure 10.7. You will see that a line has been drawn through the data and this line represents the linear relationship between the two variables. However, since the relationship is not perfect it is possible to draw several different lines 'by eye' through the diagram, each of which would look reasonable. However, each line would represent a slightly different relationship as the gradient and/or intercept on the y-axis would be different. To decide how good a particular line is, you could find the difference between each point and the line. These differences are often referred to as the 'errors' between the actual value and that predicted by the line.

These errors have been represented by vertical lines on the diagram. Note that the errors below the line are negative and those above the line are positive. If you add these errors you will find that the total error is zero. Does this prove that the line is a good one? Unfortunately not, because the zero value is only obtained by adding positive and negative values. Many more lines could be found that also would give a

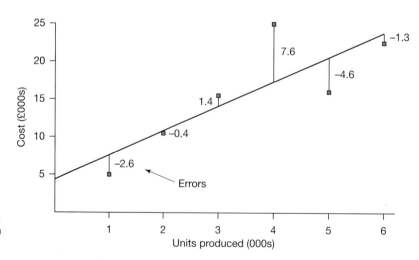

Figure 10.7
Line of best fit drawn through the data from Example 10.1

total error of zero. The errors could be added, ignoring the sign, but it can be shown that the best line or the 'line of best fit' is obtained when the sum of the squares of the errors is minimized. Squaring the errors not only removes the minus sign, but also gives more emphasis to the large errors.

The method of least squares

Linear regression involves finding that line that minimizes the sum of squares of the errors. The theory behind the *method of least squares* is beyond the scope of this book, but the application of the theory is straightforward. The most important part is to ensure that the *y* variable is the dependent variable – so, for example, the production cost depends on the number of units produced.

The linear regression model is given in the form:

the dependent variable ↘   ↙ the independent variable

$$y = a + bx$$

constants

The values of *a* and *b* that minimize the squared errors are given by the equations:

$$b = \frac{n \sum xy - \sum x \sum y}{n \sum x^2 - \left(\sum x\right)^2}$$

$$a = \frac{\sum y}{n} - b \frac{\sum x}{n}$$

You can think of *b* as the slope of the regression line and *a* as the value of the intercept on the *y*-axis (value of *y* when *x* is zero).

Activity 10.7

Calculate the regression line for the production cost data given in Example 10.1 (page 241).

You will probably realize that there are many similarities between the formula for *b* and that for *r*, the product moment correlation coefficient. Since the correlation coefficient has already been calculated for this data (Activity 10.4), you can note that:

$$\sum x = 21, \quad \sum y = 94.5,$$
$$\sum xy = 387.5 \quad \text{and} \quad \sum x^2 = 91$$

Substituting these values into the equations for *a* and *b* gives:

$$b = \frac{6 \times 387.5 - 21 \times 94.5}{6 \times 91 - 21^2} = 3.2429$$

and

$$a = \frac{94.5}{6} - \frac{(3.2429 \times 21)}{6} = 4.3999$$

The regression equation for this data is therefore:

$$y = 4.4 + 3.24x$$

That is: cost $= 4.4 + 3.24 \times$ units. This suggests that for every 1 unit (1000) rise in production volume, the production cost would rise, on average, by 3.24 units (£3240), and that when nothing is produced ($x = 0$), the production cost would still be £4400. This probably can be explained by factory overhead costs that are incurred even when there is no production.

In order to estimate the value of y for a particular value of x, this x value is substituted into the above equation.

Activity 10.8

Calculate the cost of production for production volumes of

(a) 2500 units
(b) 20 000 units

Have you any reservations regarding the costs obtained?

To obtain the cost of production for these two cases you would simply substitute the values of 2.5 and 20 into the equation $y = 4.4 + 3.24x$.

That is:

(a) $y = 4.4 + 3.24 \times 2.5 = 12.5$

So 2500 units would cost about £12 500 on average.

(b) $y = 4.4 + 3.24 \times 20 = 69.2$

and 20 000 units would cost £69 200 on average. However, 20 000 units is well outside the range of data used in the original analysis. You cannot be certain that the relationship between cost and volume will remain linear outside this range and so it would be unwise to place too much reliance on the predicted figure.

Coefficient of determination

Before a regression equation can be used effectively as a predictor for the dependent variable, it is necessary to decide how well it fits the data. One statistic that gives this information is the *coefficient of determination*. This measures the proportion of the variation in the dependent variable explained by the variation in the independent variable. It is given by r^2, which is the square of the product moment correlation coefficient.

Activity 10.9

What is the value of r^2 for the production cost data of Example 10.1?

The value of r is 0.8190, so $r^2 = 0.671$, which means that 0.67 or 67% of the variation in production cost is explained by the production volume. Alternatively, 33% of the variation is *not* explained.

Automatic methods of analyzing (paired) bivariate data

It is of course possible to use a calculator or a spreadsheet to carry out many of the calculations described in this chapter. Although a spreadsheet is by far the most useful method of analyzing bivariate data, a calculator can do most of the basic calculations, as the next activity illustrates.

Activity 10.10

Use the statistical functions on your calculator to find the regression coefficients (a and b) and Pearson's correlation coefficient (r) for the data in Example 10.1.

The instructions below refer to the Casio fx83ES and the fx85ES models. These are both popular calculators (the 85ES is a solar/battery powered model) and cost less than £10. If you have a different calculator you will need to refer to the instruction book. Whatever the make and model of your calculator, always repeat the calculation as a check that you have input the numbers correctly.

Before you start, clear the calculator by the following steps:

1 Press the keys $\boxed{\text{Shift}}$ $\boxed{9}$

Choose to clear all by

2 Press $\boxed{3}$ $\boxed{=}$

Then

3 Press $\boxed{\text{AC}}$

To enter the STAT mode

Press $\boxed{\text{Mode}}$ $\boxed{2}$

And $\boxed{2}$ for paired data

The Units produced (1, 2, 3, 4, 5, 6) are entered as the x data and the Production cost (5.0, 10.5, 15.5, 25.0, 16.0, 22.5) as the y data.

When all the data has been entered press $\boxed{\text{Shift}}$ $\boxed{1}$

Then press $\boxed{7}$ for regression.

This allows you to obtain the two coefficients (called A and B) as well as the correlation coefficient (r)

You should get $A = 4.4$; $B = 3.24$ and $r = 0.8189$. (Remember to delete the chosen statistic each time otherwise it gets included in the data.)

However, a standard scientific calculator will not be able to provide you with scatter diagrams of your data. Being able to easily create scatter charts is a major advantage of using a spreadsheet to analyze bivariate data.

Activity 10.11

Use a spreadsheet to draw a scatter chart of the data in Example 10.1.

Figure 10.8 is a screen shot of the first stage in creating a scatter chart in Excel 2010. The steps for creating a scatter chart in Excel are the same as for other charts (see Creating charts with Excel 2010 in Chapter 4, page 72). The final scatter diagram has already been shown in Figure 10.5 (page 242).

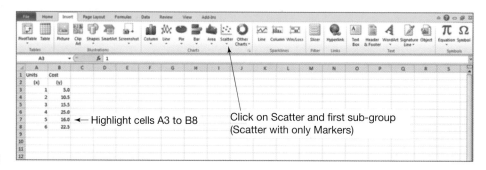

Figure 10.8
Using Excel 2010 to create a scatter chart

As well as creating charts, Excel can also be used to calculate the regression and Pearson's correlation coefficients. In finding the correct function to use you may find Table 10.8 useful: it lists the most commonly used bivariate functions. Figure 10.9 shows how the functions have been applied to the data for Example 10.1.

Table 10.8 Commonly used bivariate functions in Excel

Function	Meaning
=CORREL (x-values, y-values) or =PEARSON (x-values, y-values)	Calculates the Pearson product moment correlation coefficient r
=SLOPE (y-values, x-values)	Calculates slope of regression line
=INTERCEPT (y-values, x-values)	Calculates intercept of regression line
=RSQ (x-values, y-values)	Calculates r^2
=FORECAST (8, y-values, x-values)	Predicts y for $x = 8$ from the linear regression equation

	A	B	C
1	Units	Cost	
2	1	5	
3	2	10.5	
4	3	15.5	
5	4	25	
6	5	16	
7	6	22.5	
8			
9	Pearson's correlation coefficient (using CORREL)		=CORREL(A2:A7,B2:B7)
10	Pearson's correlation coefficient (using PEARSON)		=PEARSON(A2:A7,B2:B7)
11			
12	Slope of regression equation (b)		=INTERCEPT(B2:B7,A2:A7)
13	Intercept of regression equation (a)		=SLOPE(B2:B7,A2:A7)
14			
15	Coefficient of determination (r-square)		=RSQ(A2:A7,B2:B7)
16			
17	Forecast for x = 8		=FORECAST(8,B2:B7,A2:A7)
18			
19			

Figure 10.9
Excel's bivariate functions applied to data from Example 10.1

Notice that for the Slope, Intercept, RSQ and Forecast functions it is most important that you put the *y* values first. You might notice too that there is no function for Spearman's correlation coefficient in Excel.

Activity 10.12

Use the Forecast function in Excel to predict the production cost for a volume of 8000 units.

You should have got a value of £30 343.

Activity 10.13

Add the regression line (the line of best fit) to the scatter diagram.

It is possible to use Excel to calculate the predicted *y* values for given *x* values and then this new data series could be plotted on the same chart as the original data. However, an easier method is to use the Trendline facility within Excel. To add the regression line, click on the Layout tab within the Chart Tools and then click on Trendline which is in the Analysis Group. Select the Linear Trend. The regression line will be inserted as you can see in Figure 10.10.

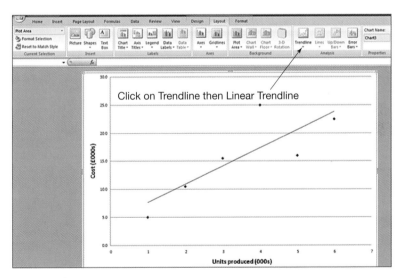

Figure 10.10
Adding the regression equation to a scatter diagram

It could be useful to extend the axes to enable the chart to be used for predictions.
Again click on the Layout tab if not already selected and click on the Axes group. Choose Primary Horizontal Axis and then More Primary Horizontal Axes Options. Under Axes Options change the Maximum from Auto to Fixed and change the maximum value to 10.0
Do the same for the Primary Vertical Axes and give it a maximum value of 40.
Now click on Trendline again and More Trendline Options. Under Forecast Forward enter 4 units to extend the trendline to a production volume of 10000 units (see Figure 10.11).

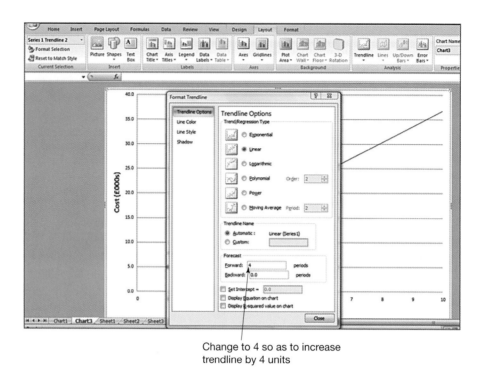

Figure 10.11
Using the Excel
Trendline Options

Change to 4 so as to increase
trendline by 4 units

Activity 10.14

Use your chart to predict the cost of production for a volume of 8000 units.

From Figure 10.12 you will see that the predicted volume is just over £30 000, which agrees with the value obtained in Activity 10.12. Of course extrapolating the regression line assumes that the line remains linear outside the range of collected data. This reservation has already been mentioned in the solution to Activity 10.8.

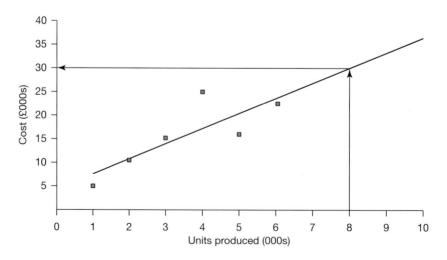

Figure 10.12
Using the regression
line for forecasting

SPSS and scatter diagrams

SPSS can create a scatter diagram within the Graphs/Chart Builder menu. We will use the data from Example 10.1 to demonstrate the use of this routine. Click on Scatter/Dot and drag the Simple Scatter into the Gallery window. Now drag Units into the horizontal axis and Cost into the vertical axis (see Figure 10.13). Click on OK and you get the chart shown in Figure 10.14

Click on Graphs and Chart Builder

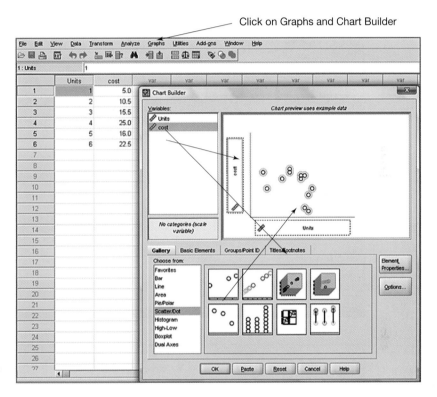

Figure 10.13
The Scatter routine in SPSS

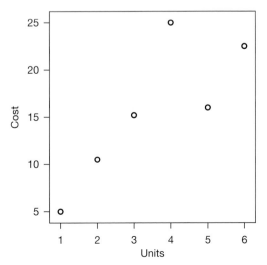

Figure 10.14
Options for a scatter diagram in SPSS

SPSS and linear regression

Linear regression can be performed in SPSS using the regression routine under `Analysis` (see Figure 10.15). Add the two variables as before (Figure 10.16), and click `OK`. Part of the output is shown in Figure 10.17.

The coefficients agree with those that we calculated manually, and with those obtained from Excel.

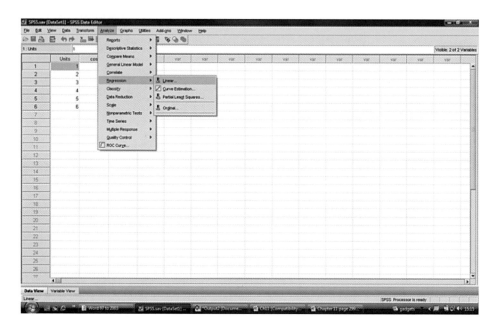

Figure 10.15
Linear regression
routine in SPSS

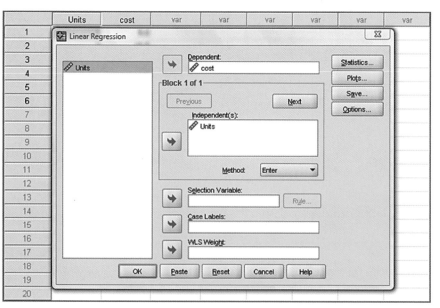

Figure 10.16
Setting SPSS for
regression analysis

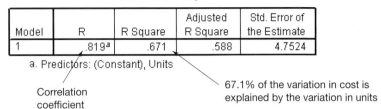

Model Summary

Model	R	R Square	Adjusted R Square	Std. Error of the Estimate
1	.819[a]	.671	.588	4.7524

a. Predictors: (Constant), Units

Correlation coefficient

67.1% of the variation in cost is explained by the variation in units

Coefficients[a]

Model		Unstandardized Coefficients		Standardized Coefficients	t	Sig.
		B	Std. Error	Beta		
1	(Constant)	4.400	4.424		.995	.376
	Units	3.243	1.136	.819	2.854	.046

a. Dependent Variable: cost

The 'a' coefficient   The 'b' coefficient

Figure 10.17
Output from SPSS

Further topics in regression

The topics we have discussed so far in this chapter are the most important in terms of understanding the general principles of correlation and regression and will be sufficient for most courses. However there are a number of more advanced topics that might be included in some courses which we will cover here. These topics generally use ideas from earlier chapters (Analysis of sample data – Chapter 8 and Testing a hypothesis – Chapter 9) and so should be understandable by most students.

To make things more 'statistical' and to aid the introduction of multiple regression we are going to modify our formula for the equation of the regression line. So instead of using $y = a + bx$, as on page 249, we are going to use the equation in the form of

$$y_i = \beta_0 + \beta_1 x_i + e_i$$

where

y_i = the value of the dependent variable of the ith value
x_i = the value of the independent variable for the ith value
β_0 = the population intercept
β_1 = the population slope
e_i = the error of prediction for the ith value ($e_i = y_i - \hat{y}$)

The method of least squares (see page 249) minimizes the sum of the squared errors. In this calculation we are assuming that the errors are normally distributed with mean of zero and standard error of the estimate of

$$s_e = \sqrt{\frac{\sum_{i=1}^{n}(y_i - \hat{y})^2}{n - 2}}$$

Hypothesis test for the slope, β_1

The parameter β_1 is only an estimate of the true population slope as it is derived from a sample. How do we know that the slope is not zero? We use the same idea as in Chapter 9 and set up the null and alternative hypotheses.

$$H_0 : \beta_1 = 0$$
$$H_1 : \beta_1 \neq 0$$

The test statistic follows a t-distribution and has value

$$t = \frac{b_1 - \beta_1}{s_b}$$

where b_1 is the sample regression slope and s_b is the standard deviation.

The formula for s_b is

$$s_b = \frac{s_e}{\sqrt{\sum_{i=1}^{n}(x_i - \bar{x})^2}}$$

$$= \frac{s_e}{\sqrt{\sum x_i^2 - \frac{\left(\sum x_i\right)^2}{n}}}$$

Activity 10.16

Using Example 10.1 (page 241) test to see if the slope is significantly different from zero.

From Activity 10.7 we know that the regression equation is $y = 4.4 + 3.24x$ (see page 250), so $b_1 = 3.24$.

The standard error can be found from Table 10.9.

$$\text{So } s_e = \sqrt{\frac{90.3436}{4}}$$

$$= 4.7524$$

You will notice that this is the same value as obtained by SPSS (Figure 10.17).

Table 10.9 Calculation of s_e

Units produced	Production cost	Predicted $\hat{y}$	Residual $y - \hat{y}$	$(y - \hat{y})^2$
1	5.0	7.64	−2.6	6.9696
2	10.5	10.88	−0.4	0.1444
3	15.5	14.12	1.4	1.9044
4	25.0	17.36	7.6	58.3696
5	16.0	20.6	−4.6	21.16
6	22.5	23.84	−1.3	1.7956
			Sum	90.3436

Next we have to calculate the value of s_b. From Activity 10.7 (page 249) we know that $\sum x_i = 21$ and $\sum x_i^2 = 91$, so

$$s_b = \frac{4.7524}{\sqrt{91 - \frac{21^2}{6}}}$$

$$= 1.136$$

You will also see this figure in Figure 10.17 under 'Std Error' for Units.

We can now calculate the test statistic

$$t = \frac{3.240}{1.136}$$

$$= 2.852 \quad \text{(which again agrees with the } t \text{ value for Units given in Figure 10.17)}$$

The critical value on 4 (that is, $n - 2$) degrees of freedom is 2.776 at 5% significance level (2 tailed). As our test statistic is greater than this value we reject H_0 and conclude that $\beta_1 \neq 0$. (In Figure 10.17 the last column headed 'Sig.' gives a value of .046. This is the p-value which was discussed in Chapter 9 and since it is below .05 or 5% we again would reject H_0.)

Confidence intervals for the slope

As well as a significance test of the slope we can calculate 95% confidence limits within which the true regression line is expected to lie. The formula is

$$b_1 - t_{(n-2, \alpha/2)} s_b < \beta_1 < b_1 + t_{(n-2, \alpha/2)} s_b$$

Because $t_{(n-2, \alpha/2)} = 2.776$, $s_b = 1.136$ and $\alpha = .05$ our confidence intervals are

$$3.24 - 2.776 \times 1.136 \quad \text{and} \quad 3.24 + 2.776 \times 1.136$$

$$= 0.086 \quad \text{and} \quad 6.39$$

As this range does not include zero it reinforces our conclusion that $\beta_1 \neq 0$.

Multiple regression

So far we have only looked at one independent variable but it is possible to have several, as in the case of the hotel regression model discussed in the Quantitative methods in action at the start of this chapter.

The population multiple regression model is

$$y_i = \beta_0 + \beta_1 x_{1i} + \beta_2 x_{2i} + \ldots + \beta_k x_{ki} + e_i$$

The assumptions required (in addition to that mentioned for the simple two variable model) to use this model are:

1 The x_{ji} values are independent variables with fixed (i.e. non-stochastic) values.
2 The expected value of the random variable y_i is a *linear* function of the independent x_{ki} variables.
3 There is no significant linear relationship between the independent variables.

When the third assumption is violated we say that the data suffers from *multicollinearity*. Whenever there are a large number of independent variables it is very likely that some of the variables will be correlated with each other. The easiest way to check for multicollinearity is to produce a correlation matrix. This is quite easy with SPSS. The correlations between the independent variables should be low although there is no specific value at which we can say that multicollinearity is present. If correlations between two independent variables are high we may find that removing one of them is the easiest solution.

Activity 10.15 demonstrates the application of multiple regression analysis to a small problem with three independent variables.

Activity 10.15

Table 10.10 gives the top 15 medal-winning countries at the 2008 Olympics. Also provided is information on the country's population, its gross national income per capita (GNI) and the average life expectancy. Is there a relationship between any of these variables and the number of medals won?

Table 10.10 Data on Olympic medal-winning countries, 2008, in order of gold medals won

Country	Total medals won	Population (millions)	GNI ($ equivalent)	Life expectancy
China	100	1324.7	5370	73
US	110	304.5	45850	78
Russia	72	141.9	14400	67
GB	47	61.3	34370	79
Germany	40	82.2	33820	79
Australia	45	21.3	33340	81
South Korea	31	48.6	24750	79
Japan	25	127.7	34600	82
Italy	28	59.9	29900	81
France	40	62.0	33470	81
Ukraine	28	46.2	6810	68
Netherlands	16	16.4	39500	80
Jamaica	11	2.7	5050	72
Spain	17	46.5	30100	80
Kenya	14	38.0	1540	53

Source: 2008 Population Reference Bureau and Wikipedia, the free encyclopedia.

We first use SPSS to obtain the correlations between all the variables to see if any of the independent variables are correlated. As you can see in Figure 10.18 there is a correlation between GNI and life expectancy. This is to be expected as both variables measure a country's affluence.

We will now use SPSS to run a regression analysis on the other variables (omitting life expectancy). The results can be seen in Figure 10.19.

Correlations		Total medals won	Population in millions	Gross national income in $	Life expectancy
Total medals won	Pearson Correlation	1	.686**	.131	.052
	Sig. (2-tailed)		.005	.641	.853
	N	15	15	15	15
Population in millions	Pearson Correlation	.686**	1	-.281	-.068
	Sig. (2-tailed)	.005		.311	.810
	N	15	15	15	15
Gross national income in $	Pearson Correlation	.131	-.281	1	.796**
	Sig. (2-tailed)	.641	.311		.000
	N	15	15	15	15
Life expectancy	Pearson Correlation	.052	-.068	.796**	1
	Sig. (2-tailed)	.853	.810	.000	
	N	15	15	15	15

**. Correlation is significant at the 0.01 level (2-tailed).

Figure 10.18
Correlation matrix for
the Olympic variables

Life expectancy and
Gross national income
are correlated

Model Summary

Model	R	R Square	Adjusted R Square	Std. Error of the Estimate
1	.764[a]	.584	.514	21.053

a. Predictors: (Constant), Gross national income in $,
Population in millions

The p-value

ANOVA[b]

Model		Sum of Squares	df	Mean Square	F	Sig.
1	Regression	7456.633	2	3728.317	8.411	.005[a]
	Residual	5318.967	12	443.247		
	Total	12775.600	14			

a. Predictors: (Constant), Gross national income in $, Population in millions
b. Dependent Variable: Total medals won

Coefficients[a]

Model		Unstandardized Coefficients		Standardized Coefficients	t	Sig.
		B	Std. Error	Beta		
1	(Constant)	11.794	12.536		.941	.365
	Population in millions	.072	.018	.784	4.041	.002
	Gross national income in $	.001	.000	.351	1.810	.095

a. Dependent Variable: Total medals won

Figure 10.19
Printout from SPSS
on the Olympic
regression results

A lot of information is provided in Figure 10.19. The *Model Summary* gives the *R* square value. The relevant figure to look at is the *Adjusted R Square* because this allows for the number of variables. The value of .514 means that the two independent variables, Population and GNI, account for just over half the variation in the dependent variable. The ANOVA table (this stands for *Analysis of Variance*) looks at the significance of the regression model. The *F*-statistic is used to measure this significance and a value of 8.411 is highly significant. The value of .005 is the *p*-value and is well below the 5% (.05) level normally accepted as significant. The final table gives the coefficients of the regression model which is described by:

Medals won $= 11.8 + .072 \times$ Pop $+ .001 \times$ GNI

How would we use this equation? If we take Great Britain as an example we have Pop $= 61.3$ and GNI $= \$34\,370$ so

$$\text{Medals won} = 11.8 + .072 \times 61.3 + .001 \times 34\,370$$
$$= 11.8 + 4.4 + 34.4$$
$$= 50.6$$

This is the predicted value and represents an error of 7.6% on the actual value.

Activity 10.16

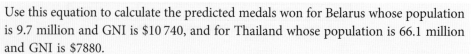

Use this equation to calculate the predicted medals won for Belarus whose population is 9.7 million and GNI is $10 740, and for Thailand whose population is 66.1 million and GNI is $7880.

Using the regression equation again we get for Belarus:

$$\text{Medals won} = 11.8 + .072 \times 9.7 + .001 \times 10\,740$$
$$= 11.8 + 0.7 + 10.7$$
$$= 23.2$$

This is not too far out from what they actually got (19).
For Thailand:

$$\text{Medals won} = 11.8 + .072 \times 66.1 + .001 \times 7880$$
$$= 11.8 + 4.8 + 7.8$$
$$= 24.4$$

This is very different from the total medals Thailand won (4).

Activity 10.17

Can you think of reasons why the regression equation doesn't work very well for countries like Thailand?

I am sure that you can think of lots of reasons! The fact that we have a constant term of 11.8 means that we will only be able to use the model to predict the number of medals won by the top sporting nations. The reason that we were not far out in predicting Belarus is that they were 16th in the table. Statistically we didn't take a random sample. Instead we chose the top 15 countries on which to base our equation. Because we are only explaining around 50% of the variation in the medals won there are obviously other factors that could explain the other 50%. The countries that did well could have a culture of competing in sporting competitions, something which would be hard to model.

Reflection

As with all statistics, it is possible to draw misleading conclusions when using correlation and regression analysis. The biggest mistake is to assume that *association* means *causation*. This is certainly not the case as you can get spurious correlations, such as the study in San Francisco that showed that the more fire engines attend a fire, the worse the damage will be! The reason for this spurious correlation is that with large fires the two variables are correlated.

There are other cases that might seem quite reasonable, such as that students who do well at school also earn higher incomes later in life. This might be a valid cause and effect, but it might also be explained in other ways – for example, it might be that students who work hard at school also work hard at their job. This is called a *lurking variable* or *hidden variable*.

It is often quite difficult to differentiate real causation from spurious association. Take the example of shoe size and reading skills. It can be shown that there is a strong association between these – but this arises only because those with bigger feet also tend to be older! In this case age is called the *confounding factor*.

In other cases there may indeed be causation, without it being obvious which factor causes the other. For example, a study in America showed that students who smoked had worse grades that those who didn't. The conclusion drawn was that students would do better if they gave up smoking. In fact, of course, it might happen the other way round: perhaps students smoke because they don't do well academically – but this conclusion is not nearly so attractive!

Key points

- A *dependent variable* is a variable that depends on one or more other (*independent*) variables.
- The *correlation* between the dependent and an independent variable can be either *positive* or *negative*, depending on whether the dependent variable increases or decreases with an increase in the independent variable.
- Spearman's correlation coefficient can be calculated on any bivariate data but it is normally used for ordinal data.
- Pearson's product moment correlation coefficient can only be used on interval scale data.
- Given a value of the independent variable, a *linear regression model* allows the value of the dependent variable to be calculated.
- The method of least squares is used to calculate the parameters in a linear regression model.

- The *coefficient of determination* determines what proportion of the *variability* in the dependent variable is explained by the independent variable.
- A test on the significance of the regression slope can be calculated either by hand or by SPSS. The same is true for the confidence interval of the slope.
- A *multiple regression model* has more than one independent variable

Further reading

There are a large number of texts on this topic at varying levels. Many texts such as Morris (2008), Curwin and Slater (2008) are aimed at the business student. Curwin and Slater has quite a good section on multiple regression as does Wisniewski (2009). A useful text for the student with good maths skills is the one by Anderson, Sweeney and Williams (2007) but it goes way beyond what most business students need.

Web links W

Answers to selected questions can be found in Appendix 2. Answers to the other questions can be found on the companion website for this book.

Practice questions

W **1** Suppose the correlation coefficient for age and earnings is 0.3. With the help of a sketch explain what this means. Define the age range to which this correlation might apply.

W **2** Suppose the correlation coefficient for age and alcohol consumption is -0.6. With the help of a sketch explain what this means.

W **3** Calculate Spearman's correlation coefficient for the following data.

x	1	2	3	4	5	6	7
y	9	6	7	9	5	2	1

W **4** A group of 6 students were monitored during their first year at university and their marks in Statistics and Management accounting were recorded. See below. Use Spearman's correlation coefficient to determine if there is any correlation between the scores in the two modules.

Student	Statistics	Management accounting
A	64%	77%
B	56%	52%
C	46%	66%
D	67%	67%
E	50%	62%
F	84%	87%

W **5** A regression line is $y = 3 + 5x$. What is the value of y if $x = 2$?

6 The data in Table 10.11 relate to the weight and height of a group of students.
   (a) Draw a scatter diagram of weight against height for the whole data. Alongside each point write either 'm' or 'f' as appropriate.

Table 10.11 Weight and height data for Question 6

Height (in)	Weight (lb)	Sex
68	148	male
69	126	female
66	145	male
70	158	male
66	140	female
68	126	female
64	120	female
66	119	female
70	182	male
62	127	female
68	165	male
63	133	male
65	124	female
73	203	male

(b) Describe your scatter diagram. Try drawing an ellipse around
  (i) all the points
  (ii) the points relating to the male students
  (iii) the points relating to the female students.

  Is there any indication that the correlation is stronger for either group?

(c) Calculate Pearson's product moment correlation coefficient for the three sets of points identified in (b) above. Comment on the values obtained. (Collect data from a group of friends and repeat the analysis.)

7 A group of students compared the results they obtained in a quantitative methods assignment and a law assignment. The results by position in a group of 50 were as follows:

Student	A	B	C	D	E	F	G	H	I
Quants	5	8	45	2	9	5	15	20	3
Law	29	17	1	11	6	18	33	3	8

Use Spearman's rank correlation coefficient to discover whether there is any correlation between position in each subject.

8 A company is investigating the relationship between sales and advertising revenue. Data has been collected on these two variables and is shown below (all figures are in £000s):

Month	Jan	Feb	Mar	Apr	May	Jun	Jul	Aug	Sep	Oct	Nov	Dec
Sales	60	60	58	45	41	33	31	25	24	23	23	23
Adv.	6.0	6.0	6.0	5.8	4.5	4.1	3.3	3.1	2.5	2.4	2.3	2.3

(a) Plot a scatter diagram of the data given in the table above. Comment on the strength of the association between the two variables.

(b) Obtain the least squares regression line and comment on how well it fits the data.

(c) What would the expected sales be, given an advertising expenditure of £5000?

9 Consider the following pairs of variables and make an assessment of the likely correlation between them. Mark each pair to show whether you expect the correlation to be positive or negative (strong or weak), or close to zero:

(a) Attendance totals and position in football league table

(b) The age of a relatively new make of car and its value

(c) The age of a vintage make of car and its value

(d) Length of education and annual earnings

(e) Level of unemployment and hire purchase sales over a period of 10 years.

10 The following data relate to the size of the electricity bill sent to 7 randomly selected customers and the time the customers took to pay the bills.

Customer no.	1	2	3	4	5	6	7
Size of bill	£100	£150	£200	£250	£330	£400	£480
Time to pay (days)	15	20	16	20	24	32	28

(a) (i) Plot the data on a scatter graph.

(ii) Use your calculator to find Pearson's correlation coefficient for the data.

(b) Determine the least squares regression equation that can be used to predict how long a bill of a given size will take to pay.

(c) Interpret your equation.

(d) Draw the line on the scatter graph.

(e) Use your equation to predict how long it will take a customer to pay:

(i) a bill of £125, and

(ii) a bill of £1000.

What reservations do you have about these predictions?

(f) The coefficient of determination for this data is 79.2%. Interpret this value.

11 A local government research unit is looking at the methods that councils use to collect rent from tenants living in houses and flats. In particular, it wants to know whether the relatively expensive door-to-door collection method is effective. A random sample of six local councils is selected and for each council the percentage of rent collected door-to-door and the percentage of total rent which is in arrears is recorded. The results are shown below.

% collected door-to-door	1	12	16	11	20	6
% of total rent in arrears	13	10	8	12	7	11

(a) Plot the data for the two variables on a scatter graph.

(b) Calculate Spearman's correlation coefficient for this data.

12 The personnel manager of a company is concerned with the high sickness records of its production staff. An analysis of its night shift revealed the figures shown in Table 10.12.

(a) Plot a scatter graph of this data. What can you deduce about the association between number of days taken off sick last year and age?

(b) Using your calculator's statistical mode or otherwise, calculate a correlation coefficient for this data.

(c) Carry out a suitable test at the 5% level to see whether there is a significant correlation between days off work and age.

(d) The least squares regression relationship between days off sick and age is:

Days off sick $= 17.4 - 0.2118 \times$ Age

(i) Plot this line on your scatter graph.

Table 10.12 Sickness records

Person	Age	Days off work last year
A	21	20
B	19	8
C	36	8
D	55	5
E	20	13
F	22	15
G	45	12
H	39	7
I	32	11
J	28	8

(ii) Do either of the numbers 17.4 or −0.2118 have a practical (*not* mathematical) meaning? If so, explain.

(iii) What prediction can you make about the days off sick for a person who is 65 years old and works on the night shift? Comment on your answer.

(iv) Calculate the coefficient of determination for this data and interpret its value.

(v) What other factors might affect days off sick?

W 13 A company believes that the monthly sales of one of its products are related to the amount spent on advertising during the previous month. It records monthly sales and advertising spend in the preceding month and obtains the data given below.

Sales (£m)	1.00	1.02	1.30	1.45	1.20	1.08	1.25
Advert. prev. month (£000s)	50	51	60	65	45	49	55

(a) Determine the regression equation for sales upon advertising.

(b) What value do you predict for next month's sales if advertising this month is (i) £40 000 (ii) £80 000. Do you have any reservations with your answers?

W 14 A company is concerned at the variability in sales at its 10 stores. There are thoughts that this variability is to do with the size of the town in which the store is situated. It is also possible that the size of store might affect sales. Another thought is that the experience of the store manager (as measured by number of years working for the company) might have an influence. The data for the 10 stores is given below:

Sales (£000s)	Population of town (000s)	Size of store (000 m²)	Years' experience
67.0	20.0	4.3	12.0
89.0	30.0	6.4	5.0
90.0	25.0	2.1	6.0
154.0	36.0	3.5	3.0
102.0	34.5	5.0	5.0
75.0	15.0	1.7	2.0
250.0	65.0	12.1	1.0
87.0	31.0	7.6	4.0
54.5	24.9	4.4	3.0
69.0	18.6	4.7	1.0

(a) Use SPSS or Excel to produce a scatter plot of sales against each of the other variables. What do you conclude from each plot?

(b) Use SPSS or another statistical package to obtain the correlation coefficients of sales against each of the other variables. Do the correlations correspond to your conclusions in part (a)?

(c) Use SPSS or another statistical package to obtain the regression equation with the largest R^2.

(d) Use your equation to obtain the predicted sales for a 6000 m^2 store in a town with a population of 28 000 people and where the manager has 12 years' experience.

(e) Comment on the data used for this investigation.

W **15** In Question 13 determine whether the regression slope is significant. Also, obtain the confidence interval for the slope.

....

Assignment

It seems reasonable to assume that the second hand price of a particular make of car is dependent on its age. Decide on a particular make and model of car and a suitable source for the data, such as your local newspaper. Collect data on the age and price of around 20 cars and use Excel to do the following:

(a) Plot a scatter graph of the data. Does the scatter graph indicate that a linear relationship exists for all or part of the range of the data?

(b) Obtain the regression equation that would enable the price of the car to be obtained given its age.

(c) Using the equation obtained in (b) above and suitable examples, illustrate how the price of a car could be found if its age was known. Within what age range is your equation valid? Why is this so?

(d) What proportion of the variability in price is explained by the age factor?

(e) Investigate whether other factors, such as engine size, would improve the fit of the regression equation

IV

DECISION-MAKING TECHNIQUES

How to make good decisions

Prerequisites	To complete this chapter successfully you should have worked through Chapter 6 (*Taking a chance: probability*).
Objectives	○ To be able to use diagrams to represent a problem situation
	○ To understand how to make decisions using payoff tables
	○ To be able to calculate expected monetary values
	○ To know how to solve problems using decision trees
	○ To be able to use Bayes' theorem in decision-making
	○ To know how to use a spreadsheet to carry out sensitivity analysis on a decision tree
	○ To be able to calculate the expected value of perfect and imperfect information
	○ To understand the idea of utility
	○ To be able to apply the SMART technique to decisions involving multiple attributes
	○ To appreciate the use of Hiview3 MCDA software
Introduction	Everyone has to make decisions from time to time. These can vary from the simple, such as 'What should I have for breakfast this morning?', to the complex, such as how to manage the UK's radioactive waste. Many decisions have to be made with incomplete information, perhaps because the problem is unclear or the outcome of a decision is uncertain or because the outcome will occur at some time in the future. Many decisions involve more than one criterion, as in the case of the radioactive waste study or choosing which house to buy. Techniques have been developed that are able to take account of *uncertainty*, and these will be discussed in the first part of this chapter. The later part of the chapter will deal with one technique for handling problems in which we have more than one criterion to consider, such as the radioactive waste decision problem described in *Quantitative methods in action*.

Quantitative methods in action: how to manage the UK's radioactive waste

Nuclear energy is a 'clean'* energy source in that it doesn't release greenhouse gases. However, nuclear energy creates radioactive waste which takes hundreds of years to decay and become safe.

To prevent this waste from contaminating the environment safe methods of disposal must be found. These methods of disposal include interim storage (man-made storage which is safe for up to 300 years), geological disposal (below-ground disposal such as boreholes) and non-geological disposal (e.g. concrete over reactors). Within each of these options there are a number of sub-options giving 14 options in total. Each of these options have advantages and disadvantages depending on what criteria (or attributes) are used to appraise them. In the UK. after wide consultation, 27 criteria were agreed on. These criteria include public safety, the environment, security, costs etc.

During 28 to 30 March 2006 a group of experts from CoRWM (Committe on Radiactive Waste Management) got together with staff from Catalyze and the London School of Economics to appraise options for managing UK's radioactive waste. This *decision conference* applied the multi-criteria decision analysis (MCDA) approach to arrive at a consensus about the relative merits of each option. Its aim was not to arrive at a 'right answer' but to provide an insight into the issues surrounding each option and to consider uncertainty in the importance of each attribute. The MCDA software Hiview3^{TM} was used to aid the analysis and the results indicated that

1 Geological disposal options are much preferred to storage options
2 The borehole option is the least preferred disposal option
3 The results are strongly influenced by just four main criteria: safety, security, burden on future generations and flexibility (ability to change if required).

The government published its white paper which broadly backed the geological disposal option on 12 June 2008.

For further information see www.corwm.org.uk/pdf/1716.

*However, since the nuclear crisis at Japan's Fukushima nuclear plant, questions have been raised about the safety of nuclear energy.

Problem formulation

Not all business problems are what they seem. Although in most text books (including this one) there is a tendency to portray a problem as well structured, this is far from the case in real life. In many cases it is not even obvious what the problem is and in these situations there is a danger that the wrong problem is solved. For example, one train company was disappointed in the sales of food and drink in its on-train buffet and thought that the reason was that items were overpriced. They therefore reduced the prices but all that they achieved was that the profit decreased – sales were exactly the same. In fact, on closer analysis they realized that the reason for the poor sales was that trains were over-crowded and passengers couldn't get to the buffet car! Whenever you are faced with a business problem you need to step back and take a holistic view. One of the best ways to do this is to draw diagrams of the problem situation. In this chapter we are going to look at several diagrams to help in identifying the problem and then more specialized diagrams to help solve a particular problem.

Mind maps

A mind map means what it says – it is simply a way of transferring your thoughts onto paper. There is no formal way of drawing a mind map and you can put things in any order. Where two things are related or causal it is a good idea to connect them up with a line or arrow. Mind maps are useful where you are trying to get a consensus among a group of people. In these situations it is usually a good idea to get each member of the group to write their thoughts on a 'post-it' note and stick it to a board or flipchart. You as facilitator can then arrange these notes into some logical sequence and from this some 'brain-storming' might be achieved.

Activity 11.1

Imagine that you are on a train and thinking about buying some food and drink from the buffet. Draw a mind map of the thoughts that might go through your mind before you make your decision.

Some ideas are shown in Figure 11.1 overleaf. These are only ideas and you may have got some better or different ones. Perhaps after drawing this map you realize that what perhaps is needed is more passenger information such as whether there is a trolley service, where the buffet car is and the prices.

Rich picture diagrams

Rich pictures were developed by Peter Checkland (1981) as part of his soft systems methodology. Instead of writing sentences as in mind maps you use cartoon-type symbols. There are some commonly used symbols (for example, 'stick men') but, generally, as long as it is clear to an observer what you are trying to say then almost anything is acceptable. (Words can also be added to make the meaning clear.) The

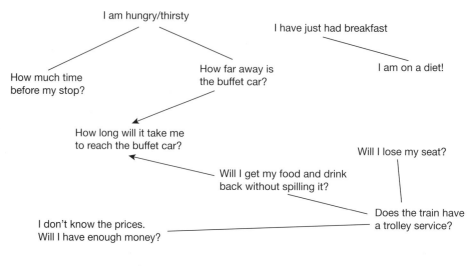

Figure 11.1
Mind map for the
buffet decision

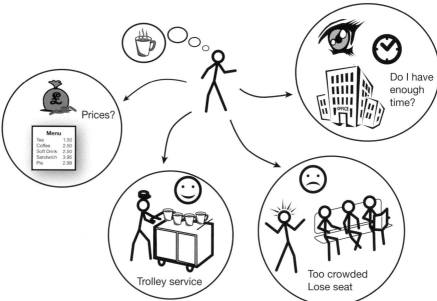

Figure 11.2
Rich picture for the
buffet decision

diagrams can be drawn by commercial drawing programs such as *Microsoft Visio 2010* although hand-drawn diagrams are quite acceptable, fun to do and more spontaneous. Figure 11.2 gives a possible rich picture diagram for the buffet problem.

Although rich pictures are a useful first step in structuring a problem they are rarely incorporated into a formal report. The next three types of diagram are more acceptable for publication.

Cognitive maps

These maps are similar to mind maps except they are more structured and attempt to explain the environment from a decision-maker's point of view. Cognitive maps or mapping began life in the field of psychology with Edward Tolman's work with rats.

They are now an essential part of a *soft systems analyst*'s tool kit. A cognitive map makes use of *constructs* and links. These constructs are statements by the decision-maker which usually lead to possible outcomes or other constructs. The constructs are linked by arrows to show the direction of the connection. To demonstrate a simple application of cognitive maps the case of the buffet problem is expanded in Example 11.1 and given from the point of view of the rail manager who has to make the decision on what to do.

Example 11.1

The manager of Avon railways is concerned at the poor sales of the buffet items [1] even after an attempt to boost sales by reducing prices [2]. Unless the buffet can produce a profit it will have to be withdrawn [3]. However this action might lose passengers to rival services [4] and therefore other solutions are being considered. It is clear that overcrowding [5] was preventing people from reaching the buffet car, and a customer survey showed that travellers were unhappy with the overcrowding in any case. Various solutions were proposed, including raising ticket prices [6] which would reduce demand [7] but this would upset passengers [8] and might cause problems with the rail regulator [9]. Another option was to increase the frequency of the service [10] or to add another coach to the trains [11]. Both these options would increase costs [12] although this cost should be offset by increased ticket and buffet sales [13]. Costs could also be reduced by having a trolley service instead of a buffet car [14]. A trolley service would also mean that the buffet car could be replaced by a passenger coach which would be a cheaper option.

Figure 11.3 shows the cognitive map drawn using these constructs. Each construct in the example is given a number so that the map is easier to follow.

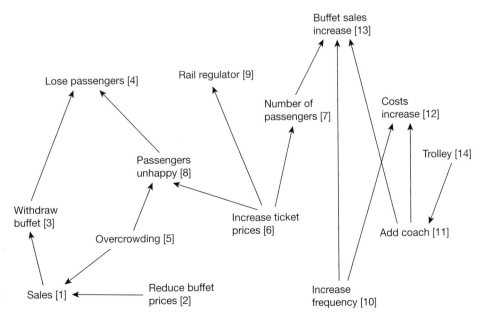

Figure 11.3
Cognitive map for the buffet sales problem

From this diagram the decision might be to investigate the option of replacing the buffet car with a passenger coach and using a trolley service instead. Of course a break-even analysis would be necessary to work out what trolley sales would be needed to pay for the passenger coach.

Causal loop diagrams

To take cognitive mapping one stage further we could show how one construct affects another by adding a '+' or '−' to an arrow head. An increase in ticket prices will reduce the number of passengers so a minus sign would be needed here, while an increase in frequency would increase costs so a plus sign would be needed at the arrow head. However the main use of causal loop diagrams is to identify *feedback loops*. A feedback loop is either reinforcing (positive) or balancing (negative). A reinforcing loop means that it is self-reinforcing and will continue to increase unless an external influence stops it. An example of a reinforcing loop is a population for which the birth rate is fixed. The population will continue to rise unless it is checked in some way. A balancing loop means that there is a dampening effect and a system will reach equilibrium. An example of a balancing loop is a central heating system which has a thermostat installed. Although the temperature may rise above the threshold it will gradually settle down to the pre-determined temperature. To find out if a loop is reinforcing or balancing you should count the number of negative signs. If this number is even you have a reinforcing loop, if odd you have a balancing loop. (a zero is counted as even number).

An example of a causal loop diagram with feedback loops is the recruitment for a master's course at a university. In this diagram there are 3 factors that can be set by the university. These are the number of places available, the level of fees, and the quality of staff and the facilities. All the other factors are influenced by these. So, if the fees charged are high the level of student expectation will be high. The level of fees charged will also affect the income. This diagram is shown in Figure 11.4.

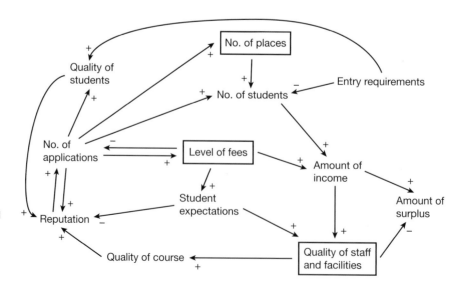

Figure 11.4
Example of a causal loop diagram for student recruitment

Source: Warwick Business School.

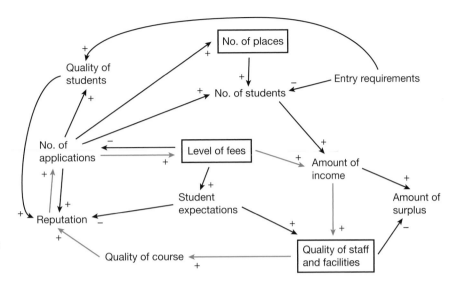

Figure 11.5
Causal loop diagram
showing one
feedback loop

There are several feedback loops in this diagram. One is shown in Figure 11.5. As this does not have any negative signs it is a reinforcing loop (of course this can be controlled by the level of fees set by the university).

Activity 11.2

Identify some more loops in the diagram and decide whether they are reinforcing or balancing.

I am sure that you found several reinforcing loops. An example is: No. of places, No. of students, Amount of income, Quality of staff and facilities, Quality of course, Reputation, No. of applications and back to start. A balancing loop is: Level of fees, Student expectations, Reputation, No. of applications and back to start. The reason that this is a balancing loop (apart for the fact that it has an odd number of negative signs) is that when student expectation is high it is unlikely that the university will be able to meet this expectation and so the number of applications for the following year's course will be lower. The fees then will need to be lower to increase the number of applications. Students paying lower fees will have lower expectations and as these expectations will be exceeded the reputation of the course will go up Of course with so many feedback loops there will be interactions between them and it will not be easy to see the overall effect. However, the main purpose of a causal loop diagram is to give a picture of the situation so that managers can see the effect of changing the factors which they control. So reducing the quality of staff and facilities would have a detrimental effect on the course. It is possible to carry out a quantitative analysis of a causal loop diagram using a technique called *systems dynamics*. This technique is covered in Pidd (2010).

Influence diagrams

The final problem-identification diagram we will look at is an *influence diagram*. This diagram is often used where there is some uncertainty present. So the sales of a product or service could be affected by the demand as well as the price charged by a competitor, both of which are uncertain and which you have little control over. As well as an arrow to show a causal relationship, as we had in a causal loop diagram, four other symbols are used:

A cloud to represent an uncontrollable input

A rectangle to represent an input you have control over

An oval to represent an output

A circle to represent an intermediate result

Figure 11.6 is an influence diagram that shows how the marketing budget (advertising), price and a competitor's pricing influence the sales of a product and the eventual profit.

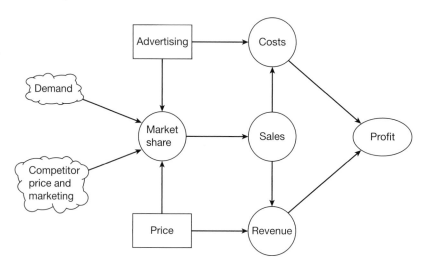

Figure 11.6
Example of an influence diagram

We will see later in this chapter how we can extend the idea of influence diagrams into *decision trees* which allow us to make decisions in conditions of uncertainty. Before then we are going to look at *payoff* tables so that numerical values can be put on some of the uncertain variables.

Payoff tables

A *payoff table* is simply a table that gives the outcome (for example, profits) of a decision under different conditions or *states of nature*. These states of nature may relate to possible demand for a product or they could be related to the national or global economy. The following are the most commonly used decision criteria.

- Maximax rule
- Maximin rule

- Minimax regret rule
- Hurwicz criterion
- Expected monetary value
- Expected opportunity loss

The *maximax* rule chooses the 'best of the best' and is a rule favoured by decision-makers who are *risk-seekers*. The *maximin* rule chooses the 'the best of the worst' and is a rule favoured by decision-makers who are *risk-averse*. The *minimax regret* rule minimizes the maximum *opportunity loss*. The opportunity loss is the loss that occurs through not taking the best option. To work out the opportunity loss you have to subtract each payoff for a particular state of nature from the best that could be achieved given that state. The *Hurwicz* criterion, like the minimax regret rule, attempts to give a compromise between the cautious maximin rule and the optimistic maximax rule. However, unlike the minimax regret rule, weights are assigned to the best and worst payoff for each decision option and the option with the highest weighted payoff is chosen.

The weighted payoff is calculated as:

$$\alpha \times \text{worst payoff} + (1 - \alpha) \times \text{best payoff}$$

The value of α (alpha) depends on the decision-maker's attitude to risk. The smaller the value, the bigger risk he is prepared to take; when $\alpha = 0$ the decision will be the same as for the maximax rule.

Expected monetary value or *EMV* is an expected value (see Chapter 7) in monetary terms. In this context it is a long-run average and is found by multiplying each payoff by the probability that this payoff will occur and adding. The option that maximizes the EMV is chosen.

Expected opportunity loss or *EOL* is essentially the same technique as the EMV method except that the probabilities are applied to the opportunity loss table and the option that *minimizes* the EOL is chosen.

Example 11.2

A car accessory company, Marla plc, has developed a new car immobilizer and has to decide whether to market the product nationwide, to sell by mail order or to sell the patent to a large chain of motor accessory shops. The cost of distributing nationwide is very high but the potential profits could also be large. There is less risk with selling by mail order but the potential profits would also be less. The safe option is to sell the patent, but in this case the chance of making large profits would be lost. How does Marla make its decision given that it has limited knowledge of the likely demand for the product? The estimated profits for each decision depend on the state of the market, which has been defined as high, medium and low. The probability that the state of the market will be high, medium or low has been estimated as 0.25, 0.3 and 0.45, respectively. The expected profits (in £000s) are given in Table 11.1 overleaf.

Table 11.1 Profits (£000s) for Marla plc

Decision	State of the market		
	High ($p = 0.25$)	Medium ($p = 0.3$)	Low ($p = 0.45$)
Nationwide	95	52	−26
Mail order	48	24	19
Sell patent	25	25	25

Activity 11.3

What are the best decisions using the maximax and maximin rules?

The largest payoff is 95 (£000s) for the 'sell nationwide' decision when the market is high. This is the decision that would be made using the maximax rule. The worst payoff for each decision is −26, 19, 25, and the highest of these is 25 so the decision under the maximin rule is to sell the patent.

Activity 11.4

What is the best decision using the minimax regret rule?

This rule requires you to create an opportunity loss table as described earlier. The largest payoff when the market is high is 95, so if the mail order option was taken instead this would mean that a 'loss' of 95 − 48 = 47 (£000s) would be made through not taking the best option. The complete opportunity loss table is shown in Table 11.2.

Table 11.2 Opportunity loss table (in £000s) for Example 11.2

Decision	State of the market		
	High	Medium	Low
Nationwide	0	0	51
Mail order	47	28	6
Sell patent	70	27	0

The largest loss for each decision is 51, 47 and 70. The smallest of these is 47, so the best decision under this rule is to sell by mail order.

Activity 11.5

What is the best decision using the Hurwicz criterion with an alpha of 0.6?

The weighted payoff is calculated from

$$\alpha \times \text{worst payoff} + (1 - \alpha) \times \text{best payoff}$$

For the decision to sell nationwide the worst payoff is -26 and the best is 95, so the weighted payoff is therefore

$$0.6 \times (-26) + 0.4 \times 95 = 22.4$$

Repeating this for the decisions to sell by mail order and to sell the patent we get:

Mail order: $0.6 \times 19 + 0.4 \times 48 = 30.6$

Sell patent: $0.6 \times 25 + 0.4 \times 25 = 25$

So under this criterion and using $\alpha = 0.6$, the decision is to go for the mail order option.

Activity 11.6

What is the best decision using the expected monetary value criterion?

Nationwide: $0.25 \times 95 + 0.3 \times 52 + 0.45 \times (-26) = 27.65$

Mail order: $0.25 \times 48 + 0.3 \times 24 + 0.45 \times 19 = 27.75$

Sell patent: $0.25 \times 25 + 0.3 \times 25 + 0.45 \times 25 = 25$

This suggests that, on average, choosing the 'mail order' option would give you a slightly higher payoff at £27 750.

Activity 11.7

What is the best decision using the expected opportunity loss criterion?

The probabilities are applied to Table 11.2, and the result is:

Nationwide: $0.25 \times 0 + 0.3 \times 0 + 0.45 \times 51 = 22.95$

Mail order: $0.25 \times 47 + 0.3 \times 28 + 0.45 \times 6 = 22.85$

Sell patent: $0.25 \times 70 + 0.3 \times 27 + 0.45 \times 0 = 25.6$

The decision that would minimize the EOL is again the mail order option. (The EMV and EOL decision rules should always agree.)

The value of perfect information

Imagine that a market research company could forecast the demand for the new car immobilizer (Example 11.2) perfectly. How much would it be worth paying for this market research? If the market research company reported that demand would be low, the best option would be to sell the patent, whereas if it said that demand would be high, the option to sell nationwide would be chosen. Of course, high demand only occurs 25% of the time, medium demand 30% of the time and low demand 45% of the time. Therefore it is possible to work out the *expected* payoff if you had this perfect information. This is called the expected value *with* perfect information. The expected value *of* perfect information (EVPI) is simply the difference between the expected value with perfect information and the best EMV.

Activity 11.8

What would be the expected value of perfect information for the payoff table given in Table 11.1?

The expected value with perfect information will be:

$$0.25 \times 95 + 0.3 \times 52 + 0.45 \times 25 = 50.6$$

The EVPI is therefore:

$$50.6 - 27.75 = 22.85, \text{ or } £22\,850$$

This is the maximum amount that a decision-maker would be prepared to pay for this information. (You should note that this is the same figure as the expected opportunity loss calculated in Activity 11.7.)

Did you know

Consumers spend millions of pounds a year on extended warranties, but are they worth it? A few simple sums will make clear that they are not. Say you bought a flat screen TV for £800 and you were offered an extended warranty for 3 years at £100. The TV will be covered for the first year under guarantee anyway but should it fail in the second or third year it could cost you £200 to £300 for repair. However TVs are generally very reliable and only about 3 out of 100 (a probability of .03) are likely to fail within the first 3 years. It would only be worth buying the extended guarantee if the expected value of the repair cost is more than the cost of the extended guarantee. The expected value is .03 × 300 = £9. Even if the repair cost £500 the expected value is still only £15. The chance of a failure would have to be over 30% to be worth buying the extended warranty but who would want to buy a product if one-third of them fail! This argument is true for extended warranties on all products, even those like washing machines that have a higher failure rate. Clearly it doesn't make financial sense to buy extended warranties and the Office of Fair Trading (OFT) has launched an investigation into the practice (*Guardian*, 14 April 2011).

Decision trees

Payoff tables are useful when there is only one decision to make, but often a sequence of decisions are necessary. This is called *multiple-stage* decision-making and for these cases decision-makers generally prefer to use *decision trees*. Decision trees are similar to probability trees (see Chapter 6) except that as well as probabilistic (or chance) branches there are also decision branches. Decision branches allow the decision-maker to compare alternative options, while the chance branches handle the probabilistic nature of an outcome. The skeleton of a single-stage decision tree is shown in Figure 11.7.

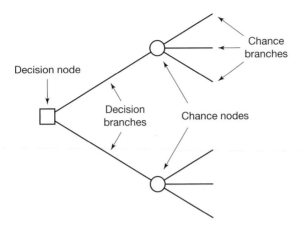

Figure 11.7
Decision tree

The square node represents the point where the decision is made, while the round nodes represent the point at which chance takes over. The decision tree is drawn from left to right, but to evaluate the tree you work from right to left. This is called the *roll back* method. You first evaluate the EMV at each chance node and then at the decision node you select the 'best' EMV (don't forget, 'best' can be lowest cost as well as largest profit).

Although a decision tree is not normally used for single-stage decision problems the next activity continues to use Example 11.2 since we know what the answer is using the EMV criterion.

Activity 11.9

Use the decision tree approach to solve Example 11.2.

The decision tree for this problem has been drawn in Figure 11.8, and you will see that the outcomes for each decision and state of the market have been written at the end of each probabilistic branch. As before, the best decision is to sell by mail order.

The next problem illustrates a multi-stage decision problem.

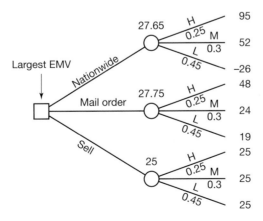

Figure 11.8
Decision tree for
Marla plc

Example 11.3

The Delma Oil company has obtained government approval to drill for oil in the Baltic Sea. This area is known to contain oil deposits and industry sources believe that there is a 50% chance that oil will be found in a commercially viable quantity. The cost of the drilling programme is believed to be £30m but this could be more than offset by the potential revenue, which is put at £100m at today's prices.

The company could carry out test drillings at different sites, which would only cost £5m. From historical data, tests are likely to indicate a viable field 65% of the time. However, these tests are not completely reliable and the probability that they are correct is only 0.7. That is, if the tests are positive there is a 70% chance that a viable quantity of oil will be found, and if negative there is only a 30% (100 − 70) chance that oil will be found in a viable quantity.

The company could sell its rights to drill in the area, but the revenue obtained will depend on the outcome of the tests (if carried out) and are as follows:

Tests indicate oil	£35m
Tests don't indicate oil	£3m
No tests carried out	£10m

Activity 11.10

 What decisions should the company make given this information?

This problem involves two decisions. The first decision is whether to test drill and the second decision is whether to start a drilling programme. In order to solve this decision problem you would carry out the following three steps:

Step 1

Draw the decision tree. This is shown in Figure 11.9. You will see that the decision nodes have been numbered 1, 2 and 3 while the chance nodes have been labelled as a, b, c and d. The values at the end of each branch of the tree represent the *net* outcome. For instance, if drilling is carried out without any tests and oil is found, the net outcome is a profit of £100m − £30m = £70m, whereas if no oil is found a loss of £30m is made.

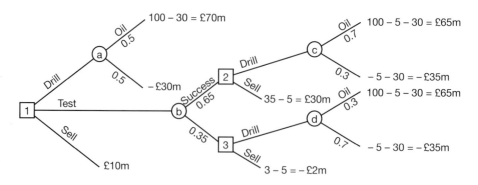

Figure 11.9
Decision tree for the
Delma Oil company

Step 2

Working from the right, the EMV at the chance nodes a, c and d are calculated as follows:

Node	EMV
a	$0.5 \times 70 + 0.5 \times (-30) = £20m$
c	$0.7 \times 65 + 0.3 \times (-35) = £35m$
d	$0.3 \times 65 + 0.7 \times (-35) = -£5m$

(The EMV at node b cannot be calculated until Step 3.)

Step 3

The roll back technique is now employed. At decision node 2, the decision is to either drill or sell. Sell will give you £30m, whereas drilling will give you £35m. The option that gives the largest EMV is to drill, and so this is the option that would be taken. The value 35 is put above node 2 and the sell option is crossed out. If you repeat this for node 3 you should find that the best option here is to sell. The EMV at chance node b can now be calculated and you should find that this is £22.05m $(0.65 \times 35 + 0.35 \times (-2))$. You can now go to decision node 1 and compare the three decisions. You should find the following:

Drill: £20m
Test: £22.05m
Sell: £10m

The best decision is to test first. If the test gives successful results, only then should drilling start; *otherwise* the rights should be sold for £3m. You will see this analysis illustrated in Figure 11.10.

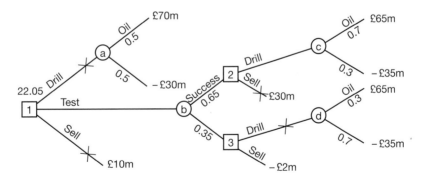

Figure 11.10
Completed decision tree for Delma Oil company

Decision trees and Bayes' theorem

In Example 11.3 you were given all the relevant probabilities, but in general you are more likely to be given just the *prior* probabilities and the *conditional* probabilities. You would then need to work out the relevant *posterior* probabilities using Bayes' theorem. You met Bayes' theorem in Chapter 6 where you used it to modify a prior probability given some new information. The next example requires you to use the same technique before you are able to solve the decision problem.

Example 11.4

A small motor component company, CleanFuel, is trying to decide whether to market a fuel additive which it claims will improve fuel consumption. Unfortunately there are a number of competitors in the market who are also working on the same product and CleanFuel knows that if it decides to market the product it will face stiff competition from other companies.

Instead of marketing the product itself, it could sell the rights to it for £2m. However, if it goes ahead and markets the product itself, it estimates that the probability that sales will be high is only 0.2. The profit resulting from these high sales is put at £10m, but if the sales are low (with a probability of 0.8), the company will end up making a loss of £1m. An alternative is to commission a market research survey to see if motorists would purchase the product. This market research would indicate either high or low sales. From past experience CleanFuel knows that this particular market research company is better at predicting high rather than low sales. When sales have turned out to be high the company has been correct 75% of the time, but when sales have been low the company has only managed a 65% success rate.

The market research is confidential, so even if the results of the research indicate low sales it will still be possible to sell the rights for £2m. Of course, CleanFuel could also decide to market the product whatever the results of the survey.

Activity 11.11

Draw a decision tree for this problem.

The tree you should have obtained is shown in Figure 11.11.

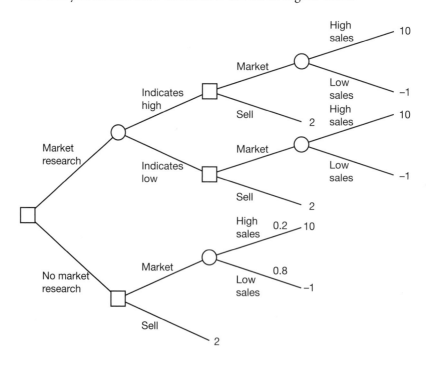

Figure 11.11
Decision tree for
Activity 11.11

Notice that there are some probabilities that we don't appear to know. These are the probability of the market research giving a high and low forecast and the probability of high and low demand given the different outcomes of the market research. These probabilities can be obtained by the use of Bayes' theorem. The prior probabilities are 0.2 for high sales and 0.8 for low sales.

Activity 11.12

Draw a probability tree diagram and calculate using Bayes' theorem the following probabilities:

P(market research indicates high sales)

P(market research indicates low sales)

P(high sales | market research indicates high sales)

P(low sales | market research indicates high sales)

P(high sales | market research indicates low sales)

P(low sales | market research indicates low sales)

Note: For this activity you may find it helpful to refer back to page 137.

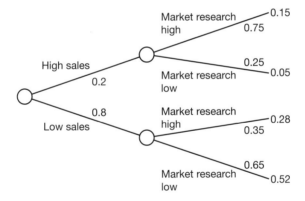

Figure 11.12
Probability tree diagram for Activity 11.12

Figure 11.12 gives the probability tree diagram, where you will see that the joint probabilities have been added to the end of each branch.

P(market research indicates high sales)	$= 0.15 + 0.28 = 0.43$
P(market research indicates low sales)	$= 1 - 0.43 \quad = 0.57$
P(high sales|market research indicates high sales)	$= \dfrac{0.15}{0.43} \quad = 0.349$
P(low sales|market research indicates high sales)	$= 1 - 0.349 \quad = 0.651$
P(high sales|market research indicates low sales)	$= \dfrac{0.05}{0.57} \quad = 0.088$
P(low sales|market research indicates low sales)	$= 1 - 0.088 \quad = 0.912$

These probabilities can now be added to the decision tree and the tree rolled back to show that the best decision is to commission the market research and only to market the product if the research suggests that the sales will be high, and otherwise to sell the rights. You can see the final tree in Figure 11.13.

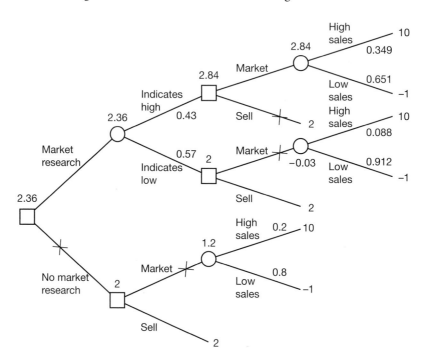

Figure 11.13
The completed decision tree for Example 11.4

The preceding calculations did not make any reference to the cost of market research. It would be important for CleanFuel to know whether the cost of the market research was reasonable. An upper limit to how much to spend on market research is relatively easy to work out as it is the difference between the 'market research' and 'no market research branches' in Figure 11.13. The 'no market research' branch implies that the rights to the product will be sold for £2m.

Activity 11.13

What is the maximum amount of money it would be worth CleanFuel paying for the market research?

The difference between the two branches is £0.36m (2.36 − 2). This is called the *expected value of imperfect information* (EVII) as it takes account of the fact that the market research is not completely reliable. CleanFuel should therefore not pay more than £0.36m for the market research.

Sensitivity analysis

The major difficulty with decision analysis is estimating the probabilities and the expected returns. In many cases the probabilities are simply best guesses. In decision analysis, the sensitivity of the recommended decision to changes in any of the estimated values should be investigated. The most effective way to look at how sensitive the final decision is to changes in the probabilities is to see how big a change in one of the probabilities is necessary for you to change your decision. If only a small change in probability is required then you would say that the decision is sensitive to the value of the probability. If it would take a large change in probability then you could say that the decision is insensitive to changes in the probability and that the decision is *robust*. To investigate the sensitivity of the decision it is normal to find the probability that makes you *indifferent* between two decisions.

Activity 11.14

How much can the probability of a successful test in the Delma Oil company problem (Example 11.3) be allowed to vary before the decision changes from 'test first' to 'drill without test'?

You might have tried to solve this activity by trial and error, but this is not recommended as it can be tedious and there are better methods available. As the probability of success falls the EMV at node b will also fall. When this EMV becomes £20m we will be indifferent to 'test first' and 'drill without test'. To find this point of indifference we could calculate the EMV at node b using a different value of the probability of success. The original value and the new EMV could then be plotted and the point of indifference found graphically. To illustrate this method let us calculate the EMV using a probability of success of 0.4. The EMV at node b will then be:

$$0.4 \times 35 + 0.6 \times (-2) = £12.8m$$

This and the original value are plotted on the graph shown in Figure 11.14. The line between the two points intersects the £20m gridline at a probability of just under 0.6. From this we can deduce that the decision will change once the probability falls below

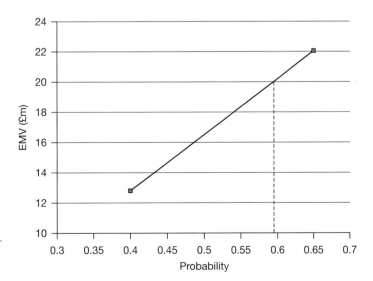

Figure 11.14
Graphical method for solving sensitivity analysis problems

this figure. Since the original probability was 0.65 this is a relatively small change in probability. We can therefore say that the decision whether to test drill or not is quite sensitive to the probability of a viable oil field.

An alternative algebraic method is to call the probability p and the EMV at node b then becomes:

$$35 \times p + (-2) \times (1 - p) = 35p - 2 + 2p$$
$$= 37p - 2$$

The decision will change when the value of this expression is less than £20m. That is:

$$37p - 2 < 20$$

that is, $37p < 22$

therefore, $p < 0.595$

which agrees with the answer found from the graphical method.

Activity 11.15

Investigate the sensitivity of the decision on whether to carry out market research or not for the CleanFuel problem (Example 11.4) to changes in the probability of the market research company successfully predicting high sales.

When sales were high the success rate of the market research company was given as 75%; that is, the probability of success when sales were high was 0.75. To investigate changes in this probability we would need to determine what this probability would have to become for the decision to change from 'conduct market research' to 'don't conduct market research'. This problem is much more difficult to solve than for Activity 11.14 as any change in this probability makes many changes within the decision tree itself. The most effective method of carrying out sensitivity analysis on complex decision problems is to use the *goal seeking* routine in Excel. In fact, it is a good idea to use a spreadsheet for all decision tree problems as you can then see immediately the effects of changing any of the inputs, such as the probabilities or outcomes. To do this it is advisable to use the *drawing* toolbar in Excel to draw the tree diagram and enter the inputs as parameters at the top of the sheet. You can then enter formulae at appropriate points in the diagram. Figure 11.15 is a screen shot of the worksheet for the CleanFuel problem.

The probabilities of the market research company making accurate forecasts when sales are high and low respectively can be seen in cells B1 and B2 and have been labelled as 'x' and 'y'. The value we are interested in is contained within cell B1. The Goal Seek routine can be found in the Data Tools group within the Data tab. Click on What-If Analysis and then Goal Seek. The Set cell is the cell that currently contains the value of 2.36, which we want to change to the value 2 (the EMV without market research). The By changing cell is cell B1, which currently contains the value 0.75. The dialog box for the Goal Seek routine can be seen in Figure 11.16.

The result of using Excel's Goal Seek can be seen in Figure 11.17, where you will see that the probability 'x' which is necessary to make you indifferent between market

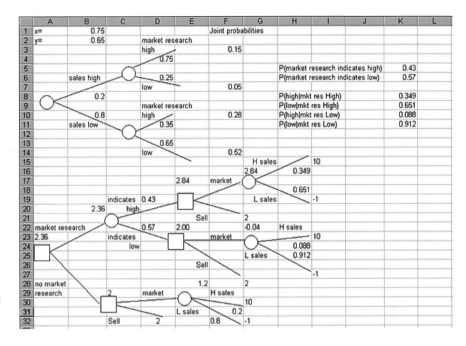

Figure 11.15
The decision tree for
Example 11.4 added
to an Excel
spreadsheet

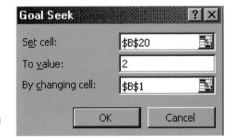

Figure 11.16
The Goal Seek dialog
box

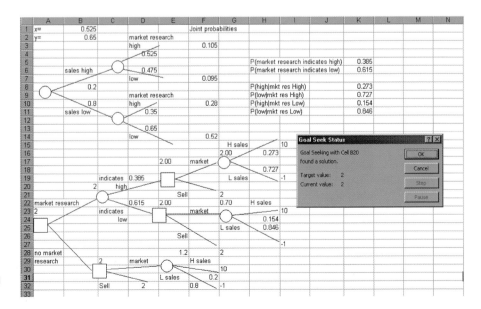

Figure 11.17
Result of using Goal
Seek in Excel

research and no market research is 0.525. This means that if the probability of successfully predicting high sales fell from 0.75 to below 0.525 the decision would change from 'carry out market research' to 'don't carry out market research'. This is quite a large difference so we could say that the decision is fairly insensitive to changes in this probability.

Activity 11.16

Investigate the sensitivity of the decision on whether to carry out market research or not for the CleanFuel problem (Example 11.4) to changes in the probability of the market research company successfully predicting low sales.

You should have found that the probability 'y' has now become 0.5, which is not such a large fall as in the probability of successfully predicting high sales. The decision is therefore more sensitive to changes in this probability.

Utility

The EMV criterion is a very useful and popular method for choosing between a number of alternatives. However, its main drawback is that it takes no account of the decision-maker's attitude to *risk*. Some decision-makers are *risk-seekers* – they are prepared to take the risk of making a loss if there is also a chance (even if this chance is small) of making large gains. Other decision-makers are *risk-averse* – they would always choose the safe option to avoid the risk of making a loss. One method of taking a decision-maker's attitude to risk into account is to evaluate their *utility* function. This converts monetary values into a scale between 0 and 1 in such a way that the change in the utility reflects changes in the decision-maker's preference for different amounts of money. In order to obtain this information, the decision-maker is asked a number of questions.

Example 11.5

The owner of Marla plc (Example 11.2) has called in a firm of consultants to help her decide on the best decision for her company. Table 11.3 is a repeat of the data already provided earlier in this chapter.

Table 11.3 Profits (£000s) for Marla plc

Decision	State of the market		
	High ($p = 0.25$)	Medium ($p = 0.3$)	Low ($p = 0.45$)
Nationwide	95	52	−26
Mail order	48	24	19
Sell patent	25	25	25

To determine the owner's attitude to risk, the consultants asked the question:

'Would you prefer to accept a sum of £52 000 or to enter a lottery where the chance of winning £95 000 is 60% and the chance of losing £26 000 is 40%?'

The owner thought for a few seconds and decided that she would rather take the £52 000. The interviewer then kept raising the probability of winning the lottery until he reached the point where the owner could not make up her mind which option she would prefer; that is, she was indifferent between taking the £52 000 or entering the lottery. This occurred at a probability of 0.9. This procedure was repeated for the sum of £25 000 and £19 000, and the probability at which she was indifferent between the certain sum of money (£25 000 or £19 000) and entering the lottery was 0.7 and 0.65 respectively.

The approach to finding a decision-maker's utility function by the method described above is called the *probability-equivalence* approach. The largest of all the possible payoffs in the decision is given the utility of 1 and the smallest the utility of 0. In Table 11.3 we have the following values (in £000s) to consider: 95, 52, 48, 25, 24, 19, −26. The largest value, 95, is given the utility of 1 and the smallest value, −26, is given the utility of 0. From the answers to the owner's questions we are now able to work out her utility (u) for values of £52 000, £25 000 and £19 000 as follows.

$$u(52) = 0.9u(95) + 0.1u(-26)$$
$$= 0.9 \times 1 + 0.1 \times 0 = 0.9$$

So once the point of indifference has been established, the utility for a particular monetary value is simply the probability of the best outcome of the lottery.

Activity 11.17

Find the utility of the remaining monetary values.

$$u(25) = 0.7 \qquad u(19) = 0.65$$

Unfortunately we do not have the utilities of either £48 000 or £24 000 (although as £24 000 is so close to £25 000 we could assume it is about 0.69). To find £48 000 we can draw a graph of utility against monetary value as shown in Figure 11.18. Interpolating this graph we can estimate the utility of £48 000 as about 0.87.

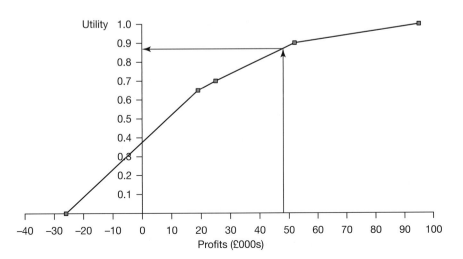

Figure 11.18
Graph showing the utility function for Example 11.5

The final step is to substitute the monetary values in Table 11.3 with the calculated utility values and find the decision that maximizes the expected utility.

Activity 11.18

Calculate the expected utilities for each decision and decide on the best option using this criterion.

Table 11.4 gives the utility values for each alternative and state of nature.

Table 11.4 Profits (£000s) for Marla plc

Decision	State of the market		
	High ($p = 0.25$)	Medium ($p = 0.3$)	Low ($p = 0.45$)
Nationwide	1	0.9	0
Mail order	0.87	0.69	0.65
Sell patent	0.7	0.7	0.7

The expected utilities are:

Nationwide: $0.25 \times 1 + 0.3 \times 0.9 + 0.45 \times 0 = 0.52$

Mail order: $0.25 \times 0.87 + 0.3 \times 0.69 + 0.45 \times 0.65 = 0.72$

Sell patent: $0.25 \times 0.7 + 0.3 \times 0.7 + 0.45 \times 0.7 = 0.7$

The decision has not changed – it is still 'sell by mail order' but there is now very little to choose between this and the risk-free option 'sell patent'. Notice too that there is now a bigger difference between 'sell nationwide' and the other two options. This reflects the fact that the owner is risk-averse – she doesn't want to risk the possible loss of £26 000.

Figure 11.18, which we drew previously, is a graph of the owner's utility function. You will notice that this has a concave shape. For a decision-maker who is a risk-seeker you would get a curve that is convex and for someone who is risk-neutral you would get a straight line. Figures 11.19 and 11.20 illustrate these different utility functions. Figure 11.21 is the utility function for someone who is risk-seeking at lower monetary levels but risk-averse at higher monetary levels.

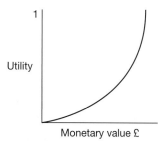

Figure 11.19
A curve of the utility function for a decision-maker who is risk-seeking

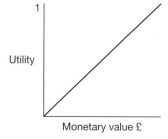

Figure 11.20
A curve of the utility function for a decision-maker who is risk-neutral

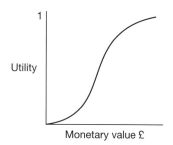

Figure 11.21
A curve of the utility function for a decision-maker who is both risk-seeking and risk-averse

Did you know

Peter Drucker (2003) wrote:

'A decision is a judgement. It is a choice between alternatives. It is rarely a choice between right and wrong. It is at best a choice between 'almost right' and 'probably wrong' – but much more often a choice between two courses of action neither of which is probably more right than the other.'

Multi-criteria decision-making (MCDA)

The techniques you have met so far have involved a single objective (for example, to maximize expected monetary value). However, in many real-life situations decision-makers have a number of conflicting objectives. Those involved in the managing radioactive waste study in *Quantitative methods in action*, for instance, may wish not only to minimize the overall cost but also to minimize the risk to the environment. Similarly, in choosing a new house you might need to consider several criteria, including price, location, type and size. Clearly it is unlikely that you will get all the features you want, so you will have to decide which are most important. For personal choices such as choosing a house it may not be necessary to use any formal techniques, but for larger problems it is important to use a formal method that can be documented. In this section you will meet a simple but powerful technique called *SMART* (Simple Multi Attribute Rating Technique). This technique was developed by Edwards (1971), and has been applied to a wide range of situations.

The underlying method behind the SMART technique is quite simple. Decision makers decide on a set of criteria that they feel are important to their problem. In simple cases there may be just a few criteria; in more complex cases there may be a hierarchy of criteria. In these cases it is useful to draw a *Value Tree* which shows the different levels of criteria in a tree structure. The value tree for the radioactive waste example is shown in Figure 11.22 where at the top of the tree there are two main criteria, costs and non-financial benefits. The non-financial benefits are then broken down into what CoRWM called headline criteria. (These headline criteria can also be thought of as objectives, so one objective is to protect the environment.)

Once the criteria have been defined it is necessary to score how well each option performs on each criterion. Important criteria will score more highly with some options than others, so it is necessary to devise some kind of scoring system. A percentage scoring system is normally used, whereby 0 represents the worst case and 100 the best. (In the radioactive waste case a 1 to 9 scale was used although this was eventually converted to a 0 to 100 scale.) Once all the options have been scored for each criterion, the decision-makers weight each criterion according to its overall importance using *swing weights*. The way this is done is to imagine all the criteria are at their worst level and to consider the swing of each from the least preferred to the most preferred level. The decision-makers then choose the criteria that they consider to be the most important in terms of this swing. In the case of the radioactive waste

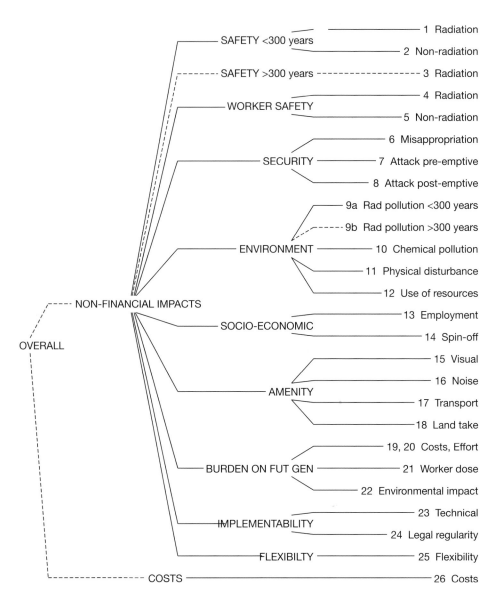

Figure 11.22
The value tree of
headline criteria and
their sub-criteria

example that had two levels, the sub-criteria were first compared. So under safety < 300 years the swing from worst to best radiation was considered to be the most important and given a value of 100. The swing from worst Non-radiation to best was considered to be only 5% as large and therefore given a value of 5. This process is repeated for all sub-criteria (where appropriate) and then the weights aggregated up to the high level criteria. After any necessary adjustments these weights are finally normalized so that they add up to 100.

To be able to compare each option the aggregate benefits across all criteria for each option are found and the option with the highest aggregate benefit will be the most preferred. However, if we now take cost into consideration there might be other options that, although do not give such high benefits, do give much lower costs.

Rather than use the technique on the complex problem of the radioactive waste example we will now demonstrate the method using the relatively simple problem of choosing a house.

Example 11.6

Suppose you have won £200 000 on the National Lottery and have decided to invest it in property. You have shortlisted five houses in your price range. You now have to decide which one of these houses to buy. To help you decide, you have made a list of the important attributes of each house. These attributes are:

- Purchase cost.
- Distance to rail station.
- Location (the attractiveness of the neighbourhood).
- Size of house (as measured by floor area).

The purchase cost of each house, together with its floor area and distance to the rail station, are shown in Table 11.5.

Table 11.5 Data for the house choice problem

House	Purchase cost	Floor area (square feet)	Distance to rail station (miles)
A	£175 000	1800	0.50
B	£160 000	1000	1.20
C	£140 000	800	0.25
D	£150 000	1200	2.50
E	£200 000	2000	0.75

Activity 11.19

Draw a value tree for Example 11.6

The value tree is shown in Figure 11.23. (This is very simple compared to the radioactive waste example!)

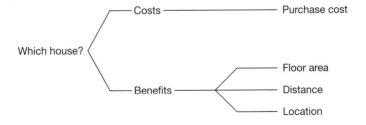

Figure 11.23
Value tree for the house purchase problem

It is now necessary to score each option on each criterion. Clearly if closeness to the rail station is important to you then you would score house C as 100 and house D as 0. For the other houses you might adopt a simple pro rata approach simply based on distance but for this exercise we will treat all criteria in the same way. The most effective means of doing this is shown below:

1 Draw a line and divide it into ten equal parts, labelling it as shown in Figure 11.24.

Figure 11.24
Assigning weights (1): dividing a line

2 Next, write your least preferred option at the zero point and your most preferred at the 100 point mark (Figure 11.25).

Figure 11.25
Assigning weights (2): marking least and most preferred options

3 Then, using your judgement, indicate the positions of the remaining options (Figure 11.26).

Figure 11.26
Assigning weights (3): marking remaining options

The diagram now reflects your feelings, not just about the order of the options but also their importance relative to each other. You have judged that based on distance houses A and E are similar and are not much below house C in preference but that house B being over a mile away is much less favourable. However house B still scores much higher than the worst choice, house D. Remember though that we are looking at just this one criterion which is independent of the other criteria.

You repeat this exercise for both the size of house and the location criteria (the location being qualitative will be much more subjective than the other two criteria) and you get the Table 11.6 showing the scores for all criteria.

Table 11.6 Scores for the three criteria

House	Floor area	Distance	Location
A	90	85	40
B	50	40	20
C	0	100	0
D	60	0	100
E	100	75	90

Activity 11.20

Based on Table 11.6 which house would you choose to buy?

Based on total score we might choose house E as it has the highest total (265). However this assumes that all criteria are equally weighted which is unlikely to be the case. To decide on the weighting to apply we use swing weights. Let us suppose that you choose location as the most important criterion: this then has a weight of 100. Floor area is the next most important criteron, and you decide that the swing from the least preferred to the most preferred size of house is only 60% as important as the swing from the worst location to the best location. Similarly you decide that distance from the rail station has a weight of 40. Figure 11.27 illustrates this process.

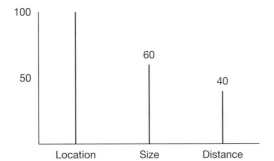

Figure 11.27
The swing weights method

The sum of these weights is 200 (100 + 60 + 40): to maintain consistency with the other weights you need to normalize them – to make the sum equal to 100 – which is easily done in this case simply by dividing by 2

Activity 11.21

Calculate the aggregate benefits for each house and decide on your preferred choice.

To calculate the aggregate measure of all these benefits for each house, we need to multiply the weight for each attribute by the normalized weight for that attribute, and add up the values. So for house A we would have:

$$(90 \times 30) + (85 \times 20) + (40 \times 50) = 6400$$

This figure should then be divided by 100 (the sum of the weights), giving 64.0. (Note: It is easier if this calculation is performed in Excel, and the function

```
=SUMPRODUCT(B2:D2,$B$9:$D$9)/100
```

can be used to calculate the aggregate benefit.) Table 11.7 overleaf shows the aggregate benefits.

For this final table the costs, too, have been included. From this table you can see that – not surprisingly – house E has the highest aggregate benefits, but it also has the highest cost. House C has the smallest aggregate benefits and the lowest cost. However, house D has quite high benefits in comparison with its cost.

To see the relationship between benefits and cost, it is a good idea to create a chart in Excel (Figure 11.28). From this chart you can see that although house A is more

Table 11.7 Aggregate benefits and costs for the house choice problem

House	Floor area	Distance	Location		Aggregate benefits	Cost (£000s)
A	90	85	40		64.0	175
B	50	40	20		33.0	160
C	0	100	0		20.0	140
D	60	0	100		68.0	150
E	100	75	90		90.0	200
Raw weights	60	40	100	Sum 200		
Normalized weights	30	20	50			

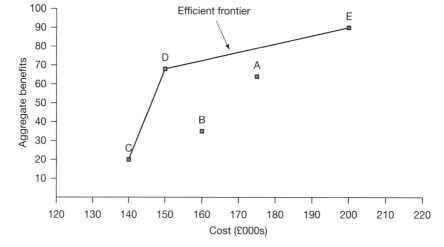

Figure 11.28
Chart of aggregate benefits versus cost

expensive than house D, it does not have higher benefits. This is also true for houses B and D. From this it should be clear that only houses C, D and E are worth considering: the other two options are dominated by these three houses. In other words, neither house A nor house B has both higher benefits *and* lower costs than any of the properties C, D and E. If we draw a line connecting C, D and E, we get what is called the *efficient frontier*. You should note that the efficient frontier will always be on the outer boundary of the plot, reflecting our wish to minimize costs whilst maximizing benefits.

The efficient frontier allows us to reduce the number of options, and with a large number of options this can be a very useful device. However, it is still necessary to decide which house out of the three is best. If you want to spend all of the £200 000 win, then house E might be best; but you could save £50 000 by choosing house D, whose aggregate benefits are only 22 points below house E.

Sensitivity analysis and MCDA software

Although you may find the basic ideas behind the SMART technique simple the process of agreeing the relevant criteria and weights can be problematic. In many large-scale MCDA problems groups of stakeholders, experts and others get together and discuss and hopefully resolve the issues. This process is called a *decision conference*. In the case of the radioactive waste management review the conference was spread over 3 days and involved 11 participants and two facilitators. The idea behind a decision conference is to agree a consensus but in many cases this is not possible. This is where sensitivity analysis can be useful as changes can be made to weights to see the effect on the overall results. In the case of the house purchase problem with only 3 criteria it would be quite simple to repeat the exercise several times. However with complex problems involving many options and criteria this is not a feasible approach. In these cases the use of software can be essential. One MCDA software is *Hiview3* produced by Catalyze. Not only does this software automate the process but it allows sensitivity analysis to be carried out easily.

Using Hiview3 you first create a value tree and add your decision criteria as you did in Activity 11.19. At the top of the tree is the *root* node which is the final decision you wish to make. This is 'Which house?' in Figure 11.23. The two main criteria are costs and benefits and beneath the benefits node are the three sub-criteria which we are to measure.

Once the criteria have been added you then score each option against each of the criteria. Hiview3 uses two types of score; constructed scales and natural scales. Constructed scales are the approach we used but you can also use natural scales for criteria that have a measurement, such as floor area. If you use a natural scale the software works out the score based on numerical values. A screen print of the criterion scores window for the location criterion is shown in Figure 11.29.

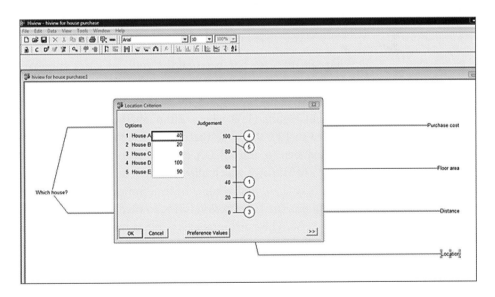

Figure 11.29
Scoring the location criterion in Hiview3

The next step is to apply the swing weighting method. To do this you click on Benefits on the tree and then choose Weight Criteria Swings Below Selected Node. You then add the agreed values as in Figure 11.30.

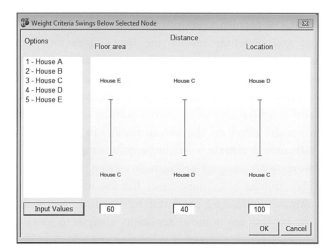

Figure 11.30
Applying swing
weights to the
Benefits node

Benefits	Weight	House A	House B	House C	House D	House E	Cumulative Weight
Floor area*	60	90	50	0	60	100	30.0
Distance*	40	85	40	100	0	75	20.0
Location*	100	40	20	0	100	90	50.0
TOTAL	200	64	33	20	68	90	100.0

Benefits Node Data

Benefits Data Breakdown

Figure 11.31
Summary of the
benefits data

When all the data has been added you can get a summary by double-clicking Benefits (see Figure 11.31). This matches the figures we obtained in Table 11.7. You can then analyze the model and obtain the efficient frontier as we did manually. This is shown in Figure 11.32 where, although the cost scale is reversed and has been normalized to 100, the same three houses are on the frontier.

The next step in any MCDA analysis is to do a sensitivity analysis. This can be easily done in Hiview3 which allows you to either summarize the whole model using the Sensitivity Down window or to examine each criterion using the Sensitivity Up option. The latter option has been used on the distance criterion and is shown in Figure 11.33. The horizontal axis is the cumulative weight of the distance criterion (as shown in Figure 11.31) which is currently 20 and shown by a vertical line. The sloping lines show how the aggregate benefits for each house change as the weight on the distance criterion changes.

Activity 11.22

How sensitive is the overall solution to changes in the weight of the distance criterion?

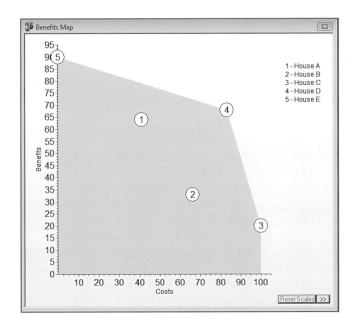

Figure 11.32
The efficient frontier

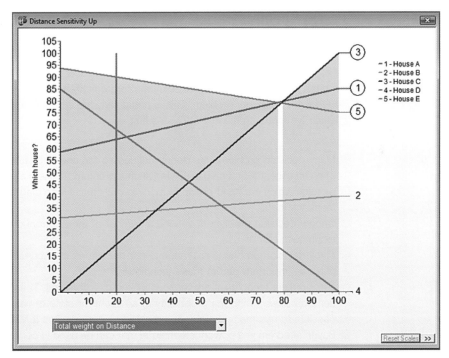

Figure 11.33
Sensitivity analysis on
the distance criterion
using Hiview3

At the current weight of 20 for the distance criterion, house E has the highest aggregate benefits. This will still be the highest option until the weight of the distance criterion reaches 80, at which point house C takes over. House E will also have the highest option even if the weight fell to zero. This analysis suggests that the solution is not sensitive to the weight of the distance criterion.

This is a very simple use of Hiview3. Those of you who wish to look at more involved MCDA problems might like to look and experiment with the models used for the radioactive waste management study. These can be downloaded from the Catalyze website (www.catalyze.co.uk/clients/casestudies/corwm) where an evaluation version of Hiview3 can also be obtained.

Reflection

The intention of this chapter is to give an insight into some decision-making techniques available to businesses. Decision-making is not an exact science, and major decisions will not be made on the basis of quantitative techniques alone. Many decisions have to take into account the wishes of the public, the shareholders and many other stakeholders. In addition many problems are not clear or well structured and require some 'problem structuring' using diagrammatic methods first.

Many decision-making techniques have weaknesses and make many assumptions. For instance, the EMV method is a long-run average, so there must be some reservation about using the technique for one-off decisions. Another issue arises when we assume a discrete range of conditions. In Example 11.4 we assumed that the market would be either high or low. This is a very arbitrary range; there could be any number of market conditions between these two extremes. This is the reason why sensitivity analysis is so important, as such an analysis makes it possible to see how robust a solution is to changes in assumptions.

With all real decision-making, one challenge is that the issues are often complex and not easy to resolve. If we can split a problem into smaller parts (divide and conquer), we can often come to an acceptable solution more quickly and more easily than if we had tried to solve the larger problem. This is particularly the case with the SMART technique, in which we focus on the key attributes first.

Key points

○ Many decision problems are poorly defined so the use of pictures and diagrams is often an essential first step in solving such a problem. These diagrams range from rich pictures which are hand-drawn to more formal causal loop diagrams which can show feedback loops.

○ Once a decision problem is defined a number of more formal diagrams and techniques can be used.

○ Many decision problems are made under conditions of uncertainty so probability plays an important part in these techniques.

○ The simplest techniques are those involving payoff tables. These then lead on to decision trees. When the probability of an event (or state of nature) is known it is possible to use the technique of expected monetary value (EMV).

○ Bayes' theorem is a powerful technique that can be used in conjunction with decision trees and allows probabilities to be adjusted when new information (such as market research) becomes available.

○ Another application of decision trees is to calculate the value of information.

○ All decisions involve risk so it is useful to ascertain a decision-maker's attitude to risk. This can be found using utility theory techniques.

○ Where a decision involves several criteria, it is possible to use a multi-attribute technique such as SMART to find the option that gives maximum benefit at the lowest cost.

Further reading

There are very many decision-making techniques and this text has indentified some of the most useful ones. For a fuller explanation of the various techniques there are many texts available. One of the best is Goodwin and Wright (2009) which has a behavioural analysis slant to it. Daellenbach and McNickle (2005) is also very good and covers both problem structuring and management science techniques. Drucker (2003) is well known for his writings on management and is useful background reading. For specific techniques, Pidd (2010) is a good text on problem structuring methods in general and systems dynamics in particular. The most well known author on problem structuring methods is Checkland (2006), although this text is not for the casual reader. An interesting paper on social utilities is the one by Edwards (1971).

Web links **W**

Answers to selected questions can be found in Appendix 2. Answers to the other questions can be found on the companion website for this book.

Practice questions

W **1** A company intends to market a new product, and it estimates that there is a 20% chance that it will be first in the market and this will give it £2m revenue in the first year. However, if it is not first in the market the expected revenue will only be £0.5m. What is the EMV?

2 Please refer to Figure 11.34 for this question and note that the objective is to maximize EMV.
   (a) What is the value of x?
   (b) What is the EMV at probabilistic node B?
   (c) What is the EMV at probabilistic node C?
   (d) What should the decision be at decision node A?
   (e) What should the value of x be in order that you will be indifferent to choosing between decision 1 and decision 2?

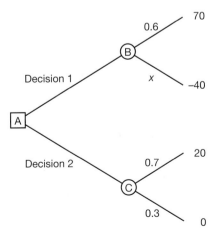

Figure 11.34 Diagram for Question 2

W 3 An inventor develops a new product. Having made the product he has three choices of what to do with it:
1 manufacture the product himself
2 allow someone else to make it and be paid on a royalty basis
3 sell the rights for a lump sum.

The profit which can be expected depends on the level of sales and is shown in Table 11.8 (in £000s).

Table 11.8 Payoff table for Question 3

	High sales	Medium sales	Low sales
Manufacture	80	40	−20
Royalties	50	30	10
Sell	20	20	20

The probabilities associated with the level of sales are 0.2, 0.5 and 0.3 for high, medium and low sales respectively.

(a) Write down the best decision using:
   (i)   the maximax rule
   (ii) the maximin rule
   (iii) the minimax regret rule

(b) Calculate the best decision using the expected monetary value.

(c) A survey might help to determine the likely level of sales. What is the maximum amount that the inventor should be prepared to pay for this survey?

W 4 An owner of a campsite is trying to decide whether to build a swimming pool, a tennis court or an indoor bar area. She can only afford to build one of these and she needs help in deciding which one to choose. The profitability of each will, to some extent, depend on the weather. If the weather if hot, campers would prefer the swimming pool, but if the summer is cool, an indoor bar will be more profitable. The owner has estimated the annual profitability (in £000s) of each option for three states of nature (the weather) as shown in Table 11.9.

Table 11.9 Payoff table for Question 4

	Weather		
	Hot	Average	Cool
Swimming pool	100	50	30
Tennis court	70	90	40
Bar	50	100	170

(a) Write down the best decision using:
   (i)   the maximax rule
   (ii) the maximin rule
   (iii) the minimax regret rule

(b) If the probability of a hot summer is 0.2 and that of a cool summer is 0.35, calculate the best decision using the expected monetary value.

5 An investment trust manager wishes to buy a portfolio of shares and he has sufficient funds to buy either portfolio A, portfolio B or portfolio C. The potential gains from the portfolio will depend upon the economy over the next 5 years and estimates (in £m) have been made as shown in Table 11.10.

Table 11.10 Payoff table for Question 5

	Growth	Stable	Recession
A	5	2	−2
B	4	7	−4
C	4	4	4

(a) Write down the best decision using:
   (i)   the maximax rule
   (ii) the maximin rule
   (iii) the minimax regret rule
(b) The manager estimates that the probability that the economy will grow over the next 5 years is 0.5, while the probability of a recession is put at 0.2. Calculate the best decision using the expected monetary value criterion.
(c) A leading economist is prepared to give more accurate estimates of these probabilities for a fee of £50 000. Would it be worthwhile employing the economist?

6 You have £1000 to invest for three months. A friend is offering you a car for £1000 which he says is half price. You believe that there is a 0.25 chance of selling it for £2000, a 0.50 chance that you could sell it for £1200 and a 0.25 that you would only get £500 for it. An alternative is to invest the £1000 in a savings account for 3 months where you would get £8.75 interest. Using the EMV criterion decide whether to buy the car or invest in a savings account.

7 A person is hard up and can't afford to pay for the car tax on his car. He needs to travel to a see his girl friend and could either get the train which would cost £50 or risk taking the car which would cost £10 in petrol. However if he risks driving without tax he believes that there is a 1 in 50 chance of being caught and fined £1000. Based on purely financial considerations what decision should he take? By how much would the chance of being caught have to change before his decision changes?

8 You are considering the purchase of some new computerized machinery for your factory, and have to decide between buying it immediately or waiting for a few months, since the price of the equipment has been falling steadily over the past year. You have been advised that, if you wait for six months, there is a 60% chance that the price will fall to £12 000; otherwise it will remain steady at £16 000.

If you buy now, the £16 000 cost can be reduced by the £2000 saving which you expect will result from the increased efficiency due to the new machine being operative over the 6-month period.

(a) Assuming that your objective is to minimize expected costs, what course of action should you take?
(b) The estimate that there is a 60% chance that the price will fall is only very rough. By how much must this probability decrease before you would be indifferent between buying the equipment now and delaying the purchase?

9 A department store has to decide whether to expand on its existing site in the town centre or to move to a new site on the outskirts. There is a possibility that a rival store may open a branch in the town centre in the near future. If this new branch does open, the first store's total profits over the next 5 years will be £10m if it does not move, as against £16m if it does.

   If the rival branch does not open, total profits for the town centre site are estimated at £40m, and for the new site at £32m. The probability of the rival branch opening is estimated to be about 70%. Which decision would maximize expected profit? (For simplicity, you should ignore factors like the time value of money.)

10 Cast Iron Construction plc (CIC) is a company specializing in high-rise office blocks. They have recently decided to consider building in third world countries and they have a choice of 2 sites. One is in the earthquake prone island of Tutamolia and the other is in the politically unstable country of Flesomnial.

   The building cost of £5m is the same for both countries and it is estimated that that the return over 10 years for each country will also be the same at £20m. However, in Tutamolia, CIC have a choice of strengthening the building at a further cost of £5m. If they do this the probability that the building will collapse if an earthquake occurs is only 0.01, whereas if no strengthening work is done the probability that the building would collapse is 0.7.

   The probability that an earthquake will occur in the next 10 years is put at 0.1. If an earthquake does occur any time during the 10 years and the building collapses the company will forfeit the return of £20m, and in addition they will have to pay compensation to the government of £10m.

   If CIC decides to build in Flesomnial there is a 20% chance that the country will be taken over by a dictator and the company will not receive any return on its investment.

   (a) Draw a decision tree for this problem and use this decision tree to determine the decision that will maximize CIC'c expected return.

   (b) The probability that an earthquake will occur is really only a guess. What should this probability become before the decision found in part (a) changes?

11 At its latest meeting, an investment club is trying to decide which investment out of 3 possible ones to buy this month.

   A member has estimated the potential returns on these investments over the next 6 months given 3 different scenarios relating to the movement of the stock market (Table 11.11).

Table 11.11 Payoff table for Question 11

Investment	Stock market movement (in £00)		
	Rising	Stable	Falling
A	150	25	−100
B	90	50	0
C	−10	10	50

(a) Write down the best decision if:
   (i)   the club was risk-seeking
   (ii) the club was risk-averse.

(b) Write down the opportunity loss table and obtain the best decision using the minimax regret criterion.

(c) If the probability of the stock market rising is 0.2 and 0.6 for a fall, calculate the best decision using the EMV criterion.

(d) What is the expected value of perfect information (EVPI)?

(e) To decide the club's attitude to risk, each member took part in an exercise designed to evaluate their utility function. The result of one member's answers are as follows:

   'I am indifferent between investing in a share that would give me a return of £9000 for certain or entering a lottery that will give me a 0.5 probability of a £15 000 return and a 0.5 probability of a −£10 000 return.'

   'I am indifferent between investing in a share that would give me a return of £2500 for certain or entering a lottery that will give me a 0.3 probability of a £15 000 return and a 0.7 probability of a −£10 000 return.'

   (i)   Sketch the member's utility function and comment on what it shows.
   (ii) From your sketch estimate the utilities for returns of £5000, £1000, £0 and −£1000. What is the best decision for the club that would maximize the expected utility?

W **12** Pizza Classic is a family-run pizza delivery company that has been in the Bristol area for over 20 years. In its current 3-year business plan it has estimated the probability of high and low demand for its pizzas as 0.55 and 0.45 respectively. It has also estimated that the net present value (using a discount rate of 10%) of income will be £750 000 if the demand is high and £375 000 if the demand is low. (The company assumed that the demand will either be high or low for all 3 years.)

The company is now considering setting up an internet site where customers could order their pizzas. The start-up costs of this venture would be £20 000 (payable now). It is believed that an internet site would increase the amount spent per customer and therefore that net income from both high and low demand would increase, as shown in the following table.

Year (end)	1	2	3
High demand	£300 000	£400 000	£400 000
Low demand	£150 000	£250 000	£200 000

If the company decides to go ahead with the plan it could employ consultants to conduct a marketing campaign. The consultants would charge £30 000 and they believe that there is an 80% chance that their campaign would be a success and customers would approve the plan. If the campaign were a success it is believed the probability of high demand would increase to 0.65. If the consultants concluded that customers would not be likely to use the site, the company would abandon the idea of an internet site.

(a) Using a discount rate of 10%, calculate the net present value for both high and low demand over the next 3 years (assume that income occurs at the end of each year and that the discount factors for years 1 to 3 are 0.9090, 0.8264 and 0.7513, respectively).

(b) Draw a decision tree for the problem.

(c) Determine the optimal decision for the company.

(d) What is the maximum amount that you would be prepared to pay the consultants?

(e) The probabilities used by Pizza Classic are really only guesses. How might you test the sensitivity of the outcome to changes in these probabilities?

13 Jayes Pharmaceutical has a number of high earning products, including the new A1 asthma spray. Preliminary sales of this product suggest that profits per unit sold amount to £10.

However, a recent report in an American journal suggests that A1 can cause an allergic reaction in up to 1% of people using the spray. The company now has a dilemma: should it continue selling the spray, knowing that there is this risk, or should it abandon it and re-market an older, less effective spray?

If it continues to sell this product and allergies develop, the company will have to compensate the buyer and the loss in profits will cost the company £20 per unit.

If the company decides to abandon the product and sell the older version it would expect to earn a profit of £1.50 per unit.

An alternative is to supply a free allergy testing kit worth £1 with each product sold. If the test is positive, the customer will get a full refund. This test is not perfectly reliable, however: the probability that the test will correctly indicate that someone will be allergic is only 0.9 and the probability that it will give a false positive reading is 0.3. The company would not be able to recover the costs of supplying this kit, so the company would effectively make a loss of £11.

(a) Draw a probability tree diagram showing the prior and conditional probabilities.

(b) Calculate the probability that the test will be positive.

(c) Calculate the following posterior probabilities:

(i) probability that a person is allergic if the test is positive.

(ii) probability that a person is allergic if the test is negative.

(d) Draw a decision tree to determine the best course of action.

(e) If the company expected to sell 500 000 of these units per year, write down the annual profits from all three courses of action.

W 14 A simple screening test can be conducted to indicate if someone has a particular medical condition or not. However the test sometimes gives incorrect results. A false positive result (when the person does not have the condition) occurs 5% of the time and a false negative result (when the person has the condition) occurs 10% of the time. It is estimated that 2% of the population have the condition.

It is possible to screen everyone at a cost of £50 per test. Those testing positive are then given treatment costing £300. Those testing negative are not given treatment but if they subsequently turn out to have the condition, treatment is expensive at £1000 per person. An alternative course of action would be to abandon the screening procedure and immunize everyone against the condition at a cost of £65 per person. No treatment costs are subsequently incurred.

Draw a decision tree for the problem and determine the most cost effective course of action.

15 A person is trying to decide between what car to buy. She has narrowed the choice down to 5 models, each costing a similar amount. Her criteria for choice of car include fuel consumption, top speed and environmental considerations. The 5 cars and the score for each criterion on each car are shown in Table 11.12.

Table 11.12 Scores for Question 15

Car	Consumption (miles/gallon)	Top speed (mph)	Environmental
A	45	90	50
B	15	140	0
C	60	80	100
D	35	100	60
E	55	110	30

She has also used swing weights on the criteria and decided that consumption is the most important criterion. Environmental considerations would have a swing weight of 60 and top speed a swing weight of 30.

(a) Convert the consumption figures and top speed into a score out of 100 by making the top value in each case 100 and the bottom one 0

(b) Based on the aggregate benefits which car should she buy?

16 The lease on a shop is due to expire and the shop owner is trying to decide which of 8 vacant premises he should rent. List possible criteria he should consider in trying to make his decision. Table 11.13 gives the scores for each criteria against each option and also the swing weights of each attribute. Plot the efficient frontier and decide which shop(s) he should consider.

Table 11.13 Data for Question 16

Shop	Criterion X	Criterion Y	Criterion Z	Rental cost (£000s)
A	100	80	0	15
B	50	60	10	8
C	50	100	100	20
D	0	55	20	10
E	30	30	80	12
F	60	0	70	16
G	75	40	30	9
H	50	90	90	18

17 Chix Laboratory has recently come up with a method of producing joints of 'chicken' from non-animal products. The process is quite revolutionary and the taste and texture of the 'meat' is believed to be indistinguishable from the real thing. The product should also have an advantage in terms of price and shelf life (the product need not be stored in a refrigerator and will stay in good condition for up to two weeks).

However, the cost of setting up production is very high at £1m and it is not at all certain that consumers will accept the product. The marketing department has assessed the risk and believe that there is only a 30% chance that consumers will approve of the product. If consumers do approve then sales are estimated to be around £2.5m p.a., but if the reaction is negative then sales will amount to no more than £0.7m p.a. (the catering market is virtually guaranteed to want the product).

The risk could be reduced by carrying out a survey to gauge public reaction to the product. From past experience this kind of survey produces accurate results 85% of the time. (That is, if the survey indicates a favourable response, the probability that a favourable response occurs is 0.85; and similarly, if the survey suggests a negative response, the probability that a negative response occurs is 0.85.) The cost of this survey would be £100 000.

The product manager assigned to this new product line is Graham Green and he has requested your help in deciding whether to commission a survey or to proceed immediately with full production. You explain that the decision is perhaps more complicated than he thinks and the following options are available to him:

1 Proceed with full production.
2 Commission a survey. Whatever the results of the survey there are two further options: to proceed with full production or abandon the project.
3 Abandon the project.

Following discussions with the marketing department, you decide that carrying out the marketing survey before going into full production will not affect the expected sales revenue. You have also assumed that the probability that the survey will indicate a favourable response is 0.3.

(a) Draw a decision tree for the problem and decide what the correct decisions should be.
(b) Investigate the sensitivity of your answer to changes in the probability of a favourable response.

....

Assignment

The case at the start of this chapter discussed the problems of radioactive waste and how to dispose of it safely. Since the catastrophe at the Fukushima nuclear plant in Japan following the tsunami in March 2011, Germany has decided to end the generation of electricity using nuclear energy by 2030. Use various diagrams to represent the situation and the choices open to countries for the generation of electricity. You should take into account factors such as global warming, peak oil and safety records of the electricity generation industry. (You will need to do some research into these and other factors.) Try and summarize the real problem and the choices open to governments.

Choosing wisely: investment appraisal

Objectives

- To understand the reasons for investment appraisal
- To know how to select projects on the basis of their payback periods
- To be able to calculate the accounting rate of return
- To be able to discount a future sum of money
- To know how to select projects on the basis of their net present value
- To be able to calculate the internal rate of return for a project
- To understand the limitations of each method

Introduction

Companies are frequently faced with the need to decide between a number of investment opportunities. As capital is usually limited, a company will want to choose the 'best' project or projects. But what do we mean by 'best', and how can we differentiate between different projects that may look equally attractive?

The projects considered in this chapter are those that require an initial capital outlay and then generate income over several years. The life of a project is of paramount importance as a sum of money that will be generated in the future will not be so attractive as money that is available in the present. This chapter looks at several methods that can be used to determine the worth of an investment.

Quantitative methods in action: banks stress test

The period from 2007 to 2011 was a difficult time for the world economy. First there was the financial crisis caused by the bursting of the United States housing bubble and the subsequent rescue of banks in the USA and Europe. Then, just as economies were starting to recover from the recession, there was a crisis in the Eurozone with first the 110bn-euro rescue package for Greece and then the 85bn-euro rescue for Ireland. Even with these huge rescue packages there are still worries over the health of the European banking system. The markets do not believe that the European banks are strong enough to withstand a second recession and they think that many large investors are too exposed to countries such as Greece and Portugal which have large debts.

In order to allay these fears the EU devised the *stress tests*. These tests were designed to see which European banks, if any, might fail given certain scenarios. The scenarios that were tested were:

- A baseline scenario that assumed a continuing recovery
- A double dip recession that lasted two years
- A double dip recession *and* another financial crisis for some European countries.

The purpose of these scenarios was to see whether banks had enough capital to survive these events. So, for instance, if house prices fell by half then mortgages made by banks would be at risk. If the bank had insufficient capital to cover these losses they would become insolvent.

All the large banks were tested, and in the UK these included HSBC, RBS, Lloyds and Barclays. However in other countries many smaller banks were tested; in Spain they tested 27 banks as these banks have a large exposure to the collapsed property market. In total 91 banks were tested, of which seven failed (five Spanish banks, one German and one Greek bank).

Sources: 'Aggregate outcome of the 2010 EU wide stress test exercise coordinated by CEBS in cooperation with the ECB', CEBS, July 2010; 'Q&A: What are the European bank stress tests for?', BBC, July 2010 (www.bbc.co.uk/news/business-10711590)

Measures of investment worth

You may think that it should be easy to judge the worth of an investment. Surely the larger the profit that will be generated, the better? Unfortunately it is not so simple as this because two projects could generate the same total profit but be quite different in the pattern of cash flows. Example 12.1 illustrates a typical case.

Example 12.1

BAS Holdings specializes in the development of out-of-town shopping centres. It is currently investigating three possible projects and these are located at Andover (A), Bristol (B) and Carlisle (C). The sites at Andover and Bristol require an investment of £4m each while the site at Carlisle requires an investment of £5m. Income from rents is guaranteed for up to 5 years, after which time BAS Holdings will transfer ownership to the local council. The net cash flows are given in Table 12.1, where year 0 refers to 'now'.

Table 12.1 Cash flows for Example 12.1

Year	Andover (£m)	Bristol (£m)	Carlisle (£m)
0	−4.0	−4.0	−5.0
1	1.0	1.5	0.0
2	1.0	2.5	0.5
3	1.0	0.5	1.5
4	1.0	0.5	2.0
5	1.0	0.0	3.0

In Example 12.1 the company has to decide which, if any, of the projects to accept. Even if all projects are profitable the company may not have the resources to proceed with them all. Perhaps it should compare each project in terms of the profit made at the end of the 5 years (4 years in the case of Bristol).

Activity 12.1

What is the total profit for each project?

The profit is simply the sum of the cash flows over the life of each project and they are shown in Table 12.2.

Table 12.2 Calculation of total profits

Year	Andover (£m)	Bristol (£m)	Carlisle (£m)
0	−4.0	−4.0	−5.0
1	1.0	1.5	0.0
2	1.0	2.5	0.5
3	1.0	0.5	1.5
4	1.0	0.5	2.0
5	1.0	0.0	3.0
Profit	1.0	1.0	2.0

On the basis of total profit the Carlisle project is best, but this project also has the largest initial investment and income is not generated until year 2. Andover and Bristol give the same profit, but notice how differently the earnings are generated. Bristol gives larger cash flows at the start, but no earnings are received in year 5, whereas Andover gives a constant flow of earnings for the full 5 years.

You should now appreciate that deciding on the best project is not a simple matter. There are several methods that can be used to compare projects and these fall into two categories. The first category is often termed 'traditional' and involves accounting procedures that do not take into account the time value of money. The second method involves procedures that *discount* future sums of money.

Did you know

> The International Monetary Fund (IMF) estimate of the total cost of the global financial crisis is $2.3 trillion (£1.5 trillion) (source: BBC 20 April 2010). In comparison, the GDP of the USA in 2010 was $14.7 trillion (source: US Department of Commerce, Bureau of Economic Analysis).

Traditional methods for comparing projects

There are two main methods in this category. These are the *payback* method and the *accounting rate of return* (ARR). The payback method simply tells you how long it takes for the original investment to be repaid.

Activity 12.2

What are the payback periods for the three projects given in Example 12.1?

You should have obtained 4 years for Project A, 2 years for Project B and 4 years for Project C. This indicates that the Bristol project is to be preferred since it takes less time for the original investment to be repaid.

The payback method is an easily understood method and favours projects that generate large cash flows early. This is an advantage since early cash flows will help a company's liquidity and also minimize risks of unforeseen problems in the future. However, this method ignores cash flows that are generated after the payback period. For example, with Project C large cash flows are generated in years 4 and 5 and this is not taken into account with the payback method.

The accounting rate of return (sometimes called the return on capital employed) is the ratio of average net income to the capital employed. The capital employed sometimes refers to initial capital and sometimes to average capital. There are also variations concerning what constitutes capital and what constitutes income. The definition used here refers to initial capital and can be expressed as follows:

$$\text{ARR} = \frac{\text{Average income (per year)}}{\text{Initial capital}} \times 100\%$$

Activity 12.3

Calculate the ARR for all three projects given in the example.

For Project A the average income is £5m/5 = £1m and the initial capital employed is £4m so the ARR is:

$$\text{ARR} = \frac{1}{4} \times 100 = 25\%$$

For Project B the average income will again be £1m (the total adds up to £5m – the same as Project A). Since the capital employed is £4m, the ARR is again 25%.

For Project C the average income is:

$$\frac{(0 + 0.5 + 1.5 + 2.0 + 3.0)}{5} = 1.4$$

Since the initial capital is £5m, the ARR is:

$$\text{ARR} = \frac{1.4}{5} \times 100$$
$$= 28\%$$

On the basis of the ARR, Project C is the better project.

The ARR is easy to calculate but it has many disadvantages, such as not allowing for timing of the cash flows. For example, Project A and Project B are ranked equal even though Project B generates larger cash flows in the first two years.

Discounted cash flow techniques

The disadvantages of the payback and the ARR methods are that they do not take into account the time value of money. If you were offered £1000 now or £1000 in a year's time, which would you take? I am sure that you would take £1000 now! However, what would be your decision if you were offered £1000 now or £2000 in a year's time? Unless you were desperate for money, you would probably prefer to wait a year and get the £2000. These two cases are clear cut. But what would be your decision if you were offered £1000 now or £1100 in a year's time? If you could put the money to good use so that after a year you would have more than £1100, then your decision should be to take the £1000 now.

It is clear from this that money in the future is not worth as much as money now, so we need some method of *discounting* future sums of money. In order to understand the idea of discounting, it is first necessary to revise the idea of *simple* and *compound* interest. Simple interest is the expression used when interest on a sum of money is calculated on the principal only. This situation occurs when the interest is withdrawn as it is earned.

Activity 12.4

You decide to invest £8500 in an investment account paying an interest rate of 5% p.a. The interest is paid out to you as it is earned. What interest would you receive at the end of each year?

The answer to this activity is 5% of £8500, which is £425.

Normally the interest is reinvested so that the interest also earns interest. In this case you would use the expression 'compound interest'.

Activity 12.5

You again decide to invest £8500 in an investment account paying an interest rate of 5% p.a. This time, however, all interest is reinvested. How much would the £8500 have grown to at the end of the 10th year?

The principal at the end of the first year is simply the original principal plus the interest earned. That is:

$$8500 + \frac{5}{100} \times 8500 = 8500 \left(1 + \frac{5}{100}\right)$$

This is £8500 + £425 = £8925.

The principal at the end of year 2 =

the principal at the start of year 2 +

the amount of interest received during the year.

That is:

$$8500 \left(1 + \frac{5}{100}\right) + 8500 \left(1 + \frac{5}{100}\right) \times \frac{5}{100}$$

This can be simplified by noting that the expression $8500 \left(1 + \frac{5}{100}\right)$ is common to both terms. The equation can therefore be factorized as follows:

$$8500 \left(1 + \frac{5}{100}\right)\left(1 + \frac{5}{100}\right) = 8500 \left(1 + \frac{5}{100}\right)^2$$

In general if you invest an initial principal P_0 for n years at an interest rate of r per cent, the principal at the *end* of the nth year is:

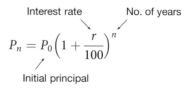

Interest rate   No. of years

$$P_n = P_0 \left(1 + \frac{r}{100}\right)^n$$

Initial principal

This is called the *compound interest* formula.

So for $P_0 = 8500$, $r = 5$ and $n = 10$,

the principal at the end of the 10th year $= 8500\left(1 + \dfrac{5}{100}\right)^{10} = £13\,846.$

Another way of expressing this is that £13 846 in 10 years' time at an interest rate of 5% is equivalent to £8500 now. This is quite a useful idea as it allows you to make a judgement on the value of some future sum of money.

Activity 12.6

You have been promised £10 000 in 5 years' time. What would this amount be worth now, assuming an interest rate of 6%?

To solve this problem the compound interest formula can be used in reverse. That is, P_n is known and you have to calculate P_0. In this case, $n = 5$, $r = 6\%$ and $P_n = 10\,000$, and the equation becomes:

$$10\,000 = P_0\left(1 + \dfrac{6}{100}\right)^5$$
$$= 1.3382 \times P_0$$

Therefore

$$P_0 = \dfrac{10\,000}{1.3382}$$
$$= £7473$$

Since this calculation will be repeated many times, you will find it easier to rearrange the compound interest formula to make P_0 the subject of the formula. That is:

$$P_0 = P_n \times \dfrac{1}{\left(1 + \dfrac{r}{100}\right)^n}$$

The expression $\dfrac{1}{\left(1 + \dfrac{r}{100}\right)^n}$ is called the *discount factor*.

For example, for $r = 6\%$ and $n = 5$, the discount factor is $\dfrac{1}{1.3382} = 0.7473$, so

$$P_0 = 10\,000 \times 0.7473$$
$$= £7473.$$

Activity 12.7

Discount the sum of £30 000 that is to be received in 4 years' time using an interest rate of (a) 2% and (b) 10%.

You should have found that the discount factors for 2% and 10% are 0.9238 and 0.6830 respectively. Therefore the discounted value of £30 000 is:

30 000 × 0.9238 = £27 714 at an interest rate of 2%

30 000 × 0.6830 = £20 490 at an interest rate of 10%

Net present value

Activity 12.8

You have been offered either £5000 in 2 years' time or £6000 in 3 years' time. Which would you accept, assuming an interest rate of 5.5%?

This is a slightly different problem in that you are asked to compare a sum of money in 2 years' time with a sum of money in 3 years' time. In order to compare the two amounts you need to have a common base. The easiest method is to find the value now of both amounts. The diagram in Figure 12.1 explains this more clearly.

The discount factors are given on top of each arrow and the value at the point of the arrow is the value now of each sum of money. This shows you that £6000 in 3 years' time is the better choice since the *present value* of £6000 is worth more than the present value of £5000 due in 2 years' time. This idea of calculating the present value of a sum of money can be extended to the case where a project generates a series of cash flows and the present value of the sum of these cash flows is required. The interest rate that is used is usually called the *discount rate* and is the *cost of capital* for the company.

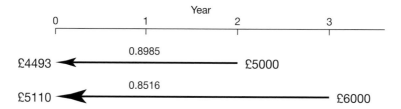

Figure 12.1
Present value of a
sum of money

Activity 12.9

In the case of BAS Holdings, the company's discount rate is 8%. Calculate the present value for each of the three projects given in Example 12.1.

The calculations are best set out in a table similar to Table 12.3.

From this table you should see that the largest present value is Project C with a total cash flow of £5.13m. However, to achieve this, a capital investment of £5m was required, whereas the other two projects only required an investment of £4m. To obtain the net profit, the investment should be deducted from the present value and, when this is done, the result is called the *net present value* or NPV.

Table 12.3 Calculation of present value

Year	Discount factor	Andover		Bristol		Carlisle	
		Cash flow (£m)	Present value (£m)	Cash flow (£m)	Present value (£m)	Cash flow (£m)	Present value (£m)
0		−4.0		−4.0		−5.0	
1	0.9259	1.0	0.9259	1.5	1.3889	0.0	0.0
2	0.8573	1.0	0.8573	2.5	2.1433	0.5	0.4287
3	0.7938	1.0	0.7938	0.5	0.3969	1.5	1.1907
4	0.7350	1.0	0.7350	0.5	0.3675	2.0	1.4700
5	0.6806	1.0	0.6806	0.0	0.0	3.0	2.0418
			3.9926		4.2966		5.1312

Activity 12.10

What is the NPV for each of the three projects?

The calculations are:

$£3.9926m − £4m = −£0.0074m$ or a loss of £7400 for Project A

$£4.2966m − £4m = £0.2966m$ or a gain of £296,600 for Project B

$£5.1312m − £5m = £0.1312m$ or a gain of £131,200 for Project C

On the basis of the NPV, Project A would result in a loss and is therefore not a profitable investment, while Project B is the most profitable investment.

When you use NPV to select one project out of many, you simply choose the project with the highest figure. You can also use NPV to make a decision about one project. In this case your decision should be as summarized in Table 12.4.

Table 12.4 Decision criterion when using NPV

NPV	Decision
Negative	Reject project
Zero	Indifferent
Positive	Accept project

Internal rate of return

The NPV method is a very useful method as it takes into account the timing of a series of cash flows. However, the decision is dependent on the discount rate used – a larger rate will reduce the NPV and could change the decision from accept to reject. An alternative approach is to calculate the discount rate that will give the NPV of zero. This is called the *Internal Rate of Return* or IRR. If the IRR for a project is greater than or equal to the cost of capital for a company, the project would be acceptable; if not, the project should be rejected. In the case of BAS Holdings, the cost of capital is 8% and any project with an IRR of at least this figure will be acceptable. Calculation of the IRR is not straightforward but an approximate value can be obtained using either a graphical approach or a linear interpolation. For both methods you need to calculate the NPV for two different discount rates. For the greatest accuracy the NPVs should be small, and preferably one should be positive and one negative. For the graphical method these points are plotted on a graph of NPV against discount rate and a line drawn between them. The point where the line crosses the horizontal axis (which represents zero NPV) can then be read from the graph.

Activity 12.11

Find the IRR for Project A.

For Project A, a discount rate of 8% gave an NPV of −£0.0074m. For most practical purposes this is virtually zero, so the IRR is about 8%. However, to get a more accurate answer you could try another discount rate, say 7.5%. The calculations for this discount rate are shown in Table 12.5.

Table 12.5 NPV calculations for a discount rate of 7.5%

Year	Discount factor	Cash flow (£m)	Present value (£m)
0		−4.0	
1	0.9302	1.0	0.9302
2	0.8653	1.0	0.8653
3	0.8050	1.0	0.8050
4	0.7488	1.0	0.7488
5	0.6966	1.0	0.6966
			4.0459

The NPV is $4.0459 - 4 = £0.0459$m. These two values have been plotted in Figure 12.2.

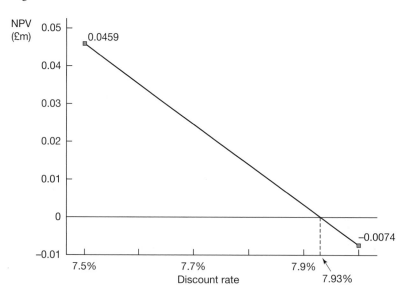

Figure 12.2
Graphical method for finding the IRR for the Andover project

You should find that the line cuts the horizontal axis at 7.93% and this is the value of the IRR for this project. To use the interpolation method the following formula can be used:

$$IRR = \frac{N_1 r_2 - N_2 r_1}{N_1 - N_2}$$

where an NPV of N_1 was obtained using a discount rate of r_1 and an NPV of N_2 was obtained using a discount rate of r_2.

So for $N_1 = 0.0459$, $r_1 = 7.5\%$, $N_2 = -0.0074$ and $r_2 = 8\%$, the IRR is:

$$IRR = \frac{0.0459 \times 8 - (-0.0074) \times 7.5}{0.0459 - (-0.0074)}$$

$$= \frac{0.42195}{0.0532}$$

$$= 7.93\%$$

This is the same as the value obtained from the graph.

Activity 12.12

Find the IRR for Project B using the graphical method.

(Hint – try discount rates of 11% and 13%.)

The NPV values calculated in Table 12.6 have been plotted in Figure 12.3 where you will see that the line joining the two points cuts the axis at a discount rate of about 12.1%.

Table 12.6 Calculations for the NPV using discount rates of 11% and 13%

Year	Discount factor @ 11%	Cash flow (£m)	Present value (£m)	Discount factor @ 13%	Present value (£m)
0		−4.0	−4.0		−4.0
1	0.9009	1.5	1.3514	0.8850	1.3275
2	0.8116	2.5	2.0290	0.7831	1.9578
3	0.7312	0.5	0.3656	0.6931	0.3466
4	0.6587	0.5	0.3294	0.6133	0.3067
5	0.5935	0.0	0.0000	0.5428	0.0000
NPV			0.0754		−0.0614

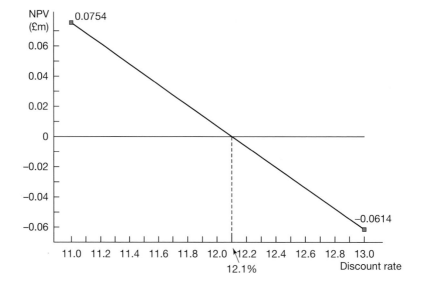

Figure 12.3
IRR for the Bristol project

Activity 12.13

Find the IRR for Project C using the formula.

Two rates have been tried: one at 6% which gave an NPV of £0.5305m and one at 8% which gave an NPV of £0.1312m. (You are recommended to do these calculations yourself.) Substituting these values into the formula gives:

$$\frac{0.5305 \times 8 - 0.1312 \times 6}{0.5305 - 0.1312} = \frac{3.4568}{0.3993}$$
$$= 8.66\%$$

The results of the IRR calculations agree with the NPV method; that is, Project A is not profitable, while Project B appears to be more profitable than Project C. The advantage of the IRR method is that it allows you to have a benchmark against which projects can be measured, and a rate of return is something that management understand. The disadvantages are that it is more difficult to calculate and does not take into account the absolute value of the cash flows. So, on the basis of IRR, a project giving an NPV of £100 might look better than a project with an NPV of £1m.

There is also the problem that in certain circumstances it is possible for the IRR method to give multiple solutions or no solution at all! It is possible to use Goal Seek in Excel to find the IRR. See Activity 11.15 (page 290) for details on using Goal Seek.

Other applications of the compound interest formula

Sinking funds

Activity 12.14

A firm wishes to purchase a machine costing £800 in 3 years' time by making 4 equal instalments (the first now, the second at the end of the first year, the third at the end of the second year and the fourth at the end of the third year – that is, when they purchase the machine) in a savings plan paying 5.2% net per annum. How much should each instalment be?

If we assume that the price of the machine will not increase then the investment plan must realize £800 at the end of the third year. If each instalment was for £200 the total amount saved would exceed £800 as a result of the interest received. If you look at Figure 12.4 you will see that the first payment will earn interest for 3 years, the second payment will earn interest for 2 years and the third payment will earn interest for just 1 year. The final payment will be made at the end of the third year and we can assume that the machine will be purchased immediately afterwards. So how would you find the correct amount to save? You could do it by trial and error but a little mathematics would be much more effective! If we call the unknown instalment x, then:

the first instalment will grow to $£x(1.052)^3$ at the end of the plan

the second instalment will grow to $£x(1.052)^2$ at the end of the plan

the third instalment will grow to $£x(1.052)$ at the end of the plan

the fourth instalment will stay at $£x$

Total amount accumulated $= x(1.052)^3 + x(1.052)^2 + x(1.052) + x$
This must equal £800. So:

$$x(1.052)^3 + x(1.052)^2 + x(1.052) + x = 800$$

Factorizing we get:

$$x[(1.052)^3 + (1.052)^2 + 1.052 + 1] = 800$$
$$x(1.1643 + 1.1067 + 1.052 + 1) = 800$$

So $4.323x = 800$ and

$$x = 800/4.323$$
$$= 185.06$$

Therefore each instalment should be £185.06.

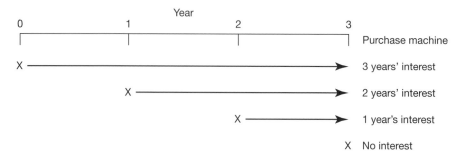

Figure 12.4
Regular savings plan

This type of savings plan is called a *sinking fund*. The method in Activity 12.14 will work for any number of years but it is possible to derive a formula (using the sum of a geometric series) that makes the calculation quicker. The formula is:

$$\frac{x\left[\left(1+\dfrac{r}{100}\right)^{n+1}-1\right]}{\dfrac{r}{100}}$$

The meaning of the symbols x, r and n is the same as before. (*Note*: Before using this formula make sure that the timings of the regular payments x correspond to those given in Activity 12.14.)

Activity 12.15

Solve the problem in Activity 12.14 using the sinking fund formula.

We again need to find x, so:

$$\frac{x\left[\left(1+\dfrac{5.2}{100}\right)^{4}-1\right]}{\dfrac{5.2}{100}}=800$$

$$x[(1.052)^{4}-1]=800\times0.052$$

$$0.2248x=41.6$$

$$x=\frac{41.6}{0.2248}$$

$$=185.05$$

which is the same as before (apart from the small rounding error).

Constant repayments

This sinking fund formula is a special case of the situation where an amount P_0 is invested followed by regular amounts x. The formula is:

$$P_n=P_0\left(1+\frac{r}{100}\right)^{n}+\frac{x\left[\left(1+\dfrac{r}{100}\right)^{n}-1\right]}{\dfrac{r}{100}}$$

Activity 12.16

You take out a 25-year repayment mortgage for £50 000 at a fixed interest rate of 8%. Repayments are made at the end of each year and will consist of part interest and part capital. Calculate the amount of the annual repayments.

Since you want the amount owed at the end of the 25-year period to be zero, then $P_{25} = 0$ and $P_0 = -50\,000$ (note: P_0 is negative because you owe £50 000).

Substituting these values together with $r = 8$, you get:

$$0 = -50\,000 \times \left(1 + \frac{8}{100}\right)^{25} + \frac{x\left[\left(1 + \frac{8}{100}\right)^{25} - 1\right]}{\frac{8}{100}}$$

$$0 = -50\,000 \times (1.08)^{25} + \frac{x[(1.08)^{25} - 1]}{0.08}$$

$$0 = -50\,000 \times 6.8485 + \frac{x[5.8485]}{0.08}$$

$$0 = -342\,425 + 73.106x$$

$$73.106x = 342\,425$$

$$x = 4684$$

So the annual repayment should be £4684.

If you multiply this amount by 25 you will get £117 100, which is the amount you would pay back over the life of the loan; that is, over double the amount you borrowed!

Activity 12.17

You can only afford to pay back £4500 per year. How long would it take you to pay back the original loan?

This time you know x but not n, so:

$$0 = -50\,000 \times \left(1 + \frac{8}{100}\right)^{n} + \frac{4500\left[\left(1 + \frac{8}{100}\right)^{n} - 1\right]}{\frac{8}{100}}$$

$$0 = -50\,000 \times (1.08)^{n} + \frac{4500[(1.08)^{n} - 1]}{0.08}$$

$$0 = -50\,000 \times (1.08)^{n} + 56\,250 \times (1.08)^{n} - 56\,250$$

$$0 = 6250 \times (1.08)^{n} - 56\,250$$

$$6250 \times (1.08)^{n} = 56\,250$$

$$(1.08)^{n} = \frac{56\,250}{6250} = 9$$

To make n the subject of the formula we can take logs of both sides:

$$\log(1.08)^n = \log(9)$$

Using laws of logs (see Chapter 1):

$$n \times \log(1.08) = \log(9)$$

$$n = \frac{\log(9)}{\log(1.08)}$$

$$= \frac{0.9542}{0.03342}$$

$$= 28.55$$

So a total of 29 years would be required to pay off the loan for an annual payment of £4500.

Depreciation

Many investments such as consumer items and machinery depreciate so that after a few years the item is worth less than it was when it was first bought. One way of depreciating an item is the *reducing balance* method. This method assumes that a fixed percentage of the initial capital value of the item is written off each year. It results in a larger depreciation in the early years, which is what you would normally expect for these types of goods. To solve these problems we can use the compound interest formula, but in this case the interest rate r is the *rate of depreciation*.

Activity 12.18

An item of machinery is bought for £30 000 and after 10 years its scrap value is £1000. Find (a) the rate of depreciation and (b) its book value after 5 years.

To solve this problem you would use the compound interest formula:

$$P_n = P_0 \left(1 + \frac{r}{100}\right)^n$$

For $P_0 = 30\,000$, $P_{10} = 1000$ and $n = 10$ you get:

$$1000 = 30\,000 \times \left(1 + \frac{r}{100}\right)^{10}$$

$$\left(1 + \frac{r}{100}\right)^{10} = \frac{1000}{30\,000}$$

$$= 0.033\dot{3}$$

$$\text{So } \left(1 + \frac{r}{100}\right) = (0.033\dot{3})^{\frac{1}{10}}$$

$$= 0.7117$$

$$\frac{r}{100} = 0.7117 - 1$$

$$= -0.2883$$

$$r = -28.83\%$$

r is negative since the capital is decreasing in value. So the depreciation rate is 28.83%.

The *book value* is the value of the asset at a particular point in time. To calculate the book value after 5 years we simply use the calculated value of r in the formula, that is:

$$P_5 = 30\,000 \times \left(1 - \frac{28.83}{100}\right)^5$$

$$= 30\,000 \times 0.1826$$

$$= £5478$$

Compound interest with continuous compounding

Activity 12.19

The sum of £5000 is invested at 6% per annum compound interest. Find the value of the investment at the end of 5 years if interest is compounded (a) annually, (b) monthly, and (c) daily.

For the annual case you would use the compound interest formula with $r = 6\%$. That is:

$$P_5 = 5000 \times \left(1 + \frac{6}{100}\right)^5$$

$$= 5000 \times 1.3382$$

$$= £6691$$

If compounded monthly, the interest rate would be 0.5% per month (6/12) and the time period would be 60 (5 × 12 months). So the value of the investment at the end of 5 years would be:

$$P_5 = 5000 \times \left(1 + \frac{0.5}{100}\right)^{60}$$

$$= 5000 \times 1.3489$$

$$= £6744.50$$

If compounded daily, the interest rate would now be 0.01644% per day (6/365) and the time period would be 1825 (5 × 365).

$$P_5 = 5000 \times \left(1 + \frac{0.01644}{100}\right)^{1825}$$

$$= 5000 \times 1.3499$$

$$= £6749.50$$

As you can see the amounts are gradually increasing as the time period gets less. In the limit (that is, when the interest is continuously compounded), the value of an investment after n years is given by:

$$P_n = P_0 e^{\frac{r \times n}{100}}$$

where r is the annual interest rate and e is the exponential function (and can be found on all scientific calculators).

$$P_n = 5000 e^{\frac{6 \times 5}{100}}$$

$$= 5000 \times 1.3499$$

$$= £6749.50$$

Reflection

Throughout our lives we are faced with financial decisions. As children we must decide whether to spend our pocket money or save it and as we get older these decisions become more complex and more frequent. So we have to decide whether to borrow money to buy a house or car and where to invest our savings. There are a large number of institutions that want our money and until the financial crisis of the late 2000s we assumed that our money would be safe and earn a good return. We certainly didn't expect that some of the major banks such as Halifax would need huge amounts of taxpayer's money to remain solvent. Nor did we realize that the financial instruments the bank use to invest our money was so complicated and risky that only analysts really understood them. The methods used in this chapter, although relatively simple, are fundamental when making decisions on where to invest money. Hopefully the financial sector will go back to some of the tried and tested methods rather than risk another potential financial meltdown!

....

Key points

○ Traditional accounting procedures do not take time into account. Examples of such methods are the *payback method* and the *accounting rate of return*.
○ Compound interest is normally applied to an investment as this means that the interest also gains interest.
○ The compound interest formula can be re-arranged so that you can work out the amount of money you need to invest now that will give you a desired sum of money in n years time.
○ Put another way this means that you can calculate what a sum of money in n years time is worth at today's prices. This is called the *discounted cash flow technique* and allows investments that mature at different times to be compared more easily.
○ When we subtract the initial investment we get the *net present value*.
○ A net present value greater than zero means that a project is worthwhile.

● The *internal rate of return* gives the discount rate that makes the net present value zero.
● The compound interest formula also allows us to calculate sinking funds, constant repayments (mortgages) and depreciation of an asset.
● It is possible to modify the compound interest formula to allow for continuous compounding.
● Table 12.7 summarizes the four different methods of investment appraisal for Example 12.1.

Table 12.7 Summary of the different methods of investment appraisal for Example 12.1

Method	Project			Decision
	A	B	C	
Payback	4 years	2 years	4 years	B
ARR	25%	25%	28%	C
NPV	−£0.0074m	£0.2966m	£0.1312m	B
IRR	7.93%	12.1%	8.66%	B

Further reading

Investment appraisal is a huge subject and is treated differently depending on the background of the authors. So an accountant would look at the subject differently from an economist and a tax expert would also have a different approach. However, for a general text that covers the material in this chapter and extends it further, but in a non-mathematical manner, the one by Lumby and Jones (1999) is a good choice.

Web links W

Answers to selected questions can be found in Appendix 2. Answers to the other questions can be found on the companion website for this book.

Practice questions

W 1 The following cash flows occur with 3 different investment opportunities. Use the payback method and the accounting rate of return to decide which is the best investment opportunity.

Year	Investment A	Investment B	Investment C
0	−20	−15	−5
1	12	0	3
2	10	10	3
3	5	5	3
4	3	5	3
5	0	5	3

W 2 One project involves an outlay of £2.5m and gets an annual net income of £1m for 5 years. Another project involves an outlay of £10m but gets no income until year 5 when the capital is repaid plus interest of £5m. Using the payback and accounting rate of return methods decide which is the most attractive project.

W 3 A buy-to-let investor is trying to decide between three properties. The first property costs £200 000 and he believes that after mortgage interest payments and expenses he will be able to get a net income of £400 per month. The second property costs £300 000 and the net income should be £500 per month while the third property costs £400 000 with a net income of £800 per month. Using the payback and accounting rate of return methods decide which property the landlord should buy. (Assume that the landlord does not sell the property and the rent does not increase.)

W 4 £10 000 is invested in a one-year fixed rate account paying 6%. What interest is payable at the end of the term?

W 5 £20 000 is invested in a 5-year fixed interest rate account paying 5%. Interest is paid out each year. What interest do you receive each year?

W 6 £20 000 is invested in a 5-year fixed interest bond paying 5% p.a. If interest is reinvested in the account how much will the bond be worth at the end of the 5 years?

W 7 £50 000 is invested at 5.5% for 6 years. If all interest is reinvested:
(a) What would be the amount accumulated at the end of the 6 years?
(b) How much interest would have been received during the 6 years?

W 8 A car is purchased for a £3000 deposit and 5 annual payments of £1000. What is the cost of the car at today's prices if a discount rate of 8% is assumed?

W 9 What is the present value of £50 000 that is payable in 5 years' time if interest rates are expected to be constant at 6% during this period?

W 10 You have been offered £20 000 in 1 year's time or £25 000 in two years' time. Which should you accept based on present values?

W 11 An annuity is a guaranteed annual income for life that is purchased through a pension plan. A particular annuity is bought with a pension pot of £50 000. If the annuity pays out £3500 p.a. for life what is the present value of this annuity assuming a life expectancy of 10 years and interest rate of 5%?

W 12 An investment costs £2m to set up and then gives an income of £0.6m p.a. for 5 years. Use the net present value method with a discount rate of 6% to decide if this investment is worthwhile.

W 13 Using the cash flows given in Question 1 and the NPV method of investment appraisal, decide which (if any) of the three investment opportunities should be undertaken. Assume a discount rate of 6%.

W 14 A project involves an investment of £2m and is guaranteed to produce an income of £0.5m each year for the next 5 years. Compare and contrast different methods for evaluating the worth of this project. Assume that the income occurs at the end of each year and that the discount rate is 7%.

15 A project costs £5m to set up, and a return of £2m p.a. for the next 3 years is guaranteed. A project will only be accepted if the internal rate of return is greater than 14%. Should the project be accepted?

16 On 1 January 2005 you invested £1000 in a building society's 5-year fixed rate account paying 5.4% net per annum. How much will be in the account on 1 January 2010 if no funds or interest are withdrawn throughout the period of the investment?

W **17** A car dealer is considering leasing some vehicles as an alternative to outright sales. The scheme she has devised requires the customer to pay an annual premium over a fixed period. If the dealer wants to accumulate £20 000 over a 3 year period what annual premium should she charge assuming an interest rate of 5.75%?

18 A car is purchased for a £4500 deposit and 5 annual payments of £1000. What is the cost of the car at today's prices if a discount rate of 7.5% is assumed?

19 A firm is considering the purchase of one of two machines. The first (machine A), costing £4000, is expected to bring in revenues of £2000, £2500 and £1500 respectively in the 3 years for which it will be operative; while the second (machine B), which costs £3900, will produce revenues of £1500, £2500 and £2000, and has the same lifetime. Neither machine will have any appreciable scrap value at the end of its life. Assuming a discount rate of 8%, compare and contrast different methods for evaluating which machine should be purchased. (Hint to calculating IRRs: a discount rate of 25% gave NPVs of −£32 and −£76 for machines A and B respectively.)

20 A company has the choice of two investments, both costing an initial £15 000. The first will yield cash flows of £6000 per year for 3 years (the first payment receivable 1 year after investment), while the second will yield a lump sum of £19 000 at the end of the 3 year period. Assuming a discount rate of 5%, which investment should be chosen? (Hint to calculating IRRs: a discount rate of 10% gave NPVs of −£79.20 and −£725.30 for investments 1 and 2 respectively.)

21 A machine which currently costs £800 will increase in price by 4% per year as a result of inflation.
   (a) What will the machine cost in 3 years' time?
   (b) If a firm wishes to purchase this machine in 3 years' time by making 3 equal instalments (the first now, the second in one year's time and the third in two years – that is, one year before the purchase), in a savings plan paying 5.2% net p.a., how much should each investment be?

22 A machine is purchased for £3750 and generates a revenue of £1310 per year for 5 years. After this time, it ceases to be productive and has no scrap value.
   (a) Assuming a discount rate of 11.2 %, calculate its net present value.
   (b) Find a discount rate at which the net present value becomes negative, and use it to estimate the internal rate of return.

23 A firm wishes to provide a sinking fund in order to replace equipment that has a life span of 10 years. If the cost of the equipment will be £1m in 10 years' time, what annual amount does it need to put aside in an account paying 7% p.a.?

24 You decide to take out a 20-year mortgage for £65 000 at an annual interest rate of 7.5%.
   (a) What would be the annual repayment?
   (b) If you could increase the annual amount paid to £7000, how much money would you save over the life of the mortgage?

W 25 What would the annual payments be on a 25-year repayment mortgage for £150 000 at a fixed interest rate of 7%?

W 26 An item of machinery is purchased for £50 000 and after 5 years will have a scrap value of £5000. What is the rate of depreciation?

27 You have just bought a car for £12 000 from a garage that promises to buy the car back from you for £5000 in 3 years' time.
(a) What is the rate of depreciation?
(b) Given this rate of depreciation, what will the car be worth at the end of the first year?

28 Which is better: a savings account paying 7% p.a. where interest is compounded annually, or an account which pays an annual rate of 5% but where the interested is compounded continuously?

··

Assignment

MOS plc is a computer software company and its main business is the development of payroll systems. Recently it has also developed a number of specialized machine control systems and the company is keen to expand into this area. However, the risks in developing these types of systems are much greater than for payroll systems. This is partly to do with the fact that there is a risk that the software will not work, but also to do with the fact that it takes much longer for the project to be completed. A payroll system can be developed in under a year, while for control systems the development time can be 2 to 3 years. The policy of the company is to lease the software for a fixed period of time and during this period the client pays an annual rental that diminishes with time.

When MOS receives a request for a piece of software, a valuation exercise takes place. This valuation exercise looks at the financial implications as well as any technical problems. For payroll systems the market is very competitive and there is very little room for manoeuvre. However, for control systems there is much more flexibility in pricing. As with any small company, MOS has a limited amount of capital available, which currently amounts to £500 000 obtained through bank loans. MOS currently pays interest at a rate of 8.5% p.a.

MOS has options on three projects. Project A and Project B are payroll systems and both involve an expenditure of less than £100 000, while Project C is a specialized control system that involves an expenditure of £500 000. Details of the expenditure and leasing rental are shown in Table 12.8.

Use investment appraisal techniques to decide which (if any) of the projects should be accepted. Write a note to the Project Manager of MOS plc explaining your results and recommendations.

Table 12.8 Information for the assignment

Year	Project A (£000s)	Project B (£000s)	Project C (£000s)
0	−60	−80	−500
1	30	40	0
2	30	20	0
3	20	20	0
4	10	20	500
5	10	5	300
6			200
7			100

Forecasting: time series analysis

Prerequisites	There are no prerequisites for this chapter apart from a basic knowledge of Excel
Objectives	○ To be able to apply the technique of moving averages to isolate the trend in a time series
	○ To understand the circumstances in which the additive and multiplicative models should be used
	○ To be able to calculate the seasonal component for both the additive and multiplicative models
	○ To be able to calculate the seasonally adjusted series
	○ To know how to apply the technique of exponential smoothing in appropriate circumstances
	○ To be able to make forecasts, and to understand the limitations of these forecasts
	○ To know how to use Excel in time series analysis
Introduction	Many variables have values that change with time, such as the weekly sales of ice cream, visits abroad by UK residents, or the daily production rates for a factory. The changing value of such variables over a period of time is called a *time series*. The analysis of time series data is very important both for industry and for government, and a large number of people are employed to do this analysis. This chapter will look at the main features of a time series, and demonstrate some popular techniques.

Quantitative methods in action: forecasting US electricity demand

Due to the economic downturn that began in late 2007 the demand for electricity in the USA actually fell by 1% in 2008 and 3% in 2009. It was the first time since records began 60 years ago that electricity demand has actually fallen in two consecutive years. This was most unexpected and not forecast. Although events like the economic downturn and the financial crisis cannot be predicted it is still necessary to make long-term forecasts for energy use because the construction of power supplies can take 20 years or more.

The US Energy Information Administration (EIA) provides forecasts of energy use based on factors such as:

○ the pace of economic recovery
○ the price of fuels
○ legislation related to energy and the environment
○ improvements in energy efficiency.

The EIA provides projections of electricity demand to 2035. Figure 13.1 shows the demand *growth* from 1950 to 2035. The scale on the vertical axis is in percentages so, although the projection is showing a decline, the actual demand is increasing. From 2008 to 2035 the actual energy consumption increases by 14%, which means that the average growth is 0.5%. As the USA expects its economic output to grow by 2.4% the difference will be taken up by more efficient use of energy. A trend line has been drawn through the graph which has been calculated using moving averages a technique that will be discussed in this chapter.

Source: Annual Energy Outlook 2010 (Energy Information Administration)

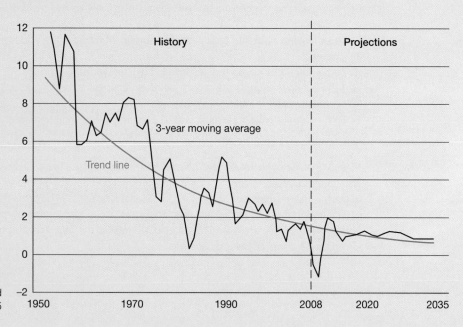

Figure 13.1
US electricity demand growth, 1950 to 2035

The decomposition model

This model assumes that a time series is made up of several components. These components are:

○ Trend
○ Seasonality
○ Cyclic behaviour
○ Randomness

The trend represents the long-run behaviour of the data and can be increasing, decreasing or constant. Seasonality relates to periodic fluctuations that repeat themselves at fixed intervals of time. Cyclic behaviour represents the ups and downs of the economy or of a specific industry. It is a long-term fluctuation and for practical purposes is usually ignored. Randomness is always present in a time series and represents variation that cannot be explained. Some time series (for example, share prices) have a very high random component and the forecasts of these series will be subject to a high degree of error.

Example 13.1

Table 13.1 consists of data relating to the sales of petrol at the Star petrol station for 3 weeks while Table 13.2 consists of the sales of sun cream by Mace Skin Care plc.

Table 13.1 Sales of petrol at the Star petrol station

Week	Day	Litres (000s)
1	Monday	28
	Tuesday	16
	Wednesday	24
	Thursday	44
	Friday	65
	Saturday	82
	Sunday	30
2	Monday	33
	Tuesday	21
	Wednesday	29
	Thursday	49
	Friday	70
	Saturday	87
	Sunday	35
3	Monday	35
	Tuesday	23
	Wednesday	31
	Thursday	51
	Friday	72
	Saturday	89
	Sunday	37

Table 13.2 Sales of sun cream by Mace Skin Care plc

Year	Quarter	Sales (£000s)
2006	1	6.00
	2	9.00
	3	12.00
	4	8.00
2007	1	8.00
	2	13.50
	3	17.00
	4	13.00
2008	1	12.00
	2	20.25
	3	30.00
	4	19.50
2009	1	18.00

Activity 13.1

Plot the two series represented by Tables 13.1 and 13.2 on graph paper (or use a spreadsheet) and compare and contrast the important features of each.

You can check your graph with the ones in Figures 13.2 and 13.3. What can you say about these graphs? You should notice that both series show a marked seasonal component since the patterns repeat themselves at regular intervals. In the case of the Star petrol station, the highest sales always occurs on a Saturday and the lowest on a Monday. The time series for the quarterly sales of sun cream by Mace Skin Care plc shows a peak in quarter 3 and a trough in quarter 1. You should also notice that the sales of sun cream appear to have increased rapidly during the 3-year period.

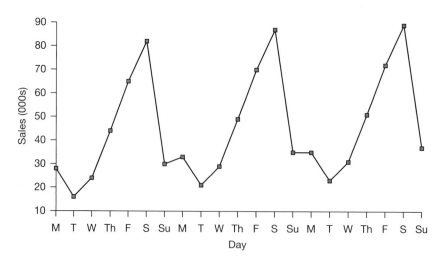

Figure 13.2
Sales of petrol at the
Star service station

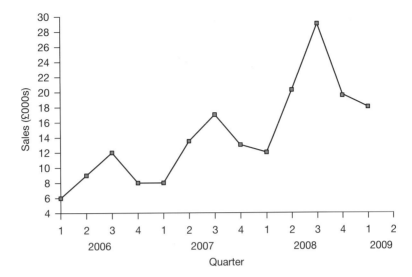

Figure 13.3
Sales of sun cream
by Mace Skin
Care plc

Isolating the trend

To isolate the trend you need to remove the seasonal fluctuations. In the case of the petrol sales the pattern repeats itself every week, so perhaps the average sales each week might be a useful calculation.

Activity 13.2

Calculate the average petrol sales for weeks 1, 2 and 3. Does this help remove the seasonal fluctuations?

The values you should have got are 41.3, 46.3 and 48.3 for weeks 1, 2 and 3 respectively. The seasonal fluctuations have certainly been removed, but then so has most of the data! This is therefore not the best of methods. However, why use Monday to Sunday as a week? Why not Tuesday to Monday or Wednesday to Tuesday? If you think along these lines you will see that many more than 3 averages can be obtained. This process is called *moving averages* since the average is moved by one time period each time. Since there are 7 days or periods in this example, you have to calculate a 7-point moving average.

The calculations for the first 3 averages are shown in Table 13.3 overleaf. Notice that the first average has been placed alongside Thursday: this is because Thursday is the middle of the week that starts on Monday.

Activity 13.3

Calculate the remaining moving averages and plot these figures on the same graph as you plotted the original series.

The complete table is shown in Table 13.4.

Table 13.3 Calculation of moving averages for petrol sales

Day	Petrol sales (000s litres)	Weekly total	7-point moving average
Monday	28		
Tuesday	16		
Wednesday	24		
Thursday	44	$28 + 16 + 24 + 44 + 65 + 82 + 30 = 289$	$289/7 = 41.3$
Friday	65	$16 + 24 + 44 + 65 + 82 + 30 + 33 = 294$	$294/7 = 42.0$
Saturday	82	$24 + 44 + 65 + 82 + 30 + 33 + 21 = 299$	$299/7 = 42.7$
Sunday	30		
Monday	33		
Tuesday	21		

NOTE: A shortcut is to notice that as you move down the table, you are simply dropping one period and adding another. That is, the total for Friday is $289 - 28 + 33 = 294$. This is particularly useful for large cycle lengths, such as 12- or 52-point moving averages.

Table 13.4 Moving averages for Activity 13.3

Day	Litres (000s)	Moving average
Monday	28	
Tuesday	16	
Wednesday	24	
Thursday	44	41.3
Friday	65	42.0
Saturday	82	42.7
Sunday	30	43.4
Monday	33	44.1
Tuesday	21	44.9
Wednesday	29	45.6
Thursday	49	46.3
Friday	70	46.6
Saturday	87	46.9
Sunday	35	47.1
Monday	35	47.4
Tuesday	23	47.7
Wednesday	31	48.0
Thursday	51	48.3
Friday	72	
Saturday	89	
Sunday	37	

The moving average figures have been superimposed on the original time series graph and are shown in Figure 13.4.

There is no doubt that the moving average has smoothed the data and therefore this second series should represent the trend. You can see from the graph that there is a slight upward movement to this trend.

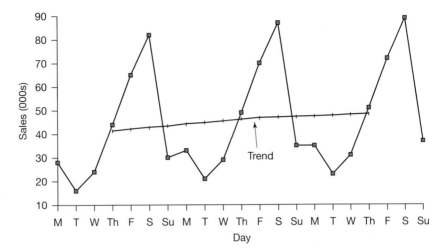

Figure 13.4
Time series graph of petrol sales with the moving averages plotted

The Star petrol station example illustrated the case where the moving average was based on an odd number of periods (7 days). However, with the sun cream series there is an even number of periods (4 quarters). The problem with this is that the middle of the year falls between quarters 2 and 3. This would not be very helpful since the original data relate to a specific quarter. (How would you plot a value between 2 quarters and what would this value mean?) To get round this problem, *centred moving averages* are used. The moving averages are worked out as before, placing the averages between periods. Pairs of averages are then taken and the average of the averages can be written down alongside a specific period. Table 13.5 illustrates the calculations for the first 2 centred moving averages.

Table 13.5 Calculation of moving averages for sun cream

Year	Quarter	Sales (£000s)	Moving average	Centred moving average
2006	1	6.0		
	2	9.0		
			8.75	
	3	12.0		$(8.75 + 9.25)/2 = 9.00$
			9.25	
	4	8.0		$(9.25 + 10.38)/2 = 9.81$
			10.38	
2007	1	8.0		
	2	13.5		

Activity 13.4

Calculate the remaining centred moving average figures for the sales of sun cream and plot these figures on the same graph as you plotted the original series.

You should have obtained Table 13.6. The centred moving averages can then be plotted, as in Figure 13.5. Notice the rapidly rising trend values.

Table 13.6 Centred moving averages for Activity 13.4

Year	Quarter	Sales (£000s)	Centred moving average
2006	1	6.00	
	2	9.00	
	3	12.00	9.00
	4	8.00	9.81
2007	1	8.00	11.00
	2	13.50	12.25
	3	17.00	13.38
	4	13.00	14.72
2008	1	12.00	17.19
	2	20.25	19.63
	3	30.00	21.19
	4	19.50	
2009	1	18.00	

NOTE: Figures have been rounded to 2 decimal places in this and subsequent tables. The figures will therefore not agree exactly to those obtained using a spreadsheet.

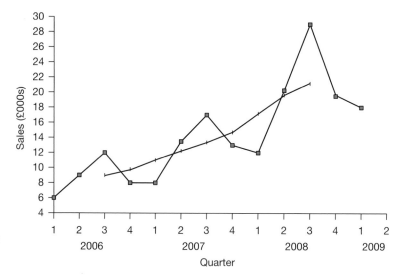

Figure 13.5
Time series graph of sun cream sales with the moving averages plotted

Isolating the seasonal component

There are two models that will allow you to isolate the seasonal component. The first is the *additive* model and is applicable if the seasonal swings are a constant difference from the trend. This means that the *difference* between the trend and a particular period remains approximately constant throughout the entire time series. The second model is the *multiplicative* model and is applicable if the seasonal swings are a constant percentage of the trend; that is, the seasonal swing will depend on the value of the trend at that point.

In equation form the additive model is:

$$Y = T + S + C + R$$

and the multiplicative model is:

$$Y = T \times S \times C \times R$$

where Y is the variable of interest, T is the trend, S is the seasonal component, C is the cyclic component and R is the random element.

Activity 13.5

By examining Figure 13.4, decide whether the additive or multiplicative model is more appropriate for the petrol sales series. Repeat this exercise for the sales of sun cream, using Figure 13.5.

You should have found that the seasonal swings about the trend for the petrol sales series appear reasonably constant, so an additive model is probably appropriate here. In the sun cream example the seasonal swings about the trend are increasing, so the multiplicative model is probably better. However, it is not always so clear cut and sometimes both models are tried and the results compared. To show this, both models will now be applied to the sun cream example.

To obtain the seasonal differences, the additive model can be rearranged as:

$$S + C + R = Y - T$$

So the value of the variable minus the trend value at that point will give you the seasonal difference plus the cyclic and random components. The cyclic component can only be isolated when values of the variable Y are available over many years (at least 20), which is rare. Usually the cyclic component is ignored, and its effect (if any) forms part of the random element.

For quarter 3 of 2006 the estimate of the seasonal difference is $12 - 9 = 3$. This tells you that sales for quarter 3 in 1999 are 3 units (£3000) above the trend. For quarter 4 of 1999 the seasonal difference is -1.81 ($8 - 9.81$), which means the sales are 1.81 below the trend.

Activity 13.6

Calculate the seasonal differences for the remainder of the data.

You should have obtained the seasonal differences shown in Table 13.7 overleaf.

If you look at these figures you will notice that for the same quarter number the seasonal difference varies. This is due to the random element. This variation can best be observed in Table 13.8, which also allows the average seasonal difference to be calculated.

The use of an average value helps to remove some of the random component. These averages should sum to zero since they should cancel out over the year. In the

Table 13.7 Seasonal differences for the sales of sun cream

Year	Quarter	Sales (£000s)	Centred moving average	Seasonal difference
2006	1	6.00		
	2	9.00		
	3	12.00	9.00	3.00
	4	8.00	9.81	−1.81
2007	1	8.00	11.00	−3.00
	2	13.50	12.25	1.25
	3	17.00	13.38	3.63
	4	13.00	14.72	−1.72
2008	1	12.00	17.19	−5.19
	2	20.25	19.63	0.62
	3	30.00	21.19	8.81
	4	19.50		
2009	1	18.00		

Table 13.8 Average seasonal differences for the sales of sun cream

Quarter	1	2	3	4	
2006			3.00	−1.81	
2007	−3.00	1.25	3.63	−1.72	
2008	−5.19	0.62	8.81		
Average	−4.095	0.935	5.147	−1.765	Sum = 0.222
Adjusted	−4.15	0.88	5.09	−1.82	Sum = 0.00

example above you will see that $-4.095 + 0.935 + 5.147 - 1.765 = 0.222$, which is clearly not zero. If each average is reduced by 0.056 $\left(\dfrac{0.222}{4}\right)$ then you will get the adjusted figures (rounded to 2 decimal places) shown in Table 13.8 and you should check that their sum is now zero.

The calculations for the multiplicative model are similar except that S is called the seasonal factor and is worked out by dividing Y by T. These factors are often expressed in percentage form by multiplying by 100. For example, the seasonal factor for quarter 3 in 2006 is:

$$\frac{12}{9} \times 100 = 133.3\%$$

Activity 13.7

Obtain the average percentage seasonal factors for the sales of sun cream by Mace Skin Care plc.

In this model a seasonal factor above 100% represents sales above the trend, and a value below 100% represents sales below the trend. The seasonal factors and average seasonal factors are shown in Tables 13.9 and 13.10 respectively.

Table 13.9 Seasonal factors for the sales of sun cream

Year	Quarter	Sales (£000s)	Centred moving average	Seasonal factor (%)
2006	1	6.00		
	2	9.00		
	3	12.00	9.00	133.3
	4	8.00	9.81	81.5
2007	1	8.00	11.00	72.7
	2	13.50	12.25	110.2
	3	17.00	13.38	127.1
	4	13.00	14.72	88.3
2008	1	12.00	17.19	69.8
	2	20.25	19.63	103.2
	3	30.00	21.19	141.6
	4	19.50		
2009	1	18.00		

Table 13.10 Calculation of average seasonal factors for the sales of sun cream

Quarter	1	2	3	4	
2006			133.3	81.5	
2007	72.7	110.2	127.1	88.3	
2008	69.8	103.2	141.6		
Average	71.3	106.7	134.0	84.9	Sum = 396.9
Adjusted	71.9	107.5	135.0	85.6	Sum = 400.0

Each average was adjusted by multiplying its value by $1.00781 \left(\dfrac{400}{396.9} \right)$, since the sum of the averages should in this case be 400.

Analysis of errors

Once you have isolated the trend and seasonal components it is a good idea to see how well the model fits the data. This is particularly important when you are not sure whether the additive or multiplicative model is the correct model to use.

For the additive model $Y = T + S$, so the Y variable can be predicted by adding the trend to the relevant adjusted average seasonal difference. For the multiplicative model $Y = T \times S$, so the prediction is made by multiplying the trend and adjusted average seasonal factor. In both cases the difference between the actual value and the predicted value gives you the error in the prediction. For example, the predicted sales of sun cream for quarter 3 in 2006 using the additive model is $9.00 + 5.09 = 14.09$. Since the actual value is 12.00, this represents an error of -2.09 ($12 - 14.09$). Using the multiplicative model the predicted value is $9.00 \times \dfrac{135.0}{100} = 12.15$ and the error is now -0.15.

Activity 13.8

Calculate the remaining errors using both the additive and multiplicative models.

The errors for both models are shown in Table 13.11 and Table 13.12. The errors should be small and show no pattern. Even with small quantities of data the easiest way to look at the errors is by means of a graph. Figures 13.6 and 13.7 show that the multiplicative model gives the smallest errors and is therefore the better model, which is what was expected.

Apart from a graphical display of the errors, it is possible to analyze them statistically. Two statistics are normally calculated, the mean absolute deviation (MAD) and the mean square error (MSE).

Table 13.11 Calculation of the errors for the additive model

Year	Quarter	Sales (£000s)	Trend	Average seasonal difference	Predicted sales (£000s)	Error
2006	1	6.00				
	2	9.00				
	3	12.00	9.00	5.09	14.09	−2.09
	4	8.00	9.81	−1.82	7.99	0.01
2007	1	8.00	11.00	−4.15	6.85	1.15
	2	13.50	12.25	0.88	13.13	0.37
	3	17.00	13.38	5.09	18.47	−1.47
	4	13.00	14.72	−1.82	12.90	0.10
2008	1	12.00	17.19	−4.15	13.04	−1.04
	2	20.25	19.63	0.88	20.51	−0.26
	3	30.00	21.19	5.09	26.28	3.72
	4	19.50				
2009	1	18.00				

Table 13.12 Calculation of the errors for the multiplicative model

Year	Quarter	Sales (£000s)	Trend	Average seasonal factor (%)	Predicted sales (£000s)	Error
2006	1	6.00				
	2	9.00				
	3	12.00	9.00	135.0	12.15	−0.15
	4	8.00	9.81	85.6	8.40	−0.40
2007	1	8.00	11.00	71.9	7.91	0.09
	2	13.50	12.25	107.5	13.17	0.33
	3	17.00	13.38	135.0	18.06	−1.06
	4	13.00	14.72	85.6	12.60	0.40
2008	1	12.00	17.19	71.9	12.36	−0.36
	2	20.25	19.63	107.5	21.10	−0.85
	3	30.00	21.19	135.0	28.61	1.39
	4	19.50				
2009	1	18.00				

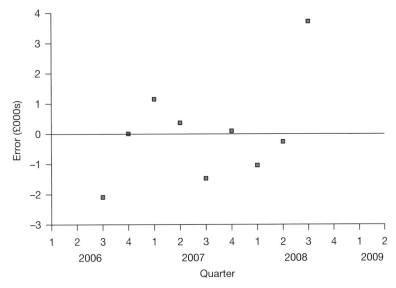

Figure 13.6
Errors for the additive model

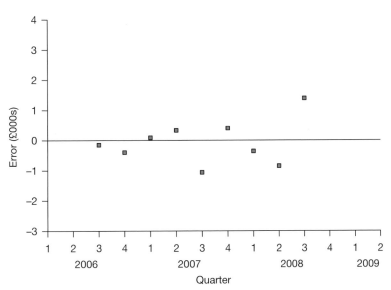

Figure 13.7
Errors for the multiplicative model

The formulae for these are:

sum the *absolute* values of the
errors (ignore the sign)

sum the *square* of the errors

$$\text{MAD} = \frac{\sum |\text{errors}|}{n} \qquad \text{MSE} = \frac{\sum (\text{errors})^2}{n}$$

The MAD statistic is simply the mean of the absolute errors (or deviations), while MSE is the mean squared errors. Both statistics are valid, but you will find that many statisticians favour the MSE statistic. One reason for this is that squaring puts more emphasis on large errors. For the sun cream example, the calculation of MAD and MSE using the errors obtained from the additive model is shown in Table 13.13.

Table 13.13 Calculation of MAD and MSE for the additive model

Year	Quarter	Actual sales (£000s)	Predicted sales (£000s)	Error	Absolute error	Squared error
2006	3	12.00	14.09	−2.09	2.09	4.3681
	4	8.00	7.99	0.01	0.01	0.0001
2007	1	8.00	6.85	1.15	1.15	1.3225
	2	13.50	13.13	0.37	0.37	0.1369
	3	17.00	18.47	−1.47	1.47	2.1609
	4	13.00	12.90	0.10	0.10	0.0100
2008	1	12.00	13.04	−1.04	1.04	1.0816
	2	20.25	20.51	−0.26	0.26	0.0676
	3	30.00	26.28	3.72	3.72	13.8384
				Sum =	10.21	22.9861
				Mean	1.13	2.55

Activity 13.9

Repeat the above calculation using the multiplicative model.

You should have obtained Table 13.14.

Table 13.14 Calculation of MAD and MSE for the multiplicative model

Year	Quarter	Actual sales (£000s)	Predicted sales (£000s)	Error	Absolute error	Squared error
2006	3	12.00	12.15	−0.15	0.15	0.0225
	4	8.00	8.40	−0.40	0.40	0.1600
2007	1	8.00	7.91	0.09	0.09	0.0081
	2	13.50	13.17	0.33	0.33	0.1089
	3	17.00	18.06	−1.06	1.06	1.1236
	4	13.00	12.60	0.40	0.40	0.1600
2008	1	12.00	12.36	−0.36	0.36	0.1296
	2	20.25	21.10	−0.85	0.85	0.7225
	3	30.00	28.61	1.39	1.39	1.9321
				Sum =	5.03	4.3673
				Mean	0.56	0.49

Both these statistics are smaller than that obtained with the additive model, demonstrating once again that the multiplicative model is better for this example.

Seasonally adjusted series

I am sure that you have heard the phrase 'seasonally adjusted' when economic time series are mentioned by the media. A common example is unemployment. If a series is seasonally adjusted it means that the seasonal component has been removed, leaving the trend component. By seasonally adjusting unemployment figures, for example, it is easy to tell what is happening to this important economic variable.

For the additive model a time series is seasonally adjusted by *subtracting* the seasonal difference, while for the multiplicative model the operation is one of *division*.

Normally this procedure is used when new data arrives and you want to see if there is any change in the trend of the series. So if you wanted to seasonally adjust the sales of sun cream in quarter 2 of 2009 you would need to divide the sales by the appropriate seasonal factor since the multiplicative model was shown to be the best model.

Activity 13.10

The sales of sun cream by Mace Skin Care plc for quarter 2 of 2009 are £28 500. Seasonally adjust this figure.

The average seasonal factor for quarter 2 is 107.5% (see Activity 13.7), so the seasonally adjusted sales are $\dfrac{28\,500}{1.075} = £26\,512.$

Forecasting using the decomposition model

One purpose of time series analysis is to use the results to forecast future values of the series. The procedure for this is to extrapolate the trend into the future and then apply the seasonal component to the forecast trend. There are various methods of extrapolating the trend. If the trend is approximately linear then linear regression could be used by assigning numerical values to time. For example, using the sun cream series, quarter 1 of 2006 would have a value 1 and quarter 1 of 2009 would have a value 13. This is explained in more detail on page 355. However, you will often find it easier to extrapolate by eye ('eyeballing') since other factors can then be considered, if necessary. If there is doubt about the future behaviour of the trend, you could make two or three different extrapolations to give different forecasts (say, an optimistic and a pessimistic one).

For the sun cream example, a possible extrapolation of the trend has been made and can be seen in Figure 13.8. The forecast trend values for the remainder of 2009 have been read off this graph and are shown below:

Quarter	2	3	4
Trend forecast	25.5	27.0	28.5

To calculate the forecast for each quarter using the multiplicative model, these trend forecasts need to be *multiplied* by the appropriate seasonal factor. For example, for quarter 2 the average seasonal factor is 107.5%, so the forecast value is $25.5 \times 1.075 = 27.41$, or approximately £27 400. For the additive model the average

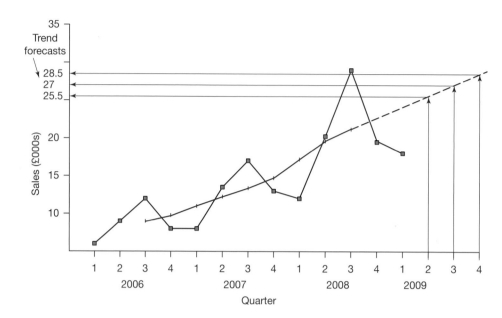

Figure 13.8
Trend forecasts for
sales of sun cream

seasonal difference of 0.88 is *added* to 25.5; that is, 26.38, or approximately £26 400. The result using the multiplicative model is likely to be more accurate since the model had smaller errors. However, any forecasts are subject to considerable uncertainty and all forecasts should be treated with caution.

Activity 13.11

Use the multiplicative model to obtain forecasts for quarters 3 and 4 of 2009.

The seasonal factors for quarters 3 and 4 are 135.0% and 85.6%, so the forecasts will be:

$$27 \times 1.350 = 36.450 \ (\text{approximately } £36\,500)$$
$$\text{and} \quad 28.5 \times 0.856 = 24.396 \ (\text{approximately } £24\,400)$$

Did you know

While statistical forecasting using time series analysis is very important many managers and analysts like to incorporate judgement into their forecasts. This is called *judgemental forecasting* and is a particularly useful method when the time series does not have a steady seasonal or trend pattern. The Bank of England uses its judgement when making forecasts about important economic indicators. (See Bank of England Inflation report February 2011, www.bankofengland.co.uk/publications/inflationreport/ir11feb.pdf)

Exponential smoothing

The technique of exponential smoothing is often used where a short-term forecast is required (that is, the next period). The formula for this technique is very simple:

Next forecast = Last forecast + α × error in last forecast

where α (alpha) is a smoothing constant. This constant takes a value between 0 and 1, so that the next forecast will simply be the last forecast plus a fraction of the last error. The error in the last forecast is the actual value minus the forecast.

To illustrate this technique, imagine that you are responsible for ensuring that the Small Brewery company has sufficient barrels available to store its beer. Full barrels are sent out and empty ones returned. You need to know how many barrels will be returned the next day to plan production. If insufficient barrels are available, beer is wasted, whereas if more barrels than expected are returned, you may have lost sales.

There are two problems with exponential smoothing. The first is what value of α to use. This can only be found by trial and error, and you may even have to change the value in the light of experience. It is usually found that a value between 0.05 and 0.3 gives the smallest values of MAD or MSE. For the Small Brewery company, a value of 0.1 has been chosen.

The second problem is how to get the first forecast, since a last forecast is required. Some people choose a suitable value while others prefer a warm-up period. Once several forecasts have been made, the starting value becomes less important anyway, but let us suppose that you have decided to use the warm-up method. You are to use the last 10 days for this purpose, and therefore your first proper forecast will be for day 11. The number of barrels returned over the last 10 days are:

Day	1	2	3	4	5	6	7	8	9	10
No. of barrels	20	13	19	19	25	17	15	13	22	20

If you take the forecast for day 2 as the actual for day 1, then the error is -7 $(13 - 20)$ and the forecast for day 3 becomes:

$$20 + (0.1 \times -7) = 19.3$$

The forecast for day 4 is now:

$$19.3 + (0.1 \times -0.3) = 19.27$$

and so on.

Activity 13.12

Continue this process to achieve a forecast for day 11.

You will probably find it easier if you use a table similar to Table 13.15. As you can see, the forecast for day 11 is 18.95 (that is, 19 barrels).

Table 13.15 Forecasts using exponential smoothing and a smoothing constant of 0.1

Day	No. barrels	Forecast	Error	α × error	Next forecast
1	20				
2	13	20.00	−7.00	−0.70	19.30
3	19	19.30	−0.30	−0.03	19.27
4	19	19.27	−0.27	−0.03	19.24
5	25	19.24	5.76	0.58	19.82
6	17	19.82	−2.82	−0.28	19.54
7	15	19.54	−4.54	−0.45	19.09
8	13	19.09	−6.09	−0.61	18.48
9	22	18.48	3.52	0.35	18.83
10	20	18.83	1.17	0.12	18.95
11		18.95			

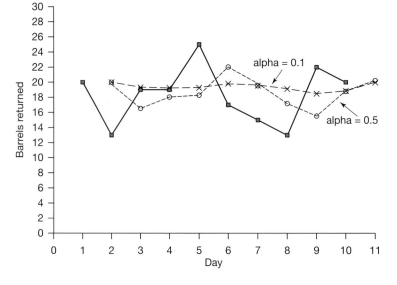

Figure 13.9
Numbers of returned barrels and forecasts using exponential smoothing

The time series of the original data and of the forecast values are shown in Figure 13.9. Also shown is the forecast using an α of 0.5, and you will see that a value of 0.1 gives a smoother series. This is generally true: the smaller the value of α, the greater the smoothing effect.

In terms of accuracy the errors can again be analyzed and MAD and MSE calculated. Using an α of 0.1, an MSE of 17.97 is obtained.

Activity 13.13

Calculate the MSE statistic using an alpha of 0.5.

By using an α of 0.5 you should have found that the MSE statistic has increased to 23.21.

Simple exponential smoothing is a very useful and easy-to-use short-term forecasting technique. However, it will lag behind a series that is undergoing a sharp change, such as a series that has a seasonal component or a steep trend. If you want to use it on seasonal data you must seasonally adjust the series first.

Using spreadsheets in time series analysis

Time series calculations can be performed using standard Excel arithmetic formula commands. The line graphs can also be created using Excel's charting tools. Both the use of formulae and charting have been met in previous chapters, so the instructions given in this section have assumed that you are reasonably proficient in these skills.

Activity 13.14

Use Excel to carry out a time series analysis (using the multiplicative model) on the data relating to the sales of sun cream (Table 13.2, page 338).

The only formula you need to create the worksheet shown in Figure 13.10 is Average. When calculating the moving average for an even period by hand it is often recommended that you leave a blank line between successive figures of the main table. This is to allow you to place the moving average in between periods. However, this is not a good idea with a spreadsheet, as you would have to leave a blank row between the data. A better method is to place the moving average in the same row as the centred moving average. So in the sun cream data the moving average would start in the third row down. You can see this in Figure 13.10. Transferring the seasonal component to the summary table is another source of error for novice spreadsheet analysts. Don't be tempted to type the figures into the table. If you do this and the data changes, your summary table will not be updated. The only data that should be typed in is the original series itself. All other figures should be formulae, as you will see in Figure 13.10.

Figure 13.10
Excel worksheet showing the time series formulae for the multiplicative model

	A	B	C	D	E	F	G
1			Sales of sun cream				
2							
3		Year	Quarter	Sales	Moving	Centred moving	Seasonal
4					average	average	factor
5		2006	1	6			
6			2	9			
7			3	12	=AVERAGE(D5:D8)	=AVERAGE(E7:E8)	=D7/F7
8			4	8	=AVERAGE(D6:D9)	=AVERAGE(E8:E9)	=D8/F8
9		2007	1	8	=AVERAGE(D7:D10)	=AVERAGE(E9:E10)	=D9/F9
10			2	13.5	=AVERAGE(D8:D11)	=AVERAGE(E10:E11)	=D10/F10
11			3	17	=AVERAGE(D9:D12)	=AVERAGE(E11:E12)	=D11/F11
12			4	13	=AVERAGE(D10:D13)	=AVERAGE(E12:E13)	=D12/F12
13		2008	1	12	=AVERAGE(D11:D14)	=AVERAGE(E13:E14)	=D13/F13
14			2	20.25	=AVERAGE(D12:D15)	=AVERAGE(E14:E15)	=D14/F14
15			3	30	=AVERAGE(D13:D16)	=AVERAGE(E15:E16)	=D15/F15
16			4	19.5	=AVERAGE(D14:D17)		
17		2009	1	18			
18							
19							
20		Quarter	1	2	3	4	
21		=B5			=G7	=G8	
22		=B9	=G9	=G10	=G11	=G12	
23		=B13	=G13	=G14	=G15		
24		Average	=AVERAGE(C21:C23)	=AVERAGE(D21:D23)	=AVERAGE(E21:E23)	=AVERAGE(F21:F23)	=SUM(C24:F24)
25		Adjusted	=C24*400%/$G$24	=D24*400%/$G$24	=E24*400%/$G$24	=F24*400%/$G$24	=SUM(C25:F25)
26							

You should have also added a chart to your spreadsheet. This chart should contain the original series and the trend. You can create this chart on a separate sheet or incorporate it as an object in the same sheet. The chart you should have used is a line graph and the instructions for creating a line chart are:

1 Highlight cells D5 to D17 and then, with the `Ctrl` key held down, highlight cells F5 to F17.
2 Click on the `Insert` tab then `Line` in `charts` group.
3 Choose `Line with Markers`.
4 Move chart to new sheet.
5 Now to get the year and quarter added to the horizontal axis first make sure that you are in the `Design` tab. Then click on `Select Data` in `Data` group and click `Edit` in `Horizontal (Category) Axis Labels` (see Figure 13.11).
6 Highlight cells B5 to C17 and click `OK`.
7 While you are still in the `Select Data Source` you can change the name for Series1 and Series2 (see Figure 13.11).
8 You can now add titles to each axis.
9 With the `Chart Tools` tab open (click on it if not), click on `Layout` then on `Axis Titles` in the `Labels` group. For both horizontal and vertical axes click on required title format.
10 Double click on each title to edit.

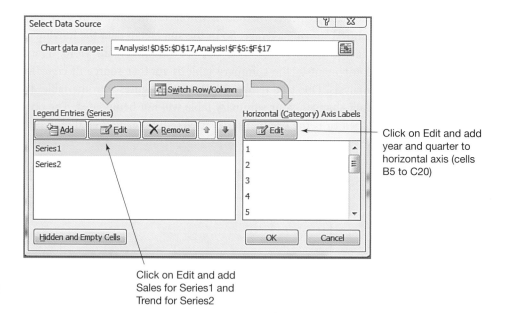

Figure 13.11
Step 2 of the Chart Wizard in Excel

The chart in Figure 13.12 is similar to Figure 13.8 which we produced earlier. The difference is that a smooth line has been drawn through the centred moving average points and extended to the end of 2009. This line has been produced using linear regression and to do this in Excel you do the following:

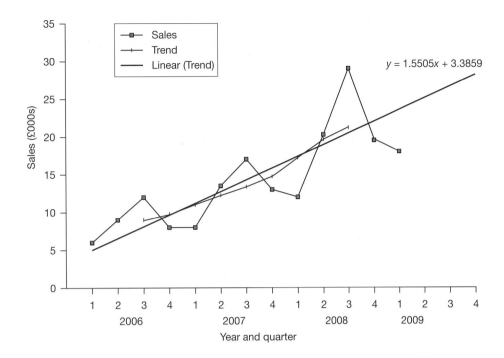

Figure 13.12
The trend line
extrapolated using
Excel

1 In the Layout tab, click on Trendline in the Analysis group then More
   Trendline Options.
2 Select the centred moving averages as the series you want to create your trendline.
3 Check the Linear button and Forecast Forward by 3.0 units so that you can
   use the chart for forecasting.
4 To obtain the linear regression equation you need to check the Display
   Equation on chart.

As you will see the trend equation is $Y = 1.5505x + 3.3859$. The Y variable is the
trend values and the x variable are the period number on the time axis, starting from
1 for quarter 1 of 2006 and ending with 13 for quarter 1 of 2009. Trend forecasts will
therefore be based on period numbers of 14, 15 and 16 and these can be substituted
into the regression equation. For example, the trend forecast for quarter 2 of 2009 is:

$$Y = 1.5505 \times 14 + 3.3859$$
$$= 25.09 \ (\text{£000s})$$

To arrive at the sales forecasts we need to multiply this value by the seasonal factor for
quarter 2 which is 1.075 (see page 342). So the sales forecast for quarter 2 is
$25.09 \times 1.075 = 26.97$ (£000s).

Activity 13.15

Calculate the trend and sales forecasts for quarters 3 and 4 of 2009.

Table 13.16 gives the figures you should have obtained for both the trend and sales
forecasts.

Table 13.16 Forecasts for quarters 3 and 4 of 2009

Quarter	x	y	Seasonal factor	Sales (£000s)
3	15	26.64	1.350	35.96
4	16	28.19	0.856	24.13

These are similar figures to those we obtained in Activity 13.11.

The disadvantage with using the Excel's forecast is that we are assuming that the trend is linear, which may not be true. *Eyeballing* has the advantage that external factors can be taken into account when arriving at forecasts.

Reflection

There are many forecasting techniques; some are quite simple, such as the ones looked at in this chapter, while others are very complex. However, the choice of forecasting method depends on the use to which the forecasts will be put, and whether it is essential that staff within an organization know how the forecasts are made. Utility companies need very accurate forecasts if they are to maintain low levels of reserves, so quite complex forecasting techniques are used. Many businesses also operate very low stock levels because stock is an expensive commodity. In manufacturing, most companies operate a 'lean' manufacturing policy, which entails stock and parts arriving *'just in time'* (*JIT*). To ensure that they don't run out of stock, some form of forecasting is needed.

Short-range forecasts are generally reasonably accurate, except perhaps for a series in which there is a great deal of variability, such as stock or commodity prices. Long-range forecasts, in contrast, which often use regression-type methods, can be horribly wrong. In 1952 IBM predicted that the total market for computers would be 52! Thirty years later, with the advent of the personal computer, IBM raised this figure to 200 000. Today IBM ships about this number every week. Alexander Bell once said that one day every city would have a telephone! Even Bill Gates is reported to have said once that '640k [memory] ought to be enough for anyone.' (See www.economicsuk.com/blog/000166.html)

Long-range forecasts are often more like star-gazing, but all businesses and governments do need to look into the future to some extent. The act of preparing forecasts helps to make an organization aware of the challenges it might one day face. There are also some engineering projects, such as a nuclear power station, that rely on forecasts because they take many years to build.

....

Key points

○ A time series can consist of a seasonal component, a trend, a long-term cycle and randomness. Unless we have over 20 years of data we normally ignore the long-term cycle.

○ To isolate the trend of a time series we take a moving average.

○ To isolate the seasonality we can either use the additive or multiplicative models. The additive model is used when the seasonal fluctuations are a constant difference from the trend. The multiplicative model is used when the seasonal fluctuations are a constant proportion of the trend.

- We can sometimes tell by looking at the time series chart which is the most appropriate model to use. If not, we can use both models and calculate the mean square error (MSE). The model with the lowest MSE is the best.
- To obtain forecasts we extrapolate the trend and then apply the seasonal difference or factor.
- For short-term forecasts, exponential smoothing is a good method.

Further reading

This text is only an introduction to the huge subject of time series and forecasting. There are a large number of more advanced models that can be used. If you have an interest in the subject and are good at maths then the text by Makridakis et al. (1998) gives a thorough coverage but is quite technical. Forecasting techniques are used in sports and the text by Eastaway and Haigh (2011) is worth reading. The Operational Research (OR) Society has published an article on 50 years of OR in sport (Wright, 2009) and part of this publication discusses forecasting models used in sport.

Web links W

Answers to selected questions can be found in Appendix 2. Answers to the other questions can be found on the companion website for this book.

Practice questions

1   You have just completed an analysis into the sales of a computer game over the past 3 years and the result is shown in Table 13.17.
   (a) Plot this series on graph paper.
   (b) From the raw data, calculate the centred moving average series and plot this on the graph. Comment on both series of data.
   (c) Use the additive decomposition model to obtain average seasonal differences for each period.
   (d) Obtain rough forecasts for 2009.

Table 13.17 Sales for Question 1

Year	Period	Sales (000s)	Year	Period	Sales (000s)	Year	Period	Sales (000s)
2006	1	30	2007	1	30	2008	1	35
	2	35		2	40		2	33
	3	35		3	38		3	37
	4	40		4	35		4	43
	5	50		5	52		5	50
	6	60		6	60		6	65

2 The personnel department of BBS plc, a large food processing company, is concerned about absenteeism among its shop floor workforce. There is a general feeling that the underlying trend has been rising, but nobody has yet analyzed the figures. The total number of shop floor employees has remained virtually unchanged over the last few years.

The mean number of absentees per day is given in Table 13.18 for each quarter of the years 2006 to 2008 and quarter 1 of 2009.

Table 13.18 Mean number of absentees for Question 2

	Q1	Q2	Q3	Q4
2006	25.1	14.4	9.5	23.7
2007	27.9	16.9	12.4	26.1
2008	31.4	19.7	15.9	29.9
2009	34.5			

(a) Plot the data on a graph (leave space for the remaining 2009 figures).
(b) Use the method of moving averages to determine the trend in the series and superimpose this on your graph. Interpret your graph.
(c) Use an appropriate method to measure the seasonal pattern in the data. Briefly give reasons for your choice of method.
(d) Use your analysis to produce rough forecasts of the mean number of absentees there will be in the remaining quarters of 2009.

3 The manager of the electrical department at a high street store has asked you to perform a time series analysis on the quarterly sales figures of the numbers of TVs sold over the past 3 years (see Table 13.19). It is advised that you use Excel for this question.

Table 13.19 Sales for Question 3

Year	Quarter	No. of sales
2006	2	100
	3	125
	4	127
2007	1	102
	2	104
	3	128
	4	130
2008	1	107
	2	110
	3	131
	4	133
2009	1	107

(a) Produce a line graph of the number of sales. (Extend your time axes up to quarter 4 of 2009.) Describe the pattern exhibited by the data.
(b) Use moving averages to calculate the trend in your data and add this to your chart.

(c) What would be the best decomposition model, the additive or multiplicative? (Hint – calculate the MSE statistic for both models.)

(d) Extrapolate the trend and using your chosen model forecast the sales for the rest of 2009.

4 The following data refers to the daily end-of-business share prices for a particular company:

112, 111, 113, 115, 114, 112, 115, 111, 111, 112, 113

Use exponential smoothing with a smoothing constant of 0.1 to forecast the price on day 12.

W. 5 Top Cycles is a small supplier of cycling equipment to the general public. In 2005 it started to sell a lightweight cycle which was an instant success; annual sales have risen from 633 units in 2005 to 765 units in 2008. However one of the problems has been in sourcing sufficient titanium for the frame. Top Cycles' manager is particularly concerned about whether the company will be able to handle demand during the last two quarters of 2009 as they have budgeted for an increase in demand of no more than 5%.

The sales by quarter for the past 4 years are shown in Table 13.20.

Use these figures to forecast demand for each quarter during 2009. Will the company be able to meet demand?

Table 13.20 Sales data for Question 5

Year	Quarter	Sales
2005	1	55
	2	122
	3	315
	4	141
2006	1	61
	2	127
	3	342
	4	148
2007	1	60
	2	136
	3	366
	4	157
2008	1	66
	2	144
	3	382
	4	173

W. 6 The chart in Figure 13.13 shows the turnover (in £000s) of Eat Well restaurant since 2005. Superimposed on the chart is the trend line.

(a) It has been suggested that a straight line could be used on the trend line. Comment on this proposal

(b) To analyze this time series a decomposition model could be used. For the additive model the mean square error (MSE) is 69.04 while for the multiplicative model it is 5.33. Based on these figures which is the best model? Explain how the chart reinforces your decision

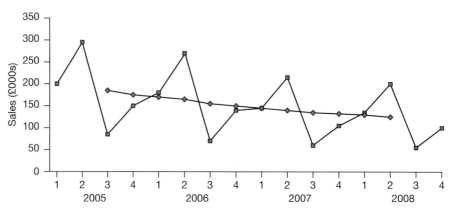

Figure 13.13 Chart for Question 6

(c) The seasonally adjusted figures for part of this series are given below. Use exponential smoothing with a smoothing constant of 0.2 to forecast the first period of 2009. Start the process in quarter 2 of 2007 using the actual 2007 quarter 1 figure as the forecast.

		Seasonally adjusted
Year	Quarter	turnover
2007	1	138.0
	2	134.6
	3	129.5
	4	124.6
2008	1	127.6
	2	125.8
	3	125.3
	4	117.7

(d) Calculate the MSE for the exponential smoothing process in (c)

W 7 The chart in Figure 13.14 shows the average daily oil consumption (in 000s barrels) from 1984 to 2007. Superimposed on this chart is an exponential forecasting line using a smoothing constant of 0.1.

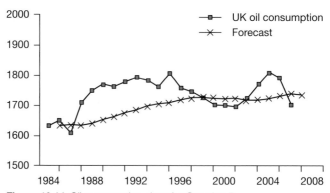

Figure 13.14 Oil consumption chart for Question 7

Source: BP Statistical Review of World Energy

(a) Comment on the use of exponential smoothing for this series.

(b) What would be the effect of increasing the value of the smoothing constant? Would a higher value be more or less useful in forecasting the consumption for 2008?

(c) Using a smoothing constant of 0.5 the forecast for 2007 was 1777. If the actual for 2007 was 1696 calculate the forecast for 2008.

W 8 The sales figures represent the number of guitars sold each quarter for the years 2004–2007.

Year	Quarter	Sales
2004	1	101
	2	125
	3	129
	4	103
2005	1	107
	2	127
	3	135
	4	108
2006	1	112
	2	131
	3	135
	4	108
2007	1	114
	2	132
	3	138
	4	120

(a) Plot a chart of this time series

(b) Calculate an appropriate moving average of the date and add this to your chart. What does this trend line tell you about the sales of guitars? Which decomposition model is likely to be the most appropriate? Why?

(c) Use both the additive and multiplicative models to isolate the seasonal component. Calculate the MSE (mean square error) for each model to determine which model is best. Is this consistent with your answer to (b)?

(d) Using your chosen model and the average seasonal component, deseasonalize the series and superimpose this on your chart. The actual sales for quarters 1 and 2 for 2008 turned out to be 115 and 132 respectively. Deseasonalize these figures and comment on whether these latest figures are consistent with the past trend.

(e) Use your trend line and the model identified in (c) to provide forecasts for quarters 3 and 4 of 2008. (It is suggested that you extrapolate the trend line by eye although you can get Excel to do it for you).

Assignment

Obtain the latest data for the overseas travel and tourism case presented in the companion website. Carry out a time series analysis of the 'all visits' data' and see if the downward trend suggested by the Office of National Statistics (ONS) is true. Obtain forecasts for quarter 3 of the year following the last quarter of your new data.

Making the most of things: linear programming

Prerequisites   There are no prerequisites for this chapter apart from a basic knowledge of Excel.

Objectives

- To be able to formulate linear programming models for both maximizing and minimizing problems
- To know how to apply a graphical method to solve two-variable problems
- To understand the concept of shadow prices, and to be able to calculate their value
- To be able to carry out a sensitivity analysis on the problem
- To know how to use Excel to solve linear programming problems
- To be able to apply linear programming to transportation problems and to multi-objective problems

Introduction   Industry, and business in general, operates with limited resources. Frequently money, material and space are scarce, and companies attempt to utilize their resources as efficiently as is possible. The technique of *linear programming* is a procedure that can provide the best solution to many problems that involve an *objective*, such as profit maximization, and a *series of linear constraints*, such as time, labour and cost. This chapter introduces the technique and applies it to simple problems that can be solved either graphically or using Excel. The technique is also extended to problems where there is more than one objective, and for transportation problems.

Quantitative methods in action: Netherlands railways uses optimization techniques

The problem with any rail network is that a failure of one part of the network can have a knock-on effect to the rest of the network because all trains use the same track and platforms. In comparison if an airline suffers a disruption the problem is generally localized and does not cause such widespread chaos.

Although the Netherlands is a small country the train network is more like a large urban network with many interconnecting routes. On the main routes there are ten trains an hour and the network is one of the most heavily used in Europe. The traditional method of scheduling rail services is a graphical method but this is not guaranteed to be optimal. It is also labour intensive and is not very flexible when trying to solve disruption problems. Optimization methods for transportation is an important research area, but these methods have not been too successful due to the complexities of most rail networks.

However an EU-funded research project called *ARRIVAL* (Algorithms for Robust and online Railway optimisation: Improving the Validity and reliAbility of Large scale systems) has changed this and specifically has helped the Netherlands develop a rail system that is one of the most efficient in Europe. Trains in the Netherlands now suffer fewer delays and have shorter waiting times between trains – and profits have risen by 40 million Euros per year.

The ARRIVAL system involves a two-pronged approach to rail planning. The first is a standard proactive approach that uses a set of algorithms to schedule trains, platform allocation, staff distribution and freight loads as efficiently as possible. Whereas many algorithms take a long time to find a good solution, the algorithms used by ARRIVAL are so efficient that they find solutions in fractions of a second. They can therefore look at a large number of alternatives to ensure that a good one is selected. The second is a reactive approach that deals with disruptions in a real-time mode. This two pronged approach is new to railway planning and the results are impressive. More and more rail companies are using it, including Berlin's U-Bahn underground network where waiting times were reduced to two minutes. There is talk of the system being used in other areas such as road navigation systems and even healthcare management.

Sources: Algorithms Provide a Model of Railway Efficiency, June 2010, *Inside OR (A publication of the OR Society)*; The ARRIVAL project (http://arrival.cti.gr/)

Basics of linear programming

Linear programming (or LP) is concerned with the management of scarce resources. It is particularly applicable where two or more activities are competing for these limited resources. For example, a company might want to make several different products, each of which makes different demands on the limited resources available. How many of each product should be made so that contribution to profits is *maximized*? Or perhaps you want to determine the quantities of raw materials necessary for a particular blend of oil that will *minimize* the cost of production.

Before these and other problems can be solved you have to *formulate* the problem in linear programming terms. This involves expressing the problem as a series of *inequations* and finding solutions to these inequations that optimize some objective. This may sound very difficult but for *two-variable* problems (for example, two products) the problem can be solved using a graphical technique. For larger problems computer software is normally used.

Linear programming requires a knowledge of elementary algebra and the drawing of straight lines. If you are a little rusty in these areas you are advised to work through appropriate sections (*Elementary algebra, Graphs and straight lines* and *Solving linear equations graphically*) of Chapter 1.

Did you know	Linear programming was developed in 1940 by George B. Dantzig who came up with the *Simplex* method. This is an algorithm for finding the best solution to problems where there are many hundreds or thousands of possible solutions. It was used extensively in the Second World War where it made a significant contribution to the war effort. For this reason it was kept a secret until 1947.

Model formulation

Before a problem can be solved by the linear programming method, a model needs to be developed. The model consists of a description of the problem in mathematical terms. In particular, the variables of the problem need to be defined and the objective decided. In addition, the *constraints* need to be expressed as *inequations*.

The next few activities will take you through the procedure using the following example.

Example 14.1

The company Just Shirts has been formed to make high quality shirts and is planning to make two types – the 'Regular Fit' and the 'Deluxe Fit'. The contribution to profits for each shirt is £5 for each Regular Fit shirt made and £8 for each Deluxe Fit shirt. To make each shirt requires cotton, of which 600 square metres is available each day, and machinists to cut and stitch the shirts. Twenty machinists are employed by the company and they each work an 8-hour day, giving 160 hours of labour in total. Each

Regular Fit shirt requires 5 square metres of cotton and takes 1 hour to make, while each Deluxe Fit shirt takes 6 square metres of cotton and 2 hours to make. The company wishes to maximize contribution to profits, so how many of each type of shirt should be made on a daily basis?

Activity 14.1

Define the variables for this problem.

You are required to determine the number of each type of shirt to produce. Let R represent the number of Regular Fit shirts that are to be made each day and D represent the number of Deluxe Fit shirts.

Activity 14.2

It is required to maximize contribution to profits. How would you express this in equation form?

If you made just one of each type of shirt, you would make a profit of £5 + £8. However, you are making R Regular Fit and D Deluxe Fit shirts, so the total profit will be $5R + 8D$. The maximum profit can be written as:

Max. $5R + 8D$

Activity 14.3

There is a limit of 600 square metres of cotton available each day. How would you express this as a constraint to production, given that each Regular Fit shirt requires 5 square metres and each Deluxe Fit shirt requires 6 square metres?

If you make R Regular Fit shirts then you will use $5R$ metres of cotton. Similarly you will use $6D$ metres of cotton to make D Deluxe Fit shirts. The sum of these two must be less than or equal to 600 square metres, so this can be written as:

$5R + 6D \leq 600$

Activity 14.4

Repeat Activity 14.3 for the labour resource.

You will use R hours for the Regular Fit shirt and $2D$ hours for the Deluxe Fit shirt and 160 hours are available each day, so the *constraint* can be written as:

$R + 2D \leq 160$

You have now formulated the problem, although you should indicate that you are only interested in positive values of R and D, and the two constraints $R \geq 0$ and $D \geq 0$ will do this for you.

To summarize, the LP formulation for this problem is:

Max. $5R + 8D$

subject to:

$$5R + 6D \leq 600$$
$$R + 2D \leq 160$$
$$R, D \geq 0$$

There are many values of R and D that will satisfy these inequations. For instance, $R = 40$ and $D = 20$ would satisfy all the constraints, so this is a feasible combination. The problem is, which combination will give the largest profit?

Graphical solution of linear programming problems

The formulation of the problem is only the start (but for many students the hardest part). You now have to solve the problem. There are many computer packages on the market that will solve LP problems, but for two-variable problems it is possible to solve the problem graphically.

If, for the moment, you replace the inequality signs by equalities, the two main constraints become:

$$5R + 6D = 600 \quad \text{(cotton)}$$

and

$$R + 2D = 160 \quad \text{(labour)}$$

Since these equations contain only two variables, R and D, they can be represented as straight lines and plotted on a graph. Two points are required to plot a straight line and it is convenient to find where they cross the axes. To do this it is simply a matter of letting $R = 0$ and calculating D, and then letting $D = 0$ and calculating R.

Activity 14.5

Plot the two equations, $5R + 6D = 600$ and $R + 2D = 160$ on graph paper.

The points where the two lines cross the axes are summarized in Table 14.1.

These two lines have been plotted on a graph (see Figure 14.1) and they mark the boundaries of the inequations. The *region* satisfying each inequation will be one side

Table 14.1 Crossing points for Activity 14.5

Constraint	R	D
Cotton	0	100
	120	0
Labour	0	80
	160	0

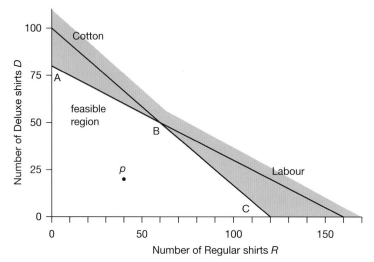

Figure 14.1
Graphical solution for
the Just Shirts
problem

of the boundary. In this example the regions for both inequations are *below* the lines. To identify the required region it is normal to shade the *unwanted* region, that is the region *not* satisfying the inequality. The region that satisfies all inequalities is called the *feasible region*: any point within this region will satisfy all the constraints. From the graph for the Just Shirts example you should be able to identify the feasible region as 0ABC.

Any point within the feasible region will satisfy all constraints, but which point or points give the largest profit? Fortunately, this can be found quite easily.

Finding the optimum – the isoprofit/cost method

The point p (40, 20) in Figure 14.1 is in the feasible region and the profit for this combination is:

$$5 \times 40 + 8 \times 20 = £360$$

However, there are other combinations of R and D that give the value of 360, since:

$$5R + 8D = 360$$

Thus the profit equation is just another straight line and can be plotted in the same way as the constraints.

That is, if $R = 0$, then $D = 45$
and if $D = 0$, then $R = 72$

This line obviously passes through the point p (see Figure 14.2). Can this figure of 360 be increased? If you try, say, a value of 500 so that $5R + 8D = 500$, you will get another straight line that is parallel to the first one. The reason for this is that the gradient of the line stays the same – it is only the intercepts on the axes that change. Such lines are called *isoprofit* lines ('iso' means same).

Activity 14.6

Place a ruler on the isoprofit line and very carefully move it away from the origin and parallel to the line. What is happening to the profit as the isoprofit line moves away from the origin? At what point does it leave the feasible region completely?

You should have found that as the line moves away from the origin the profit increases and you will find that the point B is the point that is furthest away from the origin, yet still within the feasible region. The fact that the optimum point is at a corner point of the feasible region is not a coincidence – *the optimum value will always be found at a corner point of the feasible region.*

The values of R and D at point B can be read off the graph in Figure 14.2. You should find that $R = 60$ and $D = 50$ and this gives a profit of:

$$5 \times 60 + 8 \times 50 = \pounds700$$

You may find it surprising that at the optimum solution more Regular Fit shirts are made than Deluxe Fit ones – this is because the Deluxe Fit version uses proportionately more resources.

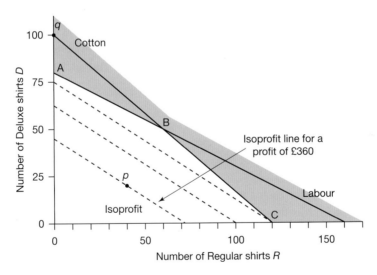

Figure 14.2
The isoprofit method

You found the value of R and D from the graph, but for greater accuracy it is recommended that the relevant equations are solved algebraically. This is particularly important when the graph shows that fractional values are involved or when it is difficult to decide which point is optimal. The method of simultaneous equations (see page 15) is used to solve for R and D and is as follows:

$$R + 2D = 160 \qquad \text{equation (1)}$$
$$5R + 6D = 600 \qquad \text{equation (2)}$$

Multiply (1) by 5 and subtract (2) from the result:

$$5R + 10D = 800$$
$$5R + 6D = 600$$
$$4D = 200$$

so:
$$D = 50$$

If $D = 50$ is now substituted back into (1):

$$R + 100 = 160$$
$$R = 60$$

This is the solution found from the graph.

NOTE: A word of warning – even if you use simultaneous equations to solve for the two variables, you must still draw the graph first. Without drawing the graph you could quite easily solve pairs of equations outside the feasible region. Also, the optimum point could be on either axis (for example, point A or C in Figure 14.2).

Finding the optimum – an alternative method

Since you now know that the optimum point must be at a corner point of the feasible region, you could work out the value of the two variables at every corner point. For example, at point A the value of R is zero and D is 80, so the profit must be $8 \times 80 = £640$.

Activity 14.7

Calculate the profits at the other corner points.

The profit for each corner point is shown in Table 14.2. These figures confirm that point B gives the greatest profit.

Table 14.2 Profit at each corner point of the feasible region

	R	D	Profit
Point A	0	80	£640
Point B	60	50	£700
Point C	120	0	£600

For feasible regions that have few corner points, this method is probably the quickest. However, it is necessary for you to understand the idea of isoprofit lines as this concept is important when looking at sensitivity analysis.

Tight and slack constraints

If you substitute the optimal values of R (60) and D (50) back into the constraints you will get the following:

Labour: $60 + 2 \times 50 = 160$

Cotton: $5 \times 60 + 6 \times 50 = 600$

Since these values correspond to the maximum quantity of both resources available, the resources are *scarce* and are called *tight* or *binding* constraints. Where a constraint has not reached its limit it is referred to as a *slack* or *non-binding* constraint. For example, if it was not possible to make more than 70 Deluxe Fit shirts, the constraint would be written as $D \le 70$. This constraint would be slack because the optimal solution has not reached this limit.

Sensitivity analysis

Linear programming is a deterministic model; that is, all variables are assumed to be known with certainty, so the quantity of cotton available each day was assumed to be exactly 600 square metres and the contribution to profits of the Regular Fit shirt was assumed to be exactly £5. Of course, in reality you will never be 100% certain about the value of many of the parameters in an LP model and the purpose of sensitivity analysis is to ask 'what if' questions about these parameters. For example, what if more cotton can be purchased, or what if the profit of a Regular Fit shirt increased to £6?

Sensitivity analysis in linear programming is concerned with the change in the right hand side of the constraints (normally the resources) and changes to the objective function coefficients (that is, the profit/costs of each variable).

Changes to the right hand side of a constraint

Both the labour and cotton resources are tight constraints, and an increase in either of these resources will increase the profit made. The reason for this is that as the right hand side of a tight constraint increases, the constraint *and* the optimum point move *away* from the origin.

This can be demonstrated by resolving the simultaneous equations with the right hand side of the labour constraint increased by 1 to 161. That is:

$R + 2D = 161$

$5R + 6D = 600$

Solving these two equations simultaneously as before gives:

$R = 58.5$ and $D = 51.25$

(Don't worry about the fractional values for the time being.) The new profit will be £702.50, an increase of £2.50. This £2.50 is called the *shadow price* of the labour resource. It is defined as the change in the value of the objective function if the right hand side is increased (or decreased) by one unit.

Activity 14.8

Calculate the shadow price of the cotton resource.

You should have found that the shadow price of the cotton resource is £0.50 per square metre. That is, an additional profit of 50p could be made for each extra square metre of cotton that could be obtained.

So if it were possible to increase labour hours (perhaps by working overtime) or to increase the supply of cotton, a potentially larger profit could be made. However, this assumes that the direct costs would not increase as well. If, for instance, overtime rates increase costs by more than £2.50 per hour, then it wouldn't be economic to increase production in this way. However, assuming it is worthwhile, how many more hours should be worked? As the labour constraint moves away from the origin, there comes a point where it moves outside the cotton constraint; this is at point q in Figure 14.2. This means that the labour resource ceases to be scarce and further increase of this resource will just add to the surplus of labour. At point q, $R = 0$ and $D = 100$, so if these values are substituted into the labour equation you get:

$$0 + 2 \times 100 = 200$$

So the labour resource can increase by 40 hours (200–160), which means that a possible $40 \times 2.50 = £100$ extra profit can be made each day.

Activity 14.9

What additional quantity of cotton would it be worth purchasing and what additional profit would result?

You should have found that the supply of cotton can be increased to 800 square metres per day, which is an additional 200 square metres. The extra profit would be £100.

Changes to the objective function coefficients

The objective function for the Just Shirts example is:

Max. $5R + 8D$

where 5 (in £) is the contribution to profits for each Regular Fit shirt made and 8 is the profit per Deluxe Fit shirt. If it were possible to reduce costs, then profits per shirt would rise, and vice versa, but would the production of 60 Regular Fit shirts and 50 Deluxe Fit shirts remain the optimal solution?

Activity 14.10

Assume that the profit on a Regular Fit shirt has decreased to £2. Redraw the isoprofit line to see if the optimum point has changed.

Figure 14.3 shows the effect on the isoprofit line of reducing the profit of a Regular Fit shirt to £2.

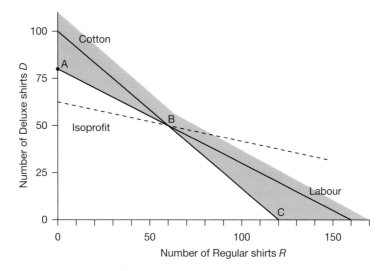

Figure 14.3
Effect on the optimum solution when the profit changes

The optimum solution has changed and is now at point A. In this solution you would make 80 Deluxe Fit shirts but no Regular Fit ones.

Although you could find the optimum point each time a change in the profit coefficient was made, it would be much easier if you knew the value of the profit that would cause a change in the optimal solution. If you let the profit be P, the isoprofit line has the equation:

$$P = 5R + 8D$$

Rearranging this equation into the form $y = mx + c$ gives:

$$D = -\frac{5}{8}R + \frac{P}{8}$$

The gradient of this line is $-\frac{5}{8}$. This gradient is simply the profit on a Regular Fit shirt divided by the profit on a Deluxe Fit shirt. If the profit on the Regular Fit shirt is £2 then the gradient of the isoprofit line becomes $-\frac{2}{8}$. Now consider what happens as the isoprofit line changes from a gradient of $-\frac{5}{8}$ to $-\frac{2}{8}$. At some point it must become parallel to the labour constraint line, and at this point the same profit will be obtained at both points A and B. (In fact all points along the line AB would give the same profit – this is known as *multiple optimal solutions*.)

To find the profit on the Regular Fit shirt that would make the isoprofit line parallel to the labour constraint, you need to work out the gradient of this line.

Rearranging the equation $R + 2D = 160$ into the standard $y = mx + c$ form will give you:

$$2D = 160 - R$$

that is, $$D = 80 - \frac{1}{2}R$$

or $$D = -\frac{1}{2}R + 80$$

The gradient is therefore $-\frac{1}{2}$.

You now need to find the value of the profit on a Regular Fit shirt that will give you this gradient. This can be done with the help of some elementary algebra (see page 8).

Let x be the unknown value of the profit. Then the gradient of the isoprofit line is $-\frac{x}{8}$ and

$$-\frac{x}{8} = -\frac{1}{2}$$

This gives $x = 4$, so if the profit of a Regular Fit shirt falls below £4 the optimum solution changes to point A on the graph ($R = 0$ and $D = 80$). This is the *lower* limit for the profit of the Regular Fit shirt. There is also an *upper* limit and you are advised to tackle the next activity.

Activity 14.11

Using the same procedure as above, calculate the *upper* value of the Regular Fit profit.

The upper limit can be found when the isoprofit line becomes parallel to BC, and since the gradient of the cotton line is $-\frac{5}{6}$ the equation becomes:

$$-\frac{x}{8} = -\frac{5}{6}$$

This gives $x = 6.67$, so if the profit on a Regular Fit shirt rises above £6.67, the optimum solution changes to point C on the graph ($R = 120$ and $D = 0$).

Activity 14.12

Calculate the range of the profit of the Deluxe Fit shirt within which the optimal solution stays the same.

This again requires you to find the lower and upper values of the profit. You should have found that this profit range is from £6 to £10.

Minimization problems

The Just Shirts example was a *maximization* problem because a solution was required that maximized the contribution to profits. However, equally important are *minimization* problems in which some objective, for example cost, is to be minimized. The general procedure for dealing with minimization problems is no different from maximization problems. A feasible region will still be obtained, but instead of moving your *isocost* line *away* from the origin, you will be moving it *towards* the origin. There must be, of course, at least one 'greater than or equal to' constraint, otherwise you will arrive at the origin!

Example 14.2

Ratkins, a local DIY store, has decided to advertise on television and radio but is unsure about the number of adverts it should place. It wishes to minimize the total cost of the campaign and has limited the total number of 'slots' to no more than 5. However, it wants to have at least one slot on both media. The company has been told that one TV slot will be seen by 1 million viewers, while a slot on local radio will only be heard by 100 000 listeners. The company wishes to reach an audience of at least 2 million people. If the cost of advertising is £5000 for each radio slot and £20 000 for each TV slot, how should it advertise?

This problem can be solved by the graphical method of linear programming because there are two variables: the number of radio adverts and the number of TV adverts.

Activity 14.13

Formulate the problem given in Example 14.2.

The formulation for this problem is as follows:

Let R = no. of radio ads, and T = no. of TV ads:

Min. $5000R + 20000T$

Subject to:
$$0.1R + T \geq 2 \qquad \text{(Minimum audience in millions)}$$
$$R + T \leq 5 \qquad \text{(Maximum number of 'slots')}$$
$$\left. \begin{array}{l} R \geq 1 \\ T \geq 1 \end{array} \right\} \quad \text{(At least one slot on each)}$$

Activity 14.14

Solve this problem using the graphical method. Is the solution sensible?

The procedure for drawing the graph is the same as that for the maximizing case. That is, it is necessary to find the points at which the constraints cut the axes. Table 14.3 gives these values.

The graph for this problem is shown in Figure 14.4. You should confirm that the feasible region is given by the area enclosed by ABC. The optimum point will be at one of these corners, and this time it is necessary for you to find the point that gives the *minimum* value. You should have found that the coordinates and hence the cost at each of the corner points are as given in Table 14.4.

Table 14.3 Crossing points for Activity 14.14

Constraint	R	T
Audience	20	2
Total slots	5	5
Min. slots for radio	1	—
Min. slots for TV	—	1

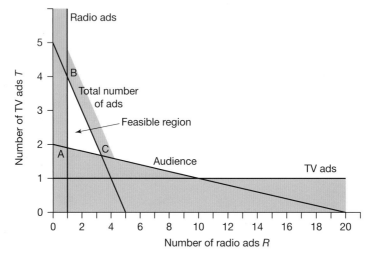

Figure 14.4
Graphical solution for
Example 14.2

Table 14.4 Solution to Activity 14.14

	R	T	Cost
A	1	1.9	£43 000
B	1	4	£85 000
C	3.33	1.67	£50 050

Point A gives the minimum cost of £43 000. This solution implies that the company should buy 1 radio advert and 1.9 TV adverts, hardly a sensible solution. Unfortunately, linear programming will give fractional values, and if this is not sensible *integer linear programming* should be used. This technique is not covered in this book, but for two variable problems a more realistic solution can often be found by inspecting the graph. In this particular case it is simply a matter of rounding the 1.9 to 2, which increases the cost to £45 000. However, do take care as rounding can often give you an *infeasible* solution. This can be avoided by checking to see that all constraints are still satisfied. In this example $R = 1$ and $T = 2$ does satisfy all 4 constraints.

Using Excel's 'Solver' to solve linear programming problems

Excel has an add-in called Solver that allows you to solve optimization problems. It may not be currently installed and if this is the case you will have to install it.

Activity 14.15

Use Solver to solve Example 14.1 (the shirt problem).

The formulation for this problem was:

Max. $5R + 8D$

subject to:

$5R + 6D \leq 600$ (cotton constraint)

$R + 2D \leq 160$ (labour constraint)

$R, D \geq 0$

where R was the number of Regular Fit shirts to make and D was the number of Deluxe Fit shirts to make.

Before using Solver you need to set up the relevant formulae and headings. The idea is to make the formulae general so that the worksheet can be used for other problems. Figure 14.5 shows one method of doing this.

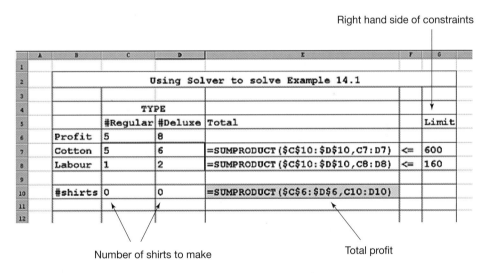

Figure 14.5
Setting up the formulae for Solver

In this worksheet, cells `C10` and `D10` have been made the cells that will contain the optimal number of shirts. The total profit to be maximized is in cell `E10`. Cells `C6` to `D8` contain the coefficients of the constraints. Cells `E7` and `E8` represent the total resources used; to calculate these figures, you multiply the number made (currently zero) by the coefficients in the constraint equations. So `5R+6D` becomes `C7×C10+D7×D10`. (It is easier to use the `=SUMPRODUCT` formula, as this allows you to use ranges: for several constraints this is much quicker.) Similarly, for the total profit you multiply the number made by the profit for each type of shirt. Again `=SUMPRODUCT` simplifies this process.

The instructions for using Solver are as follows:

1 Click on the `Data` tab and then `Solver` in the `Analysis` group. (If it is not there, you will need to add it by clicking on `Add-Ins` in `Excel Options`.)
2 Set `Objective` to `E10`.
3 Click on `Max` in the dialog box.
4 `By Changing Variable Cells` becomes `C10:D10`.
5 For `Subject to the Constraints`, click on `Add`.
6 Add the constraints one at a time. (You can add them as ranges, as the inequality constraints are the same for both.)
7 Select `Simplex LP`. Tick `Make Unconstrained Variables Non-Negative`.

The Solver parameters should match those in Figure 14.6.

The solution to the problem can be seen in Figure 14.7. The values in cells `C10` and `D10` are 60 and 50 respectively, and the profit of 700 is shown in cell `E10`. These figures agree with those that we calculated manually.

Solver can give you various sensitivity analysis reports, including changes to the objective function coefficients and changes to the right-hand side of the constraints. In the final dialog box, highlight the `Sensitivity` report.

From this report (Figure 14.8) you should be able to recognize the shadow prices and allowable changes in the objective function. For example, the profit of a Deluxe shirt can increase by £2 or decrease by £2, giving a range of £6 to £10 (the same range you found in Activity 14.12). You can also see that the right-hand side of the cotton constraint can increase by 200, which is what you found in Activity 14.8.

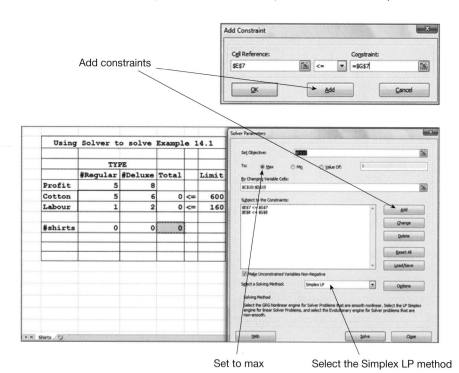

Figure 14.6
Adding the Solver constraints

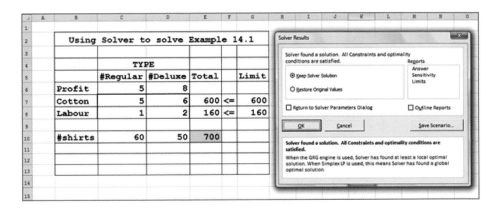

Figure 14.7
Solution found by
Solver

			Final	Reduced	Objective	Allowable	Allowable

Microsoft Excel 14.0 Sensitivity Report
Worksheet: [Activity 14.15.xls]Shirts
Report Created: 07/04/2011 20:46:33

Variable Cells

Cell	Name	Final Value	Reduced Cost	Objective Coefficient	Allowable Increase	Allowable Decrease
$C$10	#shirts #Regular	60	0	5	1.666666667	1
$D$10	#shirts #Deluxe	50	0	8	2	2

Constraints

Cell	Name	Final Value	Shadow Price	Constraint R.H. Side	Allowable Increase	Allowable Decrease
$E$7	Cotton Total	600	0.5	600	200	120
$E$8	Labour Total	160	2.5	160	40	40

Figure 14.8
Sensitivity report from
Solver

The advantage with using Solver is that you can easily make changes to the model and get updated results quickly. This is particularly true if you wanted to try adding other variables to the problem or new constraints. However it is often possible to use the sensitivity analysis report to decide if it is worthwhile adding a new product as the next Activity shows

Activity 14.16

In the Just Shirts problem (Example 14.1) consideration is being given to making a third shirt (European range). This new shirt will require 7 square meters of cotton and take 3 hours to make. If the expected contribution to profits of this new shirt would be £12 is it worthwhile making this new product? (Assume that you cannot increase either the supply of cotton or labour.)

As both cotton and labour are scarce resources then by making one European shirt you are losing profit from the other products as you will be making less of them. To solve this problem without re-running Solver you need to consider the opportunity cost involved in making one of the new shirts. The shadow price of the cotton

Table 14.5 Opportunity cost of making one European shirt

Resource	Shadow price	Resource required	Opportunity cost
Cotton	£0.5 per m²	7 m²	£3.5
Labour	£2.5 per hour	3	£7.5
		Total	£11.00

resource is £0.50 per m² so as the new shirt requires 7 m² the opportunity cost is $7 \times 0.5 = £3.5$. Similarly the shadow price for the labour resource is £2.50 an hour so the opportunity cost for making one European shirt is $3 \times 2.5 = £7.5$. The total opportunity cost is therefore $£3.5 + 7.5 = £11.00$. Table 14.5 summarizes these calculations.

As the expected contribution to profits of the new shirt is greater than £11 then it is financially worthwhile making this new shirt. However what this calculation doesn't tell you is how many of the new shirts should be made and what effect it has on the production of the other shirts. To discover this information it is necessary to amend the model and re-run Solver.

Activity 14.17

Amend your Excel model to allow for the third shirt and re-run Solver.

Letting E represent the number of European shirts to make, your new LP model should be

Max. $5R + 8D + 12E$

Subject to:

$5R + 6D + 7E \leq 600$

$R + 2D + 3E \leq 160$

$R, D, E \geq 0$

Figure 14.9 is a screen print of the results from Solver and Figure 14.10 shows the new sensitivity report.

	A	B	C	D	E	F	G	H	I
1									
2			Using Solver to solve Activity 14.17						
3									
4			TYPE						
5			#Regular	#Deluxe	#European	Total		Limit	
6		Profit	5	8	12				
7		Cotton	5	6	7	600	<=	600	
8		Labour	1	2	3	160	<=	160	
9									
10		#shirts	85	0	25	725			
11									
12									
13									
14									

Figure 14.9
Adding a new product

Microsoft Excel 14.0 Sensitivity Report
Worksheet: [Activity 14.17.xlsx]Shirts
Report Created: 08/04/2011 06:47:18

Variable Cells

Cell	Name	Final Value	Reduced Cost	Objective Coefficient	Allowable Increase	Allowable Decrease
$C$10	#shirts #Regular	85	0	5	3.571428571	1
$D$10	#shirts #Deluxe	0	-0.5	8	0.5	1E+30
$E$10	#shirts #European	25	0	12	3	1

Constraints

Cell	Name	Final Value	Shadow Price	Constraint R.H. Side	Allowable Increase	Allowable Decrease
$F$7	Cotton Total	600	0.375	600	200	226.6666667
$F$8	Labour Total	160	3.125	160	97.14285714	40

Figure 14.10
The sensitivity report after adding a new product

As you can see Solver has included the new product but at the expense of the existing Deluxe product. This is because relative to the amount of resources used the Deluxe shirt is contributing less profit than the other two products. You will also see that the profit on the European shirt can be reduced by £1 before it is not worth making – this reflects the difference between the opportunity cost calculated in Activity 14.16 and the profit of the shirt. You will also notice that the overall profit has increased from £700 to £725 even though the total number of shirts is unchanged at 110.

If you wanted to keep all three products then you would need to include a suitable constraint that specified this. This is left as an exercise for the reader.

Applications of linear programming

Wherever it is required to maximize or minimize some function it is often possible to use linear programming to solve the problem. Linear programming has been used in such diverse areas as blending of oil products, inventory problems, cash flow, networks, transportation and allocation problems, cutting problems and multi-objective problems. We will look at two problems; these being transportation problems and problems involving more than one objective.

Transportation problems

Example 14.3

The distribution manager of the BAZ oil company receives daily orders from his depots for bulk delivery of heating oil. On one particular day 4 depots request delivery of 24 500 litres in total and the 3 refineries have 40 500 litres available. Therefore there is no difficulty in meeting the order but the problem is deciding which refinery should supply which depot. The refineries are in different parts of the country and the cost of delivery from a refinery to a depot varies considerably. The cost in £ per litre from a refinery to a depot is given in Table 14.6 together with the availability (in 00s of litres) at each refinery and the requirement (again in 00s litres) at each depot.

Table 14.6 Transportation data for BAZ oil company

Refinery / Depot	A	B	C	Required
P	5	13	7	60
Q	6	4	8	35
R	5	22	20	50
S	3	9	4	100
Available	175	80	150	

Cost per litre for delivery from
refinery A to depot S

Activity 14.18

What is the objective of this problem?

Clearly we want to transport the oil as cheaply as possible so the objective is to minimize the total cost. The cost function is simply the sum of the costs of transporting the oil from each refinery to each depot. If we use x_{ij} to represent the number of litres that need to be transported from refinery i to depot j then the objective will be as follows:

$$\text{Minimize cost} = 5x_{AP} + 13x_{BP} + 7x_{CP} + 6x_{AQ} + 4x_{BQ} + 8x_{CQ} + 5x_{AR} + 22x_{BR}$$
$$+ 20x_{CR} + 3x_{AS} + 9x_{BS} + 4x_{CS}$$

Activity 14.19

What would be the constraints of the problem?

There will be 3 supply constraints. So for refinery A the sum of the amount delivered to each depot must be equal to or less than 175; that is:

$$x_{AP} + x_{AQ} + x_{AR} + x_{AS} \leq 175$$

and similarly for the other two refineries:

$$x_{BP} + x_{BQ} + x_{BR} + x_{BS} \leq 80$$
$$x_{CP} + x_{CQ} + x_{CR} + x_{CS} \leq 150$$

There will also be 4 demand constraints. So for depot A the amount delivered from each refinery is equal to or less than 60; that is

$$x_{AP} + x_{BP} + x_{CP} \leq 60$$

and similarly for the other 3 depots:

$$x_{AQ} + x_{BQ} + x_{CQ} \leq 35$$
$$x_{AR} + x_{BR} + x_{CR} \leq 50$$
$$x_{AS} + x_{BS} + x_{CS} \leq 100$$

So this small problem has $4 \times 3 = 12$ variables and $4 + 3 = 7$ constraints and could be solved using Solver. (This is left as an exercise for the reader – see Question 11 in the Practice questions section at the end of this chapter). In real-life problems we could have hundreds of origins and destinations giving tens of thousands of variables and hundreds of constraints and special software would be required.

However because of the symmetry of the problem mathematicians have come up with an alternative method that for small problems can be solved without a computer. This is called the *Transportation algorithm*. The steps involved in using this algorithm are:

1 Find an initial feasible solution.
2 Test to see if the solution is optimal.
3 If not optimal, improve the solution and repeat step 2.

Step 1   Find an initial feasible solution
A feasible solution is one where all the requirements at the destinations are met and all supply at the origins is allocated. This means that:

Total supply $=$ total requirements

In the BAZ case supply exceeds requirements by 160 units ($405 - 245$). However we can make this equation true by having a dummy destination or origin. In the case of BAZ a dummy depot is required that will 'soak' up the excess capacity. The transportation cost for this dummy depot will be zero.

There are various methods of finding an initial feasible solution but the *least cost method* is probably a good compromise between a simple method that isn't very efficient (that is, takes longer to find the optimal solution) and a more complicated method that is more difficult to implement. The least cost method involves allocating as much as possible to the cheapest route (excluding the dummy route). In the BAZ case the cheapest *route* is A–S at £3 per litre. The requirement at S is 100 units and this can be met since 175 units are available at A.

Activity 14.20

Continue this process allocating as much as possible to the next cheapest route and so on.

The next cheapest route is B–Q is £4 (don't forget we have allocated the entire requirement for S so nothing can be added to route CS) and 35 units can be added to this route as 35 units are required and 80 units are available. For the next allocation you should have noted that there are two routes (AP and AR) which both cost £5. We can use either route but A–R is preferred as it avoids later having to use routes B–R and C–R which are the most expensive routes. We can now add 35 units to route C–P which completes the allocation for depot P. Finally we need to allocate 45 units and 115 units to the two dummy routes. Table 14.7 gives this feasible solution.

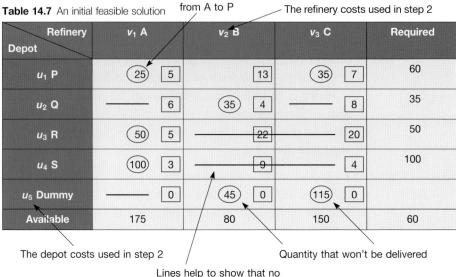

Table 14.7 An initial feasible solution

25 units delivered from A to P

The refinery costs used in step 2

Refinery / Depot	v_1 A		v_2 B		v_3 C		Required
u_1 P	(25)	5		13	(35)	7	60
u_2 Q	——	6	(35)	4	——	8	35
u_3 R	(50)	5	——	22	——	20	50
u_4 S	(100)	3	——	9		4	100
u_5 Dummy	——	0	(45)	0	(115)	0	
Available	175		80		150		60

The depot costs used in step 2

Quantity that won't be delivered

Lines help to show that no more can be added to a route

Activity 14.21

What is the cost of this initial solution?

You should have calculated the cost as follows:

$$(25 \times 5) + (35 \times 7) + (35 \times 4) + (50 \times 5) + (100 \times 3)$$
$$= £1060$$

Is this the best that can achieved; that is, is the solution optimal?

Step 2 Test to see if the solution is optimal

In order to decide if this is the optimal solution we need to calculate the *shadow prices*. If a shadow price is negative it means that for every unit that can be placed in the relevant route, this amount of money will be saved.

The way that shadow prices are calculated is as follows. Each route that is currently being used has a cost. This cost can be thought of as being made up of a cost at the depot (u) and a cost at the refinery (v). Each u and v is given a subscript (see Table 14.7) so for refinery A and depot P we have:

$$u_1 + v_1 = 5$$

Activity 14.22

Write down the equations for the other 6 routes

You should have got the following equations:

$$u_1 + v_3 = 7$$
$$u_2 + v_2 = 4$$
$$u_3 + v_1 = 5$$
$$u_4 + v_1 = 3$$
$$u_5 + v_2 = 0$$
$$u_5 + v_3 = 0$$

In order to solve for 8 variables using only 7 equations it is necessary to allocate an arbitrary value of zero to one of the variables. If $u_1 = 0$ then it is possible to solve for the other variables.

Activity 14.23

Solve for the other variables.

If $u_1 = 0$, then $v_1 = 5$ and $v_3 = 7$. We can now solve for other variables and $u_3 = 0$, $u_4 = -2$, $u_5 = -7$, $v_2 = 7$ and $u_2 = -3$.

We can now find the shadow prices of the unused routes by applying the following formula:

Actual cost − (cost at origin + cost at destination)

So for route B–P the shadow price is $13 - (0 + 7) = 6$.

Activity 14.24

Find the shadow prices of the unused routes

The shadow price of route A–Q is

$$6 - (-3 + 5) = 4$$

The shadow prices of the other unused routes are:

$$\text{B–P} = 13 - (7 - 0) = 6; \quad \text{B–R} = 22 - (0 + 7) = 15;$$
$$\text{B–S} = 9 - (-2 + 7) = 4; \quad \text{C–Q} = 8 - (-3 + 7) = 4;$$
$$\text{C–R} = 20 - (0 + 7) = 13; \quad \text{C–S} = 4 - (-2 + 7) = -1$$

As we have one negative shadow price (route C-S) the solution is not optimal – we can reduce the cost by using this route.

Step 3   If not optimal, improve the solution and repeat Step 2

As much as possible should be sent via route C–S but care must be taken to ensure that the solution remains feasible. One method of achieving this is the *stepping stone* method.

The idea behind this method is that the rows and columns must remain balanced if the solution is to remain feasible. A '+' is added to route C–S to indicate that a quantity of oil should be added to this route. It is now necessary to add a '–' to a route in the same row or column that is currently being used. C–P is the only used route in the same column and a '–' has been added to this route (see Table 14.8). Another '+' is now added to route A–P to balance this row and a '–' has been added to route A–S for the same reason. A dotted line has been drawn round the diagram to show that the loop is closed. (The loop doesn't have to be rectangular – it just needs to arrive back at the starting point.)

Table 14.8 The stepping stone method

We now need to decide how much to add to route C–S. To avoid making any quantities negative you can only add the minimum quantity of the routes with '–' sign. The two routes with a '–' sign are C–P and A–S, and the smallest quantity is route C–P at 35 units. This quantity is now added or subtracted from each of the 4 'stepping stones' identified. This gives you your new table and you now have to repeat step 2 by recalculating the us and vs.

Activity 14.25

Repeat the process until the solution is optimal.

Table 14.9 shows the new table with the new us and vs added and the shadow prices recalculated. As you will see all the shadow prices are non-negative so the solution is optimal.

Table 14.9 The optimal solution

Refinery / Depot	v_1 (5) A		v_2 (6) B		v_3 (6) C		Required
u_1 (0) P	(60) [5]	7	[13]	1	[7]		60
u_2 (−2) Q	3	[6]	(35) [4]	4	[8]		35
u_3 (0) R	(50) [5]	16	[22]	14	[20]		50
u_4 (−2) S	(65) [3]	5	[9]		(35) [4]		100
u_5 (−6) Dummy	1	[0]	(45) [0]		(115) [0]		
Available	175		80		150		

The final solution is therefore:

Refinery A should deliver 6000 litres to depot P, 5000 litres to depot R and 6500 litres to depot S

Refinery B should deliver 3500 litres to depot Q only

Refinery C should deliver 3500 litres to depot S only

The total cost is £102 500, a saving of £3500 from the initial solution.

In some cases there will be alternative optimal solutions to a transportation problem. This occurs when one or more of the shadow prices is zero. By using the stepping stone method again it is possible to find this alternative solution(s) but the cost will of course be the same.

It is also possible to prevent certain routes from being used. This is easily achieved by giving this route a very high cost.

For the problem we looked at there were 3 origins and 5 destinations (including the dummy). If you look at any of the iterations you will see that there are 7 used routes which is $3 + 5 − 1$. It is generally true that the number of used routes is the number of origins + number of destinations − 1. However in some cases the number of routes is less than this which will prevent you for calculating the u s and v s. This is called a *degenerate* solution. To get round this problem it is normal to pretend that a route is actually being used and add a zero quantity to it.

Finally remember, as in all linear programming problems, the use of the transportation algorithm is an approximation. In the case of BAZ oil we are assuming that the cost of transporting say 1000 litres of oil is equal to ten times the cost of transporting 100 litres. This of course is unlikely to be true.

The next application we will look at concerns the use of linear programming in problems where there is more than one objective or goal.

Multi-objective problems or goal programming

In the problems we have looked at so far there has been just one objective (e.g. maximize profit or minimize cost). However there are situations where there are conflicting objectives and we wish to get as close to each objective or *goal* as possible. This is called *goal programming* and is an important application of linear programming.

Example 14.4

In Example 14.1 our objective was to maximize profits for Just Shirts. Instead we now have a number of goals which are (in order of priority):

Goal 1 – to achieve a profit of at least £600
Goal 2 – to use less than 150 hours of labour in total
Goal 3 – to make at least 160 Regular shirts

In goal programming there are a number of goals which are desired although not all will be met. Each goal has a certain priority and the idea is to try and meet higher priority goals before attempting to meet lower priority ones. If we cannot meet a goal we try and get as close as possible to it. Goal programming models are all maximization problems.

The formulation of a goal programming model is slightly different to a normal LP one. In goal programming we define deviations from a goal as either + or −, so for Goal 1 we have

$$5R + 8D + d_1^- - d_1^+ = 600$$

where d_1^- = profit below £600 and d_1^+ is profit above £600. These deviations are called *deviational* variables. As we don't mind if the profit is above £600 we want to minimize d_1^- (the under-achievement of the £600 profit) and the objective we want to minimize is written as:

Minimize $P_1\, d_1^-$

If we ignore the deviational variables and plot $5R + 8D = 600$ we get the graph shown in Figure 14.11. Any point above the line satisfies Goal 1.

Activity 14.26

Now formulate the other two goals and plot the equations on the graph. Which goals can be met?

For Goal 2 we have:

$$R + 2D + d_2^- - d_2^+ = 150$$

where the deviational variables d_2^- and d_2^+ now refer to the over- and under-achievement of Goal 2. In this case we do not want to exceed 150 hours so we want to

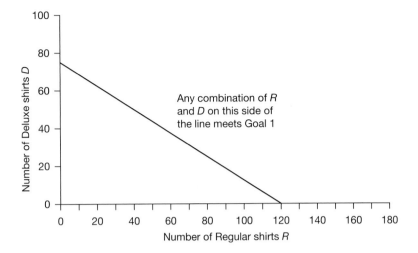

Figure 14.11
Goal 1

minimize d_2^+. Just taking the first two goals the objective function becomes:

Minimize $P_1 d_1^- + P_2 d_2^+$

The line $R + 2D = 150$ has now been plotted and shown in Figure 14.12. As you can see we can meet the first two goals in the feasible area given by ABC.

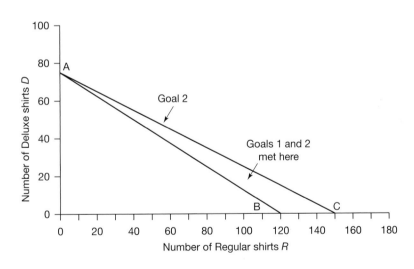

Figure 14.12
Goals 1 and 2

The third goal is defined as:

$R + d_3^- - d_3^+ = 160$

We also want to minimize d_3^- as this represents the under-achievement of Goal 3. The total deviation we want to minimize is therefore:

Minimize $P_1 d_1^- + P_2 d_2^+ + P_3 d_3^-$

This is plotted in Figure 14.13 where you will see that Goal 3 cannot be met.

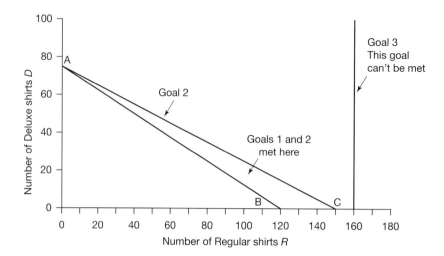

Figure 14.13
Goals 1, 2 and 3

Activity 14.27

What is your recommended solution and how far does this solution over- or under-achieve each goal?

Anywhere in the area ABC will meet the first two goals. The nearest point to Goal 3 is C which is $R = 150$ shirts and $D = 0$ shirts Substituting these values into each goal constraint we get:

Goal 1

$5 \times 150 + 8 \times 0 = £750$; so $d_1^- = £0$ and $d_1^+ = £150$

Goal 2

$150 + 2 \times 0 = 150$; so $d_2^+ = 0$ hours and $d_2^- = 0$ hours

Goal 3

$d_3^- = 160 - 150 = 10$ shirts and $d_3^+ = 0$ shirts

So we under-achieve Goal 3 by 10 shirts

Use of Solver in goal programming

To use Solver we must include the deviational variables and solve in a sequential fashion, starting with the highest priority goal. The relevant deviational variable is minimized in each iteration and we continue until all goals are achieved or until a better solution cannot be found.

Figure 14.14 shows the Excel model for Example 14.4. Note that the left hand side (LHS) now contains both the original and deviational variables relevant to that constraint. Figure 14.15 shows the Solver parameters. In the first iteration we want to minimize d_1^-. As expected this gives us a value of d_1^- of zero (Figure 14.16). In the

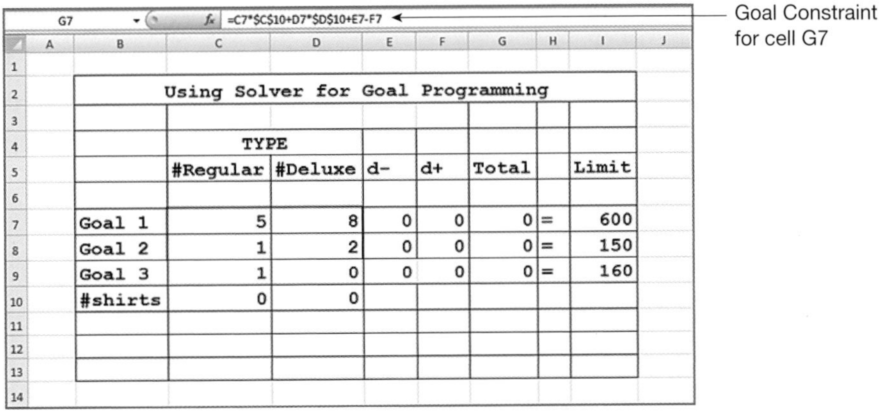

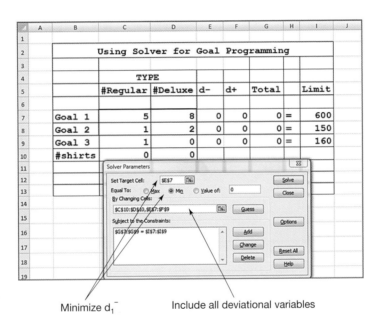

Goal Constraint for cell G7

Figure 14.14
The Excel model for Example 14.4

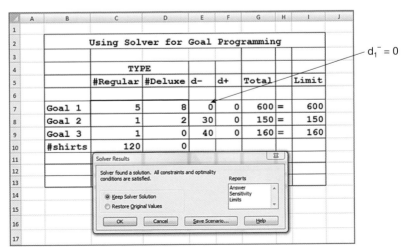

Minimize d₁⁻   Include all deviational variables

Figure 14.15
Setting up Solver for the first iteration

Figure 14.16
Solver results after first iteration

next iteration we want to minimize d_2^+ but we also want to keep $d_1^- = 0$ so we include this into the constraint (Figure 14.17). Again we get the expected result of $d_2^+ = 0$ so in the final iteration we include this as a further constraint while minimizing d_3^- (Figure 14.18). The final result is shown in Figure 14.19 which you will see agrees with that produced manually.

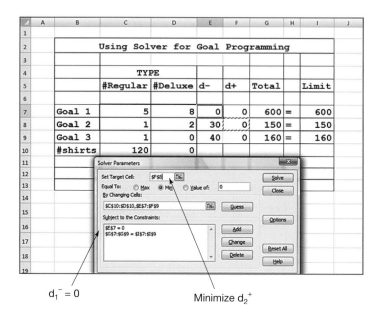

Figure 14.17
Setting up second iteration of Solver

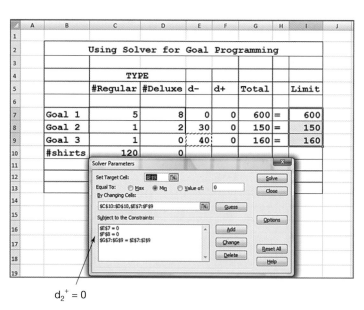

Figure 14.18
Final iteration of Solver

		TYPE						
		#Regular	#Deluxe	d−	d+	Total		Limit
	Goal 1	5	8	0	150	600	=	600
	Goal 2	1	2	0	0	150	=	150
	Goal 3	1	0	10	0	160	=	160
	#shirts	150	0					

Using Solver for Goal Programming

Figure 14.19
Final result of the
Solver analysis

$d_3^- > 0$ so Goal 3 cannot be met.
Best solution is to produce 150 Regular shirts

Reflection

Solving an LP problem involves three phases. These are:

1 Formulate the problem so that it can be solved (matrix generator).
2 Solve it (optimizer).
3 Interpret the output (report-writing).

When using Solver, the first phase required the use of Excel to create the 'template' or matrix from which Solver could be used. Solver was then used to find the optimum solution. It also created reports, which it placed in a separate worksheet.

Although Solver can be used for problems with several variables and constraints, it is not very good for real-life problems where there are hundreds, if not thousands, of variables and constraints. In these cases specialist software is normally used, as Solver would be far too slow to set up and solve the problem.

Matrix-generation and report-writing software can be spreadsheet-based, or an algebraic MP language such as AMPL, MPL for Windows and XPRESS can be used. One of the most popular is MPL for Windows, as this allows you to input data in the same way for an LP formulation. For really large problems, however, AMPL or XPRESS are more powerful.

There are several optimizers on the market, including CPLEX, OSL, XPRESS and Lindo. All optimizers accept input from all matrix generators.

Many problems such as train scheduling are too complex for standard LP methods to be used. In these instances special algorithms or *heuristics* have to be used which, although they will not guarantee optimal solutions, do usually produce good solutions. However, since many millions of alternatives often have to be evaluated the algorithms need to be very efficient and powerful computers need to be used to arrive at a solution in a realistic time period. The ARRIVAL system discussed in the *Quantitative methods in action* at the start of this chapter is able to produce good solutions extremely quickly.

Key points

- Linear programming is a method that finds the best solution amongst many possible solutions. It is an optimizing technique.
- The method requires an objective function, which can be either maximize or minimize, and a set of linear constraints.
- For two variable problems a graphical method can be used, but for more than two variables it is necessary to use *Solver* or a special purpose optimizer.
- One of the most important parts of a linear programming approach is the information obtained from a *sensitivity analysis*. This analysis gives the marginal value of a resource and the sensitivity of the solution to changes in the objective coefficients.
- There are many applications of linear programming including production problems, blending problems, capital rationing, transportation problems and problems involving more than one objective.
- Although transportation problems can be solved by the LP algorithm the *transportation algorithm* can be used to solve this type of problem.
- Goal programming is used to solve LP problems with more than one objective.

Further reading

Linear programming is an operational research (OR) technique and any text with OR or management science in the title will almost certainly include this technique. There is quite a lot of maths involved in the LP algorithm but fortunately it is not necessary for the business student to know details of how the algorithm works. In fact most students think that formulating the problem already contains too much maths! However for the student who wants to find out more about this important technique then the book by Anderson et al. (2008) is a good choice.

Web links W

Answers to selected questions can be found in Appendix 2. Answers to the other questions can be found on the companion website for this book.

Practice questions

W 1 A particular linear programming problem is formulated as follows:

Min. $Z = 2500x + 3500y$

Subject to:

$5x + 6y \geq 250$

$4x + 3y \geq 150$

$x + 2y \geq 70$

$x, y \geq 0$

Draw these constraints on graph paper and determine the optimum solution.

2 A manufacturer produces two products, P and Q, which when sold earn contributions of £600 and £400 per unit respectively. The manufacture of each product requires time on a lathe and a polishing machine. Each unit of P requires 2 hours on the lathe and 1 hour on the polishing machine, while Q requires 1 hour on each machine. Each day, 10 hours are available on the lathe and 7 hours on

the polishing machine. Determine the number of units of P and Q that should be produced per day to maximize contribution.

3 A manufacturer produces a component for diesel engines and a similar component for petrol engines. In the course of production, both components must pass through a machine centre and a testing centre. Diesel engine components spend 4 hours in the machine centre and 2 hours in the testing centre. Petrol engine components spend 2 hours in each centre. There are 16 hours available per day in the machine centre and 12 hours in the testing centre. A contract with a customer stipulates that at least 3 diesel engine components must be produced per day.

Each diesel component that is produced earns a contribution of £60 and each petrol component earns £45. How many units of each component should be manufactured each day in order to maximize contribution?

4 Bright Lights Ltd manufactures light bulbs for general household use. One design is used in microwave ovens and two types are produced: a low wattage and a high wattage version. The company obtains the glass shells from a supplier who can only supply a maximum of 1500 shells a day. The fitting and testing of the bulbs takes place on special machines of which there are one of each (for fitting and for testing) and both machines are available for 10 hours a day. The time to fit and test is different for the two bulbs, as shown in Table 14.10. Also shown is the contribution to profits for each bulb. The company's objective is to maximize contribution and they want to know how many bulbs of each type they should produce each day.

Table 14.10 Data for Question 4

	Low wattage	High wattage
Fitting (seconds)	20	30
Testing (seconds)	10	30
Contribution (pence)	5	7

(a) Formulate the problem as a linear programming model.
(b) Use Excel Solver to obtain the daily number of each bulb to produce so as to maximize contribution to profits.
(c) How much of each resource (glass shells, fitting time and testing time) are unused at the optimal solution? Would it be worth increasing any of these resources, and, if so, why?

W 5 A company has been set up in Bristol to manufacture rowing dinghies. Currently it has plans to produce a basic and a deluxe version. The two dinghies are similar and both take 1.5 days to manufacture. However, the deluxe version is much stronger and the profit is higher, as can be seen in Table 14.11.

Table 14.11 Details for Question 5

	Basic	Deluxe
Resin	10 kg	16 kg
Glass Fibre Mat	30 m	50 m
Profit	£50	£80

Due to safety regulations, the company is only allowed to store a limited amount of the raw material, which is 200 kg of resin and 900 m of mat. The required raw material is delivered on a daily basis.

The basic dinghy is likely to be a good seller, but it is assumed that the deluxe dinghy will be limited to a maximum of 9 per day. All boats produced by the end of the day are delivered to a distribution depot as there are no storage facilities available at the plant.

(a) If the current labour force is 27, use the graphical method of linear programming to demonstrate that there are multiple solutions to the problem. Hence suggest a sensible mix of dinghies to produce on a daily basis and show that this results in a profit of £1000 per day.

(b) (i) What is the shadow price of the resin resource?

(ii) As a result of improved storage facilities more resin can be held at the plant. What is the maximum amount of resin that would be worth storing, and how would this affect the profit calculated in (a)?

W **6** Revor plc has one production line for the manufacture of the ELEN PLUS and ELEN SUPER ignition systems. Both models use similar components in their manufacture but the SUPER model usually requires more of them and takes longer to produce. Relevant details are shown in Table 14.12.

There are supply problems for components A and B and daily usage is limited to 400 and 250 respectively. For component C, the company has entered into a contract with its supplier to take at least 150 per day.

It is also found that at least twice as many ELEN PLUS models are sold as ELEN SUPER, so production should reflect this fact.

The contribution to profits for the PLUS and SUPER models are £60 and £85 respectively.

You can assume that there are 60 employees engaged in the production of these ignition systems and that each employee works an 8-hour day.

(a) Formulate this as a linear programming problem, assuming that it is required to maximize profits.

(b) Use the graphical technique of linear programming to determine the optimal numbers of ELEN PLUS and ELEN SUPER models to produce each day. What is the daily profit associated with this production?

(c) Identify the scarce resources (tight constraints) for this problem. For each determine the shadow price. It is possible to purchase additional quantities of component A from an alternative supplier at a premium of £10 per component. Would it be worthwhile?

(d) The unit costs associated with the production of these systems is known to vary. However, the selling price is only changed annually. How much can the profit on the ELEN PLUS model be allowed to vary before the optimal solution found in (b) changes?

Table 14.12 Details for Question 6

	ELEN PLUS	ELEN SUPER
No. of component A	4	8
No. of component B	2	3
No. of component C	0	10
Manufacturing time (hours)	5	7

7 A company is planning a radio and TV advertising campaign and it has decided that it must use at least 60 adverts, have no more than 50 radio adverts, have at least as many radio as TV adverts and not exceed a budget of £34 000

A radio advert is not as effective as a TV advertisement and the industry assigns a rating to each of the media to indicate their relative effectiveness. For radio the rating is 200 whereas TV gives a rating of 600.

(a) Assuming it is required to maximize the ratings, use the graphical technique of linear programming to find the number of each type of advertisement.

(b) What constraints are binding? What would happen to the overall rating if the maximum number of radio advertisements was increased to 100?

(c) How much could the rating on TV advertisements be reduced before the solution changes?

8 A wealthy investor has £550 000 in a bank account that she wishes to invest and is considering four general types of investment, which are: Government bonds, Corporate bonds, FTSE 100 stocks, Aim stocks

The goal of the investor is to maximize the rate of return on the money invested, where the annual expected return for each investment type is 4%, 5%, 6% and 8%, respectively. Any money not invested in one of these investment type remains in the bank where it earns interest at 3%.

The investor has decided to invest at least £50 000 on corporate bonds and that no more than £300 000 will be put into investments with an element of risk (i.e. corporate bonds and stocks). In addition she decides that at least one half of the money invested in the above 4 ways will go into stocks. Also no more than 25% of the money invested will go into the very risky Aim stocks.

(a) Formulate this problem as a four-variable linear programming problem

(b) This problem was solved using Solver and part of the output from Solver is shown in Figure 14.20.

(i) Use the output to describe the optimum investment plan, the amount of money left in the bank account and the annual yield from this plan in percentage terms.

(ii) It may be possible to relax the constraints regarding the minimum amount to invest in Corporate Bonds *or* the maximum amount to be invested in the riskier investments. Investigate both possibilities and make recommendations on which constraint should be relaxed, by how much and the resulting increase in return.

Adjustable Cells

Name	Final Value	Reduced Cost	Objective Coefficient	Allowable Increase	Allowable Decrease
Government bonds	200000	0		1E+30	0.015
Corporate bonds	50000	0		0.040	1E+30
FTSE 100 Stocks	125000	0		0.020	0.080
Aim Stocks	125000	0		1E+30	0.020

Constraints

Name	Final Value	Shadow Price	Constraint R.H. Side	Allowable Increase	Allowable Decrease
Constraint 1	500000	0	550000	1E+30	50000
Constraint 2	50000	-0.040	50000	100000	25000
Constraint 3	300000	0.050	300000	25000	200000
Constraint 4	0	0.015	0	50000	200000
Constraint 5	0	-0.005	0	500000	500000

Figure 14.20 Solver output for Question 8(b)

(iii) Use the printout to investigate the effect on the variables in solution of reductions in the rate of return of the four investments. Only consider one change at a time. Explain why the allowable decrease in the rate of return for Corporate Bonds is infinite.

9 Aquila is a specialist car manufacturer and currently it has two models; the LXT and HXT. The contribution to profits for the LXT is £580 and for the HXT it is £440.

During manufacture each product has to pass through 3 workshops: the Body shop, the Assembly shop and the Painting shop. LXT requires 5 hours in the Body shop, 9 hours in the Assembly shop and 7 hours in the Painting shop. The HXT model requires 10 hours in the Body shop, 2 hours in the Assembly shop and 5 hours in the Painting shop. Each shop works 40 hours per week. There is also a requirement that at least 60% of the total weekly output must be for the model LXT.

(a) Formulate this problem as an LP model (assuming that the objective is to maximize profit).

(b) Use the graphical technique of linear programming to determine how much of each model to make and the profit as a result of this production schedule.

(c) Which constraints are binding and how much slack (or surplus) do the non-binding constraints have?

(d) Solver shows that the range of the profit for the LXT for this solution to remain optimal is from £220 to £1980. Using your graph explain what will happen outside this range.

(e) The firm is considering the introduction of a new model ZXT which requires 4 hours in the Body shop, 2 hours in the Assembly shop and 1 hour in the Painting shop. If the shadow prices of the Body shop, Assemble shop and Painting shop are £35, £45 and £0 respectively determine the minimum contribution to profit that would be needed to make the production of the ZXT worthwhile.

(f) A major customer complains about the quality of the upholstery for the cars they receive. After investigating the issue, management decide that the interior of all cars should be cleaned as a separate process rather than in the Paint shop. LXT would require 5 hours for cleaning and HXT would require 4 hours. Management estimate that 30 hours could be made available for this new process without affecting the availability of resources in the other three shops. Would the introduction of the cleaning process change the optimal production plan already produced?

10 A baker wants to bake two types of family pie, Shepherd's Ecstasy and Lentil Puff. Both pies require two secret ingredients (A and B), both of which are in short supply. Shepherd's Ecstasy requires 0.5 kg of ingredient A and 0.25 kg of ingredient B, while Lentil Puff requires 0.4 kg of ingredient A and 0.7 kg of ingredient B. The maximum daily amount of ingredients A and B available is 6 kg and 14 kg respectively. The baker plans to sell each Shepherd's Ecstasy pie for £3 and each Lentil Puff pie for £2.50. The variable costs work out at £1.50 for each pie (any fixed costs are negligible).

Only one baking is done each day and the oven that is used to bake the pies can only hold 30 pies. A local restaurant has a daily order of 5 Lentil Puff pies which must be met.

(a) Formulate the problem assuming that the objective is to maximize profits.

(b) Use a graphical technique to determine how many of each pie that the baker should bake each day and the profit they will make.

(c) If a reduction of £0.25 was made to the selling price of Shepherd's Ecstasy how would your solution change?

(d) This problem was solved using Solver and the sensitivity analysis report is shown in Table 14.13.

Table 14.13 Data for Question 10

Constraints						
Cell	Name	Final value	Shadow price	Constraint RH side	Allowable increase	Allowable decrease
$D$6	A	6	3	6	8.5	4
$D$7	B	5.5	0	14	1E+30	8.5
$D$8	Oven	13	0	30	1E+30	17
$D$9	Restaurant	5	−0.2	5	10	5

(i) The restaurant has asked the baker to increase its order from 5 to 7 pies each day. What would be your response?

(ii) The baker could get hold of another 3 kg of ingredient A at an extra cost of £1 per kg. Would this be worthwhile and if so what would be the increase in profits?

(iii) The baker is considering making a 3rd type of pie which she has called the Corn Delight. This pie will use 0.6 kg of secret ingredient A and 0.1 kg of secret ingredient B. The profit on this pie would be £1.65. Should she go ahead with this new pie?

W. 11 Solve the transportation problem in Example 14.3 (page 381) using Solver and the model developed in Activities 14.18 and 14.19.

W. 12 The computer distributor Riglen owns 3 warehouses. These are at Watford, Bristol, and Birmingham. Goods are delivered to retail outlets in London, Wales, the North West (NW), the North East (NE) and the South West (SW).

Goods from the warehouses are delivered in standard size boxes. The requirements for one particular day last week are shown in Table 14.14.

Table 14.14 Delivery requirements for Question 12

Retail outlets	Number of boxes
London	530
Wales	350
NW	450
NE	500
SW	400

It is not always possible to fully meet demand and any shortfall is made up on the next delivery. This was the case for the day being considered and the following number of boxes were allocated for delivery to the 5 regions by the 3 warehouses:

Watford (Wat): 500 boxes;   Birmingham (Birm): 900 boxes;
Bristol (Bri): 500 boxes.

Table 14.15 Average cost per box for Question 12

Warehouse	London	Wales	NW	NE	SW
			Destination		
Wat	1.80	5.00	5.00	7.10	2.90
Birm	4.50	4.10	3.40	10.00	4.70
Bri	3.30	2.20	4.70	7.90	2.10

The average cost per box is shown in Table 14.15.

(a) Use the transportation algorithm to allocate the goods from each warehouse to each retail outlet as cheaply as possible. What is the cost of your allocation?

(b) Is there an alternative solution to the one found in part (a). What is it?

(c) What would be the additional cost per box of using the Bristol to London route.

(d) If more efficient vehicles could be used on the Birmingham to North East route the cost per box would be reduced. By how much does this cost have to fall before it becomes economic to use this route?

W 13 Revor plc, a car component manufacturer, has factories at Aberdeen, Bristol and Colchester. It sells its goods to a national distributor which owns 4 warehouses, located in different parts of the UK. Due to the recession, the quantity required by the supplier has fallen but Revor has not reduced its production capacity. Excess capacity is stored on the factory premises.

Goods purchased by the supplier are transported to its warehouse by container. The cost (in £00s per container) from each factory to each warehouse is shown in Table 14.16. Also shown is the normal weekly production at each factory and the requirements at each warehouse.

Table 14.16 Data for Question 13

Warehouse	Aberdeen	Bristol	Colchester	No. of containers required
P	5	13	7	60
Q	*	4	8	35
R	5	22	25	50
S	3	9	4	100
No. of containers available	175	80	150	

*For operational reasons it is not possible to deliver to warehouse Q from Aberdeen

(a) the current transport plan is as follows:

Aberdeen to warehouse P   25 containers
Aberdeen to   R   50 containers
Aberdeen to   S   100 containers
Bristol to   Q   35 containers
Colchester to   P   35 containers

Calculate the cost of this plan and show that it is not the cheapest plan that could be achieved.

(b) Use the transportation algorithm to find the optimum solution. What is the cost of this solution?

14 The Global energy company produces two products; convection heaters and thermal heaters. Both products require a two step production process involving wiring and assembly. If X1 = numbers of convection heaters produced and X2 = number thermal heaters produced the LP model is given by:

Profit = 7 X1 + 6X2
Subject to
2X1 + 3X2 $\leq$ 12 (wiring hours)
6X1 + 5X2 $\leq$ 30 (assembly hours)
X1, X2 $\geq$ 0

(a) What is the optimal solution?
(b) The company now sets up the following goals:
Goal 1 to produce a profit of £30
Goal 2 to fully utilize the available wiring hours
Goal 3 to avoid overtime in the assembly department
Goal 4 to meet a contract to produce at least 7 convection heaters.

W. 15 Question 4 referred to the Bright Lights company that manufactures light bulbs. For this question you are asked to consider 3 goals. These are (in this order) to use all 1500 bulb shells a day, to restrict the testing machine to 8 hours a day and to achieve a profit of at least £100. Can these goals be met?

....

Assignment

The food department at Riglen plc has brought out a new breakfast cereal called Hi-Fibre, which uses a concentrated form of fibre developed by Riglen's research laboratory. This product has been test marketed in a few selected areas and the consumer reaction has been favourable. However, several of the people questioned said that they would prefer a higher fibre content, so Dave Smith, the Product Manager, has decided to meet this demand with an additional product called Hi-Fibre Plus. This product will have double the fibre content of Hi-Fibre and will require additional cooking time. The selling price of Hi-Fibre Plus will be greater than for Hi-Fibre and the contribution to profits also will be higher. For Hi-Fibre the contribution will be 12p per 500 g packet, and for Hi-Fibre Plus it will be 15p per 500 g packet.

During the period of test marketing, 500 packets of the product were produced each day. However, from a commercial point of view at least 2500 packets of each product must be produced daily and it is expected that demand will soon exceed this figure. Dave's problem is that he is unsure of the quantities of each product to produce. Even if he assumes that he can sell all that he makes, the resources at his disposal are limited. The storage area can take a maximum of 12 000 packets, so total daily production of the cereal cannot exceed this figure. He has one oven and one packaging plant that operates for 12 hours a day and the supply of concentrated fibre is, for the moment, restricted to 120 kg per day. There is no practical limit to the other ingredients.

Dave Smith has asked you to use LP to solve his production problem and he has given you some additional information:

	Hi-Fibre	Hi-Fibre Plus
Cooking/packaging	3 seconds	5 seconds
Fibre content	5 g	10 g

All figures are based on 500 g of cereal.

(a) Formulate this problem in LP terms with the objective of maximizing contribution to profits.

(b) Use the graphical technique of linear programming to solve this problem.

(c) How much of each resource (that is fibre, storage space and the working day) is left after the optimal quantities of cereal are produced? Which resources are 'scarce' (that is, all used up)?

(d) Is it worthwhile increasing any of the scarce resources, and if so by how much? The additional cost of increasing fibre production is £20 per kg; storage space would work out at 20p per packet; and extending the working day would incur costs of £30 per hour.

(e) Would the optimal solution change if the profit contribution of either product changed?

(f) The sales department believes that the demand for Hi-fibre Plus will be greater than that for Hi-Fibre. If this is correct, production of Hi-Fibre Plus needs to be higher than Hi-Fibre. What increase in profit contribution of Hi-Fibre Plus will be necessary if the total profit is to remain the same?

Planning large projects: network analysis

Objectives

- To know how to construct an activity-on-node network to represent a project
- To be able to calculate the earliest and latest start and finish times for each activity
- To be able to calculate the float for each activity, and to identify the critical path
- To be able to draw a Gantt chart and a resource histogram to smooth the use of resources required by a project
- To know how to apply the technique of crashing
- To apply the PERT technique when activity times are uncertain

Introduction

Network analysis is a branch of mathematics (combinatorial problems) that tries to optimize the flows in a network. This network could be the flow of goods or people between cities (the 'travelling salesmen problem') or it could be the scheduling of activities in a construction project. In Chapter 14 we showed how the *transportation algorithm* could be used to solve particular types of linear programming problems. The objective of the transportation algorithm was to minimize the cost of transporting goods from a set of origins to a set of destinations. In this chapter we will concentrate on a rather different type of network problem where the objective is to minimize the time taken to complete a project which consists of a set of interrelated activities. Although it is possible to use linear programming to solve this type of problem we will use a method often called *critical path analysis*, which for small problems can be solved by hand. This method identifies the activities that must start on time and cannot be delayed. These *critical* activities form a path (or paths) through the network and the time taken to complete this path gives the minimum time for the project to be completed. There are two different approaches to obtaining the critical path and in this chapter we will use the *Activity-on-node* method. We will also look at ways of scheduling resources in a project using a *Gantt* chart and resource histogram and we will look at a method for reducing the time of a project using a technique called *crashing*. Finally we will consider how uncertainty in activity times can be handled.

Quantitative methods in action: 2012 Olympic Games

Any large construction project requires careful planning to ensure that the project is completed on time and on budget. Of course many projects over-run in time and in budget and, although embarrassing and usually expensive in penalties, these over-runs are often accepted as inevitable. However there are some large projects where an over-run in time would be a disaster. One example is the staging of the Olympic Games. When Great Britain won the bid for the 2012 Games the organizers were adamant that their Games would not suffer the same fate as Athens in 2004 when the infrastructure was completed with barely hours to spare.

The Olympic Delivery Authority took possession of the Olympic site in July 2007 and spent the next ten months clearing the site of 30 buildings and contaminated soil. This in itself needed careful planning as there were many contractors involved using large earth moving equipment, cranes etc. The contractors cannot have expensive equipment lying idle so it was important that everything was planned down to the last detail.

The actual construction started in May 2008 with around 4000 concrete columns to reinforce the stadium area. Temporary bridges and roadways were built to enable construction to take place. Early in 2009 the steel structures that support the stadium roof were put in place. The stadium was completed on 29 March 2011 which was the target set in May 2008. It was also completed under budget. More than 240 UK businesses were involved in the construction and 5250 people have worked on the project during the three years it took to construct. This was a huge undertaking and the management team would have had to:

1 Develop an optimum plan in deciding what had to be done and when.
2 Allocate resources efficiently.
3 Set up control functions to ensure that the project stayed on schedule and within budget.
4 Have contingency plans in case critical activities were delayed.

As we shall see in this chapter there are accepted methods of devising an optimal plan and ensuring that resources are used efficiently. There are also methods that can speed up the critical activities by utilizing more resources. Although the examples used in this chapter are very small these methods will work for any size of project. However, once a project has more than about 100 activities computer software is essential to do all the number crunching.

As well as overseeing the construction of the venue the Olympic Committee are also 'stress' testing systems to ensure that everything runs smoothly. They have a lab in Canary Wharf where they are running and analyzing 'virtual' races. By the time the Olympics start there will be a team of 5000 involved in the testing using 880 PCs, 130 servers and 110 network switches in analyzing results and other crucial data created from the 35 sporting events that will be available in 2012.

Sources: 'Start of construction on the Olympic Stadium', Olympic Delivery Authority, May 2008; '2012 London Olympics "still on budget"', BBC, 14 February 2011 (www.bbc.co.uk/news/uk-england-london-12445712)

The activity-on-node method

This technique allows the time of the project and the slack (or *float*) of individual activities to be determined. If an activity has zero float you would say that it is *critical* because any delay in that activity would delay the entire project.

Before *critical path analysis* (or *CPA*) is used it is necessary to make a list of all the activities, their durations and which activities must immediately precede them.

Once this list has been completed, you should represent the project by the means of a diagram. The diagram used in this book uses the *activity-on-node* method. The basic diagram for this method is shown in Figure 15.1. The nodes represent the activity, and the lines the dependencies between activities.

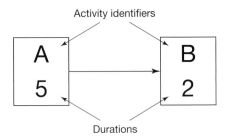

Activity identifiers

Durations

Figure 15.1
Activity-on-node

Example 15.1

You have just obtained planning permission to build a garage and you are now in the process of planning the project. With a little help from a friendly builder you have made a list of activities that need to be completed, the durations of these activities and the order in which they can be tackled. This list is shown in Table 15.1.

Table 15.1 Details of the garage building project

Activity	Description	Immediate preceding activities	Duration (days)
A	Obtain bricklayer	–	10
B	Dig the foundations	–	8
C	Lay the base	B	1
D	Build the walls	A and C	8
E	Build the roof	D	3
F	Tile the roof	E	2
G	Make window frames	–	3
H	Fit the window frames	D and G	1
I	Fit glass to frames	H	1
J	Fit the door	E	1
K	Paint the door and window frames	I and J	2
L	Point the brickwork	D	2

Activity 15.1

Draw the network for the garage problem using the activity-on-node method.

The basic diagram for the garage problem is shown in Figure 15.2. You will see that the name of each activity is displayed in the box together with the duration. You will also see that there are start and end nodes. This is to ensure that every activity has at least one line entering and one line leaving its node.

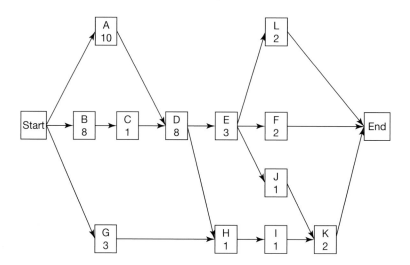

Figure 15.2
The network for the garage problem

For this method you need to display 4 additional pieces of information on each node: the earliest start time of the activity (EST), the latest start time (LST), the earliest finish time (EFT), and the latest finish time (LFT). This information should be displayed as in Figure 15.3.

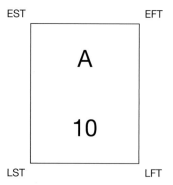

Figure 15.3
Information displayed on each node

In order to calculate the EST and EFT a *forward pass* is made through the network. If the start is at time zero, then the EST of activities A, B and G is zero and their EFT is 10, 8 and 3 respectively. The EST of activity C must be 8, since it can start as soon as B is completed. However, what about activity D? This activity cannot start until both A and C are completed, and as A is completed later than C, then activity A determines the EST of D, which must be 10. This is the general rule when calculating the EST – if there are two or more choices the EST is the *larger* of the EFTs of the preceding activities. From this you will see that the EST of K must be 22 and not 20.

Activity 15.2

Continue the forward pass through the network and add this information to your network. How long will it take you to complete the project?

You can now check your answers with Figure 15.4. From this diagram you will see that the project will take 24 days in total.

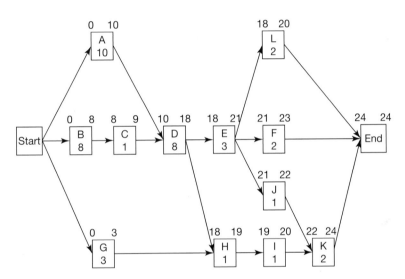

Figure 15.4
A forward pass through the network

To enable the LFT and LST to be calculated a *backward pass* is made through the network, starting at the END node. The LFT of activities F, K and L must be 24 since the project is only complete when all these activities have been completed. The LST of F, K and L must all be 22 days since the duration of all three activities is 2 days. To calculate the LFT of all other activities involves a process similar to that for the forward pass, with one difference, which is that when there is a choice, the *smallest* value is chosen.

Activity 15.3

Continue the backward pass through the network.

The completed network is shown in Figure 15.5 overleaf.

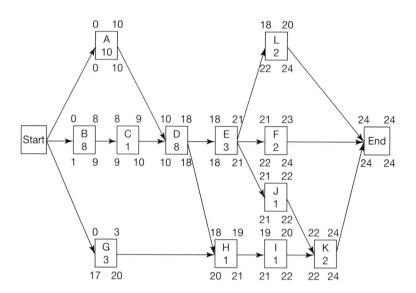

Figure 15.5
The completed network

The float of an activity

The float or slack of an activity is the difference between the EST and LST (or between the EFT and LFT) for each activity. For example, activity D has a zero float since the EST and LST are the same (10), while activity F has a float of 1 day $(22 - 21)$.

Activity 15.4

Obtain the floats for the remainder of the activities. Which activities are 'critical'; that is, have no float?

You should have obtained the information shown in Table 15.2.

Table 15.2 Calculation of the floats

Activity	EST	LST	Float
A	0	0	0
B	0	1	1
C	8	9	1
D	10	10	0
E	18	18	0
F	21	22	1
G	0	17	17
H	18	20	2
I	19	21	2
J	21	21	0
K	22	22	0
L	18	22	4

From this you can see that activities A, D, E, J and K have zero floats and are therefore *critical*. Any delay in the start or finish times of these activities would delay the entire project by the same amount. The other activities could be delayed by up to their float without affecting the overall project time. For example, activity B (dig foundations) could be delayed by one day, but this activity would then become critical. You will notice that the critical activities form a path through the network – this is called the *critical path*. However, it is possible to have more than one critical path, as you will see in *Cost scheduling*, below.

Did you know

> In its broader sense network analysis is being used in a wide range of fields. One such use is *social network analysis* where it is used to find links between people, groups, organizations, computers etc. It has been used in tracking the spread of diseases and in tracking people belonging to a terrorist organization.
> See www.orgnet.com/sna.html.

Resource scheduling

Activities of a project often involve resources of one kind or another. In the garage building example, labour is the obvious resource since each activity requires people to do the work. Perhaps you have asked a friend or neighbour to help and the two of you intend to help the bricklayer and do the less skilled jobs.

Example 15.2

For each activity in the garage building project you decide how many people are required to do these jobs, and you get the list shown in Table 15.3.

Table 15.3 Resource requirements for the garage project

Activity	No. of people required
A	0
B	2
C	2
D	1
E	1
F	2
G	1
H	1
I	1
J	2
K	1
L	1

Since some activities, such as digging the foundations and making the window frames, can take place at the same time, the number of people required at a particular time may be greater than the availability. However, it may be possible to delay non-critical activities, such as making the window frames, sufficiently to avoid this problem. The critical path network cannot easily solve this problem because this network is designed to show the *order* in which activities take place rather than *when* they take place. A better chart to use is the *Gantt* chart. A Gantt chart is like a bar chart that has been turned on its side. The horizontal axis is time and each activity is represented by a bar; the start of the bar is initially the EST and the end of the bar is the EFT. The float of an activity is represented by a dotted line.

Activity 15.5

Draw the Gantt chart for the garage project.

This chart is shown in Figure 15.6.

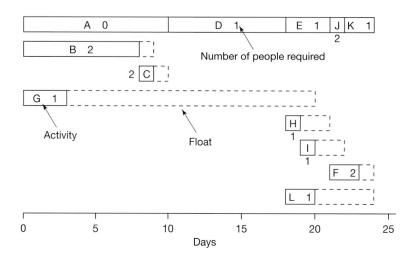

Figure 15.6
The Gantt chart

You will see that the bars representing the critical activities have all been placed on one line – this is because each activity follows one another on the critical path. The non-critical activities should, however, be placed on separate lines so that their floats can be clearly shown. The number of people required has been added to each bar. From this you can see that 3 people are required during the first 3 days $(0 + 2 + 1)$.

Activity 15.6

Repeat this procedure for the entire project. When are more than 2 people required?

The figures are shown in Table 15.4. You can see that more than 2 people are required on several occasions. You might find this easier to see on the *resource histogram* in Figure 15.7.

Table 15.4 Daily resource requirement

Day	Number of people required
First 3 days	3
Next 6 days	2
Next day	0
Next 8 days	1
Next 2 days	3
Next day	1
Next day	4
Next day	3
Next day	1

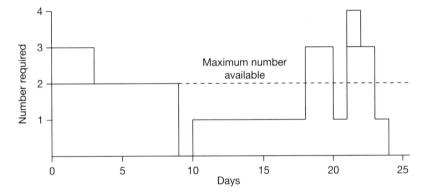

Figure 15.7
The resource
histogram

From this histogram you will see clearly the peaks and troughs in the resource requirements. If a peak could be moved into a trough, the net result would be a smoother histogram. A perfectly smooth histogram would mean that the resource is being fully utilized and no further savings would be possible. In the case of the garage it would be possible to delay the start of activity G (make window frames) until day 9, since G has a float of 17 days. This would mean that from the start of the project until day 12, 2 people would be required all the time. The peaks at the end of the project are not so easy to solve. If the start of activity F (tile the roof) was delayed by its float of one day, the peak of 4 people during day 21 could be reduced by 1, so 3 people are required for much of the latter part of the project. The alternative to increasing the number of people is to extend the project. For example, if the critical activities J (fitting the door) and K (painting) were delayed until activity F had been completed, the completion of the project would be delayed by 2 days but only 2 people would be required for the entire time.

Cost scheduling

A very important resource in network analysis is money. This resource is usually so important that a separate technique has been devised to solve problems posed by financial considerations. This technique is called *crashing*.

It is usually desirable to reduce the time a project takes because there are often financial advantages in doing so. For example, the Department of Transport pays a bonus to contractors who complete a road building or repair project early (and a penalty is charged if the project time is overrun). It is often possible to speed up the completion of an activity at an extra cost. This cost may be incurred because a machine is hired or because more people are employed. The reduced duration is called the *crashed* duration, and the increased cost is called the *crashed* cost.

Example 15.3

It is possible to reduce the time for completing activities B, D, E, F, G, K and L of the garage building project by employing additional labour. If this is done costs will increase for these activities. Table 15.5 gives you the durations and costs for all activities.

Table 15.5 Cost details for the garage project

Activity	Normal duration (days)	Crash duration (days)	Normal cost	Crash cost
A	10	10	£5	£5
B	8	2	£100	£700
C	1	1	£200	£200
D	8	5	£800	£1700
E	3	2	£500	£900
F	2	1	£200	£400
G	3	1	£150	£550
H	1	1	£50	£50
I	1	1	£20	£20
J	1	1	£20	£20
K	2	1	£30	£130
L	2	1	£100	£200

Activity 15.7

What is the normal total cost of the project?

The total cost is simply the sum of *all* the activities, since all must be completed. This is £2175. If some of the activities are crashed this cost will increase. The question is which activities should be crashed in order to reduce the project time to a minimum but without incurring unnecessary costs.

Activity 15.8

Would it be worth crashing all the activities identified above?

The answer to this question is no because not all the activities are on the critical path. Even if they were, some of the activities are more economic to crash than others. For instance, activity D costs £300 per day to crash (an extra cost of £900 and a time reduction of 3 days) while activity E costs £400 per day. The objective of crashing should be to find the minimum project duration at the minimum extra cost. In order to satisfy this objective it is first necessary to find the crash cost per day for each activity. This is necessary as the crashing can make non-critical activities become critical.

Activity 15.9

Calculate the cost per day for activities B, D, E, F, G, K and L using the information given in Table 15.5.

This calculation is summarized in Table 15.6.

Table 15.6 Daily cost of crashing

Activity	Max. reduction by crashing (days)	Extra cost	Crash cost/ day
B	6	£600	£100
D	3	£900	£300
E	1	£400	£400
F	1	£200	£200
G	2	£400	£200
K	1	£100	£100
L	1	£100	£100

The next step is to write down all the paths through the network together with their durations. (Path GHIK can be ignored because it has a relatively short duration.)

Activity 15.10

Make a list of all major paths through the network.

You should have found 8 major paths, which are shown in Table 15.7.

Table 15.7 Paths through the network

Path	Duration
ADEJK	24
BCDEJK	23
ADEF	23
ADHIK	22
BCDEF	22
BCDHIK	21
ADL	20
BCDL	19

Activity 15.11

Which path should be reduced first and which activity should be crashed?

Path ADEJK should be reduced first as it the longest path through the network and therefore the critical path. Activities D, E and K can be crashed, but, of the 3, K is the cheapest. If K is crashed by 1 day then not only will the duration of path ADEJK be reduced by 1, but so will paths BCDEJK, ADHIK and BCDHIK. The project duration has now been reduced by 1 day at a cost of 100, but path ADEF is now critical, in addition to ADEJK.

Activity 15.12

Continue to crash the network. What is the minimum project time and what activities should be crashed to keep the crashing cost to a minimum?

Both ADEF and ADEJK must now be crashed together as they are both critical. Both D and E are common to these 2 paths and, since D is the cheapest, this will be crashed by 3 days at a cost of £900. Finally, E is crashed by 1 day to reduce the project duration to 19 days at a cumulative extra cost of £1400. No further crashing is worthwhile because it is not possible to crash both critical paths (only F has any crashing capability left). You might find it easier to write the necessary steps in a table similar to the one shown in Table 15.8.

Table 15.8 Steps involved in crashing the network

Path	Duration	Step 1	Step 2	Step 3
ADEJK	24	23	20	19
BCDEJK	23	22	19	18
ADEF	23	23	20	19
ADHIK	22	21	18	18
BCDEF	22	22	19	18
BCDHIK	21	20	17	17
ADL	20	20	17	17
BCDL	19	19	16	16
Activities crashed		K – 1	D – 3	E – 1
Extra cost		£100	£900	£400
Cumulative extra cost		£100	£1000	£1400

Activity 15.13

You are paying someone £150 per day to help you. How does this affect your recommended minimum project time?

It would be worthwhile crashing K because for an expenditure of £100 you would save £150; a net gain of £50. However, it wouldn't be worthwhile crashing D because for each day saved it has cost you £150 (£300 − £150). So minimum project time is 23 days.

In many construction projects there is a penalty if you exceed the agreed project time and a bonus if you complete the project in less time.

Activity 15.14

As well as the £150 daily overheads you have agreed to hire a cement mixer for 20 days at a fixed cost of £1000. If you keep this mixer for longer than 20 days you will pay an additional £100 per day but if you return it before the 20 days are up you will get a refund of £50 per day. How does this affect your crashing strategy?

Table 15.8 has been redrawn (Table 15.9) showing how the different costs are made up to give the total variable costs for a range of project times from 24 days to 19 days. These variable costs have then been plotted against project duration (Figure 15.8). From both table and chart you will see that the optimum project duration is 23 days as this gives the lowest cost of £3850.

Table 15.9 Total costs including penalty and bonus costs

Duration (days)	24	23	22	21	20	19
Crash cost (£)	0	100	300	300	300	400
Cumulative crash cost (£)		100	400	700	1000	1400
Overheads (£)	3600	3450	3300	3150	3000	2850
Penalty/bonus (+/−) (£)	400	300	200	100	0	−50
Total (£)	4000	3850	3900	3950	4000	4200

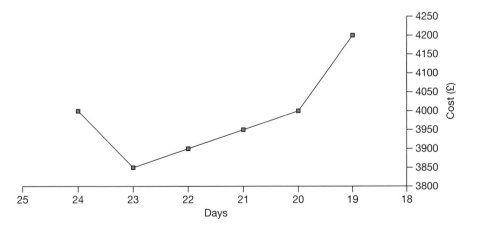

Figure 15.8
Chart showing cost function

Handling uncertainty in time estimates (the PERT method)

So far it has been assumed that all activity times are known with certainty. In practice most times will be an estimate and therefore the overall project time will be subject to error. Usually the best we can do is to have an optimistic time which would be fine if everything went according to plan, and a pessimistic time if the worst happened. You could of course analyze two networks; the first network using optimistic times and the second using the pessimistic times. You would then have a range of times within which the project would be expected to finish. An alternative is to use the PERT method (Programme Evaluation and Review Technique). This approach is useful where some or all of the activities have been carried out in the past and a good deal of information on their durations is available. In addition to being able to obtain an optimistic time (t_o) and a pessimistic time (t_p), a most likely time (t_m) is required. The most likely time is the time that occurs most frequently (the mode). The equations for calculating the mean activity time ($\bar{t}$) and the variance of the activity times (σ_t^2) are

$$\bar{t} = \frac{t_o + 4t_m + t_p}{6}$$

$$\sigma_t^2 = \left(\frac{t_p - t_o}{6}\right)^2$$

These calculations are repeated for each activity where uncertainty is present and the network analysis is then conducted in the normal way, but using the mean activity times.

Following the calculation of the project time and critical path the total variance in the project time can be found by adding the variances on the critical path. (If there are two or more critical paths the largest variance is used.) If it is now assumed that the project times are normally distributed the ideas of Chapter 7 can be applied. For example, we could calculate the probability that the project will exceed a certain time.

Activity 15.15

In Table 15.10 the optimistic, pessimistic and most likely times have been added to the garage building project of Example 15.1 (see page 405). Calculate the expected times and variance for each activity.

The calculation of the expected time and variance for Activity A are:

$$\bar{t} = \frac{6 + 4 \times 9 + 14}{6}$$
$$= 9.33 \text{ days}$$

and

$$\sigma_t^2 = \left(\frac{14 - 6}{6}\right)^2$$
$$= 1.78$$

Table 15.10 Using PERT on the garage project

Activity	Optimistic time (days)	Pessimistic time (days)	Most likely time (days)
A	6	14	9
B	6	12	9
C	1	1	1
D	7	10	8
E	2	5	4
F	2	2	2
G	2	5	4
H	1	1	1
I	1	1	1
J	1	1	1
K	2	2	2
L	1	3	2

These calculations are repeated for each activity (a spreadsheet is recommended) and the following table should have been obtained.

Activity	Optimistic time	Pessimistic time	Most likely time	Expected time	Variance
A	6	14	9	9.33	1.78
B	6	12	9	9.00	1.00
C	1	1	1	1.00	0.00
D	7	10	8	8.17	0.25
E	2	5	4	3.83	0.25
F	2	2	2	2.00	0.00
G	2	5	4	3.83	0.25
H	1	1	1	1.00	0.00
I	1	1	1	1.00	0.00
J	1	1	1	1.00	0.00
K	2	2	2	2.00	0.00
L	1	3	2	2.00	0.11

Note that some variances are zero. This is because the three time estimates were identical, so there was no uncertainty with the times of these activities.

Activity 15.16

Has the critical path changed? You will need to repeat Activities 15.2, 15.3 and 15.4 to check this. What is the expected time to complete the project now?

You should have found that the critical path is still A, D, E, J and K but the time has increased to 24.33 days.

Activity 15.17

Find the probability that the project will take longer than 26 days.

To solve this activity it helps to draw a sketch of the normal distribution. This is done in Figure 15.9. As you see we need to calculate the area of the right hand tail.

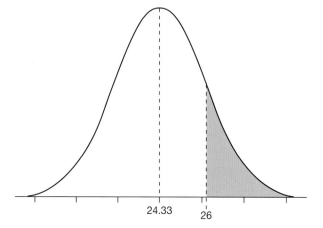

Figure 15.9
The normal distribution for Activity 15.17

24.33   26

To solve a normal distribution problem we need the standard deviation. To find the standard deviation we first add up the variance for each activity on the critical path:

$$1.78 + 0.25 + 0.25 + 0 + 0 = 2.28$$

and then square root this value to get 1.51 days.
Using the formula

$$Z = \frac{x - \text{mean}}{\text{standard deviation}} \quad \text{(see page 167)}$$

we get

$$Z = \frac{26 - 24.33}{1.51}$$
$$= 1.11 \text{ standard deviations}$$

Looking this value up in the normal tables we find that the probability is 0.1335. So there is a 13.35% chance that the project will take longer than 26 days.

PERT makes assumptions about the form of the distribution of activity times and also the normality assumption of the project time. This normality assumption is quite important for working out the probability that a project will take more (or less) time than a specific time. For large projects with hundreds of activities this assumption is quite reasonable but for small projects like the garage one the assumption is probably doubtful.

Did you know

Reflection

Critical path analysis is one of the most useful and easily understood techniques in the analyst's 'toolbox'. Software such as Microsoft Project™ is available which can help in applying this technique.

Many large contracts have a bonus/penalty clause with legally binding project durations and costs. The Wembley National Stadium was a case in point as the original estimate by the contractor was for £326.5m, and it was due to have been completed in 2003. In the end the overall cost was £900m and it opened just in time for the 2007 FA Cup final! The construction company, Multiplex, were originally blamed for the delays but they are now suing the engineering consultants Mott MacDonald for £253m claiming that their services were inadequate and that the saga had damaged their reputation (*The Observer*, 16 March 2008). At the other extreme, the 2012 Olympic Park was completed ahead of schedule although the final cost was a lot higher than originally forecast at £2.35bn.

Key points

- There are two main methods for planning and monitoring a project: the *activity-on-node* and the *activity-on-arrow* methods. In this chapter we have used the former procedure.
- *Critical path analysis* identifies the minimum time in which the project can be completed, together with the *critical activities* and the *float of the non-critical activities*.
- A *Gantt chart* is effective in showing when activities occur. By using such a chart it is often possible to reduce the *resources* required for a project.
- In some cases the total *duration* of a project can be reduced by reducing the duration of individual activities. The technique of *crashing* allows this reduction to be carried out at minimum additional cost.
- Activity times are rarely known with certainty and to allow for this a technique called PERT can be used. However, this technique makes assumptions which may not be valid for small projects.

Further reading

As mentioned at the start of this chapter there are two methods for constructing a network. The one used here and also by Anderson et al. (2008) is the activity-on-node method. Many texts such as Morris (2008) and Curwin and Slater (2008) use the activity-on-arrow method. Certainly the activity-on-arrow diagram looks neater but students usually find the activity-on-node method more logical. It is also the method used by Microsoft® Project and other project management software. For details of Microsoft® Project see www.microsoft.com/project/en/us/default.aspx.

Web links W

Answers to selected questions can be found in Appendix 2. Answers to the other questions can be found on the companion website for this book.

Practice questions

W **1** Please refer to Figure 15.10 for this question.

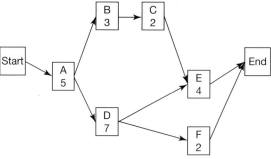

Figure 15.10 Diagram for Question 1

(a) How long will the project take?
(b) How much float has activity D?
(c) How much float has activity F?
(d) If activity B takes 3 weeks longer than expected, will the project be delayed?
(e) If activity B requires 3 people continuously, D requires 2 people and C requires 1 person, how many people are required during week 6?

W **2** Yachtsteer manufactures a self-steering device for pleasure yachts and, as a result of increased competition from foreign manufacturers, it has decided to design and manufacture a new model in time for the next Boat Show. As a first step in planning the project, the major tasks and durations have been identified (Table 15.11). Draw a network to represent the logical sequence of tasks and determine how long it will be before the new product can be marketed.

Table 15.11 Details for Question 2

	Task		Time (weeks)	Preceding tasks
A		Design new product	8	–
B		Design electronics	4	–
C		Organize production facilities	4	A
D		Obtain production materials	2	A
E		Manufacture trial gear	3	C, D
F		Obtain electronic circuit boards	2	B
G		Decide on yacht for trials	1	–
H		Assemble trial gear and electronics	2	E, F
I		Test product in workshops	3	H, G
J		Test product at sea	4	I
K		Assess product's performance	3	J
L		Plan national marketing	4	K

W **3** Shipways boatyard undertakes spring refits on cabin cruisers and yachts, and in the past the company has received complaints from customers regarding the time taken to complete the job. As a consequence the Project Manager, Alan Waters, has decided to carry out a critical path analysis on the cabin cruiser refit. Table 15.12 gives, for each activity, the duration, immediate preceding activities and the number of yard assistants required.

Table 15.12 Details for Question 3

Activity	Description	Duration (days)	Immediate preceding activities	Yard assistants required
A	Bring craft up slipway	1	–	2
B	Check and overhaul seacocks, etc.	3	A	1
C	Scrape and prepare hull for painting	7	A	2
D	Paint hull	4	C	1
E	Remove engine	2	A	3
F	Overhaul engine	16	E	1
G	Clean and paint engine bilges	3	E	1
H	Refit engine	3	F and G	3
I	Apply antifoul paint to hull	2	D and H	2
J	Refloat	1	B and I	2

NOTE: The reason that I follows from both D and H is that a boat must be refloated no more than 48 hours after the antifouling paint has been applied. Antifouling should not therefore be started until the boat is ready for the water.

(a) Draw the network and determine how long the refit will take. What are the critical activities and how much float do the non-critical activities have?

(b) (i) Draw a Gantt chart and resource histogram for the refit. What is the maximum number of yard workers required and when is this required?

   (ii) Unfortunately there are only 4 yard workers available during the period of the refit. Using your Gantt chart and/or histogram, reschedule the activities so that no more than 4 yard workers will be required.

4 Revor plc are urgently planning the production of their new lightweight car battery, the 'Epsilon'. They would like to exhibit their battery at a trade fair, which is to take place in 48 weeks' time. Various activities have to be completed before production can start, and these are shown in Table 15.13.

Table 15.13 Activities for Question 4

	Task	Preceding tasks	Duration (weeks)
A	Clear area	–	20
B	Commission consulting engineers to design equipment	–	2
C	Receive consultant's report	B	10
D	Place equipment out to tender	C	1
E	Obtain equipment	D	6
F	Install equipment	A, E	30
G	Recruit additional staff	C	6
H	Train new staff	G	4
I	Order and obtain materials	–	16
J	Pilot production run	F, H, I	3
K	Advertise new product	–	2

(a) Draw the network and show that it is not possible to start production within 48 weeks. What are the critical activities and how much total float do the non-critical activities have?

(b) It is possible to 'crash' (i.e., reduce the duration of) certain activities at increased cost. These activities are shown in Table 15.14.

Table 15.14 Crash and cost details for Question 4

Activity	Crashed duration (weeks)	Normal cost (£000s)	Crashed cost (£000s)
A	18	4	10
E	5	1	3
F	28	15	27
I	8	0.5	8.5
J	2	16	26

   (i) Ron Smith, the Production Manager, suggests that only activity I need be crashed because this is the cheapest option and allows the greatest reduction in time to be made. Explain why this would not help the situation.

   (ii) It has been estimated that for every week over 48 weeks that this project takes, a loss of £8000 is made as a result of lost profits. Decide on the strategy that will minimize the sum of crashed costs and loss of profits.

5 A painting and decorating firm has decided to use critical path analysis in order to plan its next job. The activities of this job are as shown in Table 15.15.

Table 15.15 Activities for Question 5

Activity	Description	Duration (days)	Preceding activities	Number of operatives
A	Order materials	3	None	0
B	Remove curtains and cover furniture	0.5	None	1
C	Wash interior woodwork	2	B	1
D	Sand exterior woodwork	1	None	2
E	Paint ceilings	2	A & C	2
F	Paint interior woodwork	4	E	3
G	Paint exterior woodwork	5	A & D	2
H	Hang wallpaper	2	F	4
I	Remove covers and replace curtains	0.5	H	1
J	Clean up and depart	0.5	G & I	4

(a) Draw a network representing the sequence of activities and the interdependencies between them.

(b) Determine how long it will take to complete the job and identify the critical activities.

(c) If it were to rain for 4 out of the 5 days allocated for painting the exterior woodwork, what effect would this have on the duration of the job? (Assume that it is dry for the remaining time.)

(d) It has now been decided to analyze the labour requirements for this job. Using graph paper, draw a Gantt chart for the job (assuming earliest start times apply). What is the maximum number of operatives required and when does this occur? Unfortunately, only 4 operatives are available. Explain how this will affect the time taken to complete the job.

W 6 A construction company is planning the building of a warehouse. The activities to complete the projects are shown in Table 15.16.

Table 15.16 Activities for Question 6

Activity	Duration (days)	Immediate predecessor
A	4	None
B	2	None
C	4	A, B
D	2	C
E	6	D
F	3	D
G	4	E
H	5	G, F

(a) Draw a suitable network diagram for this project.

(b) What is the project duration and what are the critical activities?

(c) On further discussion it is apparent that there is some uncertainty over the duration of Activity B. The project manager thinks that, although 2 days is the most likely time, it can be completed in as little as 1 day or if the weather is poor it can take as much as 7 days. Based on this information decide if the project duration and critical activities might be different from that found in part (b)

(d) For every day over 20 days the company will have to pay a penalty of £6500. There are also overheads of £1000 per day. What is the current total cost of the project?

(e) It is possible to reduce the time (crash) some activities so as to reduce the project time. Table 15.17 gives the daily cost of crashing and the maximum time that the activities can be crashed. So for instance Activity A can be crashed by 1, 2 or 3 days at a daily crash cost of £5000. Which activities should be crashed so that the total cost of the project is minimized?

Table 15.17 Crash details for Question 6

Activity	Crash cost per day (£000s)	Maximum number of days that the activity can be crashed
A	5	3
B	3	1
C	15	1
E	7	1
H	20	2

Note: Activities not listed cannot be crashed.

W. **7** A company has just won a contract to refurbish a hotel. The sequence of events from gaining the contract to completion is given in Table 15.18.

Table 15.18 Activity data for Question 7

Activity	Predecessor activities	Duration (weeks)
A	–	5
B	–	6
C	A	3
D	B	3
E	–	7
F	C, D, E	4

(a) Draw the network representing the sequence of activities and the interdependencies between them, identify the critical activities, the minimum time required to complete the project and the slack (float) of the non-critical activities

(b) If activity A took 2 weeks longer than expected what increase in completion time would result and what activities are now critical?

(c) After some consultation with the hotel management it is decided to try and speed up the refurbishment by reducing (crashing) some activities. Table 15.19 gives the maximum crashing that can be achieved for each activity and the cost per week of this crashing.

Table 15.19 Crashing data for Question 7

Activity	Cost per week (£000s) of crashing	Maximum crashing available (weeks)
A	5	1
B	12	3
C	13	1
D	15	1
E	1	2
F	20	2

What activities would need to be crashed to reduce the project time to 11 weeks at minimum cost?

What is the maximum reduction at minimum cost that could be achieved?

8   TG UK services and repairs gaming machines and their agreement with Global Casino is that a fee and repair time for a particular job is agreed in advance. In addition, for every hour over the agreed repair time TG UK will pay Global £100, while for every hour below the time Global will pay them £100. For the latest contract a fee of £10 000 has been agreed with a repair time of 12 hours.

In the past TG UK have overrun repair times and have had to pay a penalty. For the latest contract TG UK have decided to apply some network planning to the activities and you have been given the task of recommending the appropriate course of action. After some investigation you have agreed the activities required in repairing this group of machines together with the expected durations and normal costs. This information is provided in Table 15.20. You also discover that it is possible to reduce some of these durations by 'crashing' activities. Table 15.20 also gives the maximum reduction possible and the hourly crash cost for each activity (note Activity A cannot be crashed).

There are also overhead costs to consider which total £100 per hour.

Table 15.20 Activity data for Question 8

Activity	Immediate predecessors	Normal duration (hours)	Normal cost	Crash cost per hour	Maximum reduction (hours)
A	–	3	£50	N/A	0
B	A	3	£200	£100	1
C	B	4	£500	£330	2
D	B	4	£100	£20	3
E	B	6	£300	£150	3
F	C, D, E	5	£500	£1000	1

(a) Using the normal durations draw a network representing the sequence of activities and the inter-dependencies between them.

(b) Identify the critical activities, the minimum time required to complete the project and the slack (float) of the non-critical activities.

(c) Taking into account the normal costs, overheads and penalty costs what would be the net profit if the project took the time found in part (b)?

(d) You now decide to see if crashing some of the activities reduces the company's costs and, therefore, make a larger profit. What strategy would you recommend in order to maximize the profit obtained from this contract? State clearly which activities should be crashed and by how much time. What would be the overall profit resulting from this strategy?

W **9** A market research agency has been engaged to carry out a customer survey following a promotional campaign for a company's range of products.

The conduct of the survey consists of the activities shown in Table 15.21.

Table 15.21 Activities for Question 9

Activity		Preceding activity	Duration (weeks)	No. of staff required
A	Draft the survey proposals	–	2	3
B	Obtain client's agreement	A	3	2
C	Recruit interviewers	A	2	2
D	Design and test questionnaire	B	1	1
E	Train interviewers	D,C	3	5
F	Order free gift samples	B	5	0
G	Select towns for use in survey	A	1	1
H	Set up a 'base' in each town	G	3	5
I	Carry out the survey	E,F,H	6	2
J	Analyze the results	I	5	2
K	Prepare report and make the presentation to the client	J	3	2

(a) Construct a network to illustrate the activities that have to be undertaken, and establish the earliest and latest start and finish times. Hence find the critical path and the total time taken to complete the survey.

(b) Draw a Gantt chart for this survey and determine how many staff are required during each day of the survey. (You can assume that the agency staff members are skilled in all tasks).

(c) If other agency commitments restrict the number of persons that can be assigned to this survey to 7, can the project be completed without any delays?

10 A household products company has decided to launch a new 'greener' washing powder. After some discussion the marketing department has agreed on the ten activities that need to be done before the national campaign is launched. However there was some argument about how long three of the activities will take so three estimates were used for these activities: the optimistic time, the pessimistic time and the most likely time. Details of the activities and these time estimates are shown in Table 15.22.

It is imperative that the national campaign be launched within 32 days.

Table 15.22 Activities for Question 10

Activity	Description	Immediate predecessors	Optimistic time	Pessimistic time	Most likely time
A	Arrange meetings	None	2	2	2
B	Design publicity material	A	3	3	3
C	Design TV advertising	A	2	7	3
D	Design newspaper advertising	A	2	6	3
E	Specifications sent to ad agency	C and D	1	1	1
F	Preparation of TV and radio ads	E	10	10	10
G	Distribution of washing powder within trial area	None	3	3	3
H	Run campaign in trial area	B, F and G	6	6	6
I	Assess results	H	2	2	2
J	Arrange national campaign	I	3	6	5

(a) Use the PERT method to calculate the mean activity time for activities C, D and J.

(b) Draw a network diagram and for each activity determine the earliest start time, the earliest finish time, the latest finish time and the latest start time. Add this information to a table and find the float (slack) for each activity. Hence determine the critical path and the expected time before the national campaign can be launched.

(c) Assuming that the distribution of project times is normally distributed, find the probability that the campaign can be launched within 32 days.

....

Assignment

There have been recurring problems with the food canning process at Riglen plc and a decision has been taken at Board level to replace the machinery with more modern computer-controlled equipment. Holder and Holder Consulting Engineers have been commissioned to advise on the system to purchase and their report is expected in 5 weeks' time. Although the fine details of the recommended system will not be known until this report has been received, the essential characteristics of all the alternatives are the same. Planning for the installation can therefore start immediately, and this is important because during the installation all food canning has to be contracted out and this will be expensive.

In order to ensure that the project is completed as quickly as possible and at minimum cost, you have been asked to use the relevant network analysis techniques on the data given in Table 15.23. You should also note that fitters are to be employed on a fixed-term contract, and it is important that only the minimum number necessary are recruited.

Table 15.23 Details for the assignment

Activity	Description	Duration	Immediate predecessors	Fitters required	Cost (£000s)
A	Obtain report	5	–	0	5
B	Remove existing machinery	4	–	8	3
C	Purchase new machinery	5	A	0	50
D	Purchase electrics	7	A	0	15
E	Purchase computers	6	A	0	25
F	Install machinery	4	B and C	5	5
G	Install computers	3	E	6	5
H	Connect electrics	3	F and D	2	4
I	Recruit and train staff	6	–	0	3
J	Pilot production run	1	G and H	6	6
K	Prepare for full production	4	I and J	5	2

(a) Draw the network and calculate the start and finish times for each activity. How long will the project take, and what are the critical activities?

(b) Draw a Gantt chart for this project. What is the maximum number of fitters required, and during what weeks does this occur? What is the minimum number of fitters required that will still allow the project to be completed in the time found in (a) above?

(c) An attempt is to be made to reduce the total project time since for every week's reduction a saving of £10 000 can be achieved through not having to contract out the week's canning. This will be possible because some activities such as B can be completed in less time than scheduled. Of course, this reduction in time will be at an increased cost. The activities that can be reduced (crashed) in time are given in Table 15.24.

(i) What is the total normal cost of the project, including the £10 000 per week canning charge?

(ii) Using the figures above, calculate for each activity the cost of reducing the time by one week.

(iii) Starting with the critical path, make a list of all paths through the network. Alongside each path write down the duration in weeks of the path.

(iv) Try and reduce the critical path to the same duration as the next largest in the cheapest way possible. Now reduce both paths until the duration is equal to the next highest path and so on. Repeat this until no further reduction is possible. What is the new total cost of the project?

(v) What is the project duration that will minimize the total cost of the project?

Table 15.24 Cost of crashing activities

Activity	Normal time (weeks)	Crashed time (weeks)	Normal cost (£000s)	Crashed cost (£000s)
B	4	2	10	16
D	7	6	15	21
F	6	3	5	20
G	3	2	5	12
K	4	3	2	10

Bibliography

Anderson et al. (2007) *Statistics for Business and Economics*, Thomson.

Anderson et al. (2008) *An Introduction to Management Science*, 12th edition, Thomson.

Barboianu, C. (2006) *Probability Guide to Gambling: The Mathematics of Dice, Slots, Roulette, Baccarat, Blackjack, Poker, Lottery and Sport Bets*, Infarom.

Blastland, M. and Dilnot, A. (2007) The *Tiger That Isn't: Seeing Through a World of Numbers*, Profile Books.

Checkland, P. (1981) *Systems Thinking, Systems Practice*, Wiley.

Checkland, P. (2006) *Learning for Action: A Short Definitive Account of Soft Systems Methodology, and its Use Practitioners, Teachers and Students*, Wiley.

Collis, J. and Hussey, R. (2009) *Business Research: A Practical guide for Undergraduate and Postgraduate Students*, 3rd edition, Palgrave Macmillan.

Curwin, J. and Slater, R. (2008) *Quantitative Methods for Business Students*, 6th edition, Thomson.

Daellenbach, H.G. and McNickle, D.C. (2005) *Management Science: Decision-making through Systems Thinking*, Palgrave Macmillan

Drucker, P. (2003) *The Essential Drucker: The Best of Sixty Years of Peter Drucker's Essential Writings on Management*, Collins Business.

Eastaway, R. and Haigh, J. (2011) *The Hidden Mathematics of Sport: Beating the Odds in Your Favourite Sports*, Portico.

Edwards, W. (1971) *Social Utilities*, Engineering Economist, Summer Symposium Series 6.

Field, A. (2009) *Discovering Statistics using SPSS*, Sage Publications.

Fowler, F. (2009) *Survey Research Methods*, 3rd edition, Sage Publications.

Goodwin, P. and Wright, G. (2009) *Decision Analysis for Management Judgement*, 4th edition, Wiley.

Haigh, J. (2000) *Taking Chances*, Oxford University Press.

Lumby, S. and Jones, C. (1999) *Fundamentals of Investment Appraisal*, Thomson Learning.

Makridakis et al. (1998) *Forecasting: Methods and Applications*, 3rd edition, Wiley.

McClave, J. and Sincich, T. (2006) *Statistics*, 10th edition, Prentice Hall.

Morris, C. (2007) *Essential Maths for Business and Management*, Palgrave Macmillan.

Morris, C. (2008) *Quantitative Approaches in Business Studies*, 7th edition, Prentice Hall.

Pallant, J. (2010) *SPSS Survival Manual: A Step by Step Guide to Data Analysis using SPSS*, 4th edition, Open University Press/McGraw-Hill.

Pidd, M. (2010) *Tools for Thinking in Management Science*, 3rd edition, Wiley.

Rowe, N. (2002) *Refresher in Basic Mathematics*, 3rd edition, Continuum International Publication Group.

Sheldon, R. (2010) *Introduction to Probability Models*, 10th edition, Academic Press.

Sussman, F. and Freed, J.R. (2008) *Adapting to Climate Change: A Business Approach*, Pew Center on Global Climate Change.

Swift, L. and Piff, S. (2010) *Quantitative Methods*, 3rd edition, Palgrave Macmillan.

Tukey, J.W. (1991) 'The Philosophy of Multiple Comparisons', *Statistical Science*, 6: 100–16.

Tversky, A. and Kahneman, D. (1974) 'Judgment under Uncertainty: Heuristics and Biases', *Science*, 185: 1124–31.

Wisniewski, M. (2009) *Quantitative Methods for Decision Makers*, 5th edition, Prentice Hall.

Wright, M. (2009) '50 years of OR in Sport', *Journal of the Operational Research Society*, 60: S161 –S168.

Appendix 1

Statistical tables

The normal tables

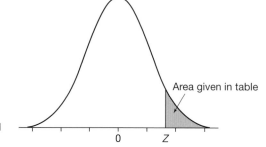

Figure A1.1
The standard normal distribution

Z	0.00	0.01	0.02	0.03	0.04	0.05	0.06	0.07	0.08	0.09
0.0	0.5000	0.4960	0.4920	0.4880	0.4840	0.4801	0.4761	0.4721	0.4681	0.4641
0.1	0.4602	0.4562	0.4522	0.4483	0.4443	0.4404	0.4364	0.4325	0.4286	0.4247
0.2	0.4207	0.4168	0.4129	0.4090	0.4052	0.4013	0.3974	0.3936	0.3897	0.3859
0.3	0.3821	0.3783	0.3745	0.3707	0.3669	0.3632	0.3594	0.3557	0.3520	0.3483
0.4	0.3446	0.3409	0.3372	0.3336	0.3300	0.3264	0.3228	0.3192	0.3156	0.3121
0.5	0.3085	0.3050	0.3015	0.2981	0.2946	0.2912	0.2877	0.2843	0.2810	0.2776
0.6	0.2743	0.2709	0.2676	0.2643	0.2611	0.2578	0.2546	0.2514	0.2483	0.2451
0.7	0.2420	0.2389	0.2358	0.2327	0.2296	0.2266	0.2236	0.2206	0.2177	0.2148
0.8	0.2119	0.2090	0.2061	0.2033	0.2005	0.1977	0.1949	0.1922	0.1894	0.1867
0.9	0.1841	0.1814	0.1788	0.1762	0.1736	0.1711	0.1685	0.1660	0.1635	0.1611
1.0	0.1587	0.1562	0.1539	0.1515	0.1492	0.1469	0.1446	0.1423	0.1401	0.1379
1.1	0.1357	0.1335	0.1314	0.1292	0.1271	0.1251	0.1230	0.1210	0.1190	0.1170
1.2	0.1151	0.1131	0.1112	0.1093	0.1075	0.1056	0.1038	0.1020	0.1003	0.0985
1.3	0.0968	0.0951	0.0934	0.0918	0.0901	0.0885	0.0869	0.0853	0.0838	0.0823
1.4	0.0808	0.0793	0.0778	0.0764	0.0749	0.0735	0.0721	0.0708	0.0694	0.0681
1.5	0.0668	0.0655	0.0643	0.0630	0.0618	0.0606	0.0594	0.0582	0.0571	0.0559
1.6	0.0548	0.0537	0.0526	0.0516	0.0505	0.0495	0.0485	0.0475	0.0465	0.0455
1.7	0.0446	0.0436	0.0427	0.0418	0.0409	0.0401	0.0392	0.0384	0.0375	0.0367
1.8	0.0359	0.0351	0.0344	0.0336	0.0329	0.0322	0.0314	0.0307	0.0301	0.0294
1.9	0.0287	0.0281	0.0274	0.0268	0.0262	0.0256	0.0250	0.0244	0.0239	0.0233
2.0	0.0228	0.0222	0.0217	0.0212	0.0207	0.0202	0.0197	0.0192	0.0188	0.0183
2.1	0.0179	0.0174	0.0170	0.0166	0.0162	0.0158	0.0154	0.0150	0.0146	0.0143
2.2	0.0139	0.0136	0.0132	0.0129	0.0125	0.0122	0.0119	0.0116	0.0113	0.0110
2.3	0.0107	0.0104	0.0102	0.0099	0.0096	0.0094	0.0091	0.0089	0.0087	0.0084
2.4	0.0082	0.0080	0.0078	0.0075	0.0073	0.0071	0.0069	0.0068	0.0066	0.0064
2.5	0.0062	0.0060	0.0059	0.0057	0.0055	0.0054	0.0052	0.0051	0.0049	0.0048
2.6	0.0047	0.0045	0.0044	0.0043	0.0041	0.0040	0.0039	0.0038	0.0037	0.0036
2.7	0.0035	0.0034	0.0033	0.0032	0.0031	0.0030	0.0029	0.0028	0.0027	0.0026
2.8	0.0026	0.0025	0.0024	0.0023	0.0023	0.0022	0.0021	0.0021	0.0020	0.0019
2.9	0.0019	0.0018	0.0018	0.0017	0.0016	0.0016	0.0015	0.0015	0.0014	0.0014

3.0	0.00135	3.1	0.000968	3.2	0.000687	3.3	0.000483	3.4	0.000337

Table of the *t*-distribution

The table gives the *t*-value for a range of probabilities in the upper tail. For a two tailed test the probability should be halved.

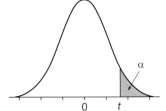

Figure A1.2
The *t*-distribution on
ν degrees of freedom

				Probability (α)				
ν	0.2	0.1	0.05	0.025	0.01	0.005	0.001	0.0001
1	1.376	3.078	6.314	12.706	31.821	63.656	318.3	3185.3
2	1.061	1.886	2.920	4.303	6.965	9.925	22.328	70.706
3	0.978	1.638	2.353	3.182	4.541	5.841	10.214	22.203
4	0.941	1.533	2.132	2.776	3.747	4.604	7.173	13.039
5	0.920	1.476	2.015	2.571	3.365	4.032	5.894	9.676
6	0.906	1.440	1.943	2.447	3.143	3.707	5.208	8.023
7	0.896	1.415	1.895	2.365	2.998	3.499	4.785	7.064
8	0.889	1.397	1.860	2.306	2.896	3.355	4.501	6.442
9	0.883	1.383	1.833	2.262	2.821	3.250	4.297	6.009
10	0.879	1.372	1.812	2.228	2.764	3.169	4.144	5.694
11	0.876	1.363	1.796	2.201	2.718	3.106	4.025	5.453
12	0.873	1.356	1.782	2.179	2.681	3.055	3.930	5.263
13	0.870	1.350	1.771	2.160	2.650	3.012	3.852	5.111
14	0.868	1.345	1.761	2.145	2.624	2.977	3.787	4.985
15	0.866	1.341	1.753	2.131	2.602	2.947	3.733	4.880
16	0.865	1.337	1.746	2.120	2.583	2.921	3.686	4.790
17	0.863	1.333	1.740	2.110	2.567	2.898	3.646	4.715
18	0.862	1.330	1.734	2.101	2.552	2.878	3.610	4.648
19	0.861	1.328	1.729	2.093	2.539	2.861	3.579	4.590
20	0.860	1.325	1.725	2.086	2.528	2.845	3.552	4.539
21	0.859	1.323	1.721	2.080	2.518	2.831	3.527	4.492
22	0.858	1.321	1.717	2.074	2.508	2.819	3.505	4.452
23	0.858	1.319	1.714	2.069	2.500	2.807	3.485	4.416
24	0.857	1.318	1.711	2.064	2.492	2.797	3.467	4.382
25	0.856	1.316	1.708	2.060	2.485	2.787	3.450	4.352
26	0.856	1.315	1.706	2.056	2.479	2.779	3.435	4.324
27	0.855	1.314	1.703	2.052	2.473	2.771	3.421	4.299
28	0.855	1.313	1.701	2.048	2.467	2.763	3.408	4.276
29	0.854	1.311	1.699	2.045	2.462	2.756	3.396	4.254
30	0.854	1.310	1.697	2.042	2.457	2.750	3.385	4.234
35	0.852	1.306	1.690	2.030	2.438	2.724	3.340	4.153
40	0.851	1.303	1.684	2.021	2.423	2.704	3.307	4.094
45	0.850	1.301	1.679	2.014	2.412	2.690	3.281	4.049
50	0.849	1.299	1.676	2.009	2.403	2.678	3.261	4.014
60	0.848	1.296	1.671	2.000	2.390	2.660	3.232	3.962
80	0.846	1.292	1.664	1.990	2.374	2.639	3.195	3.899
100	0.845	1.290	1.660	1.984	2.364	2.626	3.174	3.861
∞	0.842	1.282	1.645	1.960	2.327	2.576	3.091	3.720

Table of the chi-square distribution

This table gives chi-square values for a range of probabilities and degrees of freedom.

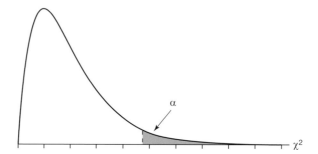

Figure A1.3
The chi-square
distribution on ν
degrees of freedom

Probability (α)

ν	0.995	0.99	0.9	0.1	0.05	0.025	0.01	0.005	0.001
1	0.000	0.000	0.016	2.706	3.841	5.024	6.635	7.879	10.827
2	0.010	0.020	0.211	4.605	5.991	7.378	9.210	10.597	13.815
3	0.072	0.115	0.584	6.251	7.815	9.348	11.345	12.838	16.266
4	0.207	0.297	1.064	7.779	9.488	11.143	13.277	14.860	18.466
5	0.412	0.554	1.610	9.236	11.070	12.832	15.086	16.750	20.515
6	0.676	0.872	2.204	10.645	12.592	14.449	16.812	18.548	22.457
7	0.989	1.239	2.833	12.017	14.067	16.013	18.475	20.278	24.321
8	1.344	1.647	3.490	13.362	15.507	17.535	20.090	21.955	26.124
9	1.735	2.088	4.168	14.684	16.919	19.023	21.666	23.589	27.877
10	2.156	2.558	4.865	15.987	18.307	20.483	23.209	25.188	29.588
11	2.603	3.053	5.578	17.275	19.675	21.920	24.725	26.757	31.264
12	3.074	3.571	6.304	18.549	21.026	23.337	26.217	28.300	32.909
13	3.565	4.107	7.041	19.812	22.362	24.736	27.688	29.819	34.527
14	4.075	4.660	7.790	21.064	23.685	26.119	29.141	31.319	36.124
15	4.601	5.229	8.547	22.307	24.996	27.488	30.578	32.801	37.698
16	5.142	5.812	9.312	23.542	26.296	28.845	32.000	34.267	39.252
17	5.697	6.408	10.085	24.769	27.587	30.191	33.409	35.718	40.791
18	6.265	7.015	10.865	25.989	28.869	31.526	34.805	37.156	42.312
19	6.844	7.633	11.651	27.204	30.144	32.852	36.191	38.582	43.819
20	7.434	8.260	12.443	28.412	31.410	34.170	37.566	39.997	45.314
21	8.034	8.897	13.240	29.615	32.671	35.479	38.932	41.401	46.796
22	8.643	9.542	14.041	30.813	33.924	36.781	40.289	42.796	48.268
23	9.260	10.196	14.848	32.007	35.172	38.076	41.638	44.181	49.728
24	9.886	10.856	15.659	33.196	36.415	39.364	42.980	45.558	51.179
25	10.520	11.524	16.473	34.382	37.652	40.646	44.314	46.928	52.619
26	11.160	12.198	17.292	35.563	38.885	41.923	45.642	48.290	54.051
27	11.808	12.878	18.114	36.741	40.113	43.195	46.963	49.645	55.475
28	12.461	13.565	18.939	37.916	41.337	44.461	48.278	50.994	56.892
29	13.121	14.256	19.768	39.087	42.557	45.722	49.588	52.335	58.301
30	13.787	14.953	20.599	40.256	43.773	46.979	50.892	53.672	59.702
35	17.192	18.509	24.797	46.059	49.802	53.203	57.342	60.275	66.619
40	20.707	22.164	29.051	51.805	55.758	59.342	63.691	66.766	73.403

Random numbers

12	85	40	82	01	41	63	79	74	52	36	99	88	95	48	36	16	92	30	25
34	60	21	38	60	26	04	92	74	50	89	44	31	60	32	16	92	61	99	49
84	52	18	42	80	06	40	13	16	25	17	50	64	96	20	80	86	58	32	62
93	05	34	11	73	18	40	35	11	37	91	74	76	13	00	29	25	06	09	71
63	52	01	80	92	45	92	24	76	70	33	98	94	89	32	46	68	13	12	36
66	36	10	31	45	56	57	08	00	03	71	70	83	84	19	39	75	92	64	44
81	44	02	80	27	97	53	89	47	28	49	87	52	46	45	70	08	27	88	31
49	81	00	26	55	57	46	35	28	09	28	04	22	60	42	95	08	60	11	05
44	42	44	14	27	68	57	05	13	37	26	66	53	18	40	07	86	46	83	02
51	10	93	10	28	30	49	97	90	83	55	58	34	17	66	20	74	21	25	60
11	46	45	26	34	26	03	45	01	96	18	64	44	33	51	90	44	44	87	64
23	06	64	21	03	70	90	02	15	15	32	58	79	67	31	95	24	46	99	62
72	56	98	93	72	19	76	08	81	36	34	56	26	83	69	45	84	92	07	75
38	73	91	20	23	77	91	65	12	16	51	04	49	97	65	52	26	07	92	58
45	87	47	52	23	43	97	21	15	01	25	10	54	67	52	54	70	07	52	81
55	56	23	80	11	94	25	58	32	14	82	12	23	65	70	86	94	87	21	61
18	14	53	18	72	30	19	17	89	72	92	60	33	97	74	24	19	34	70	15
00	57	11	98	91	42	96	53	90	18	98	60	28	03	84	74	41	48	40	20
78	82	27	80	48	49	49	39	97	36	57	03	17	96	00	54	69	05	41	58
15	10	24	85	32	12	04	86	10	97	57	12	51	86	66	45	45	39	74	66
13	36	32	91	89	62	11	65	74	43	00	82	06	12	17	72	99	11	28	82
12	20	77	48	47	12	84	93	58	10	29	39	01	85	19	56	48	73	86	39
15	41	97	91	45	95	26	40	05	78	69	34	39	27	93	10	00	57	28	66
63	35	48	34	24	58	14	26	02	25	86	92	42	84	67	04	16	91	92	95
63	76	07	92	20	91	57	99	96	48	11	68	40	46	72	32	31	76	24	94
82	38	83	43	15	86	77	70	67	97	99	83	53	95	93	20	50	02	50	91
43	60	00	82	81	16	56	75	80	73	69	20	90	99	13	08	91	50	35	51
53	62	23	20	66	21	71	03	55	38	26	44	96	93	71	59	74	00	55	90
65	77	15	58	24	44	77	70	88	47	51	55	31	35	10	64	88	90	03	42
32	22	01	55	92	45	79	40	61	21	50	36	42	66	28	15	39	44	80	38
88	79	17	92	26	95	17	60	90	27	25	16	97	73	01	73	94	48	36	19
46	41	10	10	03	98	37	02	05	83	54	89	63	65	68	12	86	01	72	16
12	93	20	18	02	48	17	76	89	45	41	57	48	19	22	00	05	83	87	52
39	69	29	38	80	48	15	13	30	80	22	31	40	25	68	30	44	67	66	86
34	26	06	45	46	12	63	44	70	22	12	70	34	12	15	03	15	37	50	70
36	33	21	88	57	38	06	99	87	56	50	17	49	11	70	08	09	57	77	35
48	43	62	41	63	12	50	13	95	88	57	38	58	60	93	83	79	86	18	91
85	01	42	75	32	20	88	07	97	96	70	21	01	76	90	17	65	55	61	03
95	54	15	04	88	07	48	06	11	03	24	04	67	41	56	43	96	30	53	35
00	33	65	58	72	61	68	76	88	92	79	49	27	95	01	63	99	68	49	53
97	06	25	63	21	57	42	24	38	87	02	90	33	10	28	46	88	74	58	44
38	98	93	21	89	19	20	14	30	84	36	51	32	64	11	01	88	98	42	14
87	80	11	29	93	56	52	85	93	16	82	83	85	07	42	47	37	01	84	23
24	25	15	18	36	37	19	44	88	60	03	52	68	00	08	92	47	23	97	96
46	95	83	45	40	70	72	47	60	02	02	96	33	00	16	13	70	38	02	35
80	37	03	89	19	56	01	10	18	03	69	46	32	95	50	00	28	95	25	83
87	37	59	61	25	79	39	08	68	33	80	67	12	60	27	38	07	30	06	98
39	97	55	52	41	93	06	61	46	80	66	06	34	80	18	28	72	41	06	77
56	96	90	80	95	47	70	53	41	69	73	88	15	91	19	50	61	43	66	30
21	25	33	25	68	64	01	99	66	64	26	09	71	53	27	35	06	33	50	56

Cumulative binomial probabilities

This table gives the probability of r or fewer successes in n trials, with the probability p success in a trial.

		p						
n	r	0.01	0.05	0.1	0.2	0.3	0.4	0.5
5	0	0.9510	0.7738	0.5905	0.3277	0.1681	0.0778	0.0313
5	1	0.9990	0.9774	0.9185	0.7373	0.5282	0.3370	0.1875
5	2	1.0000	0.9988	0.9914	0.9421	0.8369	0.6826	0.5000
5	3	1.0000	1.0000	0.9995	0.9933	0.9692	0.9130	0.8125
5	4	1.0000	1.0000	1.0000	0.9997	0.9976	0.9898	0.9688
6	0	0.9415	0.7351	0.5314	0.2621	0.1176	0.0467	0.0156
6	1	0.9985	0.9672	0.8857	0.6554	0.4202	0.2333	0.1094
6	2	1.0000	0.9978	0.9842	0.9011	0.7443	0.5443	0.3438
6	3	1.0000	0.9999	0.9987	0.9830	0.9295	0.8208	0.6563
6	4	1.0000	1.0000	0.9999	0.9984	0.9891	0.9590	0.8906
6	5	1.0000	1.0000	1.0000	0.9999	0.9993	0.9959	0.9844
7	0	0.9321	0.6983	0.4783	0.2097	0.0824	0.0280	0.0078
7	1	0.9980	0.9556	0.8503	0.5767	0.3294	0.1586	0.0625
7	2	1.0000	0.9962	0.9743	0.8520	0.6471	0.4199	0.2266
7	3	1.0000	0.9998	0.9973	0.9667	0.8740	0.7102	0.5000
7	4	1.0000	1.0000	0.9998	0.9953	0.9712	0.9037	0.7734
7	5	1.0000	1.0000	1.0000	0.9996	0.9962	0.9812	0.9375
7	6	1.0000	1.0000	1.0000	1.0000	0.9998	0.9984	0.9922
8	0	0.9227	0.6634	0.4305	0.1678	0.0576	0.0168	0.0039
8	1	0.9973	0.9428	0.8131	0.5033	0.2553	0.1064	0.0352
8	2	0.9999	0.9942	0.9619	0.7969	0.5518	0.3154	0.1445
8	3	1.0000	0.9996	0.9950	0.9437	0.8059	0.5941	0.3633
8	4	1.0000	1.0000	0.9996	0.9896	0.9420	0.8263	0.6367
8	5	1.0000	1.0000	1.0000	0.9988	0.9887	0.9502	0.8555
8	6	1.0000	1.0000	1.0000	0.9999	0.9987	0.9915	0.9648
8	7	1.0000	1.0000	1.0000	1.0000	0.9999	0.9993	0.9961
9	0	0.9135	0.6302	0.3874	0.1342	0.0404	0.0101	0.0020
9	1	0.9966	0.9288	0.7748	0.4362	0.1960	0.0705	0.0195
9	2	0.9999	0.9916	0.9470	0.7382	0.4628	0.2318	0.0898
9	3	1.0000	0.9994	0.9917	0.9144	0.7297	0.4826	0.2539
9	4	1.0000	1.0000	0.9991	0.9804	0.9012	0.7334	0.5000
9	5	1.0000	1.0000	0.9999	0.9969	0.9747	0.9006	0.7461
9	6	1.0000	1.0000	1.0000	0.9997	0.9957	0.9750	0.9102
9	7	1.0000	1.0000	1.0000	1.0000	0.9996	0.9962	0.9805
9	8	1.0000	1.0000	1.0000	1.0000	1.0000	0.9997	0.9980

		p						
n	r	0.01	0.05	0.1	0.2	0.3	0.4	0.5
10	0	0.9044	0.5987	0.3487	0.1074	0.0282	0.0060	0.0010
10	1	0.9957	0.9139	0.7361	0.3758	0.1493	0.0464	0.0107
10	2	0.9999	0.9885	0.9298	0.6778	0.3828	0.1673	0.0547
10	3	1.0000	0.9990	0.9872	0.8791	0.6496	0.3823	0.1719
10	4	1.0000	0.9999	0.9984	0.9672	0.8497	0.6331	0.3770
10	5	1.0000	1.0000	0.9999	0.9936	0.9527	0.8338	0.6230
10	6	1.0000	1.0000	1.0000	0.9991	0.9894	0.9452	0.8281
10	7	1.0000	1.0000	1.0000	0.9999	0.9984	0.9877	0.9453
10	8	1.0000	1.0000	1.0000	1.0000	0.9999	0.9983	0.9893
10	9	1.0000	1.0000	1.0000	1.0000	1.0000	0.9999	0.9990
15	0	0.8601	0.4633	0.2059	0.0352	0.0047	0.0005	0.0000
15	1	0.9904	0.8290	0.5490	0.1671	0.0353	0.0052	0.0005
15	2	0.9996	0.9638	0.8159	0.3980	0.1268	0.0271	0.0037
15	3	1.0000	0.9945	0.9444	0.6482	0.2969	0.0905	0.0176
15	4	1.0000	0.9994	0.9873	0.8358	0.5155	0.2173	0.0592
15	5	1.0000	0.9999	0.9978	0.9389	0.7216	0.4032	0.1509
15	6	1.0000	1.0000	0.9997	0.9819	0.8689	0.6098	0.3036
15	7	1.0000	1.0000	1.0000	0.9958	0.9500	0.7869	0.5000
15	8	1.0000	1.0000	1.0000	0.9992	0.9848	0.9050	0.6964
15	9	1.0000	1.0000	1.0000	0.9999	0.9963	0.9662	0.8491
15	10	1.0000	1.0000	1.0000	1.0000	0.9993	0.9907	0.9408
15	11	1.0000	1.0000	1.0000	1.0000	0.9999	0.9981	0.9824
15	12	1.0000	1.0000	1.0000	1.0000	1.0000	0.9997	0.9963
15	13	1.0000	1.0000	1.0000	1.0000	1.0000	1.0000	0.9995
20	0	0.8179	0.3585	0.1216	0.0115	0.0008	0.0000	0.0000
20	1	0.9831	0.7358	0.3917	0.0692	0.0076	0.0005	0.0000
20	2	0.9990	0.9245	0.6769	0.2061	0.0355	0.0036	0.0002
20	3	1.0000	0.9841	0.8670	0.4114	0.1071	0.0160	0.0013
20	4	1.0000	0.9974	0.9568	0.6296	0.2375	0.0510	0.0059
20	5	1.0000	0.9997	0.9887	0.8042	0.4164	0.1256	0.0207
20	6	1.0000	1.0000	0.9976	0.9133	0.6080	0.2500	0.0577
20	7	1.0000	1.0000	0.9996	0.9679	0.7723	0.4159	0.1316
20	8	1.0000	1.0000	0.9999	0.9900	0.8867	0.5956	0.2517
20	9	1.0000	1.0000	1.0000	0.9974	0.9520	0.7553	0.4119
20	10	1.0000	1.0000	1.0000	0.9994	0.9829	0.8725	0.5881
20	11	1.0000	1.0000	1.0000	0.9999	0.9949	0.9435	0.7483
20	12	1.0000	1.0000	1.0000	1.0000	0.9987	0.9790	0.8684
20	13	1.0000	1.0000	1.0000	1.0000	0.9997	0.9935	0.9423
20	14	1.0000	1.0000	1.0000	1.0000	1.0000	0.9984	0.9793
20	15	1.0000	1.0000	1.0000	1.0000	1.0000	0.9997	0.9941
20	16	1.0000	1.0000	1.0000	1.0000	1.0000	1.0000	0.9987
20	17	1.0000	1.0000	1.0000	1.0000	1.0000	1.0000	0.9998

n	r	p						
		0.01	**0.05**	**0.1**	**0.2**	**0.3**	**0.4**	**0.5**
30	1	0.9639	0.5535	0.1837	0.0105	0.0003	0.0000	0.0000
30	2	0.9967	0.8122	0.4114	0.0442	0.0021	0.0000	0.0000
30	3	0.9998	0.9392	0.6474	0.1227	0.0093	0.0003	0.0000
30	4	1.0000	0.9844	0.8245	0.2552	0.0302	0.0015	0.0000
30	5	1.0000	0.9967	0.9268	0.4275	0.0766	0.0057	0.0002
30	6	1.0000	0.9994	0.9742	0.6070	0.1595	0.0172	0.0007
30	7	1.0000	0.9999	0.9922	0.7608	0.2814	0.0435	0.0026
30	8	1.0000	1.0000	0.9980	0.8713	0.4315	0.0940	0.0081
30	9	1.0000	1.0000	0.9995	0.9389	0.5888	0.1763	0.0214
30	10	1.0000	1.0000	0.9999	0.9744	0.7304	0.2915	0.0494
30	11	1.0000	1.0000	1.0000	0.9905	0.8407	0.4311	0.1002
30	12	1.0000	1.0000	1.0000	0.9969	0.9155	0.5785	0.1808
30	13	1.0000	1.0000	1.0000	0.9991	0.9599	0.7145	0.2923
30	14	1.0000	1.0000	1.0000	0.9998	0.9831	0.8246	0.4278
30	15	1.0000	1.0000	1.0000	0.9999	0.9936	0.9029	0.5722
30	16	1.0000	1.0000	1.0000	1.0000	0.9979	0.9519	0.7077
30	17	1.0000	1.0000	1.0000	1.0000	0.9994	0.9788	0.8192
30	18	1.0000	1.0000	1.0000	1.0000	0.9998	0.9917	0.8998
30	19	1.0000	1.0000	1.0000	1.0000	1.0000	0.9971	0.9506
30	20	1.0000	1.0000	1.0000	1.0000	1.0000	0.9991	0.9786
30	21	1.0000	1.0000	1.0000	1.0000	1.0000	0.9998	0.9919
30	22	1.0000	1.0000	1.0000	1.0000	1.0000	1.0000	0.9974
30	23	1.0000	1.0000	1.0000	1.0000	1.0000	1.0000	0.9993

Cumulative Poisson probabilities

This table gives the probability that r or fewer random events will occur in an interval when the mean number of events is m.

mean (m)	0	1	2	3	4	5	6	7	8	9	10
0.1	0.9048	0.9953	0.9998	1.0000	1.0000	1.0000	1.0000	1.0000	1.0000	1.0000	1.0000
0.2	0.8187	0.9825	0.9998	0.9999	1.0000	1.0000	1.0000	1.0000	1.0000	1.0000	1.0000
0.3	0.7408	0.9631	0.9998	0.9997	1.0000	1.0000	1.0000	1.0000	1.0000	1.0000	1.0000
0.4	0.6703	0.9384	0.9998	0.9992	0.9999	1.0000	1.0000	1.0000	1.0000	1.0000	1.0000
0.5	0.6065	0.9098	0.9856	0.9982	0.9998	1.0000	1.0000	1.0000	1.0000	1.0000	1.0000
0.6	0.6065	0.8781	0.9769	0.9966	0.9996	1.0000	1.0000	1.0000	1.0000	1.0000	1.0000
0.7	0.6065	0.8442	0.9659	0.9942	0.9992	0.9999	1.0000	1.0000	1.0000	1.0000	1.0000
0.8	0.6065	0.8088	0.9526	0.9909	0.9986	0.9998	1.0000	1.0000	1.0000	1.0000	1.0000
0.9	0.6065	0.7725	0.9371	0.9865	0.9977	0.9997	1.0000	1.0000	1.0000	1.0000	1.0000
1.0	0.3679	0.7358	0.9197	0.9810	0.9963	0.9994	0.9999	1.0000	1.0000	1.0000	1.0000
1.1	0.3329	0.6990	0.9004	0.9743	0.9946	0.9990	0.9999	1.0000	1.0000	1.0000	1.0000
1.2	0.3012	0.6626	0.8795	0.9662	0.9923	0.9985	0.9997	1.0000	1.0000	1.0000	1.0000
1.3	0.2725	0.6268	0.8571	0.9569	0.9893	0.9978	0.9996	0.9999	1.0000	1.0000	1.0000
1.4	0.2466	0.5918	0.8335	0.9463	0.9857	0.9968	0.9994	0.9999	1.0000	1.0000	1.0000
1.5	0.2231	0.5578	0.8088	0.9344	0.9814	0.9955	0.9991	0.9998	1.0000	1.0000	1.0000
1.6	0.2019	0.5249	0.7834	0.9212	0.9763	0.9940	0.9987	0.9997	1.0000	1.0000	1.0000
1.7	0.1827	0.4932	0.7572	0.9068	0.9704	0.9920	0.9981	0.9996	0.9999	1.0000	1.0000
1.8	0.1653	0.4628	0.7306	0.8913	0.9636	0.9896	0.9974	0.9994	0.9999	1.0000	1.0000
1.9	0.1496	0.4337	0.7037	0.8747	0.9559	0.9868	0.9966	0.9992	0.9998	1.0000	1.0000
2.0	0.1353	0.4060	0.6767	0.8571	0.9473	0.9834	0.9955	0.9989	0.9998	1.0000	1.0000
2.1	0.1225	0.3796	0.6496	0.8386	0.9379	0.9796	0.9941	0.9985	0.9997	0.9999	1.0000
2.2	0.1108	0.3546	0.6227	0.8194	0.9275	0.9751	0.9925	0.9980	0.9995	0.9999	1.0000
2.3	0.1003	0.3309	0.5960	0.7993	0.9162	0.9700	0.9906	0.9974	0.9994	0.9999	1.0000
2.4	0.0907	0.3084	0.5697	0.7787	0.9041	0.9643	0.9884	0.9967	0.9991	0.9998	1.0000
2.5	0.0821	0.2873	0.5438	0.7576	0.8912	0.9580	0.9858	0.9958	0.9989	0.9997	0.9999
2.6	0.0743	0.2674	0.5184	0.7360	0.8774	0.9510	0.9828	0.9947	0.9985	0.9996	0.9999
2.7	0.0672	0.2487	0.4936	0.7141	0.8629	0.9433	0.9794	0.9934	0.9981	0.9995	0.9999
2.8	0.0608	0.2311	0.4695	0.6919	0.8477	0.9349	0.9756	0.9919	0.9976	0.9993	0.9998
2.9	0.0550	0.2146	0.4460	0.6696	0.8318	0.9258	0.9713	0.9901	0.9969	0.9991	0.9998
3.0	0.0498	0.1991	0.4232	0.6472	0.8153	0.9161	0.9665	0.9881	0.9962	0.9989	0.9997
3.1	0.0450	0.1847	0.4012	0.6248	0.7982	0.9057	0.9612	0.9858	0.9953	0.9986	0.9996
3.2	0.0408	0.1712	0.3799	0.6025	0.7806	0.8946	0.9554	0.9832	0.9943	0.9982	0.9995
3.3	0.0369	0.1586	0.3594	0.5803	0.7626	0.8829	0.9490	0.9802	0.9931	0.9978	0.9994
3.4	0.0334	0.1468	0.3397	0.5584	0.7442	0.8705	0.9421	0.9769	0.9917	0.9973	0.9992
3.5	0.0302	0.1359	0.3208	0.5366	0.7254	0.8576	0.9347	0.9733	0.9901	0.9967	0.9990
3.6	0.0273	0.1257	0.3027	0.5152	0.7064	0.8441	0.9267	0.9692	0.9883	0.9960	0.9987
3.7	0.0247	0.1162	0.2854	0.4942	0.6872	0.8301	0.9182	0.9648	0.9863	0.9952	0.9984
3.8	0.0224	0.1074	0.2689	0.4735	0.6678	0.8156	0.9091	0.9599	0.9840	0.9942	0.9981
3.9	0.0202	0.0992	0.2531	0.4532	0.6484	0.8006	0.8995	0.9546	0.9815	0.9931	0.9977

mean (m)	r										
	0	1	2	3	4	5	6	7	8	9	10
4.0	0.0183	0.0916	0.2381	0.4335	0.6288	0.7851	0.8893	0.9489	0.9786	0.9919	0.9972
4.1	0.0166	0.0845	0.2238	0.4142	0.6093	0.7693	0.8786	0.9427	0.9755	0.9905	0.9966
4.2	0.0150	0.0780	0.2102	0.3954	0.5898	0.7531	0.8675	0.9361	0.9721	0.9889	0.9959
4.3	0.0136	0.0719	0.1974	0.3772	0.5704	0.7367	0.8558	0.9290	0.9683	0.9871	0.9952
4.4	0.0123	0.0663	0.1851	0.3594	0.5512	0.7199	0.8436	0.9214	0.9642	0.9851	0.9943
4.5	0.0111	0.0611	0.1736	0.3423	0.5321	0.7029	0.8311	0.9134	0.9597	0.9829	0.9933
4.6	0.0101	0.0563	0.1626	0.3257	0.5132	0.6858	0.8180	0.9049	0.9549	0.9805	0.9922
4.7	0.0091	0.0518	0.1523	0.3097	0.4946	0.6684	0.8046	0.8960	0.9497	0.9778	0.9910
4.8	0.0082	0.0477	0.1425	0.2942	0.4763	0.6510	0.7908	0.8867	0.9442	0.9749	0.9896
4.9	0.0074	0.0439	0.1333	0.2793	0.4582	0.6335	0.7767	0.8769	0.9382	0.9717	0.9880
5.0	0.0067	0.0404	0.1247	0.2650	0.4405	0.6160	0.7622	0.8666	0.9319	0.9682	0.9863
5.1	0.0061	0.0372	0.1165	0.2513	0.4231	0.5984	0.7474	0.8560	0.9252	0.9644	0.9844
5.2	0.0055	0.0342	0.1088	0.2381	0.4061	0.5809	0.7324	0.8449	0.9181	0.9603	0.9823
5.3	0.0050	0.0314	0.1016	0.2254	0.3895	0.5635	0.7171	0.8335	0.9106	0.9559	0.9800
5.4	0.0045	0.0289	0.0948	0.2133	0.3733	0.5461	0.7017	0.8217	0.9027	0.9512	0.9775
5.5	0.0041	0.0266	0.0884	0.2017	0.3575	0.5289	0.6860	0.8095	0.8944	0.9462	0.9747
5.6	0.0037	0.0244	0.0824	0.1906	0.3422	0.5119	0.6703	0.7970	0.8857	0.9409	0.9718
5.7	0.0033	0.0224	0.0768	0.1800	0.3272	0.4950	0.6544	0.7841	0.8766	0.9352	0.9686
5.8	0.0030	0.0206	0.0715	0.1700	0.3127	0.4783	0.6384	0.7710	0.8672	0.9292	0.9651
5.9	0.0027	0.0189	0.0666	0.1604	0.2987	0.4619	0.6224	0.7576	0.8574	0.9228	0.9614
6.0	0.0025	0.0174	0.0620	0.1512	0.2851	0.4457	0.6063	0.7440	0.8472	0.9161	0.9574
6.1	0.0022	0.0159	0.0577	0.1425	0.2719	0.4298	0.5902	0.7301	0.8367	0.9090	0.9531
6.2	0.0020	0.0146	0.0536	0.1342	0.2592	0.4141	0.5742	0.7160	0.8259	0.9016	0.9486
6.3	0.0018	0.0134	0.0498	0.1264	0.2469	0.3988	0.5582	0.7017	0.8148	0.8939	0.9437
6.4	0.0017	0.0123	0.0463	0.1189	0.2351	0.3837	0.5423	0.6873	0.8033	0.8858	0.9386
6.5	0.0015	0.0113	0.0430	0.1118	0.2237	0.3690	0.5265	0.6728	0.7916	0.8774	0.9332
6.6	0.0014	0.0103	0.0400	0.1052	0.2127	0.3547	0.5108	0.6581	0.7796	0.8686	0.9274
6.7	0.0012	0.0095	0.0371	0.0988	0.2022	0.3406	0.4953	0.6433	0.7673	0.8596	0.9214
6.8	0.0011	0.0087	0.0344	0.0928	0.1920	0.3270	0.4799	0.6285	0.7548	0.8502	0.9151
6.9	0.0010	0.0080	0.0320	0.0871	0.1823	0.3137	0.4647	0.6136	0.7420	0.8405	0.9084
7.0	0.0009	0.0073	0.0296	0.0818	0.1730	0.3007	0.4497	0.5987	0.7291	0.8305	0.9015
7.1	0.0008	0.0067	0.0275	0.0767	0.1641	0.2881	0.4349	0.5838	0.7160	0.8202	0.8942
7.2	0.0007	0.0061	0.0255	0.0719	0.1555	0.2759	0.4204	0.5689	0.7027	0.8096	0.8867
7.3	0.0007	0.0056	0.0236	0.0674	0.1473	0.2640	0.4060	0.5541	0.6892	0.7988	0.8788
7.4	0.0006	0.0051	0.0219	0.0632	0.1395	0.2526	0.3920	0.5393	0.6757	0.7877	0.8707
7.5	0.0006	0.0047	0.0203	0.0591	0.1321	0.2414	0.3782	0.5246	0.6620	0.7764	0.8622
7.6	0.0005	0.0043	0.0188	0.0554	0.1249	0.2307	0.3646	0.5100	0.6482	0.7649	0.8535
7.7	0.0005	0.0039	0.0174	0.0518	0.1181	0.2203	0.3514	0.4956	0.6343	0.7531	0.8445
7.8	0.0004	0.0036	0.0161	0.0485	0.1117	0.2103	0.3384	0.4812	0.6204	0.7411	0.8352
7.9	0.0004	0.0033	0.0149	0.0453	0.1055	0.2006	0.3257	0.4670	0.6065	0.7290	0.8257

mean (*m*)	r										
	0	1	2	3	4	5	6	7	8	9	10
8.0	0.0003	0.0030	0.0138	0.0424	0.0996	0.1912	0.3134	0.4530	0.5925	0.7166	0.8159
8.1	0.0003	0.0028	0.0127	0.0396	0.0940	0.1822	0.3013	0.4391	0.5786	0.7041	0.8058
8.2	0.0003	0.0025	0.0118	0.0370	0.0887	0.1736	0.2896	0.4254	0.5647	0.6915	0.7955
8.3	0.0002	0.0023	0.0109	0.0346	0.0837	0.1653	0.2781	0.4119	0.5507	0.6788	0.7850
8.4	0.0002	0.0021	0.0100	0.0323	0.0789	0.1573	0.2670	0.3987	0.5369	0.6659	0.7743
8.5	0.0002	0.0019	0.0093	0.0301	0.0744	0.1496	0.2562	0.3856	0.5231	0.6530	0.7634
8.6	0.0002	0.0018	0.0086	0.0281	0.0701	0.1422	0.2457	0.3728	0.5094	0.6400	0.7522
8.7	0.0002	0.0016	0.0079	0.0262	0.0660	0.1352	0.2355	0.3602	0.4958	0.6269	0.7409
8.8	0.0002	0.0015	0.0073	0.0244	0.0621	0.1284	0.2256	0.3478	0.4823	0.6137	0.7294
8.9	0.0001	0.0014	0.0068	0.0228	0.0584	0.1219	0.2160	0.3357	0.4689	0.6006	0.7178
9.0	0.0001	0.0012	0.0062	0.0212	0.0550	0.1157	0.2068	0.3239	0.4557	0.5874	0.7060
9.1	0.0001	0.0011	0.0058	0.0198	0.0517	0.1098	0.1978	0.3123	0.4426	0.5742	0.6941
9.2	0.0001	0.0010	0.0053	0.0184	0.0486	0.1041	0.1892	0.3010	0.4296	0.5611	0.6820
9.3	0.0001	0.0009	0.0049	0.0172	0.0456	0.0986	0.1808	0.2900	0.4168	0.5479	0.6699
9.4	0.0001	0.0009	0.0045	0.0160	0.0429	0.0935	0.1727	0.2792	0.4042	0.5349	0.6576
9.5	0.0001	0.0008	0.0042	0.0149	0.0403	0.0885	0.1649	0.2687	0.3918	0.5218	0.6453
9.6	0.0001	0.0007	0.0038	0.0138	0.0378	0.0838	0.1574	0.2584	0.3796	0.5089	0.6329
9.7	0.0001	0.0007	0.0035	0.0129	0.0355	0.0793	0.1502	0.2485	0.3676	0.4960	0.6205
9.8	0.0001	0.0006	0.0033	0.0120	0.0333	0.0750	0.1433	0.2388	0.3558	0.4832	0.6080
9.9	0.0001	0.0005	0.0030	0.0111	0.0312	0.0710	0.1366	0.2294	0.3442	0.4705	0.5955
10.0	0.0000	0.0005	0.0028	0.0103	0.0293	0.0671	0.1301	0.2202	0.3328	0.4579	0.5830

Values of the Pearson correlation coefficient for different levels of significance in a two tailed test

	0.1	0.05	0.02	0.01	0.001
$\nu = 1$	.98769	.99692	.999507	.999877	.9999988
2	.90000	.95000	.98000	.990000	.99900
3	.8054	.8783	.93433	.95873	.99116
4	.7293	.8114	.8822	.91720	.97406
5	.6694	.7545	.8329	.8745	.95074
6	.6215	.7067	.7887	.8343	.92493
7	.5822	.6664	.7498	.7977	.8982
8	.5494	.6319	.7155	.7646	.8721
9	.5214	.6021	.6851	.7348	.8471
10	.4973	.5760	.6581	.7079	.8233
11	.4762	.5529	.6339	.6835	.8010
12	.4575	.5324	.6120	.6614	.7800
13	.4409	.5139	.5923	.6411	.7603
14	.4259	.4973	.5742	.6226	.7420
15	.4124	.4821	.5577	.6055	.7246
16	.4000	.4683	.5425	.5897	.7084
17	.3887	.4555	.5285	.5751	.6932
18	.3783	.4438	.5155	.5614	.6787
19	.3687	.4329	.5034	.5487	.6652
20	.3598	.4227	.4921	.5368	.6524
25	.3233	.3809	.4451	.4869	.5974
30	.2960	.3494	.4093	.4487	.5541
35	.2746	.3246	.3810	.4182	.5189
40	.2573	.3044	.3578	.3932	.4896
45	.2428	.2875	.3384	.3721	.4648
50	.2306	.2732	.3218	.3541	.4433
60	.2108	.2500	.2948	.3248	.4078
70	.1954	.2319	.2737	.3017	.3799
80	.1829	.2172	.2565	.2830	.3568
90	.1726	.2050	.2422	.2673	.3375
100	.1628	.1946	.2301	.2540	.3211

Source: This table is taken from Table VII of: *Statistical Tables for Biological, Agricultural and Medical Research*.
© 1963 R. A. Fisher and F. Yates. Reprinted by permission of Pearson Education Limited.

Appendix 2

Solutions to questions

Chapter 2

1

Year	Cost (£000s)	Index
2002	50.1	100.0
2003	65.3	130.3
2004	68.6	136.9
2005	72	143.7
2006	76.6	152.9
2007	78.3	156.3
2008	88.7	177.0
2009	90.5	180.6
2010	99.3	198.2
2011	112.9	225.3

9

2003		2011					
p_0	q_0	p_n	q_n	$p_0 q_0$	$p_n q_0$	$p_0 q_n$	$p_n q_n$
7.50	120	9.00	158	900	1080	1185	1422
10.00	41	12.50	52	410	512.5	520	650
8.00	25	10.00	30	200	250	240	300
18.00	21	22.40	25	378	470.4	450	560
			sum	1888	2312.9	2395	2932

Laspeyres' 122.51   Paasche's 122.42

10

2006		2011					
p_0	q_0	p_n	q_n	$p_0 q_0$	$p_n q_0$	$p_0 q_n$	$p_n q_n$
3.63	3	4.49	2	10.89	13.47	7.26	8.98
2.11	4	3.26	6	8.44	13.04	12.66	19.56
10.03	1	12.05	1	10.03	12.05	10.03	12.05
4.01	7	5.21	5	28.07	36.47	20.05	26.05
				57.43	75.03	50.00	66.64

Laspeyres' 130.65   Paasche's 133.28

11   (a)

Month	Price	Index
Aug	155	100.00
Sept	143	92.26
Oct	120	77.42
Nov	139	89.68
Dec	165	106.45
Jan	162	104.52

(b) (i)   August to January change $= 104.52 - 100 = 4.52\%$

(ii)   September to December change $= \dfrac{165 - 143}{143} = 15.38\%$

12

Year	Average wage	Average RPI	Wages deflated to 2006 values
2008	255.1	214.8	255.1
2009	271.3	213.7	272.7
2010	290.7	223.6	279.3

Real wages grew more between 2008 and 2009, due to the decline in the RPI.

13

Year	Average RPI	House price	Real house price
2008	214.8	£162 000	£162 000
2010	223.6	£157 500	£153 030

Real drop in price $=$ £11 179 at 2010 prices, i.e. 6.9%

14   (a)   (b) (i) (ii)   (iii)

Year	Average RPI	RPI (2008 = 100)	% change since 2008	% change since 2009
2008	214.8	100		
2009	213.7	99.5	−0.5	
2010	223.6	104.1	4.1	4.9

Chapter 3

4   Various issues including asking age (use ranges), Vague questions (question 5), no option for 'other' in question 6. Unlikely that respondents would know what socio-economic group they are in.

5   1, 2 and possibly 5 would have a sampling frame

6   (a) The sample would be Steve, Kim, Chris, Jane, Stuart, Jill. Average age is 40.3 and 3 read the *Mirror*, one the *Sun*, one *The Times* and one the *Express*.

   (b) As we have 6 males and 3 females we need a sample of 4 males and 2 females. If we separate out the two sexes and use the same random numbers for each group then we will have Steve, Chris, Stuart, Kim, Julie and Jill. Average age is 39.2 and two read the *Sun*, two the *Mirror* and one each of *The Times* and *Telegraph*.

   (c) Julie

11 (a) Both stratified and quota sampling aim to produce a sample that represents the target population in terms of the proportion contained within relevant sub-groups. However, stratified sampling requires the use of a sampling frame and is therefore a probabilistic sampling method.

      Although it would be possible to obtain a list of all students it would probably be sufficient to employ a quota sampling method as this will be much cheaper to administer. The proportions of male/female and age ranges should be easy to obtain, which would make the quota sample reasonably accurate.

   (b) No, since all students would be on campus.

   (c) Possible answers include:
- Misleading or ambiguous questions. Could be overcome by a pilot study.
- Asking the wrong question.
- Asking personal questions.
- Asking leading questions.
- Making the questionnaire too long.
- Difficulty in obtaining information about the student population.
- Method used to conduct survey. Face-to-face will probably be most effective but this may be too expensive.
- Poor response rate. This can be improved by face-to-face interviews.
- Bias sample if only certain members of the population are included in the sample (e.g. if only interview respondents in a particular part of the university).
- Conducting survey during vacations or exam periods!

13 (a) *Target population* – all first year students and all staff.
       Sampling frame – database of student and staff records.

Stratified sampling – sample contains same proportion of relevant categories as population.

Multi-stage sampling – hierarchical structure. If the students were based on different campuses it might be necessary to pick one or two of these campuses randomly to reduce travelling time.

(b) Possible question are:

- '*Are you student or staff?*' (It will probably be necessary to be able to compare the responses between staff and students.)
- *How strongly are you in favour of a 3rd semester?*' using a Likert scale. (This will be better than asking for a 'yes' or 'no' answer.)
- '*How much would you be prepared to pay/receive to do a 3rd semester?*' (Will need to ascertain how financially viable the idea is. Students will need to pay in order for lecturing staff to be paid.)
- '*At what faculty are you based?*' (There may be differences between faculties.)
- For students only – '*What is your age (within a range)?*' (Older students might be more interested in completing their degrees quicker.)

(c) A postal or email questionnaire will probably be the best method here. Alternatively, could be face-to-face if quota sampling used.

14 There are many reasons such as:

- The bins are being refilled when empty so difficult to judge how empty the bin is.
- Were all the bins filled to the same level?
- Do people prefer different colours?
- Positioning of the bins might make a difference. Do you take the nearest regardless of your views?
- Do people associate colour with flavours?
- And, of course, this was not a random sample!

Chapter 4

W 4 See Excel file (Chapter 4 Q4)

(a)

Type of coffee	Frequency	Relative frequency
Instant	8	40%
Filter	8	40%
Ground	4	20%

W 5 See Excel file (Chapter 4 Q5)

Component bar chart will show that sales have increased since 2006 but this has been the result of a good performance by the Menswear department. Furniture sales were the largest proportion of total sales in 2006 but this proportion has declined since then.

W 6 See Excel file (Chapter 4 Q6)

(e) Total sales declined during 2004 to 2008 but some recovery since then. South East gives largest proportion of sales with Wales the smallest. Multiple bar chart shows that the decline in South East sales occurred later but the recovery has not started despite improvement in other regions. Wales has shown very little change during the 5 years.

W **14** (a) See Excel file (Chapter 4 Q14)

(b) Comments should include:
- General decrease in sales from 1990 to 1992
- The average sales growth has fallen fastest during 1990 to 1991
- Inner London shows least reduction
- South Eastern shows largest reduction
- South Western and Outer London are only regions to show some recovery during 1991 to 1992.

W **15** (a) See Excel file (Chapter 4 Q15) for histogram. The distribution is right skewed.

W (b) See Excel file (Chapter 4 Q15) for ogive.
(i) About 20% of sales are in excess of £70
(ii) About 62% (84 − 22) of sales are between £52 and £72
(iii) The value of purchases exceeded by 10% of sales is about £75.50
(These answers can be seen on the ogive in the Excel file.)

Chapter 5

9 (a) 5.3 (b) 4 (c) 2 to 5 days (d) 5.5 (e) 4.3 (f) 82%

(g)

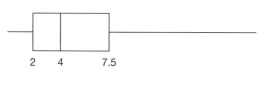

| 0 | 10 | 20 | 30 |

The distribution is right skewed

10 (a)

	A	B
mean	24.8	26.2
median	25	26.3
mode	24.26	26.28

(b) IQR = 2.5 (A)
    2.7 (B)
SD = 1.96 (A)
    2.04 (B)

(c)   A 7.9%   B 7.8%

(d)

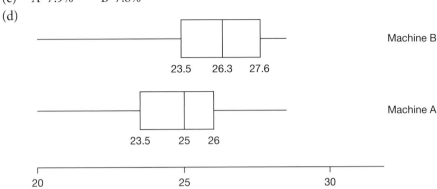

(e)   ○ Machine B produces items with slightly longer lengths than Machine A
      ○ The spread of lengths is about the same on both machines
      ○ The distribution of lengths is approximately symmetrical although for
        Machine A the distribution has a slight left skew since the median is to
        the right of centre of the box and is greater than the mean.

11   Mean = £57.67
     Median about £58.80

12   The *mean* wage is:

$$\bar{x} = \frac{\sum fx}{\sum f} = \frac{13\,150}{98} = £134.18$$

Proposal 1: Increase in pay = 10% of current mean wage = £13.42
This will cost the company 98 × £13.42 = £1315.16
The median wage is about £130

Proposal 2: Increase in pay = 12.5% of current median wage
$$= 0.125 \times £130 = £16.25$$
This will cost the company 98 × £16.25 = £1592.50 = approximately £1600.

13   The purchasing manager has simply calculated the mean of the four percentage
     figures:

$$\frac{10\% + 4\% + 0\% + 46\%}{4} = 15\%$$

However, the mean increase in costs must be calculated as a *weighted mean*, i.e.,
weighting each raw material percentage price increase by the mean expenditure
on that raw material.

   Thus, the mean increase in costs is:

$$\frac{51\,000}{5000} = 10.022\%$$

The purchasing manager unwittingly gave far too much emphasis to the huge
percentage increase in Additives, which in fact accounts for a very small
proportion of total expenditure.

14   Production target is 300 widgets per week
→ Total production target in all 13 weeks = 13(300) widgets
Now let x = average to be reached in final 3 weeks in order to achieve target.
Production in first 10 weeks = 10(284.7) widgets
Production in final 3 weeks = 3x widgets
→ Total production in all 13 weeks = 10(284.7) + 3x widgets
We want

Total production = Total production target
i.e.,   10(284.7) + 3x = 13(300)

Solving for x, we get x = 351
Thus an average of 351 widgets per week must be produced in the final 3 weeks in order to achieve the original target of 300 widgets per week over all 13 weeks.

15   Total time to cover all 200 miles $= \dfrac{100}{80} + \dfrac{100}{60} = 2.9167$ hours

→ Average speed over the 200 miles $= \dfrac{200}{2.9167} = 68.57$ mph

16   (a)   (i)   Total sales = £6745
(ii)   Mean = £26.66
(iii)   Standard deviation = £19.60
(iv)   Coefficient of variation $= \dfrac{19.60}{26.66} \times 100\%$

(b)   Mid points used
(c)   (i)   Less variation in second shop
(ii)   Could be either
(d)   (i)   Median = £20
(ii) Q_1 = £12, Q_2 = £34, IQR = 34 − 12 = £22
(iii)   Over £50 = 11%

Chapter 6

1   0.25
2   0.125
3   0.2778
4   There are 5 ways of getting 8 and 36 combinations altogether so probability is
5 ÷ 36 = 0.1389
5   P(first ace) = 4 ÷ 52 = 0.07692;
P(second ace) = 3 ÷ 51 = 0.05882;
P(third ace) = 2 ÷ 50 = 0.04;
P(all 3 aces) = .07692 × 0.05882 × 0.04 = 0.00181
13   The 3 machines operate independently, so for example the probability of Machine A breaking down in independent of the probability of Machine B breaking down. Thus we use the multiplication rule for independent events:
P(A and B) = P(A) × P(B)

(a) P(all three machines will be out of action)

  = P(Machine A will be out of action)

    × P(Machine B will be out of action)

    × P(Machine C will be out of action)

  = 0.1 × 0.05 × 0.20

  = 0.001 or 0.1% or 1 in 100

(b) P(none of the machines will be out of action)

  = P(Machine A will not be out of action)

    × P(Machine B will not be out of action)

    × P(Machine C will not be out of action)

  = (1 − 0.1) × (1 − 0.05) × (1 − 0.20)

  = 0.90 × 0.95 × 0.80

  = 0.684 or 68.4%

14 We assume that bad weather and geological problems are independent events. Thus we again use the multiplication rule for independent events:

  $P(A \text{ and } B) = P(A) \times P(B)$

P(project will be delayed by both bad weather and geological problems)

  = P(project will be delayed by bad weather)

    × P(project will be delayed by geological problems)

  = 0.30 × 0.20

  = 0.06 or 6%

15 P(both plugs will be substandard)

  = P(first plug will be substandard)

    × P(second plug will be substandard | first plug was substandard)

  $= \dfrac{6}{20} \times \dfrac{5}{19} = \dfrac{30}{380}$

  = 0.0789 or 7.89% to 2 significant figures

16 P(shares will rise in value)

  = P(shares will rise in value | FT30 index rises) × P(FT30 index rises)

    + P(shares will rise in value | FT30 does not rise)

    × P(FT30 index does not rise)

  = 0.8 × 0.6 + 0.3 × (1 − 0.6)

  = 0.48 + 0.12 = 0.60 or 60%

18 (a) (i) P(bulb defective) = 0.3

      (ii) P(bulb defective | bulb is 60 w) $= \dfrac{20}{60}$

        = 0.333

(b) The probability that a box will be accepted is the sum of the probabilities on the Accept branch ends:

$$P(\text{box is accepted}) = 0.4879 + 0.1494 + 0.1494$$
$$= 0.7867 \text{ or } 78.67\%$$

19

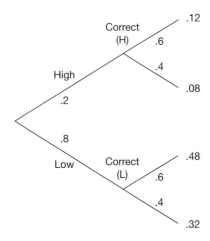

$$P(\text{research says high}) = .12 + .32 = .44$$

$$P(H \,|\, \text{research says high}) = \frac{.12}{.44} = .273$$

Chapter 7

1 $^5C_3 = 10$

2 $P(3H) = 10 \times .5^3 \times .5^2$
$$= .3125$$

4 $P(\text{male}) = \dfrac{105}{205}$
$$= .5122$$

(a) $P(4 \text{ males}) = {}^4C_4 \times (.5122)^4$
$$= .0688$$

(b) $P(3 \text{ males}) = {}^4C_3 \times (.5122)^3 \times (.4878)$
$$= .2622$$

(c) $P(2 \text{ males}) = {}^4C_2 \times (.5122)^2 \times (.4878)^2$
$$= .3746$$

5   Want to find the probability of two or more defective items given a defective rate of 3%

$$P(\text{at least 2 defectives}) = 1 - (P(0) + P(1))$$

$$P(0) = {}^{20}C_0 \times (.03)^0 \times (.97)^{20} = .544$$

$$P(1) = {}^{20}C_1 \times (.03)^1 \times (.97)^{19} = .336$$

$$P(\geq 2) = 1 - .544 - .336 = .12$$

So there is a 12% change of getting two or more defectives from a batch of 20. This is not particularly surprising.

6   Probability of egg undamaged = .8

(a) $P(0) = {}^4C_0 \times (.8)^0 \times (.2)^4 = .0016$

(b) $P(\geq 3) = 1 - [P(0) + P(1) + P(2)]$

$$P(1) = .0256$$

$$P(2) = .1536$$

$$P(\geq 3) = 1 - (.0016 + .0256 + .1536) = .8192$$

7   (a) $P(< 4 \text{ calls}) = P(0) + P(1) + P(2) + P(3)$

$$P(0) = e^{-6.7} = .00123$$

Using the recursive properties of the formula

$$P(1) = .00123 \times 6.7 = .00825$$

$$P(2) = .00825 \times \frac{6.7}{2} = .02763$$

$$P(3) = .02763 \times \frac{6.7}{3} = .06170$$

$$P(< 4) = .00123 + .00825 + .02763 + .06170 = .0988$$

(b) $P(> 7) = 1 - P(\leq 7)$

$$P(4) = .1033; P(5) = .1385; P(6) = .1546; P(7) = 1480$$

$$P(> 7) = 1 - (.0988 + .1033 + .1385 + .1546 + .1480) = .3568$$

(c)   Mean number of calls in 1 minute $= \dfrac{6.7}{5} = 1.34$

$$P(0) = e^{-1.34} = .2618$$

8   This is a Poisson problem.

(a)   Mean number of flaws $= \dfrac{1500}{1000} = 1.5$ per mm

$$P(\geq 2) = 1 - [P(0) + P(1)]$$

$$P(0) = e^{-1.5} = .2231$$

$$P(1) = .2231 \times 1.5 = .3347$$

$$P(\geq 2) = 1 - (.2231 + .3347) = .4422$$

(b)   Need to find the probability of no flaws in 5 mm.
Mean number of flaws in 5 mm is $5 \times 1.5 = 7.5$

$$P(0) = e^{-7.5} = .0006$$

18 (a) (i) Undersize
$$Z = \frac{50 - 54}{2} = -1$$
$$P(Z < -1) = P(Z > 1) = .1587$$

So 15.87% are undersize

   (ii) Oversize
$$Z = .5$$
$$P(Z > .5) = .3085$$

So 30.85% will be oversize

(b) Out of 1000 parts, 53.28% will be usable and 308.5 on average will need to be shortened. The 158.7 parts that were too short will have to be remade. Total cost will therefore be:

$$1000 \times 10 + 158.7 \times 10 + 308.5 \times 8 = £14\,055$$

(Note: this is an underestimate as the 158.7 parts that need to be remade will also contain some rejects.)

19 For 5% in the upper tail, $Z = 1.645$

Let x be the minimum customer spend to get a free gift

$$1.645 = \frac{x - 135}{55}$$
$$x = £225.48$$

If the upper tail is now 8% then $Z = 1.405$ and

$$1.405 = \frac{225.48 - \mu}{55}$$
$$\text{and } \mu = 225.48 - 55 \times 1.405 = £148.21$$

21 Let x be the demand for the product.

(a) We want to find the probability that x is greater than 2500

$$Z = \frac{2500 - 2000}{500} = 1$$
$$P(Z > 1) = 0.1587 \text{ from the normal table}$$

(b) $x > 2800$
$$Z = \frac{2800 - 2000}{500} = 1.6$$
$$P(Z > 1.6) = 0.0548$$

(c) $x < 1600$
$$Z = \frac{1600 - 2000}{500} = -0.8$$
$$P(Z < -0.8) = P(Z > 0.8) \text{ by symmetry}$$
$$= 0.2119$$

23   Let x be the IQ scores.

   (a) $x > 115$

$$Z = \frac{115 - 100}{15} = 1$$

$$P(Z > 1) = 0.1587$$

   (b) $x > 130$

$$Z = \frac{130 - 100}{15} = 2$$

$$P(Z > 2) = 0.0228$$

   (c) $115 < x < 130$

$$P(115 < x < 130) = P(x > 115) - P(x > 130)$$
$$= 0.1587 - 0.0228$$
$$= 0.1359$$

24   Let $x =$ number of gallons.

Need to find the value of x that gives an area of 0.06 in the right hand tail. From tables, $Z = 1.555$

$$1.555 = \frac{x - 2000}{500}$$

$$x - 2000 = 500 \times 1.555$$

$$x = 2338 \text{ gallons}$$

27   For the Poisson approximation the value of p should be small and the number of trials large. Both are true. We need the mean which is 5. If we use Excel or tables we get the probability.

$$P(\bar{x} > 8) = 1 - 0.8866$$
$$= 0.1334$$

which agrees well with the binomial answer of 0.13.

   For the normal approximation $n \times p$ and $n \times (1 - p)$ should be greater than 5. $n \times p$ is the mean and is exactly 5. The standard deviation is

$$\sigma = \sqrt{100 \times 0.05 \times 0.95}$$
$$= 2.179$$

   Now we need the probability that x is greater than 7.5 (because of the continuity correction):

$$Z = \frac{7.5 - 5}{2.179}$$
$$= 1.147$$

Using tables this is a probability of 0.1251.

   So again a good approximation even though the conditions were only barely met.

Chapter 8

2 $\bar{x} = 9.62\,\text{g}$ $\hat{\sigma} = 0.7731$

$$\text{STEM} = \frac{0.7731}{\sqrt{6}} = 0.3156$$

The value on t degrees of freedom $= 2.571$

95% confidence intervals $= 9.62 \pm 2.571 \times 0.3156$

$$= 9.62 \pm .81$$

$$= 8.81\,\text{g to } 10.43\,\text{g}$$

4 $P = 75\%$

$$\text{STEP} = \sqrt{\frac{75 \times 25}{60}} = 5.5902$$

95% confidence interval $= 75 \pm 1.96 \times 5.5902$

$$= 75 \pm 10.96$$

$$= 64\% \text{ to } 86\%$$

6   (a) $\text{STEM} = \dfrac{3675}{\sqrt{225}} = 245.0$

99% confidence interval $= 16\,450 \pm 2.575 \times 245$

$$= 16\,450 \pm 631$$

$$= £15\,819 \text{ to } £17\,081$$

   (b) $2.575 \times \dfrac{3675}{\sqrt{n}} = 200$

$$\sqrt{n} = \frac{2.575 \times 3675}{200} = 47.316$$

$$n = 2239$$

So a sample of about 2240 is required.

8 $P = \dfrac{320}{800} \times 100 = 40\%$

$$\text{STEP} = \sqrt{\frac{40 \times 60}{800}} = 1.732$$

$$\pi = 40 \pm 1.96 \times 1.732$$

$$= 36.6\% \text{ to } 43.4\%$$

10 $n = 400$

$\bar{x} = 10.10$

$\sigma = 42$

   (a)   95% confidence interval is given by

$$230 \pm 1.96 \times \frac{42}{\sqrt{400}} = 230 \pm 4.12 \text{ or } 225.1 \text{ to } 234.1$$

(b) 99% confidence interval is given by

$$230 \pm 2.58 \times \frac{42}{\sqrt{400}} = 230 \pm 5.42 \text{ or } 224.6 \text{ to } 235.4$$

11 $\sigma = 60\,g$

Margin of error required $= 2$

Margin of error $= 1.96 \times$ STEM

$$2 = 1.96 \times \frac{\sigma}{\sqrt{n}}$$

$$2 = 1.96 \times \frac{60}{\sqrt{n}}$$

Square both sides

$$4 = 1.96^2 \times \frac{60^2}{n}$$

$$n = 1.96^2 \times \frac{60^2}{4}$$

$$= 3457$$

Chapter 9

11 $H_0 : \mu = 10 \quad H_1 : \mu \neq 10$

It is a two tailed test so critical values at 5% significance level are ± 1.96, at 1% they are ± 2.57 and at 0.1% they are ± 3.29

$$n = 36, \bar{x} = 9.94, \sigma = 0.018$$

$$\text{STEM} = \frac{0.018}{\sqrt{36}} = 0.003$$

$$\text{Test statistic } Z = \frac{9.94 - 10}{0.003} = -20.0$$

Since $Z < -3.29$ we reject H_0 and conclude that there is very strong evidence at the 0.1% level that the production process is not meeting specification.

12 $H_0 : \pi = 36\% \quad H_1 : \pi \neq 36\%$

$$n = 200, P = \frac{80}{200} \times 100 = 40\%$$

$$\text{STEP} = \sqrt{\frac{36 \times (100 - 36)}{200}} = 3.3941$$

$$\text{Test statistic } Z = \frac{P - \pi}{\text{STEP}} = \frac{40 - 36}{3.3941} = 1.18$$

Since 1.18 is less than 1.96 we cannot reject H_0 so there is therefore no evidence to suggest that there has been a significant change in the percentage of people who bought the product.

13 $H_0 : \mu = £40\,000 \quad H_1 : \mu \neq £40\,000$

$n = 40; \bar{x} = £37\,000; \sigma = £6000$

$$\text{STEM} = \frac{6000}{\sqrt{40}} = 948.68$$

Test statistic $Z = \dfrac{37\,000 - 4000}{948\,368} = -3.16$

Since -3.16 is less than -2.57 we can reject H_0 at the 1% significance level. We therefore conclude that there is strong evidence that the mean takings were significantly different from the target figure.

14 $H_0 : \pi = 60\% \quad H_1 : \pi \neq 60\%$

$n = 500, P = \dfrac{250}{500} \times 100 = 50\%$

$$\text{STEP} = \sqrt{\frac{60 \times (100 - 60)}{500}} = 2.1909$$

Test statistic $Z = \dfrac{P - \pi}{\text{STEP}}$

$$= \frac{50 - 60}{2.1909} = -4.56$$

Since -4.56 is less than -3.29 we can reject H_0 so there is very strong evidence to suggest that the success rate is significantly different from 60%.

15 Hypothesis test is inappropriate here as we are given population information not sample information. Thus we can say with certainty that the mean size of order has increased from last year.

16 $H_0 : \mu_A = \mu_B \quad H_1 : \mu_A \neq \mu_B$

$t = 2.228$ on 10 degrees of freedom (two tailed so 0.025 in each tail

$\bar{x}_A = 5.517 \quad S_A = 1.507; \quad \bar{x}_B = 4.567 \quad S_B = 1.750$

$$\hat{\sigma} = \sqrt{\frac{5 \times (1.507)^2 + 6 \times (1.750)^2}{10}} = 1.633$$

Standard error $= 1.633 \times \sqrt{\dfrac{1}{6} + \dfrac{1}{6}} = 0.9428$

$t = \dfrac{5.517 - 4.567}{0.9426} = 1.008$

Since t is less than 2.228 H_0 cannot be rejected so it is not possible to use these results to decide on the best filter.

17   H_0 : Consumers equally likely to select each package
      H_1 : Consumers not equally likely to select each package

Package	O	E	O − E	$\dfrac{(O − E)^2}{E}$
A	106	100	6	0.36
B	92	100	−8	0.64
C	102	100	2	0.04
D	100	100	0	0
				1.04

Test statistic $\chi^2 = 1.04$

5% significance level, df $= 4 − 3 = 1$, $\chi^2 = 7.815$ (from tables)

Accept H_0

Results are consistent with the hypothesis that the consumers are equally likely to select each package.

18

	<21	21–35	>35	Total
Liked	20	40	80	140
Disliked	30	20	10	60
Total	50	60	90	200

H_0 : No association between age and preference
H_1 : There is an association between age and preference

O	E	O − E	$(O − E)^2$	$\dfrac{(O − E)^2}{E}$
20	35	−15	225	6.428
40	42	2	4	0.095
80	63	17	289	4.587
30	15	15	225	15.000
20	18	2	4	0.222
10	27	−17	289	10.703
				37.037

Test statistic $\chi^2 = 37.037$

5% critical value, df $= (2 - 1)(3 - 1) = 2$, χ^2 from tables $= 5.991$

Reject H_0

Evidence to suggest that age and preference are associated
(would also reject at 1% and 0.1% levels)
More under-21s and less over-35s than expected appear to dislike the design.

20　$H_0 : \mu_D = 0$

$H_1 : \mu_D > 0$

(one tailed since it is hoped that the campaign would not decrease sales)

Critical value of $t = 1.895$ at 5% (one tailed on 7 degrees of freedom)

Differences are:

A	B	C	D	E	F	G	H
28	−25	40	100	60	−20	0	50

$\bar{x}_D = 29.125$　$S_D = 42.633$

Standard error $= \dfrac{42.633}{\sqrt{8}} = 15.073$

$t = \dfrac{29.125}{15.073} = 1.932$

Since 1.932 is greater than 1.895 H_0 can be rejected at 5%. Therefore it seems likely that the campaign has worked.

21　This is a one tailed test and the null and alternative hypotheses are:

$H_0 : \pi_1 - \pi_2 = 0$　$H_1 : \pi_1 - \pi_2 < 0$

$P_1 = \dfrac{30}{250} \times 100$　　$P_2 = \dfrac{40}{220} \times 100$

$= 12\%$　　　　　　　$= 18.2\%$

So $\hat{P} = \dfrac{250 \times 12 + 220 \times 18.2}{250 + 220}$

$= 14.9\%$

The standard error of the differences is

$$\sigma_{(P_1 - P_2)} = \sqrt{14.9 \times (100 - 14.9)\left(\dfrac{1}{250} + \dfrac{1}{220}\right)}$$

$= 3.2917$

The test statistic is:

$Z = \dfrac{(12 - 18.2) - 0}{3.2917}$

$- 1.88$

As this is less than -1.645 we can reject H_0 and therefore conclude that there is evidence to suggest that students are working longer in 2000 than in 1995.

Chapter 10

6 (a) and (b) See Excel file (Chapter 10 Q6) for scatter graph.
The scatter graph shows there is strong positive association between height and weight for males but much weaker for females.
(c)   All data: $r = 0.760$; males: $r = 0.906$; females: $r = 0.0102$

7 $R = -0.3875$

8 See Excel file (Chapter 10 Q8) for scatter graph.
(a)   The scatter graph suggests that there is a strong association between sales and advertising expenditure and that this is a positive association.
(b) $y = -0.24 + 9.292x$, where y is sales and x the advertising expenditure. The coefficient of determination is 93.3 per cent so it appears that the regression explains the data quite well.
(c)   £46 200

9 (a)   Positive (weak for league as a whole but probably strong for a particular club)
(b)   Negative, strong
(c)   Positive, weak
(d)   Positive, strong
(e)   Negative, strong

10 (a)   (i)   See Excel file (Chapter 10 Q10)
(ii) $r = 0.8898$

(b) $a = 11.129$, $b = 0.04037$
So time to pay $= 11.13 + 0.0404 \times$ size of bill

(c)   The 11.13 is the minimum time to pay (in days) and for every £1 increase in the size of bill the time to pay will increase by 0.0404, i.e. the marginal increase.

(d)   See Excel file (Chapter 10 Q10)
(e)   (i)   for £125 time to pay $= 11.13 + 0.0404 \times 125$

$= 16.18$ or just over 16 days
(ii)   for £1000 time to pay $= 11.13 + 0.0404 \times 1000$

$= 51.53$ or 51.5 days

The prediction for £1000 is unreliable because it is outside the range of data (the largest amount is only £480).
(f)   79.2% of the variation in time to pay is explained by the size of the bill. The remaining 20.8% is not explained by this factor. (Other factors might help in explaining this remaining variation.)

W. **11** (a) See Excel file (Chapter 10, Q11)

(b)

% collected	Rank	% arrears	Rank	d	d^2
1	6	13	1	5	25
12	3	10	4	−1	1
16	2	8	5	−3	9
11	4	12	2	2	4
20	1	7	6	−5	25
6	5	11	3	2	4
				Sum	68

$$R = 1 - \frac{6 \times 68}{6(6^2 - 1)}$$

$$= 1 - 1.943$$

$$= -0.943$$

W. **12** (a) See Excel file (Chapter 10 Q12)

There is a moderate negative association between days off sick and age.

(b) Using the calculator function Pearson's correlation coefficient,

$r = -0.5717$

Spearman's

x	21	19	36	55	20	22	45	39	32	28
y	20	8	8	5	13	15	12	7	11	8
Rank x	8	10	4	1	9	7	2	3	5	6
Rank y	1	7	7	10	3	2	4	9	5	7
d	7	3	−3	−9	6	5	−2	−6	0	−1
d^2	49	9	9	81	36	25	4	36	0	1

$$\sum d^2 = 250$$

$$r_S = 1 - \frac{6 \times 250}{10 \times 99}$$

$$= 1 - 1.515$$

$$= -0.515$$

(c) $H_0 : r = 0 \quad H_1 : r \neq 0$

Critical value on 8 df $= .6319$ for Pearson's

So cannot reject H_0. There is no evidence of a significant correlation.

(d) (ii) 17.4 is for someone aged 0 and so has no practical meaning. The -0.2118 means that for every year older the days off work reduces by 0.2118

(iii) $17.4 - 0.2118 \times 65 = 3.6$ days. But 65 is outside the range of the data and the prediction is unreliable.

(iv) $r^2 = .3268$ or 32.7%. This tells us that only about 33% of the variation in days off sick is explained by age.

(v) Length of service, sex, marital status, health, etc.

Chapter 11

2 (a) 0.4; (b) 26; (c) 14; (d) Decision 1; (e) 0.509

9

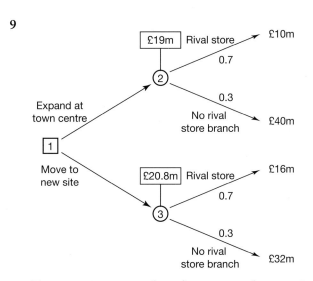

To maximize expected profit, move to the new site.

10 (a)

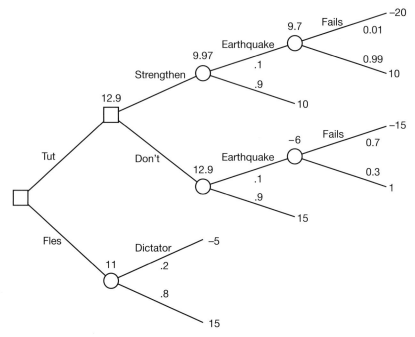

Best decision is to invest in Tutamolia but not to strengthen the building, giving an EMV of £12.9m

(b) $-6p + 15(1 - p) = 11$

$21p = 4$

$p = 0.19$

If probability greater than 0.19 then should choose Flesomnial. (Note: This won't affect decision for Tut branch as the 9.97 value will be reduced.)

11 (a) (i)   This would be the maximax rule and would choose Investment A

(ii)   This would be the maximin rule. Max$(-100, 0, -10) = 0$. Would choose Investment B.

(b)

Investment	Rising	Stable	Falling	Largest loss
A	0	25	150	150
B	60	0	50	50
C	160	40	0	160

Min$(150, 60, 160) = 60$ so choose Investment B

(c)   EMV A $= -25$, B $= 28$ and C $= 30$ so choose Investment C

(d)   The expected value with perfect information

$= .2 \times 150 + .2 \times 50 + .6 \times 50 = 70$, so EVPI $= 70 - 30 = 40$

(e)　(i)　$u(150) = 1.\ u(-100) = 0;\ u(90) = .5;\ u(25) = .3$

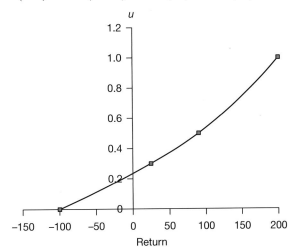

(ii)　$u(50) = .4.\ u(10) = .25;\ u(0) = .2;\ u(-10) = .15$

Expected utilities are therefore:

A:　$.2 \times 1 + .2 \times .3 + .6 \times 0 = .26$

B:　$.2 \times .5 + .2 \times .4 + .6 \times .2 = .3$

C:　$.2 \times .15 + .2 \times .25 + .6 \times .4 = .32$

So the best investment is still C.

13　(a)

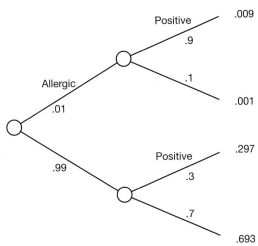

(b)　$P(\text{test positive}) = .009 + .297 = .306$

(c)　(i)　$P(\text{allergic}\,|\,\text{positive}) = \dfrac{.009}{.306} = .0294$

　　　(ii)　$P(\text{allergic}\,|\,\text{negative}) = \dfrac{.001}{.694} = .0014$

(d)

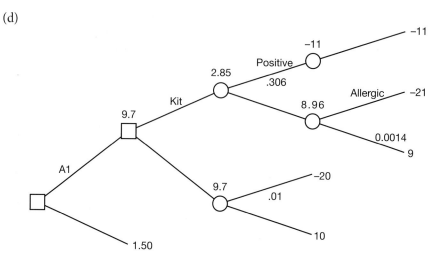

So should sell the A1 product but don't supply kit in order to maximize the EMV

(e)   If supply kit annual profit = $500\,000 \times 2.85 = £1\,425\,000$

If don't supply kit profit = $50\,000 \times 9.7 = £4\,850\,000$

If sell older version profit = $50\,000 \times 1.50 = £750\,000$

Chapter 12

15   See Excel file (Chapter 12 Q15). The Goal Seek function can be used to find the value of r to give a NPV of zero. This was found to be 9.7% and as this is less than 14% the project should not be accepted.

16   $P_0 = £1000$, $r = 5.4\%$, $n = 5$

$$P_5 = 1000 \times \left(1 + \frac{5.4}{100}\right)^5$$

$$= 1000 \times 1.30078$$

$$= £1300.78$$

18   Need to discount the 5 annual payments of £1000. So cost at today's prices is £8546

19

	Machine A	Machine B
Profit	$6000 - 4000 = 2000$	$6000 - 3900 = 2100$
Payback	$2 \times \dfrac{4}{4.5} = 1.8$ years*	$2 \times \dfrac{3900}{4000} = 1.95$ years*
ARR	$\dfrac{2000}{4000} = 50\%$	$\dfrac{2000}{3900} = 51.3\%$

*Note: It could be argued that the payback is 2 years for both if it is assumed that the revenue is obtained at the end of each year

Machine B is better on profit and ARR but not on payback

		Machine A		Machine B	
	Discount factor	Cash flow	Present value	Cash flow	Present value
0		−4000	−4000	−3900	−3900
1	0.9259	2000	1851.9	1500	1388.9
2	0.8573	2500	2143.3	2500	2143.3
3	0.7938	1500	1190.7	2000	1587.7
		NPV	1185.9		1219.9

Machine B is preferred as it has a higher NPV

Machine A		Machine B	
Discount rate	NPV	Discount rate	NPV
8	1186	8	1220
25	−32	25	−76

An IRR of about 24.5%
Using formula:

$$\frac{1186 \times 25 - (-32) \times 8}{1186 - (-32)} = \frac{29\,906}{1218}$$

$$= 24.6\%$$

For Machine B the IRR is 24.0%

Not much difference although Machine A has a slightly higher IRR and would therefore be preferred using this measure

20

	Investment 1	Investment 2
Profit	$8\,000 - 15\,000 = 3000$	$19\,000 - 15\,000 = 4000$
Payback	3 years	3 years
ARR	$\dfrac{6000}{15\,000} = 40\%$	$\dfrac{6333}{15\,000} = 42\%$

Investment 2 gives a better profit and ARR

		Investment 1		Investment 2	
	Discount factor	Cash flow	Present value	Cash flow	Present value
0		$-15\,000$	$-15\,000$	$-15\,000$	$-15\,000$
1	0.9524	$6\,000$	$5\,714.3$	0	0.0
2	0.9070	$6\,000$	$5\,442.2$	0	0.0
3	0.8638	$6\,000$	$5\,183.0$	$19\,000$	$16\,412.0$
		NPV	$1\,339.5$		$1\,412.9$

Investment 2 gives a higher NPV

Using formula

$$\frac{1340 \times 10 - (-79.2) \times 5}{1340 - (-79.2)} = \frac{13\,796}{1419.2}$$

$$= 9.7\%$$

Using formula:

$$\frac{1413 \times 10 - (-725.3) \times 5}{1413 - (-725.3)} = \frac{17\,756.5}{2138.3}$$

$$= 8.3\%$$

So Investment 1 gives a higher IRR and is preferred on this measure.

21 (a) $P_3 = 800(1.04)^3$

$$= £899.89$$

(b) Let instalment $= x$

First instalment will grow to $x(1.052)^3$ at the end of the plan
Second instalment will grow to $x(1.052)^2$ at the end of the plan
Third instalment will grow to $x(1.052)$ at the end of the plan

Total amount accumulated $= x\{(10.52)^3 + (1.052)^2 + 1.052\}$

$$= 3.322296x$$

Machine will cost £899.89 so

$3.32296x = 899.89$

and

$$x = \frac{899.89}{3.32296}$$

$$= £270.81$$

Instalments should be £270.81

22

Year	Cash flow	Present value
0	−3750	−3750
1	1310	1178
2	1310	1059
3	1310	953
4	1310	857
5	1310	770

(a) NPV = £1067

(b) By trial and error (using Excel) a discount rate of 25% gives a NPV of −£227.

Using formula

$$IRR = \frac{1067 \times 25 - (-227) \times 11.2}{1067 - (-227)} = \frac{29\,217.4}{1294}$$

$$= 22.6\%$$

23 The annual amount can be found from:

$$\frac{x\left[(1.07)^{11} - 1\right]}{.07} = 1\,000\,000$$

$$15.78x = 1\,000\,000$$

$$x = £63\,371$$

An annual investment of £63 371 would give a sinking fund of £1m in 10 years.

24 (a) $$0 = -65\,000(1.075)^{20} + \frac{x\left[(1.075)^{20} - 1\right]}{.075}$$

$$0 = -276\,110 + 43.305x$$

$$x = £6376$$

So annual repayment would have to be £6376

(b) This time we know the annual repayment (£7000) but need to find n, the number of years to pay off the loan.

$$0 = -65\,000(1.075)^n + \frac{7000[(1.075)^n - 1]}{.075}$$

$$28\,333 \times (1.075)^n = 93\,333$$

$$(1.075)^n = 3.294$$

$$n \times \log(1.075) = (3.294)$$

$$n = 16.48 \text{ years}$$

How much money is saved: Paying £7000 for 16.48 years gives a total of £115 374 and paying £6376 for 20 years gives a total of £127 520. So save £12 146.

27 (a) $5000 = 12\,000 \times (1 + r/100)^3$

$$1 + \frac{r}{100} = (.4167)^{\frac{1}{3}}$$

$$= .7469$$

$$r = -25.3$$

So the rate of depreciation is -25.3%

(b) At end of first year

$$P_1 = 12\,000 \times (1 - .253)$$

$$= £8964$$

So car will be worth £8964 after one year.

28 Take £1000 invested for one year.

If compounded annually at 7%

$$P_1 = 1000 \times 1.07$$

$$= £1070$$

If compounded continuously at 5%

$$P_1 = 1000 \times e^{\frac{5}{1000}}$$

$$= £1051$$

So better to use the first option.

Chapter 13

W 1 (a) and (b)   See Excel file (Chapter 13 Q1)

(c) Average seasonal differences (adjusted) are -10.05, -6.17, -5.38, -4.72, 8.66, 17.66

(d) Forecasts using regression line through CMA

		Trend forecast	**Forecast**
2009	1	43.5	33.4
	2	43.6	37.4
	3	43.7	38.3
	4	43.8	39.1
	5	43.9	52.5
	6	44.0	61.6

W 2 (a)   See Excel file (Chapter 13 Q2)

The additive model is best as it gives smallest MSE.

(b) and (c)   See Excel file (Chapter 13 Q2)

(d) Forecasts

Period	Trend	Sales
2	26.7	22.9
3	27.5	18.6
4	28.3	32.5

W **3** (a) and (b) See Excel file (Chapter 13 Q3)

(c) The additive is the better model as it has the lower MSE (0.04 compared to 0.55 for multiplicative).

(d) Forecasts are

Quarter	Trend	Sales
2	123.5	112.1
3	124.5	136.0
4	125.5	138.1

W **4** See Excel file (Chapter 13 Q4)

Forecast on day 12 is 112.4.

Chapter 14

2 Let P = number of units of product P and

Q = number of units of product Q

Max $600P + 400Q$

Subject to

$2P + Q \leq 10$

$P + Q \leq 7$

$P, Q \geq 0$

Solution is $P = 3$ and $Q = 4$ giving a profit of £3400.

3 Let D = number of diesel engines and

P = number of petrol engines to be produced each day

Max $60D + 45P$

Subject to

$4D + 2P \leq 16$

$2D + 2P \leq 12$

$P \geq 3$

$D \geq 0$

Solution is $D = 3$ and $P = 2$ giving a profit of £270.

4　(a)　Let L = number of low wattage bulbs to produce each day

Let H = number of high wattage bulbs to produce each day

$20L + 30H \leq 36\,000$　　　$(10 \times 60 \times 60)$

$10L + 30H \leq 36\,000$

$L + H \leq 1500$

$L, H \geq 0$

W.

(b)　See Excel file (Chapter 14 Q4) for Solver solution.

Solution is $L = 900$ and $H = 600$ giving a profit of 8700p (£87)

(c)　There are 9000 seconds (2.5 hours) left in testing but both Fitting and Supply of shells are scarce resources. The shadow price of the Fitting resource is .2p per second (£7.20 per hour) and 1p per extra shell. Increasing either the fitting time or the number of shells would increase total profits.

7　(a)　50 radio and 30 TV ads giving a total rating of 28000

(b)　Radio and budget constraints binding. Shadow price of radio ads constraint is 50 so If radio ads increased by 50 then extra rating would be $50 \times 50 = 2500$

(c)　Can't reduce TV ads rating

8　(a)　Let x_1 = Amount invested in government bonds

Let x_2 = Amount invested in corporate bonds

Let x_3 = Amount invested in FTSE 100 stocks

Let x_4 = Amount invested in Aim stocks

Max $.04x_1 + .05x_2 + .06x_3 + .08x_4 + .03(550,000 - x_1 - x_2 - x_3 - x_4)$

i.e. Max $16\,500 + .01x_1 + .02x_2 + .03x_3 + .05x_4$

s.t

$$x_1 + x_2 + x_3 + x_4 \leq 550\,000$$
$$x_2 \geq 50\,000$$
$$x_2 + x_3 + x_4 \leq 300\,000$$
$$x_1 + x_2 - x_3 - x_4 \leq 0$$
$$x_1 + x_2 + x_3 - 3x_4 \geq 0$$
$$x_1, x_2, x_3, x_4 \geq 0$$

(b)　(i)　£200 000 in government bonds, £50,000 in Corporate bonds, and £125,000 in each of FTSE 100 and Aim stocks. This means that £50,000 is left in the bank. Total return is

$200 \times .04 + 50 \times .05 + 125 \times .06 + 125 \times .08 + 50 \times .03$

$= £29\,500$

As a percentage on capital invested $= 5.36\%$

(ii) The shadow price for constraint 2 is $-.04$ which means that reducing the RHS increases the return. Can reduce RHS by 25 000 so increase in return would be $25000 \times .04 = £1000$.

The shadow price for constraint 3 is 0.05 so increase the RHS by the maximum which is 25000. Increase in return would be $5000 \times .05 = £1250$. So better to increase the RHS of constraint 3.

(iii) The allowable decreases for x_1, x_2, x_3, x_4 are .015, infinite, .08 and .02 respectively. The implication of this is that x_1 would have to fall to 2.5% which is below the bank rate. x_2 and x_3 would mean a negative rate so is not realistic. x_4 could fall to 6% and still remain in solution. The allowable decrease for corporate bonds is infinite because constraint 2 says that must have at least £50,000.

14 (a) Solution is to make 3.75 convection heaters and 1.5 thermal heaters giving a profit of £35.25

(b) Solution is same as part (a). Can meet all goals except Goal 4 (short by 3.25 convection heaters)

Chapter 15

5 (a)

(b) Job will take 12 days and critical activities are A, E, F, H, I and J
(c) Job delayed by 0.5 days
(d) 5 people required between days 6 and 8.
Not possible to have F and G at the same time. If F starts as soon as G has finished project will be delayed for 3 days.

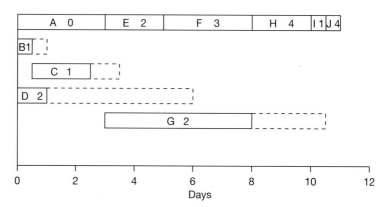

W 8 (a) See Excel file (Chapter 15 Q8)

   (b) Critical activities are A, B, E and F

   Time = 17 hours

   Slacks are C = 2 hours and D = 2 hours

   (c) Normal cost = £1650, penalty cost = £500 and overheads = £1700

   Profit = 10000 − 1650 − 500 − 1700 = £6150

   (d) D is not on critical path

Path		B 1	E 2	C 1, D 1, E 1
ABEF	17	16	14	13
ABDF	15	14	14	13
ABCF	15	14	14	13
Crash cost	–	£100	£300	£500
Penalty cost	£500	£400	£200	£100
Overheads	£1700	£1600	£1400	£1300
Total	£2200	£2100	£1900	£1900

So crash by 4 hours (same cost as only crashing by 3 hours but better to finish earlier)

Crash B by 1 hour

   C by 1 hour

   D by 1 hour

   E by 3 hours

Total cost = £1650 + £1900 = £3550

Profit = £10 000 − £3550 = £6450

10 (a)

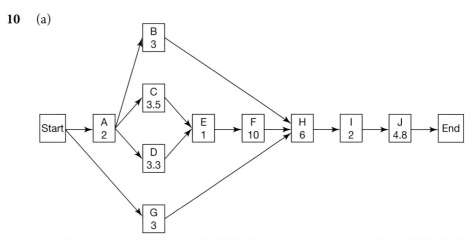

Activity	t_o	t_p	t_m	μ	σ^2
C	2	7	3	3.5	0.6944
D	2	6	3	3.5	0.4444
J	3	6	5	4.8	0.25

(b) Details of the EST and LST and floats are given below.

Activity	EST	EFT	LFT	LST	Float	Critical?
A	0	2	2	0	0	Y
B	2	5	16.5	13.5	11.5	N
C	2	5.5	5.5	2	0	Y
D	2	5.3	5.5	2.2	0.2	N
E	5.5	6.5	6.5	5.5	0	Y
F	6.5	16.5	16.5	6.5	0	Y
G	0	3	16.5	13.5	13.5	N
H	16.5	22.5	22.5	16.5	0	Y
I	22.5	24.5	24.5	22.5	0	Y
J	24.5	29.3	29.3	24.5	0	Y

Activities A, C, E, F, H, I are critical. Expected time before the national campaign can be launched is 29.3 days.

(c) The variance of the critical path is $0.6944 + 0.25 = 0.9444$ (Note: Activity D is not on the critical path), so the standard deviation is 0.9718.

To find the probability that expected time is greater than 32 days we need to calculate the Z value which is

$$Z = \frac{32 - 29.3}{0.9718}$$
$$= 2.77$$

From tables this give a probability of 0.0028

So there is a 0.28% chance that the expected time will exceed 32 days, which means that there is a probability of $100 - 0.28 = 98.72\%$ that the launch can take place within 32 days.

Index